Freiburger Schriften zur Forst- und Umweltpolitik

Band 10

Institutional change and social conflicts over forest use in the Northern Bolivian Amazon

Sergio Antonio Ruiz

Verlag Dr. Kessel

Remagen-Oberwinter 2005

1. Auflage 2005
Tel.: 02228-493

Fax: 01212-512382426

eMail: nkessel@web.de

Homepage: www.forstbuch.de, www.forestrybooks.com

Druck: www.business-copy.com

ISBN: 3-935638-74-4

To my parents, who forged my past and

to Susi, Adriano and Chiara, builders of my present and future

To the memory of Werner Hanagarth, my friend and adviser

Acknowledgements

I do wish to give special mention to certain people, without whom I could never have realised my objectives.

I will begin by thanking the sponsors of the CIFOR/BMZ II Project for financing the four years of research, as well as the translation of my work. Likewise, I wish to thank my '*Doktorvater*', Professor Dr. Michel Becker, whose knowledge and human qualities I lack the time to learn. Thank you also to Dr. Wil de Jong, CIFOR coordinator in Indonesia, for his constant concern for the achievement of good results, for the academic follow-up and his friendship. I am equally grateful to my second academic adviser, Professor Volker Kohler, for the interesting way in which he supported my work.

For those who facilitated my stay in the northern Amazon, I am at a loss to express my feelings. To René and Carmen Boot, as well as to Oscar Llanque and Armelinda Zonta, in charge of the main counterpart organisation PROMAB-IPHAE for their friendship towards my family and their support for my work in Riberalta. To Cora von Ostern of SNV-Cobija for her unconditional support for my activities in Cobija. To Mario Moreno, leader of the Indigenous Union of the region and to René Salomón, former director of INRA-national until 2002 for placing his trust in me when signing the cooperation agreements with our project.

The regional list extends to all those who provided information without any objections. To the INRA agents in Cobija, especially to my great friend Limberg Rosel; to the SIF agents of Cobija and Riberalta, where Engineer Forero, José Luis Osinaga, Fabián Soliz, Javier Baldiviezo and Dr. Seone stand out. Thanks also to 'Chichi' Fong, president of the *Barraquero* Association; to Fermín Terrazas, Luis Rojas, Carlos Mamio and Manuel Cuadiay, 'great' leaders of the Rural Federations of Pando and Vaca Diez.

To all my interviewees, who offered their time and knowledge during the long and 'boring' chats, especially to all those that took part in the case studies. I refer in particular to Eisen Vaca, Carolina Peralta, Julio Cesar Blacazar, to my compatriot Marcelo Vega '*El Sapito*', Yaskara Hayasida, Agustín Vargas, Antonio Banderas, to Wilder and Walter Rojas, Francisco Waada, Marco Cartagena, and to all the members of the Hecker family.

The CIFOR/BMZ II Project integrated me into a group of young researchers with whom I shared my ideals and passion for the northern Bolivian Amazon. I refer here to my 'research twin' Carmen Gottwald, and to my companions Gunther Hentschel, Roberto Maldonado, Johannes Stahl and Andrea Garzón: the value of their work strengthened my knowledge of the study area.

To the old and new '*Mumler*', colleagues of the 'Market and Marketing' section of the University of Freiburg, especially to Dr. Lothar Isfort, Dr. Dietmar Stoian, Dr. Christian Held, Dr. Barbara Schneider, Dr. Jochen Statz, Dr. Carol Grossmann, Michaela Haug, whose observations and criticisms served to arouse my academic curiosity. Nor could I forget my '*gute Fee im Büro*', Mrs Barbara Mattheiß.

Thanks also to my 'Zamorano' colleagues Dr. Rolando Kapmeyer and Dante Fuentes for their critical perspective and broad theoretical knowledge.

I also consider it important to name the people who corrected the writing of my work; in Spanish, particularly Luis Valencia of CIFOR, as well as Carmen Boot, Gustavo Cornejo and Cristina Ruiz. I also appreciate John Savage's translation work into English, and I appreciated especially the English review by David Butler Manning.

'The ant work', such as the transcription of interviews, setting up a database and the bibliography record was masterfully done by Enrique Correa in Riberalta. In Germany the cartography preparation was possible thanks to the help of Britta Hackenber, Felix Seidel and Sofía Garzón.

I would like to dedicate the last paragraph to my family; firstly to my companion and wife Susanne and to my two children, Adriano and Carmen Chiara for having allowed me to carry out this challenge, especially for having shared the marvellous experience of living in Riberalta with me; in the heat, surrounded by mosquitoes, 'thieves' and other typical tropical things.

My thanks go out to my mother 'Malolita'. She was always present at the most important moments in my life. To my sisters, Cristina and Raquel, and to all of my great Bolivian family, including my brother-in-law and seven nephews whose positive attitude towards life constantly raised my spirits at the most critical times. And of course to my in-laws, Bojan and Karola Peroci, not only for providing their basement and having it transformed into my office, but also for helping my family and taking care of my children, often replacing me in my duties as father.

To all, and to the many others I have failed to mention,

muchas gracias.

Landau, Germany October 2005 Sergio Antonio Ruiz

Index

Glossary

Almendra — Synonym for Brazil nut, generally when it is ready for marketing.

Baldía — Relates to land without an owner; synonym used locally to identify state or unoccupied land.

Barbecho — Area of cleared forest that has not been in production for more than three to six years.

Barraca — Production establishment involved mainly in the exploitation of non-timber forest products. Main private institution in non timber forest products (NTFPS) extraction.

Barraca holder — The *Barraca* claimant; synonym for *patron* or *barraquero*

Barraquero — Synonym for *barraca* holder or *patron*

Barrica — Trading unit of the Brazil nut in its shell, used in the area of influence of the city of Cobija, as well as in Peru and Brazil. A *barrica* is equal to approximately to 66 kg, or three *cajas*.

Beneficiadora — Industrial plant where NTFPs are processed, mainly Brazil nuts and palm hearts.

Bolacha — Trading unit of semi-processed rubber in the field that becomes firm to facilitate transport and resembles a ball that weighs from 30 to 70 kg.

Caja — Trading unit of the Brazil nut in its shell, used in the area of influence of the city of Riberalta. A *caja* weighs from 22 to 26 kg.

Capataz — Confidant of the b*arraquero*; in charge of directing, overseeing and administering the activities inside the *barraca*.

Casa Suárez — Biggest extractivist company established in the region, initially involved in the quinine and then the rubber trade. Went bankrupt in 1940.

Castaña — Edible forest fruit, from the *Bertholletia excelsa* species; synonym for nut, Brazil nut, *Paranuss* (German), and in recent years also known as the Amazon nut.

Castañero — The Brazil nut gatherer; synonym for *zafrero*.

Caucho — Latex extracted from the *Hevea brasiliensis*; synonym for *goma* or *siringa*.

Centro — Territorial division of the NTFP establishments; in relation to the production, number of harvesters and service infrastructures.

Chaco — Land area destined for cultivating agricultural products; in general not bigger than two hectares with production intended for family consumption.

Chaqueo — Preparation of the *chaco* through the felling and burning of the forest cover; generally takes place during the driest months of the year (August and September).

Chisme — Rumours whispered to discredit or to weaken the position of the opposing groups in conflict.

Chiverio — Synonym for conflict in the common language.

Clientelismo — Asymmetric relationship between a person of higher social and economic status (*patrón*) and one from a lower level (client) resulting in an advantage for both, which also creates certain social, economic and political interdependences.

Colocación — Area of three *estradas* assigned to the *siringueros*; in the past used for rubber production; synonymous today with Brazil nut *centres*.

Contratísta — Person hired by the *patrón* that assumes the responsibility of recruiting *zafreros* and responding for a quantity of product agreed in the *habilito*.

Enganche	Institution that regulated the recruitment of the labour force of the *barraca*, under a group of almost compulsive measures destined to guarantee they remained long-term.
Estrada	Trail that leads around the rubber trees and is used by the *siringueros* during the rubber of collection process. Officially one *estrada* was composed of 150 rubber trees.
Fabrico	Annual rubber production; each of the two rubber seasons (Apr.-Jun./Jul. and Sept.-Nov./Dec.) is referred to as a *medio fábrico*.
FES	The 'Socio-economic function' is a criteria used during *saneamiento* that measures *in situ* the activities developed by the agricultural (FES-*agraria*) and forest users (FES-*forestal*).
Fregues	Family living in the *barraca* and working for the *patrón* under deplorable conditions (without a fixed wage, without rights to resources); synonym for *peón* or *siringuero*.
Goma	Natural latex from the *Hevea brasiliensis*. Synonym for *caucho* or *siringa*.
Habilito	Private institution that governs the financial transactions in forest production activities; it usually consists of an advance from the *patrón* to the Brazil nut harvesters, in cash and/or kind, in exchange for the future supply of products extracted from the forest.
Holder	It replaces the owner; it refers to the person that owns a particular property, under either the traditional rules or according to public rights. → (Spanish) *Titular*
Latifundio	Large estate
Latifundista	Large estate holder
Legal personality	The aptitude or capacity of any person or group of people to be subject to rights and obligations, in their own name or in representation for others. It refers to the legal recognition of the collective groupings (communities or associations) by the state. → (Spanish) *personería jurídica*
Local Territorial Organisation	The basic community or local unit that occupies a certain territorial area and maintains a relationship with the public bodies of the State through the municipal government. → (Spanish) *Organización territorial de base (OTB)*
Motosierristas	Saw operator; responsible for providing illegal timber to the forest managers in the past. In legal terms the Forest Law eliminated *motosierrismo*, integrating those involved in the legal system through the ASLs.
Multiétnico II	Indigenous territory (TCO) formed by three ethnic groups: *Tacana*, *Esse Ejja* and *Cavineño*. It is located between the rivers Madre de Dios and Beni, in the southern part of Pando.
Municipality	The unit of territorial, population, political and administrative organisation inside the limits of a Section of a Province. The maximum authority within the municipal jurisdiction is the municipal government, elected by popular vote.
Palmito	Meristema apical of several species of palm; in the northern Bolivian Amazon mainly extracted from the *asaí* palm (*Euterpe precatoria*).
Patrón	Name given to the *barraca* holder by the *fregueces*. Synonym for *barraquero*. Formally rubber baron
'*Plan Soberanía*'	It was a government policy applied exclusively in the department of Pando. It catered for the placement of timber companies along the country's international borders to prevent foreign inhabitants from Brazil and Peru extracting the natural resources in Bolivia. (Plan Soberanía).
Polygon	Sections or units of area divided by the INRA technicians to execute the land titling process (*saneamiento*). In Pando, the department was divided into ten polygons.

Predio	Farm property, country property, individual or collective establishment with or without formal right to the associated resources.
Prefecture	State body responsible for departmental administration. The highest authority is the Prefect of the Department appointed by the President of the Republic.
Quebradoras	People responsible for shelling Brazil nuts; usually women hired by the shelling companies.
Saneamiento	Technical/legal process, executed by the INRA whose purpose is to clarify land ownership rights; it includes field activities (measuring the properties) and office work (analysis of the formal rights).
Settelment certificate	A document issued by the municipal government, supporting an individual or collective's occupation of land in rural areas. → (Spanish) *Certificado de asentamiento*
Siringa	Rubber.
Siringuero	Rubber collector usually answerable to the *patrón* or the foreman.
Sub-centro	Territorial division of the Brazil nut centres.
Tala y quema	Agricultural practice used to clear lands for agriculture during the dry season (July-September).
Tributary co-partnership	A transfer of the national income (from revenue, customs, etc.); 20% to be made available to the municipalities and 5% to the universities. → (Spanish) *Coparticipación tributaria*
Yaminahua-Machineri	Indigenous territory (TCO) formed by two ethnic groups: *Yaminahua* and *Machineri*. It is located on the international border with Brazil, in northwestern Pando.
Zafra	Period of Brazil nut gathering; generally from December to March.
Zafrero	Brazil nut gatherer; synonym for *castañero*.

Abbreviations

AAA	Area anual de aprovechamiento → (English) Annual harvesting areas
AARENARMAPA	Asociación Agroindustrial de Recursos Naturales del Río Manuripi de Pando
ABAN	Asociación de Beneficiadores del Noroeste
ACRA	Asociación de cooperación rural en África y América Latina
AP	Área Protegida → (English) Protected area
APEFA	Asociación de Productores Exportadores Forestales Amazónicos
ARFM	Áreas de Reserva Forestal Municipal → (English) Municipal forest areas
ASL	Asociación Social del Lugar → (English) Local Community Association
ASPROGAL	Asociación de Productores de Goma y Almendra (Riberalta)
ASPROGOALPA	Asociación de Productores de Goma y Almendra de Pando
BMZ	Bundesministerium für wirtschaftliche Zusammenarbeit und Entwicklung → (English) German Federal Ministry of Cooperation
BOLFOR	Proyecto de Manejo Forestal Sostenible
CDF	Forestry Development Center
CEJIS	Centro de Estudios Jurídicos e Investigación Social
CIDOB	Confederación de los Pueblos Indígenas de Bolivia
CIFOR	Center for International Forestry Research
CIPCA-Norte	Centro de Investigación y Producción del Campesino del Norte Amazónico
CIRABO	Central Indígena de la Región Amazónica Boliviana
CIPOAP	Central Indígena de Pueblos Originarios de la Amazonía de Pando
CFB	Cámara Forestal de Bolivia
CNRA	Consejo Nacional de Reforma Agraria
CORDEPANDO	Corporación de Desarrollo de Departamento de Pando
CPE	Constitución Política del Estado → (English) National Political Constitution
CSUTCB	Confederación Sindical Única de Trabajadores Campesinos de Bolivia
TC	Transaction costs
DISOP	Desarrollo Integral de Solidaridad y Progreso
DL	Decree Law
DS	Presidential Decree
€	Euro (currency of the European Union)
FAO	United Nations Food and Agriculture Organization
FES	Función Económico-Social

FIDA	Fondo Internacional de Desarrollo Agrícola → (English) International Fund for Agricultural Development
FMP	Forest management plan
FONABOSQUE	Fondo Nacional de Desarrollo Forestal
FSC	Forest Stewardship Council
FSUTCP	Federación Sindical Única de Trabajadores Campesinos de Pando
FSUTCVD	Federación Sindical Única de Trabajadores Campesinos de Vaca Diez
HERENCIA	"Herencia" interdisciplinaria para el desarrollo sostenible
INC	Instituto Nacional de Colonización
INE	Instituto Nacional de Estadística
INRA	Instituto Nacional de Reforma Agraria
IPHAE	Instituto para el Hombre la Agricultura y la Ecología
NIPE	New Institutional Political Economy
NGO	Non-government organisation
NIE	New Institutional Economics
NPE	New Political Economy
NTFP	Non-timber forest product
OTB	Organización Territorial de Base → (English) Local Territorial Organisation
PANFOR	Proyecto de Manejo Forestal Sostenible de Pando
PMC	Plan de Manejo de la Castaña → (English) Brazil nut management plan
POAF	Plan Operativo Annual Forestal → (English) Annual forestry operational plans
POP	Plan de Ordenamiento Predial → (English) Plot Allocation
PROMAB	Programa Manejo de Bosques de la Amazonía Boliviana
RNVSAM	Reserva Nacional de Vida Silvestre Amazónica Manuripi
SIF	Superintendencia Forestal
SFM	Sustainable Forest Management
SNV	Dutch Organization for Development Cooperation
TCO	Tierra Comunitaria de Origen
UFM	Unidad Forestal Municipal
USAID	US Agency for International Development
US$	United States Dollars
UTB	Universidad Técnica del Beni

Summary

The main objective of this study is to make a contribution to the analysis of the enforcement of state reforms in peripheral regions. In addition, the study seeks to contribute to the better understanding of the conflict situations emerging as a result of the changes to property rights over natural resources. The selected study area is located in the northern Bolivian Amazon, where the economy is largely based on the export of forest resources, mainly non-timber products, the Brazil nut (*Bertholletia excelsa*) in recent times and rubber (*Hevea brasiliensis*) in the past. The extractivist activities are an important source of work for more than 50% of the economically active population. Despite the importance of the forest sector for the Amazon population, control long remained firmly in the hands of an elitist group of forest users, mainly large *barraca* holders (between 2,500 and 100,000 ha), the traditional owners of the rubber/Brazil nut estates, and logging companies. The rest of the rural population, such as the indigenous and peasants, generally remained marginalised from the forest benefits until 1996.

The theoretical framework underlying the research is the 'New Institutional Economics' (NIE), which deals with the study of institutional change. The institutional changes analysed here pertained to property rights, expressed both in public (laws, decrees, resolutions) and in private institutions (traditions and agreements reached between individuals). According to SCHLÜTER (2001) there are three theories explaining institutional change: the 'efficiency theory', the 'public choice theory' and the 'distribution theory'. Within the scope of public choice theory, the main theoretical approach is rent-seeking, here understood as "a strategic pattern of behaviour in the political process, influencing changes with respect to property rights, the objective of which is to improve one's situation in relation to other actors". The concept of rent-seeking is used to explain the behaviour of the interest groups during the formulation and enforcement of public institutions (see chapter 5), and during conflict negotiation (see chapter 6).

The data presented in this study derive from field work carried out between August 2001 and June 2002. Qualitative tools are used, such as semi-structured interviews (personal and telephone) with forest users (n=164), representatives of private organisations (n=25), representatives of public organisations (n=20) and protagonists of conflicts (n=25). The information required for the analysis of the conflicts, presented in chapter 6, is gathered through three case studies. The conflict protagonists are the six forest user groups with the greatest access to the market.

Chapter 4 demonstrates that the enforcement of public institutions (Forest Law and INRA Law) contributed to reducing the disparities in the distribution of resources, thanks to the incorporation of new categories of property rights in favour of the community forest users (peasants and indigenous). In this order, the community area could increase from 60,000 ha in 1992 to 3 million ha by 2010 (INRA 2004). Other effects of the reforms are: 1) greater state role in the control and allocation of natural resources; and 2) the increased collection of forest duties compared with the old Forest Law of 1974. The reforms does not: 1) encourage forest users to manage the forests sustainably; 2) govern the extractivist activities in sufficient detail, especially in the rural communities and the *barracas*; 3) integrate other traditional user groups into the forest regime (informal timber suppliers, *barraca* holders and *fregueces*); 4) reduce the disparities in the distribution of the resources in the rural communities.

Chapter 5 is a contribution towards the better understanding of the adjustment process of the reforms based on the initiative of regional power groups. The starting point of the analysis was the 'institutional vacuum' of the reforms, which ignored the extractivist reality of the northern Bolivian Amazon. The institutional adjustment began in 1999 with the approval of Decree 25532, which formalised the traditional rights of the *barraca* holders. Decree 25532 was later annulled due to the social pressure exerted by the rural communities, who at the same time obtained the approval of Decree 25848, entitling a minimum of 500 ha per rural family living in a community.

Both in the process of formulation and in the decrees enforcement (25532 and 25848), the widespread ambition of the regional power groups to obtain state rents was observed (rent-seeking). In order to target their objectives the protagonist groups resorted to developing strategies on the basis of the availability of action resources (time, information, ability, experience, contacts, financial resources, etc.). Whilst the elitist groups resorted to activating their political contacts in the upper echelons of public decision-making, the rural groups resorted to pressurising the Government through the organisation of popular marches, hunger strikes and road blockades. Both strategies proved to be successful in the negotiations with the responsible state entities, which means that care must be taken when drawing conclusions on the asymmetries of power between the regional groups seeking to influence institutional change.

Chapter 6 concentrates on analysing the conflicts over the use of the forests after the application of Decrees 25532 and 25848. The reforms are considered one of the main sources of the current conflict, but not necessarily the only source. Although the reforms sought to reduce conflicts resulting from the overlap of agricultural and forest rights, they are responsible for three direct causes of conflict emergence: 1) vague definition of the tenure characteristics, mainly those pertaining to extractivist activities; 2) adaptation of the forest regime through the approval of public lower hierarchy institutions (administrative resolutions) that favoured the interests of certain user groups (public agents, sawmills, forest users with better access to information); and 3) insufficient *enforcement mechanisms* to severely sanction those who violate the laws with fines and punishments and grant incentives to the actors willing to adapt to the laws. Two other important sources of conflicts are: 1) the widespread rent-seeking behaviour of most of the regional actors; and 2) the historical social struggle between elitist groups and rural communities over access to the forests.

Chapter 6 also analyses the strategies used by the forest users to gain access to the resources. In all three case studies, the six protagonists sought to improve their legal security by complying with the laws. Many of them resorted to adapting to the public rules, either by changing their legal status, or by fulfilling certain technical and legal directives such as forest management plans, 'legal personality', 'socio-economic function' (FES), etc. The forest users whose circumstances made compliance with the law difficult resorted to radicalising their position, making public demands of the regional authorities or seizing materials and products from their adversaries. The private users (*barraca* holders), for instance, resorted to inviting forest companies to extract their products, drawing up management plans over extensive areas or maintaining close relationships with the public entities in charge of implementing the laws.

Chapter 7 contains a discussion of the results obtained from a perspective of the 'successes and failures' of the reforms. Briefly, the laws introduced contributed significantly to improving the state's management of the natural resources when compared to the previous regime. The situation in the four dimensions analysed (administrative, economic, social and environmental) improved after 1996 and was greater than the levels established by the old public institutions. Nevertheless, in none of them could the legal enforcement be considered entirely successful. A reduction in the advances of the legal enforcement is anticipated in the future, especially if the following tendencies continue: 1) increase of the administrative load of the public authorities, the result of the greater pressure exerted by the forest users towards the use of the natural resources; 2) lack of commitment and governmental will to formulate and to apply policies targeting the sustainable management of the forests; 3) increase in the gravity of the disputes over the use of the forests and little desire on the part of the forest users to solve the conflicts; and 4) lack of political will to integrate other still informal user groups.

In chapter 7 the outcomes of institutional change are also discussed based on the function of the institutions and rent-seeking behaviour, two of the main theoretical issues presented in chapter 2. With respect to the first point, the reforms ceased to fulfil important institutional functions such as the 'restriction of the expectations and interests' in relation to access to the forests, and did not solve the 'social dilemma posed by the emergence of opportunistic behaviour' like that of '*free riders*' within rural settlements. The traditional rent-seeking analysis, which basically identified the elitist groups and main state agents as rent-seekers, also demonstrated that the approval of public rules had a profound influence on other interest groups, such as forest users (community and individual), representatives of technical organisations (NGOs), forest companies (sawmills, shelling factories) and representatives of social organisations (peasant, indigenous and *barraquero* associations). Another finding of the study is that the 'imprecision' in the formulation of the reforms favours the development of rent-seeking behaviour, during the formulation of the property rights, but also, and in same dimension, during their enforcement. Certain actors profit more for the imprecise nature of the property rights, because they control more resources than others, and because they can maintain their bargaining power during the political process (as in the case of some politicians and bureaucracies).

Two conclusions are mentioned with regard to the link between rent-seeking and distribution of land: 1) rent-seeking does not always lead to the inefficient distribution of resources, it can also represent a form of social control, preventing the unbridled expansion of land ownership by privileged groups; and finally, 2) although rent-seeking can often lead to social conflicts, it also represents a valve for the reduction of violence in land conflicts, being an alternative for many 'losers under the reforms', enabling them to retain parts of their land claims.

1 Introduction

"The law is there, the trap is set"[1]
(Bolivian proverb)

1.1 The northern Bolivian Amazon as study area: Main features and problems

Bolivia is often associated with snow covered mountains, llamas grazing on the Andean hillsides and coca production. Few know the country as the first world exporter of shelled Brazil nuts (*Bertholletia excelsa*), or as the world leader in the certification of natural tropical forests, attributes that have been attained thanks to the presence of more than 50 million hectares of Amazon forest, representing one of the biggest forest reserves in South America, on the edge of the Brazilian Amazon.[2]

As part of the second phase of the international CIFOR/BMZ research project,[3] '*Developing institutions for sustainable uses of non-timber forest products*' this thesis involves 90% of the same study area investigated by STOIAN (2000) and BOJANIC (2001) in the first project phase,[4] i.e. the northern Bolivian Amazon. The main natural features of the region are: warm humid tropical climate with an average annual temperature between 24°C and 26°C with average annual precipitation between 1,834 mm and 2,774 mm distributes among October and April (ZONISIG 1997; FORONDA 2003:10). It includes an altitude range varying from 289 m to the west down to 90 m to the east. The dominant forest species are the Brazil nut (*Bertholletia excelsa*), rubber (*Hevea brasiliensis*), mahogany (*Swietenia macrophylla*), cedar (*Cedrela odorata*), *ísigo colorado* (*Tetragastris Altisima*), *ochoó* (*Hura crepitans*), and *palo maría* (*Calophyllum brasiliensis*), as well as other tree species of importance for animals, such as figs and palms available during a great part of the year, which explains the capacity of the region to sustain an important animal diversity, especially primates (FORONDA 2003:13; ZONISIG 1997). From the hydrological point of view, the northern Bolivian Amazon has also been called the 'Mesopotamia of Bolivia', due to the countless rivers that converge in the region. The rivers Beni, Madre de Dios, Tahumanu, Abuná, Orthon and Manuripi stand out, forming one of the main secondary basins flowing to the river Madeira.[5]

---

1 "*Hecha la ley, hecha la trampa*"

2 The Bolivian Amazon region has been delimited at least in five of its nine departments (Pando, Beni, and the areas to the north of Santa Cruz, Cochabamba and La Paz). I.e. that more than 50% of the whole Bolivian territory belongs to the Amazon basin. Moreover, taking into account the origin of the rivers that flow into the Rio Madera, the Amazon region would end up covering approximately 750,000 km^2, meaning three quarters of the national territory (DAVALOS 1997:23).

3 Center for International Forestry Research (CIFOR) and *Bundesministerium für wirtschaftliche Zusammenarbeit und Entwicklung* (BMZ).

4 For more information on the fist and second part of CIFOR/BMZ research project see sections 1.2.1 y 3.3.

5 Most of the rivers drain into the Rio Madeira, except for the Acre river that belongs to the sub-basin of the Purus river.

With respect to the political and administrative division, the northern Bolivian Amazon includes all five provinces of the Pando department, the province of Vaca Diez (Beni department) and the northernmost part of the Ixiamas municipality (province of Iturralde in the department of La Paz).[6] In view of the limited development of the national cartography, and the deficient national policies in relation to the geographical delimitation of the regions in Bolivia,[7] it is not possible to determine their surface area accurately. At least six different sources of information exist: For instance, the DHV report in 1993 claimed a surface area of 85,000 km^2; GAMARRA (2004) and CIDOB (1979) 86,260 km^2; BOJANIC (2001) and STOIAN (2000) 100,000 km^2; FORONDA (2003) 105,000 km^2; PACHECO and AVILA (2001) and ORMACHEA & FERNANDEZ (1989) 129,000 km^2; PAZ (1999) 130,000 km^2. The cause of the divergence in the total surface area between the sources reviewed is centred around the inclusion of the Ixiamas municipality; whether it is included entirely (PACHECO and AVILA 2001; PAZ 1999), only in part (FORONDA 2003; BOJANIC 2001; STOIAN 2000) or not at all (GAMARRA 2002; CIDOB 1979). In order to accelerate the '*saneamiento*'[8] (or land titling process), the government proceeded to define the region officially, incorporating 100% of the areas of Pando, Vaca Diez and Ixiamas.[9] As figure 1 shows, the study area selected in this thesis involves only the department of Pando (63,827 km^2) and the province of Vaca Diez (22,434 km^2), which combined represent almost 90% of the surface area defined by STOIAN (2000)and BOJANIC (2001). It lies between 9° 41' and 12° 30' south latitude and 65° 17' and 69°34' west longitude. The study area is bordered by Peru to the west an Brazil to the north and east.

In the northern Bolivian Amazon there are 700 rural settlements, distributed in 300 *barracas*[10] or private establishments for the extraction of non timber forest products (NTFP)11 and 400 rural communities STOIAN (2000).

---

[6] According to Bolivia's national constitution, the territory of the republic is divided politically into departments (9), provinces (112), sections of provinces (314) and cantons (1,385) (article 108). The municipality is the territorial and demographic' unit that is politically and administratively organized inside the limits of a section of province. The highest authority in the municipal jurisdiction is the municipal government, formed by the Municipal Council and the *Alcalde*, or mayor in English (Honorable Senado Nacional 2003:147).

[7] BOSIER 1993 (cited in PAZ 1999:185f), one of the most renowned regional planners in the Latin American environment, argued that the problem of regionalization in Latin America, is the preponderance of the deliberate political interests that proceed to establish regions without any basis in historical, sociological or anthropological elements. He claimed that such regions "*have been born as objects without yet becoming subjects*". These statements coincide with the Bolivian experience, where until recently, for purposes of implementing national programmes and projects, the government divided the country into three regions: the Andean, the Valleys and the Amazon. In the specific case of the Amazon region, its delimitation dates from 1978, as a result of the initiatives proposed by Brazil to integrate at the continental level all those countries with Amazon areas, which led to the signing of the 'Tratado de Cooperación Amazónica' (DAVALOS 1997:15).

[8] For the definition of *saneamiento* see section 1.3.3.

[9] Decree 25848: July 18th 2000

[10] For the definition of *barraca* see section 1.3.3.

[11] For the definitions of extraction and non timber forest products see section 1.3.3.

Figure 1 Locations of the Study Area

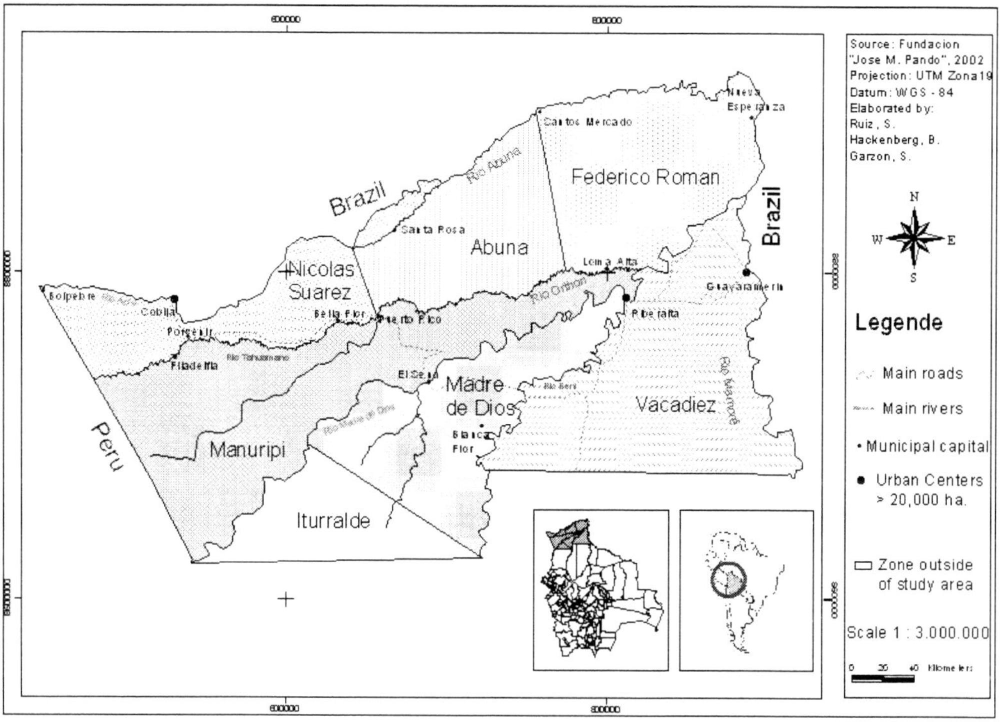

Based on field study interviews here is estimated around 550 rural settlements only for Pando and Vaca Diez, 200 of which correspond to *barracas* and 350 to rural communities.[12]

Just as in most of the Amazon regions, the history of the northern Bolivian Amazon is characterised by state abandonment, a typical feature of peripheral regions in Latin America.[13] A peripheral region is defined here as an area physically excluded from the political and administrative sphere of influence of public authorities. Put simply, it is the region not incorporated into the national development axis and, therefore, suffers the negligence and the abandonment of the government authorities. As mentioned later on, an important characteristic of the peripheral regions is the presence of strong traditional regimes that were developed by the actors themselves, given the absence of a state structure. The reasons for state abandonment of the study are were as follows: 1) the inheritance of the Spanish administration, obsessed solely with exploiting the mineral wealth of the Andean area, delegating the colonisation of the tropics to the Jesuit missionaries (PAZ 1999:65-73); 2) Bolivia has traditionally been dominated by a white and partially indigenous elite from the highlands, consisting exclusively of the social and economic white-mestizo elites of the Santa Cruz department; 3) the physical isolation and the low

[12] These estimates are based on information gathered during the field study (164 forest users interviewed), supported by data from the National Statistics Institute (INE) and preliminary *Saneamiento* data for the Department of Pando (INRA).
[13] For the definition of a peripheral region see section 1.3.3.

contribution of the region to the Gross National Product (GNP) meant the area failed to draw the attention of the state authorities; 4) a lack of interest on the part of the politicians, due to the low population density, which provides little incentive for the courting of votes (STOIAN 2000:45f); and 5) the weak parliamentary representation before the national congress, which only began to improve after the foundation of the Pando department (1938).[14]

The following is a more precise description of the study area as a peripheral region based on its administrative, economic and social features.

Administrative features

The state abandonment is clearly to perceive at the municipal administration, the lowest state administration level, where the state was only represented, basically in three of the 17 regional centres (Cobija, Puerto Rico and Riberalta) until 1994. Similar to the majority of rural regions in Bolivia, not only the state representation is weak, but also the public investment in ambits of education, health and communication is poor. Before publication of the Popular participation Law (1994), the central axis formed by the departments of La Paz, Cochabamba and Santa Cruz received some 90% of the co-participation taxes and the central government decided on the 75% of public investment. The other rural centres with important proportion of rural population were considered only as productive statements, so called *barracas,*[15] that were governed under the private norms of the rubber patrons, called *barraqueros*.

Economical features

State abandonment meant a lack of investment in infrastructure, mainly transport roads between production and industrial centres.[16] The region lacks good roads, making it difficult to access the remote communities, especially in the rainy season. The main traffic artery (600 km) incorporates only the three big cities in the region, Cobija, Riberalta and Guayaramerín and other few population centres like Porvenir, Puerto Rico and El Sena. The road is easily passable eight months of the year, and more difficult during the remaining four months. When precipitation is very strong the link to other departments is broken (see FUENTES *et al.* 2004).[17]

---

[14] Since 1938 three new senators and five deputies have represented the region's interests.

[15] For instance, the municipalities of Ingavi, Nacebe, San Pedro, Filadelfia, Bella Flor, El Sena, Porvenir,.

[16] In the absence of built roads for transport, the rivers have been important in regional development, because not only are their banks rich in rubber trees, one of the main reasons for the establishment of the *barracas*, but also for the transport possibilities they provide. Both timber and Brazil nuts continue to be transported to Riberalta (regional industrial capital) by river.

[17] Another important road in Pando is Porvenir -Chivé (189 km), which passes the community San Silvestre. At the moment 122 km of the road is in good condition (between Porvenir and San Silvestre). A great part of the population of Bolpebra uses the Brazilian highway BR-364 to travel between Cobija and San Pedro of Bolpebra. This highway is asphalted, allowing permanent traffic during the whole year (FUENTES *et al.* 2004).

This situation restricts the development of the whole potential of the forest sector, limiting the main source of income of the regional economy.[18] Especially the economic activities such as the extraction of Brazil nuts and timber have not been fully developed to date. In the case of the Brazil nut, it is estimated that presently only 30% of the production potential of the forests is being realised, estimated to be more than 320,000 tons of Brazil nuts in their shells per harvesting season (FAO 1994, cited in FORONDA 2003:25; ZONISIG 1997).[19]

Timber use at the present time is 10% of the forest potential, estimated to be 14 m³/ha for valuable species such as mahogany, cedar and oak (*Amburana cearensis*), and 24 m³/ha if the less valuable species are included (FORONDA 2003:14). However, since 1997 the study area has been the region with the highest Gross Domestic Product (GDP) per capita at national level (US$1,345) and has at the same time the biggest export index per capita, three times that of the national average (BOJANIC 2001:47). This because the exportation of Brazil nuts has a special importance for the regional economy, which increased from a few million dollars in the 1980s to above US$ 53 million in 2004. Timber production also expanded in the 1990s and contributed some US$ 15 million to the regional export in 1998 (BOJANIC 2001).[20] Even for the domestic economy, since the decline of timber exportation, mainly to the Argentinean markets (1999), the Brazil nut occupies the first place in terms of national forest exports.[21]

Extraction of non-timber forest products (NTFP), rubber in the past and today Brazil nuts, is the main source of income for rural settlements. However, in the last one hundred years both products were mainly controlled by big *barraca* holders who aspired to control near three million hectares at the beginning of 2000s. In the past the establishment of the *barracas* was favoured with the official permission on the part of the public agents, who granted widespread areas in favour of the

[18] Other economic sources in the region are palm heart extraction, small-scale gold mining, monetary remittances from Japan, the established trade with Brazil (mainly along the borders with Cobija and Guayaramerín), public sector transfers, fishing, hunting and gathering, and extensive cattle raising in the area under the influence of Cobija City (BOJANIC 2001:48ff). The agricultural sector is poorly developed in the region, because the soils are poor in nutrients. Rural agriculture is dedicated to self-consumption carried out in chacos that is created in the forest, after cutting and burning the vegetation. Each chacos is a small plot that usually is not bigger than two hectares. The main products sown are corn, rice, yucca, banana and bean (HENKEMANS 2001:116ff). Also, it is speculated that revenue from cocaine production generates US$1,600 million, which would indicate that the region, specifically Guayaramerín, is the biggest national cocaine marketing centre (PAZ 1999:214f based on a 1996 report by the La Paz DEA offices).

[19] The Brazil nut gathering period is normally between December and March. In some areas under the influence of Cobija City the Brazil nut harvest goes on until early June.

[20] The importance to the region of the forest sector also lies in the fact that it is the main source of occupation for people from rural and urban areas. Overall the forest sector consists of up to 50% of the regional labour force, offering work mainly to *zafreros* (10,000), shelling factories and their staff (6,500), chainsaw workers (2,000), transport providers, forest entrepreneurs, merchants, etc. (BOJANIC 2001:69f; Prefecture of the department of Pando 2001).

[21] The Brazil nut export value represents about 30% of the domestic forest exports. In 2000 Bolivia exported approximately US$ 33 million, falling in the two following years to US$ 27 million annually. However, in 2004 the export of Brazil nuts rose to approximately US$ 53 million, the equivalent of nearly 50% of the domestic forest exports (INE 2004).

new settlers: For example at the end of 1800s Antonio Vaca Diez requested the National Delegation award him more than 2,000 *estradas*[22] under his occupation from 1881.[23]

An other example is the '*Casa Suárez*', [24] the biggest extractivist company in the region, that had obtained the property right of 22 *barracas*, meant nearly 5 million hectares (GAMARRA 1993:34), i.e. the equivalent of nearly 50% of the area of the region. Generally the rural home of peasants and indigenous people did not profit directly from the economic benefits derived from the rubber economy: they were either removed from their original territories, or they were recruited as cheap productive labour for the extraction of forest products. The disparities in the distribution of the resources (land and forests) led to social conflicts between local forest users, which were generally solved in favour of the *barraca* holders, because the prevailing circumstances protected only their interests.

Social features

Four typical social or demographic features of peripheral regions in Bolivia are: 1) the disparities in the distribution of population, 2) the high population growth, 3) the high poverty indices and 4) pronounced differences between social classes.

With respect to the first feature, 70% of the regional population (approximately 170,000 inhabitants) resides in urban areas, mainly in the three bigger cities Riberalta (64,500), Guayaramerín (33,100) and Cobija (20,800) (INE 2002a and b). The study area represents one of the more sparsely populated regions of Bolivia: the regional population density is approximately two inhabitants per km^2, as opposed to the national average of eight per km^2, an index that decreases to less than 0.5 inhabitants per km^2 in several rural zones, such as to the north-east of Pando (Santos Mercado, Villa Nueva), Bolpebra (0.5 per km^2) and El Sena (0.3 per km^2).[25]

The second feature, the rate of high population growth, is characterised by a state of rapid flux of intra-regional (country-city) and inter-regional migration. The regional population growth rate is 3.4 % per annum due in particular to the rapid growth of cities like Cobija and Riberalta, which possess again amongst the highest growth rates at the national level, 7.3% and 5% respectively (UNDP 2003:43; INE 2002 a and b). This migratory phenomenon is not new. Even prior to

---

22 An *estrada* is a circuitous footpath connecting rubber trees and is used by the *siringueros* during the rubber harvest. The Law of December 12th 1895, decreed that an *estrada* is composed of 150 rubber trees. STOIAN (2000), declared that an *estrada* is made up of 80 to 200 rubber trees. PACHECO (1992) referred to between 120-150 trees. As yet there has been no exact determination of how many hectares make up a rubber *estrada*, as this is influenced by the density of trees present at each location. For example, in richer rubber areas the *estradas* are smaller.

23 Letter of Antonio Vaca Diez to the National Delegation, Orthon, 22 December 1893.

24 The '*Casa Suárez*' was the most important rubber company of the region. It was founded by Francisco Suárez in 1877 (London), the oldest brother of the four company owners. The company's importance resided in its absolute control over the rubber economy, from production to trade on the in international markets. Nicolás Suárez, one of the four owners, worked in the region (Cachuela Esperanza) and possessed up to 50% of the company assets. Due to the economic (nearly US $40 millions) and territorial (5 million hectares) dimensions of the company, Nicolás Suárez was called the 'Rockefeller of the rubber industry' in Bolivia, and his company the 'empire of the region'. The '*Casa Suárez*' collapsed in 1940 after the death of Nicolás Suárez, who was 88 years old (GAMARRA 1992; FIFER 1970).

25 See FUENTES *et al.* 2004

colonisation the region is characterized by the existence of strong population movements, as for example the indigenous groups of *Esse Ejja* and *Tacana*, who frequently crossed over the borders with Peru and Brazil (CIDOB 1979:207). At the beginning of the 20th century the regional population increased, due to the establishment of the *barracas* and the recruitment of thousands of workers from other regions (inter-regional migration), mainly from the north of La Paz, and the departments of Santa Cruz and Beni. After the Second World War intra-regional migration increased due to the reorganisation of the economy of the *barracas* and the emergence of 'independent communities'[26] (STOIAN 2000:191). A widespread characteristic of the region is the seasonal migratory flow of Brazil nut gatherers who move from the peri-urban areas to the rural areas between December and March. Labour migration (is not a recent phenomenon. In the '70s, before the last rubber crisis, 12.5% of the population of Riberalta (then 18,000) migrated temporarily to the rural areas to extract rubber and Brazil nuts (CIDOB 1979a: 216-7). At the present time, around 5,000 to 6,000 Brazil nut gatherers from Riberalta move to the forests to participate in the *zafra*. This is the equivalent of 10% of the city's current population (STOIAN 2000:191). When the Brazil nut harvest finishes, an reversal of the flow of migratory movement occurs. In other words, the migratory flow is away from the rural areas and towards the populated centres. The gatherers seek to find temporary jobs or in the case of an important number of young people to attend educational establishments.

The third feature, the high poverty indices, are also found in the northern Bolivian Amazon, in the less favoured regions of the country. More than 70% of the population lives below the poverty line, and nearly 30% finds itself in a situation of extreme poverty (UNDP 2003:54). A close look at the distribution of the population's poverty by municipality, allows us to conclude that in 14 of the 17 municipalities the percentage of homes with unfulfilled basic needs is greater than 80%. The absence of access to basic services (health and education) is the most important element of regional poverty (UNDP 2003:55).[27] According to FUENTES *et al.* (2004), Cobija is the only municipality with poverty indices lower than the national average, at 45.9% as compared to 58.6%. The municipalities of San Pedro, Villa Nueva, San Lorenzo, Ingavi, Gonzalo Moreno, Filadelfia and El Sena, in particular, stand out for their high poverty indices.

Finally both the current structure of the social classes and many of their effective cultural patterns, are a legacy from the time when rubber dominated the interactions between individuals.[28] According to BOJANIC, (2001) the society in the study is divided in three different classes:

- <u>Upper class:</u> mainly formed by the forest entrepreneurs (large *barraca* holders, owners of forest concessions, owners of Brazil nut factories, sawmills, etc.), the public authorities appointed by the executive and national parliamentary powers (political), and by the holders of the big *barracas*. Although this category has increased in number, its capacity

---

[26] The term 'independent community' is used synonymously with 'rural community'. For more details see section 1.3.3.

[27] In 14 municipalities more than 80% of the homesteads have no adequate access to these services, and in the other municipalities not more than 30% of the population at best has access to them (UNDP 2003:55).

[28] BOJANIC 2001:50

to negotiate and to influence the decision making process has declined. Their power is exercised through entrepreneurial organisations (ASPROGOAL[29] and CADEXNORTE[30]), social clubs and family ties.

- Middle class: formed by the public administration employees (technicians and professionals), company management staff (heads of personnel, administrators), merchants, military officers, small businessmen, teachers, small and medium *barraca* holders and NGO technicians.
- Lower class: divided into three groups: the first group includes the urban labour force, people that maintain a close link with the forest extraction activities (contractors, Brazil nut gatherers, timber retailers, chainsaw workers, Brazil nut shellers,[31] etc.), as well as transport providers, travelling salespersons, domestic employees, washerwomen, journeymen, fishermen, etc. Generally these actors belong to federations affiliated to the Bolivian Labour Union (COB), a body in charge of protecting their interests. In the second group are the members of the rural peasant and indigenous communities, as well as their local and regional representatives, who occupy positions in the peasant federations and in the indigenous unions (CIRABO[32] and CIPOAP[33]). This group has been one of those most strengthened under the reform. Under the public laws their settlements are recognized now as local territorial organisations (OTB),[34] a legal status that provides a means to land ownership, and later on to benefit from the forest resources. The last group belonging to this class is formed by individuals enjoying few privileges and rights of access to the forests, and are usually the poorest community members. The *fregueces,*[35] or permanent inhabitants of the *barracas*, and the foreign (Brazilian and Peruvian) inhabitants living in Bolivia generally occupy the areas with little access to service infrastructures, and in the case of the *fregueces*, are dependent on the conditions imposed by the *barracas* holders or *patrón*.

Given the low degree of intervention by the state, the three social classes are forced to maintain strong socio-economic interactions, specially for the use of the forests. The most relevant interrelations are between the upper and lower classes, especially between forest entrepreneurs (*barraca* holders and concessionaires) and the members of the rural communities who, in spite of being divided by the presence of social conflicts, often ask for work together because:

29 *Asociación de Productores de Goma y Almendra* (Riberalta).

30 *Cámara de Exportadores del Norte Boliviano.*

31 The Brazil nut shellers are usually women who work for the shell companies, called '*beneficiadoras*', for seven to nine months a year.

32 *Central Indígena de la región Amazónica* (Riberalta).

33 *Central Indígena y de Pueblos Originarios de Pando.*

34 The OTB is the basic community unit occupying a certain territorial space and maintains a close relationship with the public organs through its municipal government. Examples of OTBs are the urban unions (*juntas vecinales*), peasant communities and indigenous communities (Honorable Senado Nacional 2003:156).

35 The term '*freguez*' has been transformed over the course of the rubber history. At the beginning of the rubber era it was used as a synonym for the contractor that offered labour forces to the patron. Later it became synonymous with the rubber tapper (*siringuero*), or person that inhabited the *barraca* permanently under the *patron's* domain.

- Both groups have a common history that has resulted in the structuring of certain confidential positions and specialized functions. While the entrepreneurs have strong links within the industrial sector (they manage price information better, they also have better contact with the shelling factories and sawmills), the peasants and natives possess traditional knowledge, key to the timing of forest exploitation, mainly for the Brazil nut harvest.
- For some community members, the *barracas* mean alternative sources of revenue, mainly during the harvest time, where it is estimated that around 40% of the Brazil nut gatherers come from the rural areas. For the *barraca* holders to hire these people, it means lower transport costs because of the proximity of the communities to the production centres and the flexibility in the duration of the agreement of services.
- In recent times the peasants and natives have increased their control over the forests considerably, which for many entrepreneurs would mean having to give up these products if they were to ignore these groups.

Most of the interactions observed can be characterized as client relationships (in Spanish *clientelismo tradicional)*, widespread in Latin American cultures. This relationship between clients and the *patrón* can be interpreted as asymmetric, reciprocal and personal, resulting in benefits for both parties, and therefore creating natural dependencies (LEMARCHAND 1981 and SCOTT 1972 cited in PRITZL 2000:80). At the present time the social change observed in the study area saw the traditional *patrones* (*barraca* holders) partly displaced and replaced by the regional politicians (national parliamentarians and other officeholders), or by the new entrepreneurs in the forest sector (shelling factory and sawmill owners). The traditional structures and hierarchical dependences remain, however.[36]

The long tradition of rubber and Brazil nut extraction in combination with the low population density and the limited transport infrastructure have been decisive factors in maintaining the high forest cover. Although there is no consensus among specialists on the percentage of forest coverage, some estimate that more than 90% of the region is covered by forest. However, in spite of the low deforestation indices, the removal of the forests has increased since the early '90s, mainly in the areas under the influence of the cities of Riberalta and Cobija, as well as in the stretch along the main road linking these two cities. The main reason for this is the expansion of the agricultural area, especially the suitability of lands for extensive cattle raising (80%) and the increase of *chaqueos*[37] in the rural settlements (18%), as well as the commercial felling of the forests, which takes place mainly in the *barracas* (LLANQUE 2004:147ff; BOJANIC 2001; Prefectura del Departamento de Pando 2001; ZONISIG 1997).

[36] Cf PRITZL (2000:81).

[37] *Chaqueo* involves the preparation of the agricultural plots by felling and burning the woodland cover, normally occurring during the driest months (August/September).

1.2 State reform in Bolivia: the new Forest Law and Agrarian Law

A low degree of state intervention has characterised the history of several Bolivian regions since the creation the republic in 1825. With the recent approval of a very an ambitious reforms programme,[38] the government has sought to integrate such regions into the administrative and national political system. There is hardly a social, political or economic area that has not been reformed, beginning with the constitution, the public, territorial and the environmental administrations, as well as the agriculture, forest and hydrocarbon production sectors. The reforms extended to the parliament, judiciary, education, private participation in government enterprises, the distribution of public resources at municipality level and many other areas. However, following a long period of centralisation, the Bolivian reforms cannot be approved without the following aspects: 1) the establishment of democracy, after more than a decade of military dictatorships; 2) external support, to a certain extent conditioned by some international organisations (World Bank, Inter-American Development Bank, International Monetary Fund, USAID[39]); 3) the emergence of the social movements organised by the civil bodies and groups of indigenous people, as well as the country's peasants; and 4) the political will shown by the alternating governments.

This study concentrates on the analysis of two new national laws, the Forest Law (1700) and the Agrarian Law (1715), which make up the basis of the sustainable management policies of the natural resources in Bolivia. Both the Forest and the Agrarian Law are addressed when the term 'reform' is used in this study. Both laws belong to the 'second generation'[40] reform package, initiated in 1996 during the first government of Sánchez de Lozada (1993-1997). The objective of the laws analysed concentrated on bringing about institutional change to administrative, economic, environmental and social dimensions (see figure 2).

The administrative dimension is one of the most ambitious and defiant. The main interest lies in restructuring the national authorities of the public administration, such as the Forestry Development Centre (CDF)[41] in the case of the forest sector, and the National Council of Land Reform (CNRA) and the National Institute of Colonisation (INC) in the case of the agricultural sector. These three bodies were characterised by being highly bureaucratic, centralist and highly corrupt. They had great political influence, managed resources inefficiently and granted the rights to the use of resources in a non-transparent manner (HERNÁIZ & PACHECO 2001:22;

---

38 Several experts considered the programme of reform applied in Bolivia to be the most profound and most ambitious in Latin America (BIRLE 1996:9-14; ANTELO 2000:5; CRESPO 2000:9-11; REAL 2002:80).

39 U.S. Agency for International Development.

40 The rules applied during the reforms were classed into two major groups or generations: 1) the 'first generation', which in the Bolivian case began in 1985 with the Decree 21060 enforcement aimed at establishing strict measures to correct the imbalances of the Bolivian macro-economy; and 2) the 'second generation', which began with the approval of the Popular Participation Law, and later with the state's new political constitution (1995), administrative decentralisation, etc. The overall aim was to reorganize the state administration and reduce the role of the central Government (CRESPO 2000:11ff).

41 Under the old forest regulation regime, the Minister for Rural Affairs appointed the director general of the CDF. The CDF was in charge of many technical and political elements and fulfilled not only forest sector functions. Another of its responsibilities was to look after the management of protected areas and indigenous affairs.

CRESPO 2000:19; URIOSTE & BALDOMAR 1998:17; SIMAC 1990:345f). In the broad context of decentralisation policies, the Forest Law seeks to integrate the departmental (prefectures) and municipal administrations (municipal governments) in the control and allocation of the forests.

Figure 2 Objectives of the reforms of natural resource use

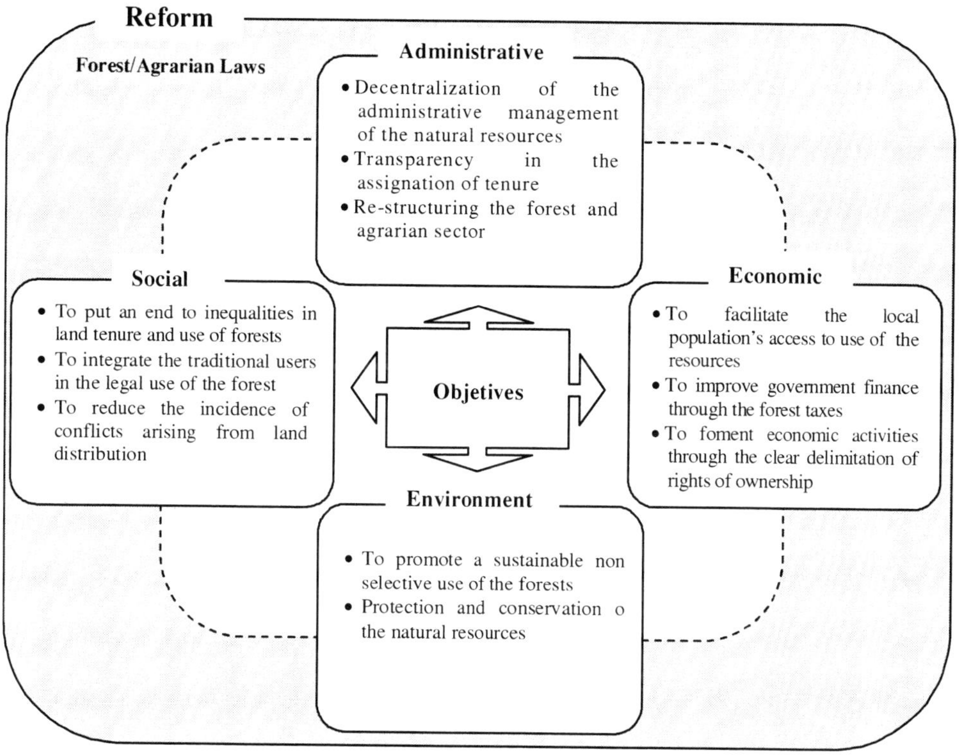

Source: RUIZ & BECKER (2003).

As a part of fiscal policy, one of the main objectives of the reforms in the economic dimension lies in increasing state incomes through the payment of forest taxes and other land revenues, with the aim of guaranteeing better technical control and eliminating the public dependence on external sources of finance. In this same dimension the legal security of the forest users is promoted, based on the more clearly defined establishment of property rights and with less overlapping of property boundaries. Also, through the provision of general access to the resources, the reform should contribute indirectly to improving the monetary incomes of the new forest users. To this end, the laws seek to diminish certain transaction costs, mainly reducing the bureaucratic process to the local population accesing natural resources.

The objective of the environmental dimension of the reforms is to contribute to Sustainable Forest Management (SFM) by means of granting forest tenures on a per hectare basis. The principles and approaches of the reforms resemble the international parameters set down by the Forest Stewardship Council (FSC) and other voluntary certification schemes (NITTLER and NASH 1999, cited in TAYTOR *et al.* 2003:67).

Lastly, in the social dimension, the integration of the traditional forest users, excluded under the previous regime, proposes the challenging goal of improving the distribution of the natural resources and putting an end to the differences in land and forest tenure.

1.2.1 Brief description of the laws under analysis

Figure 3 presents the most important contents of the Forest and Agrarian Laws that will be discussed in more detail in chapter 4.

Figure 3 Most important contents of the reform (Forest Law and Agrarian Law)

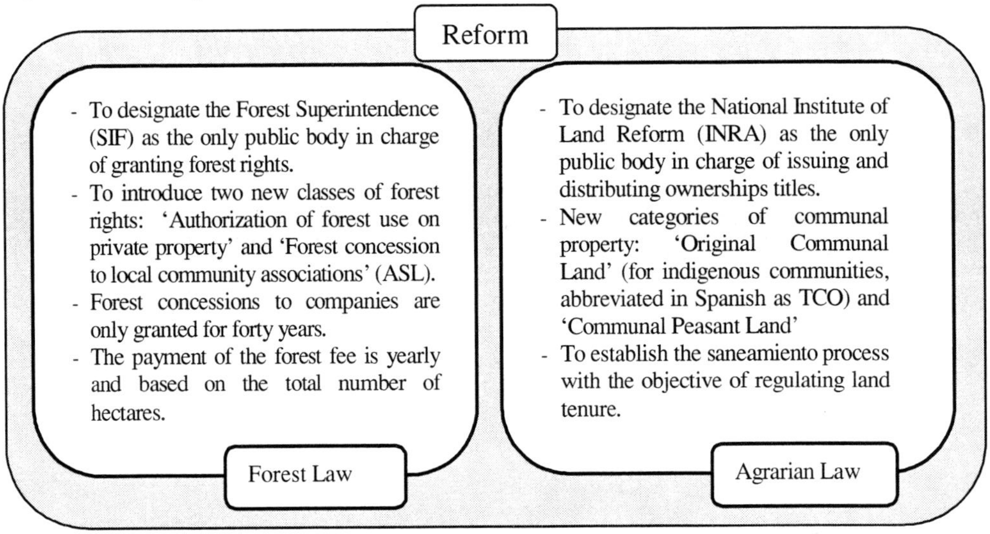

Source: RUIZ & BECKER (2003).

Forest Law (1700)

The origin of Forest Law is attributed to the initiative of the Commission of Environment and Natural Resources of the Chamber of Deputies (NITTLER 1996). The political deliberation lasted five years (1991-1996) and concluded with its approval on July 11th 1996 (PAVEZ & BOJANIC 1998; SILVA *et al.* 2002). The process of agreement of Forest Law integrated at least ten national interest groups, most notably the timber entrepreneurs, indigenous people, environmental organisations, the Bolivian president, the secretaries in charge of forest administration, international development agencies (FAO,[42] World Bank and USAID), the group of informal lumbermen, national parliamentarians, departmental civic committees, etc. (PAVEZ & BOJANIC 1998:47; 133ff). Starting from the participation principle and legal agreement, the Forest Law sought to incorporate the demands of each interest group

42 UNO for Food and Agriculture.

represented, which ultimately resulted in all of the actors getting a high percentage of their demands (PAVEZ & BOJANIC 1998:131).

Agrarian Law (1715)

The new Agrarian Law, known as '*Ley* INRA', has its origin in the chaos and corruption of the land administration in Bolivia (political influence and falsification of documents). At the end of 1992 the government was forced to intervene with two national authorities in charge of the land administration (CNRA and INC), as a measure dedicated to re-establishing law and order in the distribution and ownership of the country's rural land (URIOSTE & PACHECO 1999; HERNÁIZ & PACHECO 2001:22; CRESPO 2000:19). The political discussion, which lasted four years (1992-1996), concluded with the approval of the law of the 18th October 1996, after the 'Second Indigenous - Peasant March', which occurred between August and October 1996 (URIOSTE & BALDOMAR 1998:10). Compared with the political process accompanying the creation of the Forest Law, the Agrarian Law was discussed amongst a smaller group of actors. Seven principal interest groups were involved: the executive administration; international organisations like the World Bank and the Inter-American Bank; indigenous organisations; peasant organisations; settler organisations; agricultural managers and landowners (URIOSTE & PACHECO 1999). In contrast to the conformity of the forest interest groups, the results of the Agrarian Law did not satisfy any of the participant groups, because no party was able to realise its expectations to the full (URIOSTE & PACHECO 1999). Before any small degree of consensus could be reached among national actors, the influence of the international organisations increased, mainly that of the World Bank, which determined the course of the discussion.

In spite of the efforts behind the public acts and the urgency of the reforms, the laws ignore the socio-economic reality facing the Bolivian population and the political situation of same peripheral regions. Additionally, due to the historical state abandonment, the reforms were not discussed enough within the study region with the main representatives of the *barraca* holders and peasant associations (PAVEZ & BOJANIC 1998). For this reason the reforms are characterised by an 'institutional vacuum' in relation to the extractivist activities, harming the interests of certain forest users, and generating social disputes especially in the areas claimed by some indigenous groups or forest concessionaries which host large *barraca* holders and peasant communities.

1.3 Research structure

1.3.1 Research starting point and objectives

Part of the CIFOR/BMZ II project 'Developing institutions for sustainable use of non-timber forest products', this study is based on the recommendation of the researchers of the first project phase (CIFOR/BMZ I) 'Contributions of non-timber forest products to socio-economic development', who recommended the application of the 'New Institutional Economics' (NIE) as the theoretical framework of the study. The project deals with the investigation of the institutional change, more exactly with the change of property rights over forest resources, where the local research (inside the rural communities) was carried out by CARMEN GOTTWALD, and this study is the result of the research at regional level.

Based on my own professional experience as an advisor to the GTZ[43] (German Technical Cooperation) in relation to Bolivian environmental policy, and as an advisor to the 'Friedrich Ebert Foundation' in the study area for social and economic issues, this study concentrates on an analysis of the reform enforcement and on their impacts on the conflicts currently emerging.

The starting point of this study is the 'institutional vacuum' created by the Forest and Agrarian Laws. 'Institutional vacuum' is a fact accepted by the majority of interviewees in this study describing the exclusion in the reforms of extractivist activities in the northern Bolivian Amazon, resulting in the formal discrimination of certain forest users. For example in its initial version, the reforms did not recognise the true dimension of the *barraqueros*' and peasants' claims, fact that leads to land conflicts. In this context the investigation on conflicts presented in chapter 6 is based on three typical land struggles between the six main forest user: the 'local community associations' (so called ASLs), the peasant communities and the indigenous communities, as community groups, as well as the *barraca* holders, private landowners and forest concessionaires as individual groups.

Being aware of the fact that "*scientists rarely influence the politicians and the power to shape policies is largely out of their control*" (ALLEGRETTI 1990:253 cited in STOIAN 2000:18), this study does not directly aim to provide political instruments to improve the current regional problems. However, the study incorporates the pertinent information required to re-think some of the political decisions taken in the past, specifically in order to improve the conflict situation, as well as to promote the approval of new institutions.

The research has a general objective and three specific objectives. The general objective is to contribute to a better understanding of the reform enforcement in peripheral regions, characterised by geographical and political isolation and strongly consolidated traditional (private) institutions. The specific objectives may be formulated as follows:

1. To contribute to a better understanding of the public and private property rights that govern the management of the forests in the northern Bolivian Amazon, especially the extraction of Brazil nuts;
2. To identify the strategies of the regional interest groups in the formulation and enforcement of the public institutions; and
3. To identify the reasons for the conflicts between forest users caused by the enforcement of the reform.

[43] *Deutsche Gesellschaft für technische Zusammenarbeit* mbH

1.3.2 Research questions

Framed in the objectives of the study, are the following research questions:

1. What kind of changes does the reform introduce in relation to forest and agrarian property rights?
2. How do the private institutions change faced with the enforcement of the reform?
3. What are the direct consequences of the institutional change in the redistribution of the land and forest resources?
4. How do regional interest groups implementing the reforms react to the 'institutional vacuum'?
5. What kinds of strategies do the regional interest groups use in seeking changes to the public institutions?
6. To what extent did the reforms contribute to the current conflict situation?
7. What kinds of strategies do the protagonists use to assure their tenure or access to the forests in conflict situations?
8. In what kind of grade the reform's objectives have been implemented in the study area?

1.3.3 Terminology and some preliminary definitions

To familiarise the reader with terms frequently used, the most important are defined below.

Institutions

The term institution is ambiguous. In every day speech it is used as a synonym for organisations or groups seeking a common objective. However, in this study it has been applied in the NIE context, as a synonym for 'norms' or 'rules of the game', established by the members of a society with the purpose of guiding and/or restricting the interactions between individuals. Two types of institutions are distinguished, public and private. The first are all kinds of regulatory schemes dictated by state authorities, mainly by the executive and legislative power, in form of laws, ordinances, municipal ordinances, administrative resolutions, etc. The second includes all types of agreements between individuals, be they written or verbal, and may include agreements of services, contracts for the sale of goods, agreements on the use of the forests, rules of traditional rights and other codes that help to define the expectations of the individuals in a society. According to NORTH (1990), the public institutions together with the private institutions form the 'institutional matrix'.

Reform

Reform is a phenomenon of institutional change, which covers the group of public institutions implemented in the modernisation process of the Bolivian state since 1985. However, consistent with the focus of the study, the forest and agrarian regimes are here addressed when the term reform is used. In spite of the concentration of the analysis on forest use, the influence of the Agrarian Law cannot be ignored, because in many case access to the land access determines access to the forests. In other words, the forest regime in Bolivia is subordinate to the agrarian regime.

Regime

A regime is understood to be the group of institutions regulating certain types of activity. It includes the law itself, its regulation and the technical rules dictated through decrees, ministerial resolutions and technical guidelines issued by the bodies in charge of their enforcement and control. As with the institutions, the regimes are differentiated into public and private. In this study the private regime of the barracas is analysed, in addition to the forest and agrarian public regimes. As synonym to public regimes it is used the term of forest or agrarian legislation.

Saneamiento (land titling process)

Introduced by the Bolivian Agrarian Law, the term is defined as 'the legal and technical process that includes several activities on the land and in the office, dedicated to regularizing and consolidating the right to agrarian property'.

Interest group

An interest group is any individual or organised group of individuals able to affect or to be affected by the achievement of a purpose (FREEMAN 1984 cited in RAMIREZ 1999). An organised group does not exist without a certain interest. The interest is the main reason justifying the existence of a group, and when the source of interest between the members of a group disappears, the group weakens and may eventually disappear (BENTLEY 1908). There are several ways to classify interest groups. The classification presented in this study differentiates two groups: 1) the forest user group (individual or collective); and 2) the group of organisations (private and public). The private organisations sub-group, as proposed by NORTH (1990:5), is in turn divided into social organisations (unions of producers), technical organisations (NGO and international cooperation projects) and economic organisations (sawmills and Brazil nut factories). The public organisations sub-group (political bodies according to NORTH 1990) is divided into national organisations (ministries, parliament, INRA, etc.) and regional organisations (prefectures, municipalities, agrarian and forest regional offices) (see figure 6, chapter 3). The term social actor is synonymous with interest group.

Barraca

Barraca is a characteristic term of the northern Bolivian Amazon and refers to the most important traditional regime in the management of the forest from the institutional point of view. However, a *barraca* is also a production establishment that represents large forest areas, awarded in the past by the national government in form of concessions to the regional entrepreneurs, or as it happened in the great majority of cases, *de facto* appropriations of the forests. In the economic sense, *the barraca* is the centre where the extraction of NTFPs occurs, which at present is concentrated on Brazil nut production. In the social sense, the *barraca* is a heterogeneous rural establishment, where the *patron*, or the property holder, is an important person, just as the administrators, foremen and the families of permanent dwellers (*fregueces*). Due to the great value of rubber trees and to the ease of product transport, the *barracas* are usually located along the banks of rivers (adapted from DHV 1993 vol. C: 1).

Rural community or independent community

Similar to the *barraca*, the term 'independent community' (in Spanish *comunidades independientes*) is also characteristic of the northern Bolivian Amazon. These are community settlements in the rural areas formed by former dependent workers of the *barracas* and their families, so-called *fregueces*, who gained independence from the *patron*. However, I prefer to use the term 'rural communities', a new term introduced by the land titling process in 2000, which includes the communities formed by peasants and by indigenous dwellers.

Extraction

"*Extraction can be defined as the removal of natural resources without the provision for their replacement*" (ANDERSON 1992:215; cited in STOIAN 2000:20). The term 'extractive', derived from 'extraction', conventionally implies a destructive form of resource use. The wide spectrum of the present definition encloses the traditional timber logging in the study area, which ignores the norms of sustainable forest management (SFM). However, in the context of the rubber tappers (*siringueros*), the term 'extractive' refers to a specific economic activity that depends on the long-term maintenance of rain forest areas (ALLEGRETTI 1990:261; cited in STOIAN 2000:20).

Extractivism

Extractivism is defined as "*the systems of exploitation of forest products that are intended for sale on regional (within country), national or international markets.*" Extractivist activities are distinct from those of a hunter-gathering society whose products are only used for household consumption or local exchange (LESCURE *et al.* 1994:59 cited in STOIAN 2000:20). In the context of the Brazilian Amazon, extractivism usually excludes the large-scale extraction of timber (RODRIGUES 1996:11; cited in STOIAN 2000:20). Yet small-scale extraction either for household consumption or income generation by small producers is included (STOIAN 2000:20). Given the importance of the NTFPs for the regional economy, the term *extractivismo* in the study area is closely related with the rubber tapping and Brazil nut gathering. In order to designate the traditional timber activities terms such as 'forest exploitation' or 'timber use' (*aprovechamientos maderable*) are used. The relationship between NTFPs and extractivism is closer. The forest users, especially the *barraca* holders, wish to highlight a difference between their extractivism as an activity with little environmental impact, and conventional logging, historically widespread as an activity aimed at drawing economic benefit from the forest without considering conservation parameters.[44]

[44] Extractivism is a socioeconomic activity based on the extraction of forest products without the need to destroy the source of the resources : the forest. This type of economy is linked to a strong social movement, considering the local population as an important component for maintaining the balance of the ecosystem. Therefore, the intention is to obtain the greatest collective benefit for the rural communities (LLANQUE, *et al.* 1993:9).

Concerning the present research, influenced by the regional terminology, the term extractivism is mainly used to denote gathering NTFPs.

Non- timber forest products (NTFP)

Non-timber forest products are all biotic forest products other than timber. Given the intrinsic interdependence between the forests and its waterways, fish also falls under this definition. As with the study by STOIAN (2000), this research deliberately excludes the non-timber benefits of forests that have the character of public goods or trans-boundary significance, such as carbon sequestration, climate stabilisation, conservation of biodiversity, etc. (STOIAN 2000:21).

1.3.4 Structure of the thesis

This dissertation contains seven chapters. Chapter 2 outlines the 'New Institutional Economics' (NIE) as the theoretical framework of the study. Within the scope of NIE, in the first part of the chapter, relevant characteristics of institutional change, especially of the changes to property (rights) are presented. The second part introduces rent-seeking as a theoretical approach, used to explain the behaviour of social actors during the process of property change and the negotiations over land use conflicts. The third chapter details the methods applied in the research, emphasising the process of collecting information during the field study, the actors interviewed, the main sources of secondary information consulted, as well as the strategies executed in order to facilitate the researcher's socialisation in study area. The fourth chapter describes part of institutional change. This refers to the visible changes over the categories of property rights towards the use of the forests, the influence of the reforms on private institutions (the *barraca* regime) and the consequences of the redistribution of the forest resources of the northern Bolivian Amazon. This chapter answers the research questions 1, 2 and 3. The fifth chapter details the process of institutional enforcement of Forest and Agrarian Laws based on expectations of regional actors. A theoretical model is proposed, with the purpose of explaining the mutual influence between interest groups and public institutions, called 'cycle of institutional change'. A second model facilitating the understanding of the social interactions during the rule approval process is presented, to explain the strategies executed by two of the main regional interest groups (*barraca* holders and rural communities), in their desire to bring about changes to property rights in their favour. This chapter provides answers to the research questions 4 and 5. The sixth chapter contains an analysis of reform influence on emergence of the current land use conflicts. This chapter features a discussion of the strategies of the local actors to maintain control over the forests, based on three case studies. It provides the answers to the research questions 6 and 7. Finally, the seventh chapter answers research question 8, presenting a balance of the successes and failures in the reform enforcement in study area, based on the revision of available technical and scientific articles and on empirical results obtained during this study. In addition, the outcomes of the reform enforcement are discussed based on theoretical elements presented in second chapter, such as the functions of institutions and rent-seeking behaviour.

2 Theoretical Framework

"I open my discussion of the new institutional economics with a confession, an assertion, and a recommendation. The confession is that we are still very ignorant of institutions. The assertion is that the past quarter century has witnessed enormous progress in the study of institutions. The recommendation is that, awaiting a unified theory, we should be accepting pluralism."

(WILLIAMSON 2000:595)

2.1 Introduction

In this chapter the principle elements of the NIE are presented. The definitions of institutions and organisations are described, as well as important statements in relation to institutional change. Furthermore, this chapter emphasises the changes to property rights, so called 'property change', presenting a working definition of tenure and its 11 characteristics, which aid in the description of property rights relating to land and forest. Finally, in the third section, rent-seeking behaviour is described, as one of the main element of NIE, helping to understand the development and evolution of property rights from the point of view of regional actors. Given the variety of theoretical and methodological approaches, and disciplines that involve the NIE, two of the three empirical chapters include complementary theoretical issues, for the study of the institutions: whereas in chapter 5 two models are presented that explain the cycle of institutional change and the interrelations between interest groups and institutions, in chapter 6 the model of 'conflict escalation' is shown, as proposed by GLASL (1999), to relate the changes to forest property with the current social struggle over the use of natural resources.

2.2 The New Institutional Economics

The origins of the NIE are based in the deficiencies of the neoclassical theory. According to NORTH (1990), traditional economists ignore the institutions, with the argument that each change in the state is generated based on the operation of a perfect market. The neoclassical economic theory ignores fundamental aspects such as property rights, the asymmetric access to information and transaction costs.[45] "*The relevance of institutions in economic science lies in making the rules of how the market should be used by the participants. Having clear rules affects the economic activity because it reduces risk and uncertainty, which are highly dependent on expectations about changes in the rules of the game, raising thereby the costs related to contractual agreements* [...]"[46]

---

[45] RICHTER (1994:6ff) defined transaction costs in terms of costs for the use of the market, resulting from the following activities: 1) initiation, cost of information gathering; 2) negotiation, negotiation costs; 3) contract signing, decision costs; and 4) control of fulfilling contract and eventual sanctions for breaches, control and sanction costs (cf. PRITZL 2000:39).

[46] (WILLIAMSON 1975/1985 cited in KAPMEYER 2004:64).

The definition of institutions in the language of the NIE is broader than the more common every day use of the term. Here it does not refer to an organisation or a state administration (for example, a ministry or university), but rather "*all structures and behaviour rules, contributing to creating and stabilising the expectations of the individuals with respect to the behaviour of others*" (PRITZL 2000). These rules may be laws, decrees, contracts, and also informal social conventions carried out by the same individuals. The first type of rules count as public institutions and the second type as private institutions.[47] An organisation, in the context of the NIE, is defined as a collective and organised grouping of social actors sharing a common goal, or as SCHMOLLER (1990:61) termed it, "*the human element of the institutions*".[48] Making an analogy with sport, the institutions conform to '*rules of the game*', and the organisations to players or teams. The purpose of the rules is to define the way the game is played. The objective of each team is to win the game within that set of rules, through a combination of skills, strategies and coordination; by fair means and sometimes by foul (NORTH 1992:4f).

In spite of the seemingly precise separation of both terms in the NIE, the relationship between them has been deemed to be both close and complementary. The existence of organisations is due to the presence of rules and norms, determining attributions, responsibilities and, to a certain degree, they put temporary limits on its existence. Likewise it assumes that without organisations it would be almost impossible to implement and apply the institutional contents. This often hinders their separate identification. An example in Bolivia is the double meaning of

---

[47] In this thesis the most widely acknowledged institutional typology developed by DOUGLAS NORTH (1992), who distinguished between formal and informal institutions is not assumed. According to SCHMIDT (1999) his classification responds to two main criteria: 1) the level of formality (written or verbal), and 2) the 'enforcement mechanisms' used by the authorities in charge of the enforcement and the control of the institutions. Formal institutions are characterised as written and have recourse to the use of sanctions, such as penalties, fines and other forms of legal punishment, usually administered by government authorities. Informal institutions are verbal agreements made between members of society, executed based on the system of traditional sanctions, including punishments which have not necessarily been predetermined (isolation or shunning of the group, corporal or psychological punishment, etc.). This last type of institution is usually exercised by the members of the group or by some of its well-known bodies (SCHMIDT 1999:32ff). Often it is not possible to make a tacit differentiation between formal and informal rules. This can be observed in the Bolivian context, where the behaviour of the individuals ranges from the execution of the rules of the formal rights and rules of the *de facto* tenures. Given the weakness and the lack of transparency of the statutory control systems, the establishment of laws as formal institutions is often due to the systems of social control initiated by the actors themselves. In regions like the northern Bolivian Amazon, where traditional rights are stronger than the public laws, the state authorities are even obliged to recognise the traditional rules, when they try to establish some type of control or to acquire benefits for the public sector. At the same time, not all of the written rules are characteristic of the public system, nor do all verbal rules correspond to the social sector. For instance, due to lack of clarity of the laws, state bodies may make verbal agreements in order to implement the institutions, or community members may have recourse to write institutions directed towards the organisation of their communities, or to establish constraints over the use of the resources. For this reason, in this study a distinction has been made between public institutions and private institutions. The main distinguishing characteristic is the origin of the rules, whether they stem from the government or social spheres. Their formality remains open, as does the control or enforcement body and the sanction mechanisms.

[48] In German: "D*ie persönliche Seite der Institutionen*" (SCHOMOLLER 1990:61, cited in RICHTER & FURUBOTN 1999:8-9).

the initials INRA, which refer to Law 1715 and also to the government body in charge of implementing the Agrarian Law.[49] The focus of this study lies on the analysis of the institutions guiding the human interactions in relation to tenure and the use of the forests.

Institutions fulfil numerous social and economic functions (see table 1).

Table 1 Functions of institutions

Functions	Author / year
Providing an effective coordination and trust framework, making complex processes of human interaction more understandable and more predictable.	COMMONS (1950:104)[50]
Allowing individuals and groups of actors to cooperate successfully with others.	COLEMAN (1990)
Reducing uncertainty through the introduction of a stable (but not necessarily efficient) structure in the process of human interaction	NORTH (1990:6)
Structuring human interactions by influencing what is rational in a given situation;	KNIGHT (1992:17)
Reinforcing the predictability of human behaviour.	PEJOVICH (1995:30)
Helping to solve social dilemmas, such as 'free riding' and opportunism.	HANISCH (2003:9)
Contributing either directly or indirectly to the reduction of transaction and transformation costs, so that the markets function as flexibly and as efficiently as assumed in the neoclassical theory	FISCHER (2004:7)
Providing and limiting power, and creating a power balance between different social groups	KAPMEYER (2004).

According to NORTH (1990), the main function of institutions is to reduce uncertainty when introducing a stable structure to shape human interactions. The fact that 'institutions are not immune to change' does not contradict institutional stability. In fact, both the public and private institutions are in a permanent state of development, the main motors of change seemingly being the interests and preferences of the individuals.

Additionally institutions have to fulfil three basic conditions: 1) they are 'repetitive behaviour'; 2) they enjoy popular recognition and be shared by the members of the group; and 3) they are endowed with 'enforcement mechanisms' to be applied by third parties; for example public institutions appeal to state and its public bodies (administration, police,

[49] In Bolivia is even greater the confusion in the use of the term institution (Spanish: *institución*) also refers to the prominent personalities of the political or social environment that 'have left a mark' on society: For instance, Victor Paz Estenssoro and Hugo Banzer Suárez are called 'institutions'; both men held the office of President of the Republic of Bolivia, for four times and two times respectively. Similarly, the most important religious and traditional feasts are also called institutions, because they are considered great social events which are repeated each year, and constitute an intrinsic part of Bolivian culture.

[50] Cited in KAPMEYER 2004:65.

judiciary) enforcing the laws or private institutions appeal by the members of a group, through social control to enforce the informal arrangements (see IBARRA 2003:15).[51]

2.2.1 The institutional change

Change, as a process of transformation, can be interpreted in social and political sciences in different ways. Here it is interpreted as the form in which the institutions are created, modified or destroyed over time (NORTH 1981:5). Changes or distortions can be given in all forms and types of institutions (constitution, laws, contracts, agreements, etc.). In each case it is important to understand their reasons and consequences (RICHTER & FURUBOTN 1999:26). In Bolivia, the most popular institutional change in recent times has been the re-formulation of the public laws, known as the structural reform of the state, including among others, administrative decentralisation and the changes to the systems of resource management.

Institutional change is a complicated process, as institutions typically change incrementally rather than in discontinuous fashion. Although public rules may change overnight as a result of political or judicial decisions, private rules are much more impervious to deliberate policies (NORTH 1990:6). The persistence of the private institutions is a consequence of the intimate relationship between traditions and social customs, and subsequently, individuals better internalise their contents, adopting them as an active part of their daily lives (NORTH 1990:92). Public institutions, on the contrary, are more susceptible to transformation, following changes to the expectations and preferences of the actors, changes in relative prices, changes in the application systems and the execution of laws, and traumatic and discontinuous changes achieved by means of revolutions, conquests or natural disasters (NORTH 1990; SCHMIDT 1999:36).

In tropical countries such as Peru, Costa Rica, Bolivia, Indonesia and Cameroon alterations to forest use arising from changes to property ownership, were the result of political bargaining between several power groups. The actors are sufficiently motivated to change the relevant laws, because these are constituted in important 'action resources', allowing them to increase their rights and abilities, and also to reduce their obligations. Although the private institutions belong to these 'action resources', analysing the changes is a more complex process, because often these rules are not coded, and are, therefore, less accessible for the researcher. In this case, it is not only important to know the documented content of the norms, but also to possess a good understanding of the culture and history of the analysed environment.

WILLIAMSON (2000) provided a schema, aiding the study of institutional change on four levels of social analysis. The first level (L1) 'social embeddedness' includes the private institutions, where institutions change slowly (about every century or every thousand years), due to their spontaneous origin, minimising all kinds of deliberate choice (WILLIAMSON 2000:596f). The second level (L2), 'institutional environment' is formed by the formal rules of the game or 'public institutions'. These institutions are partly the product of evolutionary

---

51 According to KNIGHT (1992:3), 'rules of thumb' such as the maxims "*pay my bills on the day I get my paycheque*", "*get an hour of exercise five days a week*" should not be considered institutions. Although such rules may help to organise one's daily life, they are purely private constraints, idiosyncratic to the individual actor.

processes, influenced by the upper level (L1), but design opportunities are also posed (WILLIAMSON 2000:598). In spite of the recognition that the institutions at this level change quicker than the private institutions of L1, the transformation of laws and formal property rights is not frequent (occurring over decades and even centuries), unless 'destabilising events' cause the rupturing of the established rules (wars, civil demonstrations, revolutions, military coups, territorial occupations or financial crises, etc.).

The third level of social analysis (L3) deals with 'governance structures', as the perfect match between specific sets of transactions and the appropriate choice of the contractual relationships (WILLIAMSON 2000:599; HANISCH 2003:12). The changes at this level do not occur over a period of time greater than ten years (WILLIAMSON 2000:598 and HANISCH 2003:12). Finally, there is the analysis of the continuous process of resource allocation (L4). The analysis of changes to the economic incentives, and the prices and quantities of the resources is a typical feature of neoclassical economics.

The following are some general conclusions on the analysis of institutional change relating to the four levels of social interaction:

- One of the main institutional characteristics is the attitude towards change, influenced by political and economic aspects. However according to Williamson, private institutions, as well as customs, traditions, and religion have a spontaneous evolution.
- Although it is important to consider the timeframe in the analysis of institutional change, the frequency proposed by WILLIAMSON is wide and not exact, and consequently relative. According to the circumstances the institutional change may occur without defined 'time laws'. The scientific value of his statements could be depended on empiric results. In addition, it is necessary to consider external influences that accelerate change, such as civil manifestations, economic or political crises, wars, revolutions, natural catastrophes etc.
- A close non-temporal interrelation exists between levels of social interaction. Continuous changes in prices or quantities can induce future changes in the ways in which public organisations operate, as well as changes to formal property rights and the informal institutions. Conversely, changes to the influence of the upper levels should determine the allocation of resources;

2.2.2 Property rights: Change and Definition

Property rights are one central point of analysis in the NIE. They are considered to be one of the most important institutions within a society, as they define the range of privileges granted to individuals with respect to a certain object, such as management conditions. In recent years, property rights have been the topic of a number of studies, which focused on their implications for the distribution of resources. However, we know surprisingly little about the changes they undergo, mainly on their emergence and their modifications (ALSTON *et al.* 1997:146). Little is also known about the social, economic and environmental consequences, representing the introduction of new game rules, specifically in the area of natural resource management.

Like institutions, property rights can also be public or private.[52] Public property rights are characterised by regulating access to generally scarce goods, requiring the intervention of a state authority that determines 'the form of fair distribution of goods' and exercises control over them, in order to channel the behaviour of the individuals and to reduce social uncertainty. Private property rights are characterised as having applied enforcement mechanisms and are controlled by the same members of a social group. In the context of this study, an example of private property rights are the established rules inside the *barracas,* regulating the use of NTFPs. Despite this differentiation, both types of property rights share two common characteristics: 1) they should be observed and respected by the population's majority, including officeholders (PRITZL 2000:36); and 2) they not only provide the incentives for investment and other behaviour types, affecting the economy performance, they also determine the economic actors a society and define the distribution of wealth (ALSTON *et al.* 1997:146).

Therefore they usually emerge in processes of political negotiation, which determine the nature and application of the structures of rights. Put simply, they are the result of informal bargaining between small power groups, or formal negotiations involving organised groups, political representatives and government agents ALSTON *et al.* (1997:146). The following is a working definition based on DEMSETZ (1967:347):

> Property rights are an instrument of society helping individuals form expectations in relation to resource use, which they can reasonably hold in their dealings with others. These rules find expression in public institutions (laws), or private institutions (customs). The owner has the command of the community (in the broadest sense of the state) to benefit or harm oneself or others.

In addition, different property classifications and characteristics are presented, helping to illustrate the variety of property types in the study area: 1) the four types of property rights according to their analytical classification; 2) the four types of natural capital; and 3) the 11 tenure[53] characteristics in relation to natural resources.

The four types of property rights according to their analytical classification include the following rights: 1) granting the owners access to the use of resources *(usus)*; 2) allowing the owners to benefit from incomes derived coming from the use and the investment in the resource *(usus fructus)*; 3) allowing preparation or modification of the form and/or

[52] The rights to property in society are defined by rules that designate their appropriate use, control, and right of transfer. These rules may take the form of either informal rules and conventions, or formal laws enforced by the state (KNIGHT 1992:22).

[53] 'Tenure' is the set of rights that a person, or public or private entity has over certain goods. There are two alternate definitions of land tenure in the Latin American context. The first emphasises the aspects of land distribution between distinct actors and the relations generated between them. The second accentuates the forms of property rights, and access to and use of resources. SCHWEIGERT (1989) pointed out that a practical definition of land tenure should include both aspects, i.e., the distribution of the property and the property rights. Here, as was the case in the work of KUNDHANDE & LUCKERT (2000), the term tenure is also synonymous with property rights.

substance of the good possessed *(abusus)*; and 4) permitting sale or transferability of the resource to a third party *(transfer)*. These differentiated rights can be met, for example, in purchase and sale contracts, the mortgaging of a good (PRITZL 2000:34). In the northern Bolivian Amazon, this classification helps to distinguish, for example, between ownership titles over land that grant 'private owners' the right to transfer their rights, and the forest concessions that allow the holder only the right of *usus fructus* over forest.

According to BROMLEY (1991), there are four types of property regime in relation to natural capital: 'private property', 'community property', 'state property' and 'open access'. The 'private property' regime grants to an individual or group of individuals (corporation) the rights to exclude others from the use of the resources and to regulate and to control their management. Under 'community property', a clearly defined social unit, which shares the same system of authorities and collective rules, has control over the resources. The owner group has the right to exclude non-members from the benefits derived from the goods and the non-members are obliged to abide by the terms dictated by the owners. Under the category of 'state property' the rights to the resources are in the hands of the state, which makes decisions concerning the access, nature and level of exploitation permitted by its administrative authorities. Finally, 'open access' or 'non-property' implies the absence of clearly defined property rights, where access to the resources is not regulated and is free and open to all individuals, where the principle of 'first come, first served' predominates (BROMLEY 1991; SCHMIDT 1999; BROMLEY 2001). Table 2 is based on research by HANNA (1996),[54] supplementing the proposal made by BROMLEY 1991, and summarises the main owner rights and obligations in the study area.

Table 2 Rights and obligations of owners in the four types of property regimes in the study area

Regime type	Holders	Owner rights	Owner obligations	Examples
Private property	Individual	Socially and legally acceptable use; control of access to land; priority forest use	Avoidance of socially un-acceptable uses; payment of agrarian taxes; consideration of the specific national legislation	Agrarian and cattle rearing land owners; *barraca* holders with ownerships titles
Common property	Collective	Exclusion of non- members of the group; determining norms on the internal distribution of the resources	Maintain rights over space and time; transfer of rights restricted	Rural communities (peasants and indigenous); TCOs
State property	Citizens	Determine rules; exercise social control over the resources	Maintain social objectives	Protected area; lands not distributed by INRA
Open access	None	Utilisation of the resources	None	Rivers; wild fauna and flora; remote areas

Source: Adapted from HANNA 1996 (cited in KAPMEYER 2004:86)

[54] Cf. KAPMEYER 2004:86

The typology proposed by BROMLEY (1991) simplified the variety of rights regimes, yet the four types he referred to are not sufficient to apply to all of the regimes existing in the study area. "*In fact, property rights regimes combine features from different ownership categories. The academic typology of property regimes also differs significantly from the ways in which people ordinarily distinguish property rights regimes*" (KAPMEYER 2004:84). Contrary to the economic literature, individuals often refer to 'private property' as a term distinct from 'state property', a definition which may also include 'common property'. Nevertheless, the main problem caused by the academic terminology is the confusion between 'communal property' and 'open access', even between 'communal property' and 'state property'. With respect to the confusion between 'communal property' and 'open access', one of the main criticisms to HARDIN's work (1968) '*The tragedy of the common*'[55] comes from ELINOR OSTROM (1990), who has written extensively about 'common property resources'. According to OSTROM (2000), HARDIN ignores that 'communal property' incorporates institutional agreements that guide the effective management of resources, defining separately the rights of access, extraction, management, exclusion and alienation over natural resources. In addition, OSTROM (2000) remarks the presents of substantial evidence in many communal proprietorships, helping to solve effectively a wide diversity of local problems with relatively low transaction costs. Furthermore, CIRIACY-WANTRUP and BISHOP (1975) asserted that the difference between both types of property is that: "*in 'communal properties' there must be at least two groups, one which collectively controls the resources with the authority and ability to exclude the second group. On the other hand in 'open access' there is no group which can prevent any other from using the resource.*"[56]

The fact that 'open access' regimes are only applied in theory, is a second source of confusion. In most democratic countries the natural resources belong to the state, which in many cases tolerates the unregulated utilisation due to the technical and financial shortcomings of law enforcement, a common feature of the study area. Finally, confusion also exists between 'communal property' and 'state property'. The state may be viewed as a group of co-owner-like partnerships. Nevertheless, OSTROM (1990, cited in KAPMEYER 2004:85) mentioned two issues differentiating them: 1) the size of the group and its proximity to the resources. In the case of 'communal property', control over the resources is exercised by the members of the group. Resource utilisation on 'state property', on the contrary, should be regulated by state organisations and by civil society. At the same time, the communal owners are often closer to the resources than the rest of the citizenry. One means of avoiding confusion over property regimes, as well as to recognise their variations, might be to apply the tenure characteristics proposed by HALEY & LUCKERT (1990) (see table 3).[57]

---

55 HARDIN (1968) made two critical assumptions: first, that common property resources are open-access and second that such resources held in common are doomed to overexploitation since resource users are individualistic and unable to co-operate in favour of a common interest. The HARDIN model reaches the conclusion that resources must be either privatized or controlled by the state to ensure sustainable use (RICHARDS 1997:97).

56 Cf. KAPMEYER 2004:84 and OSTROM 2000.

57 HARLEY & LUCKERT researched property rights over commercial timber in Canada (see KUNDHANDE & LUCKERT 2000).

Table 3 Characteristics of property rights over natural resources

Attribute	Description
Comprehensiveness	Defines the set of natural resources over which tenure holders has control. A given type of tenure does not always confer the right to use all resources in an allotment. For example, while the rural communities can use the land for agriculture, they are restricted over the exploitation of minerals.
Exclusion	Refers to the ability of a tenure owner to prevent other users form freely enjoying the benefits of a good. For example, in a rural community the use of the land can be allocated according to individual rights, whereas the use of the forests can be a shared right between its members. Lack of exclusion may erode incentives for investment, since there is no guarantee of capturing the returns.[58]
Use Designation	Limits the types of activities that the tenure owner can carry out on a given type of tenure. In a sense, it is a form of distribution of the territory inside the properties. The stricter the assignment of use, the lower the value of the good. However, assignment of use is frequently used to ensure the continued supply of some types of natural resources.
Duration	In most cases, tenures specify the period over which property rights can be exercised. For example, private property normally infers a perpetual right. In contrast, leases of agricultural land can be for one or more seasons. The duration of tenure may have an impact on household investment decisions.
Allotment type	Refers to whether tenure specifies an area over which a owner possesses rights, or whether the tenure specifies volumes of natural resources that may be collected by the tenure owner. For example, it is common that land tenure are assigned based on a specific surface area.
Size	Refers to the spatial or volume specification of the tenure. With restricted spatial size, production can only be increased by intensifying the use of certain factors, such as labour. For example, the assignment by size of 'small agricultural property' in Bolivia means: up to 10 ha in the highlands; up to 20 ha in the valleys; up to 50 ha in the Amazon plains and up to 80 ha in the Chaco region.
Transferability	Refers to the ability of a resource owner to sell, bequeath, or gift an good (including the benefits generated by the good) to others at mutually agreed upon terms. The goods or resources transferred can take the form of sale or lease. For example, the members of the rural communities are officially limited to the sale of their properties, but in spite of this many people lease them.
Payment of taxes	Taxes may be payable by proprietors growing and/or harvesting agricultural crops or forest products. For example, timber exploitation requires all persons to buy a permit for the felling and transportation of trees. The payment of tax increases the user's costs and reduces the benefits of his tenure. However, the tax collection provides a social mechanism for profiting from resource use.
Operational requirements	Society may require that resource users adhere to certain regulations during the use of an asset. For example, the proprietors may be required to destroy corn stubble before a certain date in order to avoid plagues and illnesses. These requirements limit the proprietor's flexibility to make decisions. This attribute is in direct relationship with the 'operational control'.
Operational control	The process of defining property rights is not complete if there are no mechanisms for enforcing the conditions of tenure. Operational controls are the mechanisms for enforcing the conditions of tenure. The control mechanism may involve people that keep guard, designated by the villagers themselves, and a system of fines against those breaking the rules.
Security	Security may be defined by the perception of a tenure owner concerning his/her ability to capture benefits generated by the resource in the future, and whether changes in tenure will occur which increase or decrease the derived benefits.[59] This element of property is dependent on the socio-political environment in which the property rights are granted.

Source: Adapted from KUNDHANDE & LUCKERT (2000:7ff)

[58] CHEUNG (1970), cited in KUNDHANDE &LUCKERT (2000:7).

[59] LUCKERT (1992), cited in KUNDHANDE & LUCKERT (2000:11).

They proposed certain characteristics, which helped to classify and distinguish the tenure of resources, i.e.: the extent of the right (comprehensiveness), exclusion, use designation, duration, allotment type, size, transferability, payment of taxes, operational requirements, operational control and security (see table 3).

These characteristics were applied by KUNDHANDE & LUCKERT (2000) in their study on property rights over natural resources in the communal areas of Zimbabwe. [60] The characteristics are relevant to an understanding of the content of chapters 4 and 6, including the analysis of the changes of property rights, the overlap of public and private institutions and the emergence of conflicts. To fully understand the institutional change and the overlap of public and private institutions presented in chapters 4 and 6, it is necessary to distinguish the different variations of land tenure. Even though the state is an important protagonist in the allocation and control of resource utilisation, it is just as important to take into consideration the role of customary laws, as the overlap between both tenures types represents one of the main sources of conflict.

2.3 Theories on institutional change: Emphasis on rent-seeking

According to SCHLÜTER (2001), there are several theories which help to explain institutional change. The theories vary depending on the focus and the perspectives of the research; for example WILLIAMSON (2000) proposed different theories for each of the four levels, including the social theory (at level 1), the property rights approach, the positive political theory (at level 2), the economy of transaction costs (at level 3), and the neoclassical theory and the agency theory (at level 4). SCHLÜTER (2001:15ff) and HANISCH (2003:16ff) applied three theories in their analyses: 1) the 'efficiency theory' incorporated into the evolutionary perspective of the institutional changes, where the main mechanism of change is direct institutional competition, and where 'transaction costs', 'path dependence',[61] and 'ideology' explain the institutional change; 2) 'public choice theory' denotes an intentional perspective of changes to formal institutions, where the mechanism of change is indirect institutional competition through choice, and where the 'organisation of interests' is the main determining factor in achieving these aims; and 3) 'distribution theory', which assumes the bargaining power between the actors to be a mechanism of change, and where the factors determining change are the power relationships and the

[60] SCHLAGER & OSTROM (1992, cited in GARZÓN 2004:95f) proposed a similar classification for the identification of land tenure in common property regimes concentrating on the analysis of five criteria: 1) access: the right to enter a defined physical area and enjoy non-subtractive benefits; 2)withdrawal: the right to obtain resource units or products of a resource system; 3) management: the right to regulate internal use patterns and transform the resource by making improvements; 4) exclusion: the right to determine who will have access rights and withdrawal rights, and how those rights may be transferred; and 5) alienation: the right to sell or lease management and exclusion rights.

[61] The concept of path dependence refers to a process in which specific forms of institutional arrangements are chosen contingent of historical circumstances. Therefore, under certain conditions some technology or policy might be chosen over another even though the choice made might not necessarily be the most efficient in the long run, but the circumstances under which the choice is made can make it appear the best at the time. That is, the choice is sensitive to the initial conditions, and once an institutional arrangement is chosen it will be difficult to abandon. In this regard it is said that an institution is locked-in (NORTH 1990). The concept of path dependence brings forward the issue that what we have today is partly consequence of decisions made in the past. (cited in IBARRA, 2003:31).

ownership of the resources.[62] In the context of public choice theory, this study emphasises the analysis of rent-seeking behaviour for developing property rights. Before the presentation of the main theoretical elements of rent-seeking, it is necessary to present the definition of public choice, "*as the economic study of non market decision making, or simply the application of economics to political science*" (MUELLER 1976:395 cited in SCHLÜTER 2001).

According to SCHLÜTER, the objective of its analysis is the connection of the voters as demanders of political goods and the politicians as suppliers of political goods. The political process in the public choice theory is understood as a market, in which goods are not bought and sold for money, but traded for political goods, for example, property rights for electoral votes. Based on this rationale, DOWNS (1957:68 cited in SCHLÜTER 2001) proposed on the basis of the *homo economicus* the *homo politicus*, who, as a political actor, doesn't maximise profit but electoral votes. In this context OLSON (1995, 2000 cited in HANISCH 2003:85) employs models in the explanation of reform policies implemented in transitional and developing countries, describes politicians and bureaucracies as self interested bandits trying to extract as much as possible from their jobs and differing only in terms of whether they intend to grab more in the long term or in the short term.

2.3.1 Rent-seeking behaviour

As property rights define the distribution of wealth and political power, changes to the structure of property rights are likely to be influenced by more than pure efficiency considerations.[63] With the focus upon rent-seeking, institutional change acquires a wider perspective, explaining the interest groups behaviour and their ability to generate income without producing outputs or making a productive contribution.[64] In its most general form, rent-seeking describes the use of resources to capture a 'transfer' rather than to directly produce a good or service (FISCHER 2004:2). More in detail, the term 'rent' in the traditional economic sense means a return on some resource in excess of that which is required for its use. It is a surplus received by the owner of a resource.

---

[62] As other example, KAPMEYER (2004) presented three theories explaining the development of property rights in his study about land tenure in El Salvador: the invisible-hand theory, the naive theory and the rent-seeking theory. The invisible hand theory, also called spontaneous theory, originated with ADAM SMITH (1776), who introduced the term 'invisible hand' to suggest that: "*The individual is led by an invisible hand to promote an end which was no part of his intention*". As spontaneous theory, it seeks the origin of property rights not necessarily in the state, but rather in the nature of society (RICHTER & FURUBOTN 1999). HAYEK (1967 cited in KAPMEYER 2004) referred to institutions as being the "*results of human action but not of human design*", and introduced the term 'group selection', coming closer to an evolutionary theory of the institutional, in an almost Darwinian way. A second theory on the development of property rights described by KAPMEYER (2004) is the so called 'optimistic theory' or 'naive theory'. While the 'optimistic' point of view highlights the market as the only force pushing efficient economic organisation, critics refer to this theory as 'naive' because it ignores political processes as part of institutional change. The main limitations of the naive theory in its efforts at maximising the efficiency of property rights are that it ignores: 1) the high transaction costs caused by informational requirements in areas where the market (for example for land) is inefficient; 2) the 'path dependence', of individuals in the enforcement of institutional agreements; 3) the influence of the culture and the traditions; and 4) the interests of the individuals with bargaining power in political spheres (MLCOCH 1995:152 cited in SCHLÜTER 2001:22). About the rent-seeking theory see section 2.3.1.

[63] Cf. LIBECAP 1986, cited in KAPMEYER 2004:78.

[64] Cf. FISCHER 2004:2.

Contemporary economists, however, are more concerned with the rents accrued on resources that are socially constructed, such as patents. In this instance, an 'artificial' scarcity is created by writing rules that limit the number of producers of a particular good for a period of time. This rule allows the patent holder to act as a monopolist and reap higher than competitive prices (rents) on the sale of the protected product. Since the mid-1970s, a number of economists, including KRUEGER, TULLOCK, and TOLLISON, have expanded the discussion of rents to encompass a wide range of resources where a government creates an artificial scarcity by enacting rules (patents, import and export licenses, subsidies, professional examinations, taxi licenses, etc.) that limit access (WALKER 1998). The definition of rent may be best explained by a simplified example:[65] An inefficient company produces cars at a total unit cost of € 800 which can then be sold on the free market for € 1,000. As time passes, other companies supply better import cars at a lower cost. The company representatives have two alternatives: they may try to convince the government to ban any import as a measure to maintain jobs in the 'inefficient' domestic car industry, or the may try to improve the quality of their products by introducing improved technology and by recruiting experts. In both cases, the company can raise the retail price of cars to € 1,500, in the first case due to their monopoly position on the domestic market, and in the second case through the introduction of high technology. However the € 700 difference between the cost price and the new retail price, in the case of the monopoly example reflects a typical form of the seeking of artificial rents through political protection, here referred to as rent-seeking, and in the high technology example the difference is a factor of so-called 'profit-seeking'.[66]

In fact, examples of the distinction between 'profit-seeking' and rent-seeking in several developed countries also exist, when educated or trained persons enter the public job market after they have acquired the requirements necessary to attain certain public positions, allowing them to get income in exchange for their contributions to economic growth and social well being of their country. However, these people may also compete with numerous rent-seekers in a disloyal fashion, such as friends or relatives of public agents or political party members, for public jobs. It is often the case that these rent-seekers monopolise such public positions, without necessarily contributing to their country's development. This example illustrates the rents pursued by corrupt public agents, who are concerned only with their income, maintaining the power to make decisions, providing favours to friends, charging for future political favours, etc. Many similar examples pertaining to forest users also exist. Once they realise that the state plays an important role in resource assignment and control, they become sufficiently motivated to organise themselves and demand property changes. They do this in

---

65 The example was adapted by ideas proposed by FISCHER 2004

66 BUCHANAN (1980:3, cited in PRITZL 2000:268f) considered rent-seeking and 'profit seeking' to be contradictory on the basis of two essential differences: 1) rent-seeking does not result in an income derived from managerial activity (for example risk investment), but a source of income generated (largely) artificially by the interference of the state in the economic process and a political allocation of resources; and 2) the dispute over distribution does not flare up around the earnings and revenues obtained in the market by the different actors in the social game (managers and unions), but rather it is about distribution of positions of power and influences which guarantee the owners a sure and permanent source of rent. 'Profit seeking', on the other hand, consists of trying to obtain temporary gains that competition corrects with time. From an economic perspective, rent-seeking leads to the ineffective distribution of resources, whereas profit-seeking ultimately leads to greater efficiency.

order to gain access to forest areas, at the expense of efficient entrepreneurs, committed to consolidating their land claims based on capital investments and the production of goods.

The examples mentioned above also help to interpret the ideas put forward by OLSON (1968) in his work on the 'logic of the collective actions', where the organised interests of the elitist groups (here the car industry or the political parties) with greater access to spheres of decision have usually advantage on the diffuse interests of the consumers or popular groups, who must pay additional prices or must support inequalities in the distribution of public resources, not because they value the products as particularly good, but because they are not given the option to buy better or cheaper products or to impose their own interests. In table 4 four additional definitions of rent-seeking are presented.

Table 4 Definitions of 'rent-seeking'

Definition	Author	Attributes
Describes behaviour in the institutional sphere, where individuals make an effort to maximise the generated value of social waste, more than the generated value of social surplus.	BUCHANAN (1980:4)	Institutional sphere; social waste versus social surplus.
Includes a process of creating a scarce resource and the costs associated with gaining access to it.	WALKER (1998)	Scarce resource; costs
A procedure by means of which during the political bureaucratic process, i.e., in the political market,[67] it is sought singularly or collectively to exercise influence upon the modification of property rights.	PRITZL (2000:263)	Political market, singular or collective; changes of property rights.
An activity, mostly implying the expenditure of scarce resources, to cause and capture artificially created benefits, as well as transfers not part of society's intended income redistribution.	FISCHER (2004:34)	Expenditure of scarce resources; artificially created benefits.

This study highlights rent-seeking on the basis of three attributes:

- as an individual or collective behaviour typical of the political market, to exercise influence upon the property changes
- as an activity closely linked with the state function, where public agents become the main characters in the social fight over the distribution of the resources, wealth and power.[68]
- a form of behaviour geared towards causing and capturing artificially created benefits.

The attributes of rent-seeking help to clarify why a group might invest resources in lobbying and in making political contributions, namely in order to gain a particular modification in property rights in favour of its own members,[69] ignoring a negative effect on the overall distribution of wealth. In this context, using the rent-seeking approach one can draw conclusions in relation to the

[67] BENSON (1981) also referred to the political market as the '*black market of property rights*', where rights are assigned not on an economic or social basis, but on the basis of corruption.

[68] Cf. PRITZL 2000:264.

[69] Cf. KAPMEYER 2004:78.

"*likely winners and losers of economic and institutional change and their interaction in the political arena in specific settings*" LIBECAP (1986:228 cited in KAPMEYER 2004:78).

More about rent-seekers: they are people who steal or appropriate resources, for instance, civil servants who embezzle funds and demand bribes from their clients, or smugglers who deprive the government of income from taxes (FISCHER 2004). Rent-seekers also include entrepreneurs who lobby for measures to reduce competition so that they can sell their goods at higher prices and earn monopoly profits, or business people who bribe civil servants so that their inefficient company wins a tender. The difference that consumers and taxpayers pay for the goods and services provided by these entrepreneurs because a market is not open but protected, or because a tender has not been allocated to the highest bidder, reflects the share of income earned non-productively (FISCHER 2004:2). These examples include rent-seekers in key positions in public and private sectors. Therefore, rent-seeking is not common only to public agents, individual rent-seekers exist, as well as organised groups engaged in 'collective rent-seeking'.[70] In all cases, rent-seekers are strategists, who analyse the social and economic context, imposing their interests at the opportune moment, when they have greater political backing and better financial conditions necessary to bribe those responsible in government or enjoy greater social support from their bases enabling them to exert pressure. It is not only the good times which provide opportune moments for the rent-seekers to apply their strategies, however. Periods of crisis may also be taken advantage of to facilitate the assertion of their will, specifically when the negotiation power of the national governments has declined (because of popular rejection or the absence of a parliamentary majority). At such times the likelihood that rent-seekers will achieve their aims is increased. The distribution of the rents may increase or decrease according to the magnitude of the crisis. When a crisis intensifies, the power groups often obtain a greater relative portion of the rents, in relation to the rents and the support assigned to other groups.[71]

As successful rent-seeking activities always include some external costs, it is not uncommon that rent-seeking be linked with the emergence of social conflicts. The rent-seekers usually exhibit certain common traits. They are frequently powerful and privileged groups with great capacity for organisation, the ability to make contacts and access information, and they are usually aware of the fact that their strategies can cause conflicts. The analysis of rent-seeking strategies is a complex topic, but generally rent-seekers apply radical and solitary measures aimed at blocking the participation of third parties.

A main part of the literature assumes that rent-seeking leads to a failure in the allocation of scarce resources, so that rent-seeking is ultimately considered an unproductive and undesirable form of behaviour. The rent-seeking concept is applied to understand the behaviour of the interest groups during the formulation and enforcement of public institutions (see chapter 5), and also during the emergence of land use conflicts involving forests users, analysed in chapter 6.

---

70 TULLOCK 1993:43, cited in PRITZL 2000:263.

71 Cf. FISCHER 2004:568.

3 Research Methods

"A constructivist paradigm in methodological procedures assumes multiple realities and a subjective understanding demanding multiple methods to capture as much of this reality as possible."
(DENZIN & LINCOLN 1994).

3.1 Introduction

The regional situation was evaluated on the basis of eight research questions, formulated in accordance with the theoretical framework presented in the preceding chapter. The eight questions where directed mainly at clarifying the relationship between property changes and the emergence of land conflicts arising through the introduction of new public institutions. Relating to this the situation in the northern Bolivian Amazon presents an excellent opportunity to analyse the effects of reforms in peripheral regions, characterised historically by the existence of consolidated private institutions.

Specifically, the study deals with the analysis of property changes, beginning with the introduction of the Agrarian and Forest Law of 1996, and the overlap with the traditional *barraca* regime.[72] The focus of the research is on institutions, interest groups, and the interaction between them, as well as the strategies of the conflict protagonists.

Answering the research questions involved the selection of methodological approaches derived from social, political and institutional fields, where qualitative research methods and techniques are usually applied.[73]

3.2 Qualitative research approach

Historically, qualitative research has been overtaken by quantitative research. Qualitative research thought has been greatly developed in the Federal Republic of Germany since the 1970s. Outstanding researchers in the area of '*Qualitative Sozialforschung*' (qualitative social research) include HOPE and WEINGARTEN (1979), ZEDLER and MOSER (1983), HEINZE (1987), LAMNEK (1988) and SPÖHRING (1989) (cited in MAYRING 1999:1). In Latin America, due to influence of Spanish research, the development and application of qualitative social research only took hold in the 1990s.[74] In Bolivia, and specifically in the study area, the application of qualitative methods in social, economic and political research has been carried

---

[72] For more information concerning the *barraquero* regime see chapter 4.2.

[73] STATZ (2000:101) clarified the difference between methods and techniques. Methods constitute the systematic process applied to test and to verify theories, whereas techniques are the very specific mode of operation within a methodical process.

[74] In Mexico, for example, an increased interest in the application of qualitative methods in social sciences has been observed in the last decade (CISNEROS 2000:1).

out since 1995.[75] Contrary to the quantitative research approach, which usually measures or counts data and information, the qualitative approach seeks to systematically comprehend and interpret human behaviour, and human perceptions, intentions, opinions, experiences and values.[76] In addition to the actors and their interactions, qualitative research methods must also take into consideration the actors' environment. This is necessary in order to better understand the actors investigated and to better interpret the research data and information, which in turn is necessary for the improved credibility of the results, and conclusions derived from the research process.[77] In table 5 different features characterising both research types are highlighted. For example, in the qualitative research approach the researcher assumes the role of the main character collecting data (inside), whereas in the quantitative approach the researcher assumes a secondary role, because he is located outside from the data (see table 5).

Table 5 Characteristics of qualitative and quantitative social research

Characteristics	Qualitative research	Quantitative research
Main characteristic	Exploratory and descriptive	Confirmative and inferable
Approach	Inductive	Deductive
Methods	Open and unstructured	Standardised and structured
Orientation methods	Process orientated	Result orientated
Form of data collection	Natural, not very controlled observation	Penetrating and controlled measures
Researcher context	Next to the data (inside)	Marginal to the data (outside)
Data	Rich and deep, in the form of words, drawings, numbers, etc.	Solid and replicable, in abstract form, usually numbers
Supposition	Each phenomenon is qualitative only	All phenomena have the same qualitative structure, only in different quantities

Source: Adapted from REICHARDT & COOK (1986) and SILVERMAN (2001:25ff cited in HELD 2004).

The differences between both qualitative and quantitative research in the past gave rise to a methodological conflict that contributed to an accentuation of the contrasts between both paradigms. Nowadays, however, it is accepted as obvious that both forms of research have structural deficits, especially when they are applied separately.

In this study, the overall research approach applied was qualitative, but also involved the application of research methods for the collection of quantitative data. The application of such quantitative methods in qualitative research reduces the complex sociological data, and improves the interpretation context.[78] Furthermore, with this combination social research

75 See ASSIES 1997; PAZ 1999; STOIAN 2000; BOJANIC 2001; HENKEMANS 2001; GOTTWALD 2004.

76 ATTESLANDER (1995:11ff cited in HELD 2004).

77 MAYRING (1993:9 cited in HELD 2004).

78 KLEINING & WITT (2001:76 cited in HELD 2004).

gains in importance, validating and generalising the results, as well as neutralising the researcher's role.

3.3 Secondary data sources

In this study the main secondary data sources consulted belonged to five groups: 1) results of the CIFOR/BMZ I Programme; 2) documented scientific research and techniques from the region; 3) public institutions governing the use of natural resources (forest and land); 4) theses prepared within the scope of the CIFOR/BMZ II Programme; and 5) databases prepared by other authors.

Results of the CIFOR/BMZ I Programme

The results obtained by the researchers of the first phase of the CIFOR/BMZ research programme in northern Bolivia are one of the main sources of secondary data. Specifically, reference is made to the PhD theses presented by STOIAN (2000) and BOJANIC (2001). Not only was use made of the substance of both studies, but also of the contacts with the local partner organisation (PROMAB)[79] and databases, which contributed greatly to commencing the second research phase. The importance of both studies lies in:

- delimiting the study area according its geographical, economic, social and environmental features.
- clarifying the main regional terms such as *barraca, barraquero*, independent communities, *habilito*, etc.
- Helping to clarify the importance of the extraction of NTFPs and of timber use for the local, regional and national economy (BOJANIC 2001).
- clarifying the different typology of peasant communities and *barracas* (STOIAN 2000).

Scientific research and outstanding technical documents

Other secondary data sources are scientific and technical documents pertinent to the region published in the last decades such as from CIDOB 1979a/b (Centro de Información y Documentación de Bolivia), GAMARRA (1992), PACHECO (1992 / 1998), DHV (1993) a, b, c, d, e and f, ASSIES (1997), PACHECO & AVILA (2001), HENKEMANS (2002) and ASSIES (2002). All of these documents were selected in order to: learn about the social and economic differences between the forest users; understand the interrelations and socio-economic dependence between the interest groups, especially between *barraca* holders and the members of rural communities; provide a panoramic view of the interest groups interacting in forest use and consolidate the knowledge of the social and political reality of the study area.

[79] PROMAB stands for 'Programme for the Management of the Bolivian Amazon Forests'. It was financed until 2002 by funds provided by the University of Utrecht in Holland, with regional agreement with the Institute for Man, Agriculture and Ecology (IPHAE) and the forest engineers of the Technical University of Beni.

Public institutions

Another important secondary data source is the public rules governing natural resource use officially handed down by the Bolivian government. Figure 4 summarises the main public institutions. Based on the articles of the Agrarian regime of the Political Constitution of the Bolivian State (articles 165-176), the focus of analysis is the Forest and Agrarian legislation and all the complementary rules pertaining to property rights and the use of the natural resources. The contents of the administrative resolutions approved by the SIF and the INRA referring to forest use in the northern Bolivian Amazon were reviewed.

For the analysis of institutional change, presented in chapter 4, a historical-legal revision of the Agrarian Reform Law of 1956 and of the Forest Decree law of 1974 was made. The numerous public institutions approved since 1878, which regulate the use of the forests of the Bolivian Amazon, specifically rubber extraction, were consulted simultaneously.

Many of these laws were derogated by the legislation in force. In addition to the previously cited rules, the following laws and public ordinances were consulted: Law No. 1333 on the environment (1992); Law No. 1551 on popular participation (1994); Law No. 1654 on administrative decentralisation (1995); Law No. 2028 on municipalities (1999); Decree 25906: Re-classification of the Protected Area Manuripi (2000). Due that Decree 27572 only came into effect in June 2004, the implications and contents were not extensively incorporated into the analysis of the three thematic chapters.

Thesis work

Other valuable secondary data sources were the four research projects carried out by two graduate students (ROBERTO MALDONADO and GUNTHER HENTSCHEL) and two master students (ANDREA GARZON, and JOHANNES STAHL) within the scope of the second phase of the CIFOR/BMZ Programme.[80] The main contributions of these thesis were:

- To understand the private and public property rights of indigenous groups (*Yaminahua* and *Machineri*) (GARZON 2004);
- to understand the work of the organisations involved with the indigenous populations within the radius of influence of Cobija (GARZON 2004);
- to understand the livelihood strategies employed by the inhabitants of the rural areas (STAHL 2004);
- to supplement the information pertaining to the panorama of *barracas* and peasant tenure in the *Reserva Nacional de vida Silvestre Amazónica Manuripi* (RNVSAM) (MALDONADO 2004);
- to describe the types of social conflicts in the RNVSAM (MALDONADO 2004);
- to understand the strategies of the peasant communities' interested in benefiting from the forests and the reforms enforcement (HENTSCHEL 2004);

80 Summaries of the four research works were published by CIFOR in June 2004 (see bibliography).

Figure 4 Public institutions pertaining to natural resource use

National Constitution (1995)

Forest Law(1996)

- Res. Min. 132/97 Draft of PMF smaller than 200 ha
- Res. Min. 133/97 Guidelines on ASLs
- Res. Min. 248/98 Draft of PMF more than 200 ha
- Decree 25532 Conversion of *barracas* in forest concessions
- Decree 25838 Annulment of DS 25532
- Res. Min. 164/02 Draft of Brazil nut management plan
- Decree 27024 Adjustment of the forest tax payment

Agrarian Law (1996)

- Decree 25763 Regulation Ordinance
- Decree 25848 Modification to Decree 25763 granting a minimum of 500 ha to each peasant family and establishing land titling process in the region
- Decree 27572 which grants between 500 to 1,000 ha for the peasants and 15,000 ha for barracas holders

Research focus

Institutional change analysis

Forest Law Decree (1974)

- Decree 14459 Regulation of law (25.03.1977)
- Decree 19190 Obligation to pay timber bonuses of 11% to departments (4.10.1982)

Agrarian Reform Law (1953 -1956)

Historical regulatory frame

- Lease law by *estradas* (24.11.1883)
- Colonies and lands of the state law (13.11.1886)
- Regulatory decree of the *estradas* concessions law (15.05.1893)
- Rubber tax law (07.12.1895)
- Rubber exploitation law: awarding of rubber *estradas*, requirements for obtaining them (12.12.1895)
- *Estradas* decree: regulation of the rubber exploitation law (30. 06.1896)
- Rubber exploitation tax law (18.12.1896)
- Natives' rights decree (01.09.1897)
- Ordinance of declaration of territory of the colonies as reserved area for colonisation (25.04.1905)
- Public lands law (26.10.1905) and regulation of public lands (20.06.1907)
- Law of purchase of the lands occupied by the *barracas* (8.11.1917)
- Decree on the determination of the deeds in the proposal of 75 ha per rubber *estrada* (31.01.1919)
- Decree forbidding the felling of rubber producing trees (06.09.1925)
- Decree establishing the system of forest exploitation. 'First forest Law' (02.07.1939)
- Decree establishing that those interested in exploiting trees and bushes present their applications to the prefectures (11.11.1941)
- Decree 22407 establishing a five year ecological pause, prohibiting the grant of new forest concessions (01.01.1990)

- to understand the work of technical organisations (NGOs) and their support for rural communities in the Forest Law enforcement (HENTSCHEL 2004);
- to introduce the analysis of transaction costs in the enforcement and control of the public institutions, in the preparation of 'forest management plans' (HENTSCHEL 2004).

Other databases

In addition to data collected, seven databases compiled by other authors (see table 6) were also used.

Table 6 Databases used in this study

Database	Characteristics	Utility for this thesis
INRA (2004)	Includes preliminary results of *saneamiento* in Pando, number and area of peasant communities, private land-owners and available state areas, as well as the degree to which the rural settlements overlap with the forest concessions.	Chapter 4: Consequences of the reforms; Chapter 6: Expectations of the forest users and demarcation of conflict zones.
MALDONADO (2002)	Includes 77 interviews with forest users in the RNVSAM, containing data on production, territorial overlaps and social conflicts.	Chapter 5: Categorisation of the *barraca*.; Chapter 6: Conflicts inside the '*Manuripi*' protected area.
SIF (1997-2004)	Includes data approving technical instruments (forest management plans, annual operative plans); concessions in Pando; annual collection of forest taxes from 1997 to 2003; control inspections on illegal logging, timber transport and drafting of forest management plans.	Chapter 4: Historical diagnostic of forest distribution in the northern Bolivian Amazon; Chapter 7: Economic and environmental dimension of reform enforcement.
INRA (1957-2001)	Composed of 2,266 files and registration claims pertaining to different properties (cancelled, titled, pending, etc.). Of those, 982 registrations refer to Pando and 1,284 to the Vaca Diez province in Beni. It also includes the name of the plots holders (*titular del predio*),[81] name of the plots, ownership date, class of property, authority in charge of the registration, area in hectares, etc.	Chapter 4: Historical diagnostic of the distribution of the land in the northern Bolivian Amazon (enforcement of the agrarian regime).
ASPROGOAL (1998-2000)[82]	Includes the registration of 221 *barracas* in the study area, with data on geographic location, Brazil nut production, area, *barraca* holder[83] and overlap of *barracas* and third parties.[84]	Chapter 5: Categorisation of *barracas;* Chapter 6: Overlaps and conflicts between *barraqueros* and other forest users. Basis for figure 18.
STOIAN (2000)	Includes 173 interviews with indigenous communities, peasants, *barracas* and settlements in peri-urban areas.	Chapter 5: Establishment of the peasant communities and category-sation of *barracas*.
DHV (1993)	Includes the registration of 443 rural settlements, including peasant communities, indigenous communities and *barracas*.	Chapter 5: Number of rural communities in the Amazon region. Basis for the drafting of figure 17.

[81] 'Land holder' (*titular del predio*) is the term best suited to the situation in the region because the great majority of the rural settlements do not have consolidated property rights and are only considered 'possessors' of land, not 'owners'.

[82] The database was created from the registries of the three *barraquero* associations.

[83] The data were collected before the approval of Decree 25532.

[84] The data were collected after the approval of Decree 25532.

The databases contributed to the validation and generalisation of the findings, and increasing the representativeness of the quantitative data, as well as assisting in the creation of past and future scenarios in relation to the topics dealt with in this study. [85]

3.4 Primary data sources

Before starting to collect data it is important that the social researcher has a 'research strategy', incorporating the planning of the visits to the study area, the field study phase, the selection of the target group and, if necessary, the selection of a local counterpart, the means of accessing interviewees, the tools used to analyse data and above all to incorporate the possible limitations to be faced in the familiarisation process in the study area. The empirical research process is divided into three phases: Phase I: Pre-field study; phase II: Field study and phase III: Follow-up phase (see figure 5).

Figure 5 The three phases of empirical data collection

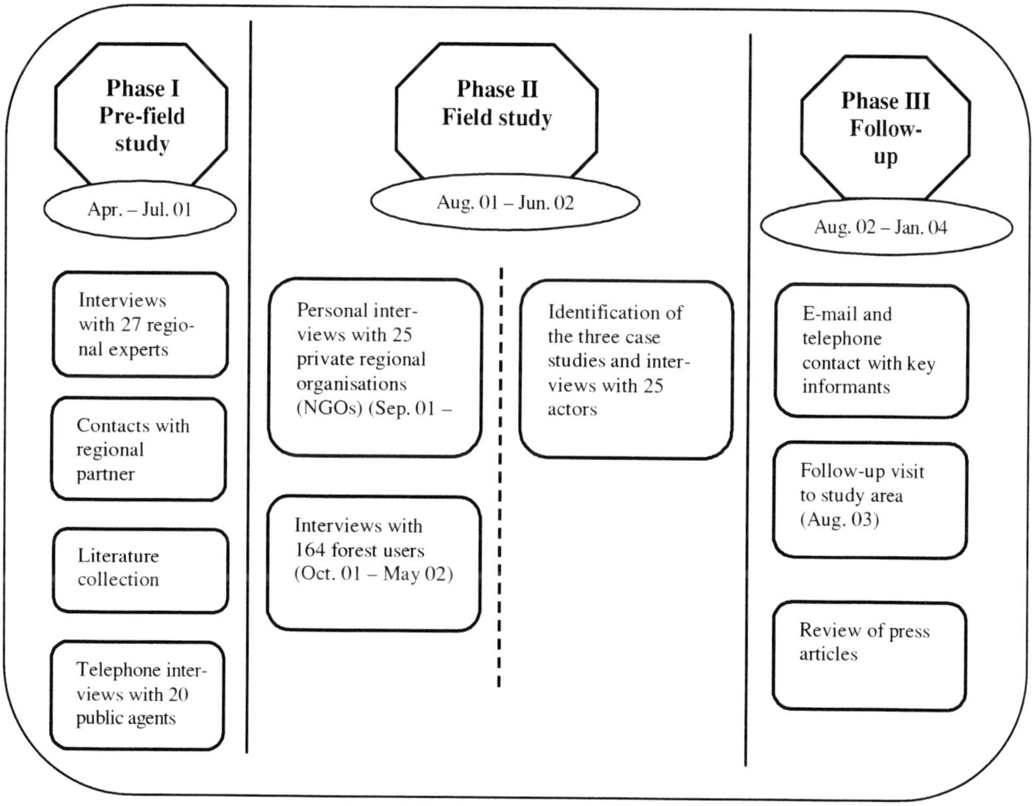

[85] The only published databases are those of the INRA (1957-2001) and the SIF (1998-2003). The INRA database is available on the internet: www.inra.gov.bo. The SIF data was structured based on the information available on the internet (www.superforestal.gov.bo) and other available technical reports.

3.4.1 Phase I: Pre-field study

It included the first contact with the study area, the first exploratory trip and the telephone interviews, conducted from Germany, with national and regional public organisations, such as municipal governments, SIF, INRA, ministry of sustainable development, and representatives of the national congress (see table 7). This phase lasted from April 2000 to July 2001.

First contact with the study area

The first contact with the study area was in April 2000, a visit outside the scope of the CIFOR/BMZ programme. Six months prior to beginning the research, I visited Riberalta as a consultant for a technical advice programme financed by the 'Friedrich Ebert Foundation'. The work involved interviewing those in charge of the regional organisations, especially NGOs (IPHAE, CIPCA, CEJIS, PROMAB, SNV-Riberalta), the peasant unions, and indigenous and *barraquero* representatives. These interviews later contributed to determining the research focus. In all interviews, the actors mentioned two main topics: the deficiency of land tenure, and the emergence of social conflicts.

The visit coincided with the enforcement process of Decree 25532, which transformed the *barracas* into NTFP concessions and led to the beginnings of the regional conflict between rural communities and *barraca* holders. At the same time, the first attempts to form alliances between the regional actors were evident.

Exploratory travel

Between January and February 2001, a visit was made to the northern Bolivian Amazon to collect data concerning the actual situation in the region in order to further elaborate the academic research proposal. Furthermore to obtain data on the socio-economic and political situation in the northern Bolivian Amazon, personal interviews were conducted with twenty local experts in Riberalta, Cobija, Puerto Rico and El Sena as well as with seven national experts responsible for implementing the forest policies in La Paz and Santa Cruz. One of the main results of this stage of the study was the establishment of contact with two local counterparts, differentiated according to the focus of the doctoral studies planned. The field study carried out by GOTTWALD took place in cooperation with the 'Centre for Research and Promotion of the Peasant' (CIPCA-Norte), whereas this study was carried out in cooperation with PROMAB. The decision to cooperate with a local counterpart means having to accept certain advantages and disadvantages during the field study. The decision to choose PROMAB as a counterpart resided in the following arguments: This is the only organisation at the regional level with experience in academic and applied research, strengthened by their collaboration with the University of Utrecht (Holland) and other international centres, such as CIFOR.[86] Since its foundation, in 1995, PROMAB has maintained close relationships with regional organisations such as the SIF-Riberalta, several municipalities, NGOs, private entrepreneur associations and concessionaires. Through its national counterpart IPHAE, PROMAB also has contacts with peasant communities and ASLs in the Vaca Diez province.

86 By the end of 2003, PROMAB had supported more than ten doctoral theses, mostly in European universities.

Lastly, PROMAB facilitated a communication and transport infrastructure (offices with telephones, fax, internet, vehicles, etc.), as well as secretarial services and field assistants.

The disadvantage of PROMAB as a counterpart was evident when setting up contacts with the peasant group in Pando and the indigenous group, as well as with representative organisations and technical advisors. Given PROMAB's cooperation with private entrepreneur associations, the rural leaders view the organisation as an opponent of their interests, restricting their access to information and contacts.[87] In order to establish contact with such rural leaders, initially margined, three other cooperation's agreements with local and national organisations were signed (INRA, CIRABO and SNV).[88] The new formal contacts not only facilitated access to secondary data on community groups, but they also facilitated the first contact with representatives of rural organisations (regional associations and local communities).

Telephone interviews

For the social researcher who is unable to be 'on site', phone interviews can be an efficient and economic means of collecting data. Telephone interviews were conducted from Germany during the months of June and July 2001, helping to: reduce the costs of personal interviews with public agents, given the great distances between their offices and the poor system of transport in the region[89] and broaden the data collection phase and to accelerate the establishment of contacts with the main organisations. The calls from Germany were rewarded with a high level of co-operation and the complete availability of the interviewees, even without previous appointment. None of the interviews were cancelled.

In comparison to the personal interviews, the telephone interviews were characterised by the high quality of data in relation to the interview run-time. The average duration was forty minutes per interview, compared with an average of more than one hour for the 'face to face' interviews. Some of the main disadvantages were: 1) in some cases the international calls raised false expectations among the interviewees, as one third of them admitted they were interested in contacting international co-operation bodies to garner funds for their organisation; 2) the researcher has to rely on the quality of the connection and is subject to continuous interruptions or two people speaking at the same time; and 3) an up-to-date list of telephone numbers for the organisations identified was not available to the author.

Table 7 shows the number of experts interviewed by organisation.

---

[87] For instance, an interview with the main NGO responsible for providing legal advice to the indigenous sector was not possible during the field study, because it considered PROMAB to be an organisation opposed to the interests of the indigenous sector.

[88] For more information see section 3.3.2.

[89] The cost of making telephone calls for the interviews from Germany was cheaper than making calls from Bolivia. At the time of the interviews, the cost from Germany was € 0.28 per minute, as opposed to € 0.35 per minute from within Bolivia, for example from La Paz to Riberalta. The cost of making calls to Bolivia from Germany has decreased greatly in recent times, from approximately € 2.50 per minute in 1995 to € 0.054 per minute in June 2005.

Table 7 Number of experts interviewed by telephone (June – July 2001)

Organisational level	Experts interviewed	Number of interviews carried out
Municipal (local governments)	Mayor or person in charge of the Municipal Forest Unit	12 municipal authorities
Regional (Riberalta and Cobija)	Office head or chief technician; regional parliamentary representative	1 INRA-Cobija 2 SIF (Riberalta and Cobija) 1 Prefecture-Pando
National (La Paz and Santa Cruz)		1ministry 1 SIF 1 INRA 1 parliamentarian[90]

The interviews with representatives of the local governments were not used completely. It was determined that both the mayors and the other municipal representatives in charge don't know in enough detail the situation in relation to the conflict over land. However these interviews provide relevant information about the inadequate technical and financial situation, the workings of the local governments and about the manner in which they assume their duties under the law, sometimes favouring certain forest user groups to the detriment of others (see chapter 7).

In summary, the execution of the first phase contributed to: focusing the research on topics of regional interest; recruiting PROMAB as the main counterpart at regional level; developing a preliminary classification of the regional interest groups, distinguishing between forest users and organisations (see figure 6). The execution of twenty telephone interviews with public agents; and the establishment of two operation centres located in Riberalta and Cobija[91] in order to cover the regional differences in relation to the dynamics of marketing products,[92] the capacity and experience of private organisations (NGOs and social unions),[93] the hierarchy in the political administration,[94] and the distribution of the rural settlements.[95]

---

90 The national parliamentary representative was interviewed during the fieldwork phase.

91 In order to give an idea of the distribution of time during the field study, 65% of the total time was spent in the Riberalta area and approximately 35% in the Cobija area. The emphasis placed on Riberalta over Cobija was partly compensated by the research carried out by ANDREA GARZÓN and ROBERTO MALDONADO in 2002.

92 Historically, Riberalta was considered the regional economic centre, due to the greater affluence of the forest enterprises, mainly Brazil nut shellers and sawmills.

93 Due to the economic and social importance of Riberalta this city attracted a greater number of NGOs and social unions than Cobija. Therefore, the organisations based in Riberalta have greater work experience, co-ordinate their work better and are able to raise greater financial resources for the execution of social and technical projects.

94 With the decentralisation process started in 1996, Cobija began to gain political weight in the region. The municipalities have started to orient themselves around the department capital more, due to financial and technical support received from the prefecture of Pando. Additionally, the establishment of the departmental directions of INRA and SIF served to strengthen the relationship between the population and the public services, previously assumed by Riberalta.

95 More peasant communities exist in Vaca Diez than in Pando, but all of the forest concessions and most of the *barracas* in the region are based in Pando.

Figure 6 Classification of the interest groups in the northern Bolivian Amazon

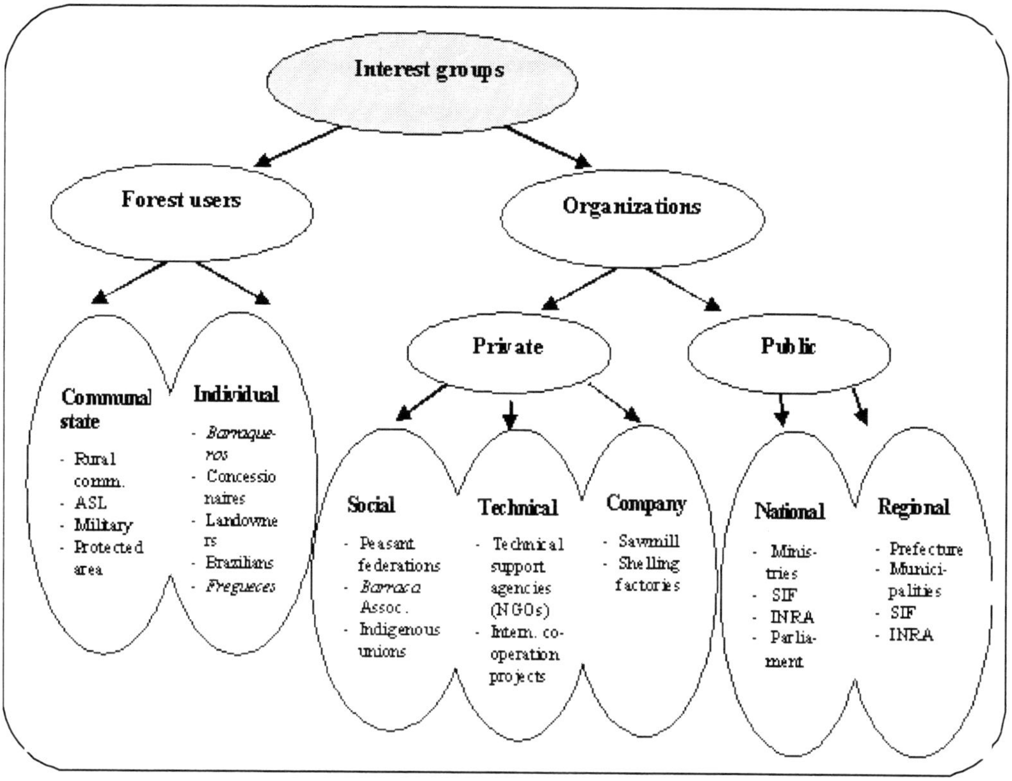

Source: Based on field study interviews

3.4.2 Phase II: The field study

The field study required that the investigated object remain in its natural environment and that the researcher go and participates in the daily life of the phenomenon under study (PATRY 1982; GIRTLER 1984; WHYTE 1984 cited in MAYRING 1999:39). The field study began August 7th, 2001 and ended June 14th, 2002. Its execution was divided into three stages: the familiarisation process, collecting regional data and the execution of case studies.

Familiarisation process

One of the main problems that the researcher faces when beginning the field phase is establishing contact with the group being studied. PARK (cited in GIRTLER 1992:54-55) compared the difficult familiarisation process a social researcher must undergo with the process that a baby must go through to become integrated into society.

In the worst cases, the society members will view the researcher as an intruder, and in the best he will be able to become a 'lawyer' of his own problems (MAYRING 1999:41). In this study, the familiarisation process was made easier by the first phase of the CIFOR/BMZ Programme and the execution of the pre-field study, which simplified the identification of local counterparts and contacting the main regional interest groups.

Given broad nature of the topic of study (analysis of social conflicts and institutions at regional level), the PROMAB contacts were not enough to reach the entire target group. Initially the 'excluded groups' were: 1) the peasant communities and their representatives, especially in Pando; 2) the indigenous population, including their NGO support sector; 3) the public organisations responsible for agrarian policies; and 4) several of the interest groups located in the city of Cobija. Thus, between August and October 2001, the first activity was to develop contacts and co-ordinate with the rest of the actors involved. Cooperation agreements were signed with the following representatives:

- The Director of the National Institute of Land Reform (INRA); this provided for access to the database on property rights and to technical reports on the saneamiento in the study area.
- The President of the Indigenous Union of the Amazon Region in Bolivia (CIRABO), who facilitated the interviews with the leaders of the indigenous communities identified for the case studies.
- The Director of the Dutch Service of Technical Co-operation (SNV) in Cobija; this was fundamental to linking up with the rest of the organisations in Pando, as well as for the research work carried out by two students (Garzón and Maldonado) and to facilitate transport to the rural settlements such as barracas, peasant communities, forest concessions and Brazilian settlements on the banks of the Karamanu and Abuná rivers.

It was not necessary to formalise the contact with the peasant and *barraquero* organisations. The relationships evolved through interviews with their leaders and visits to the organisations during the fieldwork. The contacts with the 'Peasants Union of the Provinces of Madre de Dios' and the 'Association of Rubber and Brazil nut Producers of Riberalta' (ASPROGOAL) opened the doors to further relationships with other similar unions in the region.[96]

There are two positive indicators of the familiarisation process: The low rejection index of interviews (2%) and the attempts on the part of the interviewees to obtain technical advice in relation to the research topic, particularly in relation to the content of the new institutions and the alternatives for conflict management.

Regarding to conflict management, there were four situations where the indigenous communities within *Multiétnico II* 'Indigenous Territory' (TCO) accepted the assistance of a conflict mediator, a role assumed by the author, previously the remit of the leaders of CIRABO. It was necessary in

---

96 ASPROGOAL-PA (Association of Rubber and Brazil nut Producers of Pando) and ARENARMAPA (Association of Rubber and Brazil nut Producers of the Province of Manuri) in the case of the *barraquero* sector; and the 'Peasant Unions of Pando and Vaca Diez' in the case of the peasant sector.

each case to try and separate the role of researcher and mediator. The mediator role facilitated an understanding of the relationships between individuals in conflict situations, and made possible the observation of the development of conflicts and the means whereby they were solved. At the same time, this situation helped the author to win over the trust of the regional actors, especially the indigenous population.

During the three case studies the role assumed by the author was purely that of an researcher, studying the strategies adopted and the decisions made by the conflict protagonists. In spite of the efforts made to differentiate the combination of roles, in two cases groups opposing the indigenous population (*barracas* holders) refused to grant interviews, as they were suspicious of the author's close links to the Indigenous Union (CIRABO).

These situations are difficult to avoid when researching conflicts, as the researcher is considered part of the social system, or as someone competing with other local actors (NGOs, public organisations, etc.) for information, and even for work. It is important that the researcher maintains a neutral position at all times, and is always ready to clarify the reasons for his presence if necessary, grant the same information and attention to all the interview partners and avoid exchanging information between the interviewees.

Collecting regional data

In this second stage, 'face to face' semi-structured interviews were carried out with the representatives of the private organisations (NGOs, social unions and forest enterprises) and the ten forest user groups. The interviews with the private organisations were conducted between September 2001 and January 2002, while the interviews with the forest users were conducted between October 2001 and May 2002. Both activities began in the area of influence of Riberalta and gradually moved to the Cobija area. Table 8 shows the number of experts interviewed personally according to interest group. The execution of this stage was fundamental to establishing the selection criteria for and the choice of the three case studies analysed in the following stage. During the first two phases of the empirical research, 209 interviews were carried out with 164 forest users and 45 public and private organisations.

The case studies

In qualitative social research, the term 'case study' does not describe a special data collection technique, but a focus of the research (KUTZNER 2000:56). The main idea of conducting case studies is to receive the full and permanent support of the 'cases', and to establish the complexity of the analysis process, to achieve detailed, in-depth results (MAYRING 1996 cited in KUTZNER 2000:56). The research activities took place between January and June 2002. The case studies were chosen based on the five criteria detailed in table 9.

Table 8 Personal interviews to regional experts during the field study

Interest group	Experts interviewed	Number of interviews
Private organisations	NGOs and public organisations: Head of the office or chief technician responsible.	9 national NGOs 2 international projects
	Social organisations: President of the associations of producers, president of the federations of peasants and president of the indigenous unions.	2 *barraquero* associations 3 peasant federations 2 indigenous unions 3 ASL associations
	Companies: Heads of production or enterprise owners.	2 sawmills; 2 shelling factories
Forest users	*Barraqueros:* Holders or administrators.	36
	Rural communities: Priority given to the community leader, or the person responsible for 'land and territory'.	53 peasants and 34 indigenous people
	ASL: President and members of the association.	3 (ASL associations)
	Private landowners: Property owners.	7
	Forest concessions: Holders or the responsible SIF technician.	14
	Military settlements: Those in charge of territorial issues.	9
	Brazilian settlements: Property holders.	7
	Protected area: Head of the area and head park-keeper.	1

Table 9 Criteria applied in the selection of the case studies

Criteria	Case study 1	Case study 2	Case study 3
Participation of individual and collective tenure holders with greatest access to the market.	*Barraca* holder and ASL	Private landowner and indigenous community in TCO	Forest concession and peasant community
High frequency in the answers of those responsible for the private organisations, denoting the re-gionnal importance of conflict.[97]	11 of 20 interviewees cited conflict	15 of 20 interviewees cited conflict	7 of 20 interviewees cited conflict
Participation of other regional interest groups (see figures 29, 30 and 31 in chapter 6).	Social associations, NGO, INRA, SIF, sawmills, legal counsel, UFM of municipality	Indigenous centres, NGO, social associations, INRA, SIF	Sawmills, SIF, INRA, PANFOR, technical counsels
Phase of execution of *saneamiento*	After the field study (June 2004)	Before the field study (January 2000)	During the field study (April 2002)
Geographical situation differentiated according to department and conflict zone	Riberalta/Beni; conflict zone 4 (see figure 25)	Blanca Flor/Pando; conflict zone 5	Bella Flor/Pando; conflict zone 8

97 The answers provided by the private organisations (NGOs and representatives of the forest users) were deemed parameters because their representatives revealed that they were well informed in relation to the existing social conflicts in the region.

In addition to the 209 interviews another 25 interviews were carried out during the case studies. These interviews were aimed at six conflict protagonists, the representatives of the six public organisations (three regional and three municipal), the representatives of the eight alliance groups and the five 'external actors' engaged in other conflicts with the protagonists. During this stage, many interest groups interviewed in the previous phase (interview by telephone or personal) were interviewed at least a second time. The analysis of the case studies was reinforced with the revision of documents provided by the interviewees. Among these documents were certificates of the tenures of the protagonists[98] and the history of the settlements, record books, bylaws of the communal groups, contracts established with third parties, agreements over land delimitation made with neighbours, negotiation contracts signed between conflicting parties, newspaper articles and technical reports drawn up by the regional public authorities.

3.4.3 Phase III: Follow-up phase

Due to the dynamics of topics researched, it was necessary to plan follow-up activities; the purpose of which were to fill gaps in data collected previously prior to evaluation of results.

There were three main activities in this third phase:

- Continued communication with key informants: This was the main activity involving the regional actors of Riberalta and Cobija. Some requirements for its execution were the obtaining of the addressees of key informants, and to see that communications means are available for interviewees as well as that the researcher's expenses remained low. In this instance, the main solution was the use of e-mail and telephone calls.

- Fourth visit to the study area: This took place during the first two weeks of August 2003. The visit helped to supplement the data on the tasks of the regional interest groups and to further pursue the three cases studies.

- Continued review of press articles: The purpose of this was to update social and political events within the study area. One of the obstacles is the lack of a regional newspaper available on the internet. The most important news from the northern Bolivian Amazon is only accessible through the national newspapers (La Prensa, La Razón and El Diario).

3.5 Data collection tools

An important aspect to consider when developing a research strategy is the most suitable application of the variety of qualitative tools available. Although there is a great range of qualitative techniques, which are characterised by a degree of high flexibility, the inopportune application of a qualitative tool can influence negatively the data collection process, as well as the analysis and the presentation of the results, much as the incorrect use of a hammer can

---

98 From ownership titles, approval of forest management plans, 'settlement certificates' (*certificados de asentamiento*) granted by the municipalities, proceedings of 'legal personality', agrarian judgements issued previously within the framework of the Land Reform Law, contracts of purchase and sale of goods, maps drawn up by the Bolivian Geographical Military Institute, etc.

cause serious damage in carpentry (HARDER 1974 cited in DIEKMANN 2001:17f). The tools used in this study were chosen based on the characteristics of the interviewees and the study area conditions. For example, due to the poor accessibility to the municipalities, it was decided their representatives should be interviewed over the telephone, and all interviews were done verbally due to the high levels of illiteracy, particularly in rural areas. The tools used in this study were the following:

- Structured telephone interviews with public agents;
- Semi-structured personal interviews with regional organisations;
- Semi-structured personal interviews with forest users;
- Open interviews with the conflict protagonists in the three case studies;
- Participative observation in:
    - Technical meetings of NGOs and other social organisations in the region;
    - Congresses of peasants and/or indigenous groups, as well as *barraquero* assemblies;
    - Meetings of ASLs on legal and administrative matters;
    - Conflict negotiations between *barraca* holders, peasants and indigenous communities;
    - Conflict negotiations between indigenous communities;
    - Negotiations of Brazil nut prices in Riberalta between of regional interest groups;
    - Daily life situations and activities of the protagonists in the case studies.

Four different questionnaire types were developed and applied to public agents, representatives of private organisations, forest users and conflict protagonists (see table 10)

Table 10 Differences and similarities between the questionnaire types used

Target groups	Thematic and content differences	Format differences	Similarities
Public agents	- Main actions executed in the study region - Difficulties implementing the reforms	- Rigid structures with short questions and pre-formulated answers - Maximum duration of forty minutes	- Description of the main social conflicts
Represen-tatives of private organisations	- Group's support goals - Forms of technical support given to the forest users	- Personal semi-open interview - Questions formulated in a more technical language - Duration between sixty and ninety minutes	- Interviewees' opinion of the contents of the public institutions (Forest Law and INRA Law)
Forest users	- Identification of forest and land tenure - Limitations of the reforms in meeting expectations - Size and history of settlements	- Semi-structured interview - Questions formulated in more colloquial language - Duration between sixty and ninety minutes	- Identification of the interest groups working in the region
Conflict protagonists	- Identification of discussion topics - Interests and strategies executed to gain access to forest resources - Emphasis on perceiving the institutions governing the use of natural resources	- Interviews were based on open narrations of the experience of the interviewees - The maximum duration was seven hours, spread over at least four successive visits	- Data on the special characteristics of each interest group

3.6 Data analysis

In the collecting and processing of data two types of analysis were differentiated, according to the available qualitative and quantitative data. The semi-structured interviews were designed to gather mainly qualitative information. Nevertheless they were also used to determine quantitative data such as the area of settlements, number of members per community, payment of agrarian and forest taxes. All the information gathered in the field was recorded in the form of interviews transcribed by hand. The narrative interviews conducted with the conflict protagonists were kept in notebooks. Some interviews were taped, with the prior consent of key informants.[99] The dictaphone was used mainly with two types of actors: those with whom a greater trust had been established resulting from numerous visits (especially with conflict protagonists), and representatives of organisations who provided technical information pertaining to the organisation itself or to the contents of the laws. The recordings were used to obtain more in depth details and some necessary quantitative data, as written notes on the most outstanding points were taken in all cases. Data analysis began immediately after the conclusion of each interview. In every one of the interviews qualitative and quantitative information was evaluated. The first evaluation of data helped to determine and execute the subsequent steps and to identify information gaps, which could be filled through a secondary interview, particularly in the case of the conflict protagonists. In addition, data were registered in a database created using Microsoft Excel©, divided into tables according to the type of interest group (forest users / organisations).

These groups were subdivided into different categories, represented by lines and columns, according to the topics and data to be analysed. The recorded interviews were transcribed by local people with knowledge of the subject, and also knew the popular terms used in the area of study. The transcribed interviews were subsequently read and revised at least twice, mainly in relation to the topics most relevant to the research. All of the data collected went through a second analysis, whereby unclear or incomplete data were discarded, and were supplemented according to the availability of other data sources, such as phone interviews directed at selected experts and database statistics. The interviews with the organisations and the forest users reinforced the comparative analysis of the property change presented in chapter 4. Chapter 5 was drawn up based on the interviews with public and private organisations. The first part of chapter 6, showing the conflict situation in the study area, was prepared based on the content of the reforms and the databases of SIF and INRA; both kinds of secondary data provided relevant information on institutional and land overlaps presented in figure 24. This information was triangulated with 164 face to face interviews with representatives of the most important forest user groups. In addition, figure 25 was produced as a result of the combination of secondary and primary data, and presents the ten conflict zones in the study area. From these ten identified zones, three zones were selected for the execution of case studies, the findings from each of which were prepared based on the interviews with the conflict protagonists, reviewed and supplemented with the available secondary data sources such as documents of tenure, purchase and sale contracts, foundation records and maps. All findings are presented in the following chapters in form of statements and interpretations of qualitative information; they are also presented in tables and figures.

[99] Fifteen hours of interviews were recorded during the exploratory trip and forty hours of interviews during the field study.

4 Redistribution of forest resources in the northern Bolivian Amazon: - Analysis of property changes to the public and private institutions -

"In the twelve years since 1881, I have recognised, discovered and occupied successively the rubber plantations of lower River Beni, River Orthon and River Tahuamanu. [...] The sum of *estradas* of which I am in possession is 2,041; 1,209 of which I have open and in exploitation, with the remaining 832 identified, marked and to be opened up. To legalise the ownership titles of these estates [...] I claim the award of the 2,041 *estradas* that I possess as discoverer and occupier since 1881."
(Letter written by ANTONIO VACA DIEZ to the National Delegate; Río Orthon, December 22nd 1893)

4.1 Introduction

As an introduction to the current institutional change, a brief history of the changes to Bolivian forest legislation follows, specifically the transformation of certain legal instruments and environmental policies dictated in colonial times. According to ANDALUZ (1997:4) the first public forest protection regulation was enacted between 1574 and 1575. It consisted of an ordinance dictated by the Viceroy of Toledo, whereby the felling of trees surrounding the city of Charcas[100] was prohibited, under punishment of "*one hundred lashes and the cutting to the scalp of the hair of the offender*". During the time of the republic, a few months after the foundation of Bolivia, the liberator Simón Bolívar himself dictated an ordinance on 19th December 1825. This ordinance not only provided for the conservation of the forests, but also for the plantation of up to a million trees, "*preferably in places where there is most need of them*" (ANDALUZ 1997:4). From then on, until the beginning of the rubber era in the northern Bolivian Amazon (end of the 19th century), it is estimated that no other rule intended to guide the establishment and the production of the *barracas* is known to have existed. In this context the law 'leasing by *estrada*' is considered the first institution dictated by the Bolivian state. From November 1883 to 1925 it is estimated that at least ten rules were approved, including administrative resolutions, decrees and laws, regulating the extractivist sector. According to HIRAKURI (2001), the Decree of July 2nd 1939, dictated during the Busch presidency, can be considered the first Bolivian 'forest law'.

The contemporary history of the forest regulatory scheme in Bolivia begins with the approval of Decree Law 11686 of August 14th 1974, during the dictatorial government of Banzer (1972-1977). The decree faced serious problems during the enforcement process, due to a lack of the necessary technical and financial resources on the part of the organisations responsible. The negative attitude

100 The Charcas territory from colonial times corresponds to the city of Sucre today.

of the forest entrepreneurs towards the forests further complicated the issue. With the establishment of democracy, the government of Paz Zamora (1989-1993) was fundamental to correcting the problem of the over-exploitation of the forests. This process began with the Decree of the 'Historical Ecological Pause' (January 1990), which prohibited the granting of forest contracts for a five-year period, and secondly, with the enacting of the Law on the Environment.[101] This law requires the responsible authorities to carry out an appraisal of the forests as the basis for the execution of forest management and conservation plans (art. 47). Within the scope of the sustainable development policies introduced during the first government of Sánchez de Lozada (1993-1997), the Forest Law and the Agrarian Law were enacted, officially replacing the Forest Decree Law of 1974 and the Land Reform Law of 1953.[102]

This chapter only looks at a 'small part' of the institutional change, focusing on the transformation of property rights governing the use of the forests. The main purpose of this background is to describe and to clarify the effects of the reform: firstly in terms of the formal rights (section 4.2), secondly the transformation of private institutional agreements established by the *barracas* (section 4.3), and thirdly the effect of the property rights over distribution and access to the Amazon forests (section 4.4). The fact that this investigation concentrates on the institutional analysis of *barracas* as one of the most important traditional arrangement, it doesn't mean that this study ignores other important private institutions, such as the norms within the peasant and indigenous communities. However in scope of Project CIFOR/BMZ II, the investigation of GOTTWALD (in prep.) as well as of GARZON 2004, STAHL 2004 and HENTSCHEL 2004 offer more details about this private institutions.

The following research questions were posed:

- What kind of changes do the reforms introduce in relation to forest and agrarian property rights?
- How do the private institutions change with the enforcement of the reform?
- What are the direct consequences of the institutional change in the distribution of the land and forest resources?

4.2 Public institutional change

In this section changes in forest tenure (4.2.1) and changes in agrarian tenure (4.2.2) are described.

4.2.1 Changes in forest tenure (Decree Law 1974 vs. Law 1996)

The analysis begins with the following four elements introduced by forest legislation: 1) abolition of private forest property; 2) grouping of new categories of forest tenures; 3)

---

101 Law N°. 1333 of 27th April 1992.

102 The agrarian reform was initially approved as Decree Law 3463, on 2nd August 1953 and later the Legislative Congress of 1956 elevated its rank to National Law on 29th October 1956.

historical reconciliation between agricultural and forest tenures and 4) granting of access to forest resources for the interest groups previously excluded.

4.2.1.1 Abolishment of private forest property

The Decree Law of 1974 recognises the dominion of the state over the forests (article 2) without excluding the possibility of granting private ownership of the same to the forest companies interested (articles 9, 10, 19, 22, 45, 70 and 80).

Although this disposition favoured the forest entrepreneurs, in practice this legal instrument was never implemented. One of the main reasons was the subscription of use contracts, and thus entrepreneurs quickly consented to the utilisation of forests with lower enforcement costs. On the other hand, when opting for private property, the forest companies gave up two of the most important advantages of the system: access to limitless areas of forest and the selective extraction of the most sought-after species on the market. Another of the comparative advantages of the felling authorisations '*derechos de monte*' was the low cost of accessing the forests, which could be easily circumvented by the owners. Law 1700 put an end to the legal status of forests as private property, instead providing for the granting of property rights exclusively for the use of forest resources.

4.2.1.2 Grouping of forest tenures

The Forest Law contains three types of 'felling authorisations' in a category called 'forest concessions' (see table 11).

Table 11 Comparison of the forest tenures between the old and new legislation

Forest Decree Law 1168 (1974) (art. 25-I-III)	**Forest Law 1700 (1996)** (art. 28 and art. 29 II)
Authorisation of single use	Forest concession (timber and non-timber resources)
Annual felling authorisation	Authorisation of forest use on private property
Short, medium and long-term authorisations	Permission to extract
Authorisation for the harvesting of secondary forest products	

Source: Forest Decree law (1974); Forest Law (1996).

This change not only affects the form, but also the concept of granting tenures. The differences between both classes of tenures have not been sufficiently analysed in several technical and scientific reports. There are six attributes distinguishing between both tenures: the authority in charge of granting the concessions, the duration of the right, the transfer possibilities, the payment of the forest patent, the type of use, and the development of the use of alternative forest species.[103]

103 For more information see RUIZ 2004a:29

In the case of the utilisation of the Amazon forests two types of tenures are distinguished: those regulating commercial timber logging and those centred on the extraction of NTFPs.

Changes in timber rights

The forest concession was and continues to be the most common legal instrument in the region with respect to the timber trade. The current forest concessions arose in response to policies applied by the government in 1993. With the approval of the '*Plan Soberanía*',[104] the government granted 19 long-term use contracts between 1993 and 1995. Two years later, with the approval of the forest legislation, all of these use contracts were subjected to a process of voluntary conversion executed by the SIF. The 19 companies with long-term use contracts received their forest concessions through administrative resolutions of the SIF.

Changes in extractivist rights

In relation to the property rights for rubber and Brazil nut extraction, the government has granted the *barraca* holders concessions for the use of NTFPs since 1920. In the '40s, the Bolivian Development Corporation (CBF) was the authority in charge of authenticating concessions. However, in 1985, the Regional Development Corporations of Pando and Beni assumed responsibility for the extraction of NTFPs, in spite of the Decree Law of 1974, which delegated responsibility for the granting of 'harvest authorisations for secondary forest products' to the of Forestry Development Centre (CDF) (DHV 1993d:21; Forest Law 1996:art. 25 II). Currently, there are two legal alternatives governing the commercial or traditional use of NTFPs in areas where they are of significance: Firstly, based on the forest timber concessions granted, the additional extraction of NTFPs is permitted, with prior adaptation of the Forest Management Plan (FMP). This alternative allows the concession holders to pass over this right to a third party, in the event of not being interested or not being able to extract the resources, with previous subscription of subsidiary contracts with the interested parties supervised by the SIF (Forest Law 1996: art. 29 II). Secondly, the forest concessions may be granted for this purpose, giving priority to the traditional users, rural communities and local community associations (ASL)[105] (Forest Law 1996: art. 31 i).

Few of the companies of Pando were found to comply with article 29 of Forest Law, requiring the adaptation of forest management plan to extract NTFPs. Of the 11 concession recipients interviewed during the field study, only three claimed to have complied with the regulation requiring the adaptation of their management plans. Two further entrepreneurs claimed not to harvest Brazil nuts themselves. The six remaining companies availed of the Brazil nut crops, but with serious restrictions due to the lack of infrastructure (four

[104] The '*Plan Soberanía* ' (Sovereignty Plan) was a government policy applied exclusively in the department of Pando. It catered for the placement of timber companies along the country's international borders to prevent foreign inhabitants from Brazil and Peru extracting the natural resources within the department. This plan was institutionalised by a National Ministerial Resolution, which was approved by the CDF directory of Pando in 1993 (Presencia 18th November 1993).

[105] For more information about the ASL see section 4.2.1.4

companies), and in certain cases they claimed that the Brazil nut use provided for within their concession was carried out by third parties (five companies). In other words, 70% of the concessions remain informal, as according to the regulations they should present at least subsidiary contracts with third parties.

With the enforcement of the new forest regime, the only attempt to register the *barracas* as 'NTFP concessions' was made at the beginning of 2000, in line with Decree 25532 enacted 1999. Enforcement process did not take place because shortly after approval of the institutions, the government had to back down due to the pressure exercised by the peasants and indigenous people of the region (see chapter 5). In practice, the users of the Amazon forests experienced great difficulty implementing their rights to extract NTFPs provided for in 1974 and 1996. Seemingly, the entrepreneurs had little interest in being granted authorisation to harvest these products. Put simply, the '*barraquero* regime' continues to regulate extractivism in the region.[106]

4.2.1.3 Reconciliation between forest and agrarian tenures

The reforms reduce the possibility of overlapping forest and agrarian tenures, as the concessions are granted in area units and not volume units, and because forest tenures are subject to the results of the *saneamiento* of the agrarian plots.

At the same time, the Forest Law grants high-priority forest tenures to the agrarian property owners, which means the direct exclusion of third parties from the utilisation of the forests inside private and community properties. These new rights are implemented under the 'authorisation of forest use in private property' instrument. The enforcement of this category could eventually even exceed the areas occupied by the current forest concessions, if as has been estimated some 3 million hectares or more become titled property in the coming years, in line with the Decrees 25548 and 27572 (June 2004), granting at least 500 ha to each peasant family living in every community.

4.2.1.4 Socialisation of access to the forest resources

Decree Law of 1974 excluded from access to forest resources any forest user who is not incorporated as a forest entrepreneur. Article 4 (d) is one of the few paragraphs of this ruling that makes reference (in a general and unconvincing way) to the incorporation of the rural class in the benefits of forest production. Under the old regime, the indigenous peoples were called 'wild tribes' (*tribus selvícolas*), protected by the CDF authorities to guarantee their survival (art. 119-120).

---

[106] The DHV (1993d:21) report on land ownership indicates that very few cases of awarding forest tenures were known in Pando. Most of the existing authorisations were granted by CDF in return for political favours by certain regional entrepreneurs. This situation is difficult to confirm, because neither CDF Pando nor CDF Riberalta has reliable permanent registries on forest tenures over NTFP use. Upon reviewing the CDF archives in Pando it was discovered that in 1994 of the 15 registered forest companies, nine were granted an authorisation to use timber forest resources exclusively. The six remaining companies either provided services or were furniture, parquet or palm hearts factories. None of 15 companies possessed a specific authorisation for the harvesting of Brazil nuts (CDF Regional Nor-oeste 1994: Registry of forest companies, unpublished technical report).

Before the reform enforcement, 40% of the domestic forest area (approximately 21 million hectares) was in the hands of fifty forest companies, with less than 173 use contracts granted (CONTRERAS & VARGAS 2001:4; PACHECO 2000:8; BOJANIC 2001:42). With the introduction of Law 1700, the forest use area decreased drastically. From 1997 up until 2001, the area granted to forest companies declined, while the area under the management of new forest users increased (LLANQUE & ZONTA 2002; cited in RUIZ 2004:32a).

In breaking up the hegemony of the entrepreneurial sector with almost exclusive access to the forests, the new forest legislation seems to have completed at least one of its main social objectives (see figure 2). Currently, 12% of the total Bolivian forest area (approximately 6.5 million hectares) is being used legally by new forest users (SIF 2001: administration report). Although the granting of forest concessions continues to be the common legal instrument (78%), 7% of the total area is being managed as TCO, 6% as ASL, 4% as private estates, and the rest in forest concessions dedicated to research or in 'private reserves of natural patrimony' (RPPN) (SIF 2002; cited in RUIZ 2004:32a).

In the study area, apart from the long term forest concessions, forest users can access the forest resources through the enforcement of three other legal categories: 1) forest concessions such as ASL; 2) forest use in TCO; and 3) forest use in private and communal estates (see following section). The first legal instrument of the ASL was established directly under Forest Law, whereas the second and the third instruments were provided for under Agrarian Law and Popular Participation Law.[107]

The local community associations (ASLs)

The ASL category was created to provide for the formal access of formerly illegal user groups to forests, in the past made up of the chainsaw operators, so called *motosierristas*, and timber merchants.[108] An ASL is a group of organised people, enjoying the recognition of its municipality by means of a legal status. An ASL may be composed of traditional users, rural communities, indigenous people and other users of forest resources (Forest Law Regulation, Decree 24453 1996: art. 1-II TO). Local governments can declare as municipal forest area (ARFM) an area not greater than 20% of the public forests within their jurisdiction and to bid on concessions granted to the ASL (Forest Law 1996: art. 25a). In fact the enforcement

[107] The Law of Popular Participation establishes that the basic requirement for recognition as a peasant or indigenous community is the submission of a 'legal personality'. Once the members of the community complete this procedure, it will be able to receive land including forests (see figure 13).

[108] The operators of chainsaws or '*motosierristas*' form an active part of forest extraction system in Bolivia. Traditionally, local elites contracted small-scale operators, providing them with chainsaws, boats and provisions and sending them in search of valuable wood. The *motosierristas*, once equipped, made difficult trips into the interior of the forests in search of wood in remote and isolated areas. Later, the trees were cut illegally and '*cuartoneaban*' (cut using chainsaws), a process in which the wood was generally wasted. The *motosierristas* later sold the extracted wood to the contractors, who paid them a small proportion of the overall value of the wood used. The wood was later 'laundered' through concessionaires with political connections, who obtained the necessary certificates. This type of adjustment was typically strengthened by the debts between contractors and *motosierristas*, which fortified their bonds. Corrupt local government agents and politicians generally 'defended' this illegal activity and received part of the benefits. This mainly occurred on a small scale, and was generally tolerated and even supported by the inhabitants of the zone (CONTRERAS & VARGAS 2001:31).

reveals that seven of the 17 municipalities in the study area have proceeded to demarcate their ARFM (see figure 7), thanks to the technical support of organisations like BOLFOR[109] in Riberalta and PANFOR[110] in Cobija.

Figure 7 Locations of claims over Municipal Forest Areas (ARFMs)

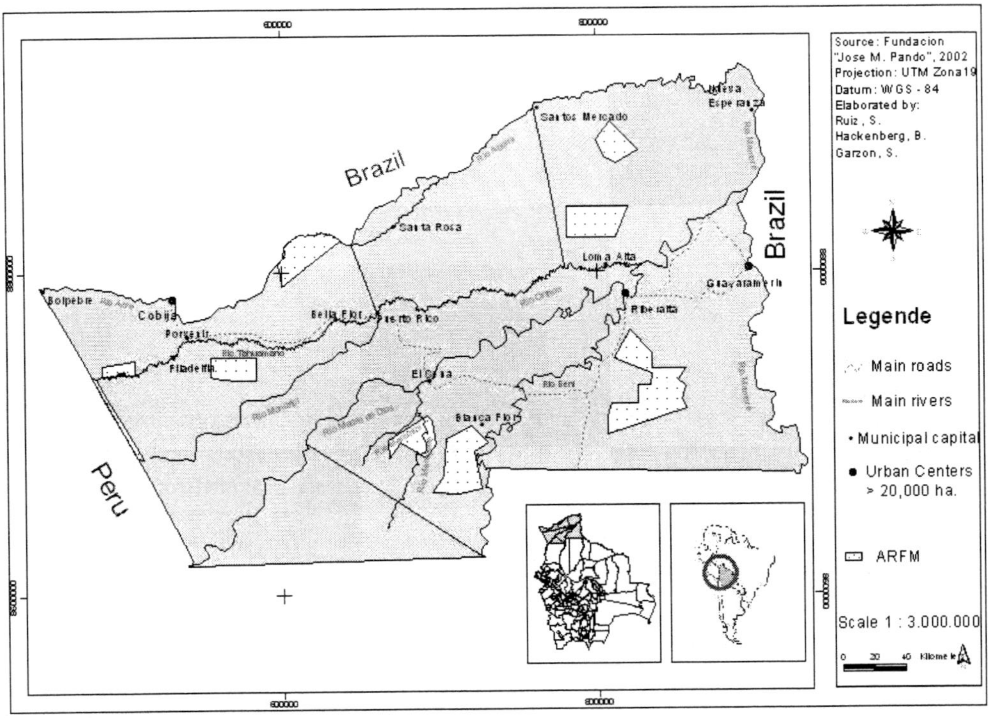

The process of ARFM delimitation was carried out in the office, locating the forest spaces based on two basic suppositions: abundance of forest species and 'absence' of property rights of third parties. This situation led to several social actors questioning the genuineness of the process of demarcation of ASLs together with other user groups, such as rural communities, *barraca* holders and 'private landowners'.

Compared against other Bolivian regions, the constitution of ASLs in study area is poor.[111] According to the field data, only four ASLs were organised in Vaca Diez province,[112] and so

109 Sustainable forest management project, dependent on the Bolivian government, with USAID financing.

110 PANFOR, 'Project of Sustainable Forest Management of Pando', is under the umbrella of the BOLFOR project and is financed by funds provided by the US government. It was under the control of the prefecture of the department of Pando until June 2002.

111 According to SIF statistics, 15 ASLs exist at national level with effective forest rights, occupying 407,700 ha (SIF 2002:8).

112 Two in the Municipality of Riberalta (El Verdum and APEFA) and two in the Municipality of Guayaramerín (Las Maras and 26 de Junio).

far only one has been able to take advantage of the forests. The establishment of ASLs in the department of Pando is even less advanced, with no association in existence as yet.

Only six ARFMs have been identified thus far, and only in a preliminary way, and this has again taken place in an office[113] not in the field. The process of demarcation of the ARFMs and the subsequent creation and consolidation of the ASLs has been put on hold until the land titling process has been concluded.

The indigenous territories (TCOs)

The second legal means of forest socialising access is elucidated in article 32 (II) of the Forest Law and article 3 (III) of the Agrarian Law, referring to forest use in the TCOs. These articles guarantee the indigenous peoples the exclusivity of collective use in their forests. Just as in the case of the ASLs, the regional experience in the use of the forests inside the TCOs is poorer than in the rest of the country.[114]

By early 2004, four indigenous communities had requested approval from the SIF for forest management plans for areas smaller than 200 hectares, corresponding to a total area of 800 hectares (see table 12). This is not a significant area when one considers that in 2001 around 315,000 hectares corresponding to two TCOs were granted: *Multiétnico II* (289,470 ha) and *Yaminahua-Machineri*, (26,470 ha). The forest legislation continues to pose a challenge for the indigenous communities in terms of forest use on their lands, given the strong technical, financial and administrative demands that they represent for their owners (REAL 2002:vii).

Another element impeding forest use inside the TCOs is disagreement between the members. The inhabitants of the TCOs do not dare to intrude upon the area of forest use fearing that it will generate social conflicts within their communities. This situation will not change as long as differences in the level of access to information exist among TCO inhabitants, and while the rules concerning the allocation of resources to individual actors and the distribution of earnings remain unclear. In the *Multiétnico* II TCO, most of the communities agree upon preventing their leaders from taking part in any type of negotiation of their timber resources, without the prior consent of all of the inhabitants and of the Indigenous Unions of the Bolivian Amazonian Region (CIRABO).[115]

The authorisation of forest use on private property

Finally the legal provision capable of changing the course of the utilisation of Bolivian Amazon forests in the event that the 300 rural communities due to be declared title-owners decide to carry out the community use of natural resources is presented. Three years after the execution of the land titling process, community forest management in the rural communities is a reality, made possible by granting of 500 ha/family and the interest of a great number of regional power groups. According to SIF data, by October 2003 three peasant communities

---

[113] El Sena, Santos Mercado, Villa Nueva, Bolpebra, Filadelfia, Bella Flor.

[114] Up until 2001, the SIF had authorised 11 forest use permits in TCOs nationally, encompassing a total of 444,400 hectares.

[115] Along with the CIPOAP, the CIRABO is the main social organisation representing indigenous interests in the region.

come up with general plans for forest management (PGMF), encompassing a total area of about 88,000 ha. However only 155 ha were approved (see table 12).

Table 12 'Community forest management plans' submitted to SIF (Administration 2003)

Rural Community	Type of community	Requested area (ha)	Approval process	Support organisation	Observations
Exaltación	Indigenous TCO '*Multiétnico* II'	200	In progress	Sawmill	Technical part concluded, legal part to be approved.
Santa Ana	Indigenous TCO '*Multiétnico* II'	200	In progress	Sawmill	Technical part concluded, legal part to be approved.
Tres Estrellas	Indigenous TCO '*Multiétnico* II'	200	Approved	Sawmill	
San Pedro	Indigenous TCO '*Yaminahua-Machinerí*'	200	In progress	NGO / BOLFOR	Technical part concluded, legal part to be approved.
Loma Alta	Peasant	35,209	In progress	NGO / Sawmill	1,000 ha supporting by NGO and 838 ha by sawmill, both in approval process
Reserve	Peasant	26,216	Approved	Sawmill	PGMF presented. To date 155 ha. approved
Santa Teresa	Peasant	26,685	In progress	Sawmill	There are two areas of 333 ha and 403 ha, both in approval process.

Source: Based on personal interviews with the Pando Forest Superintendence technician (August 10th 2003).

For the forest users in the northern Bolivian Amazon, the 'authorisation of forest use on private property' represents comparative advantages over other legal instruments, such as the ASL, TCO or even the forest concession, for the following reasons:

- Sufficient availability of forest area, guaranteeing sustainable commercial management;
- Facilities for the execution of technical and legal steps, because the SIF is one of the main organisations promoting this system;
- High level of legal security, once the land titling process guaranteeing the exclusivity of the use of the resources is concluded; and
- The payment of the forest duty should be applied based on the area utilised annually, which represents approximately 5% of the total area of the concession.

4.2.2 Institutional change in agrarian tenure (Law 1956 vs. Law 1996)

The nation's agrarian regime, specified in the CPE, constituted the basis for the formulation of the '*Ley INRA*'. Articles 1 and 171 of the national constitution open up a range of possibilities for the original populations with the declaration of Bolivia as a 'multiethnic and pluricultural' country and with the recognition of the right to the use of natural resources within their TCOs. As with the Land Reform Law of 1953, the Agrarian Law implicitly recognises the original dominion of the Bolivian state over the land (Agrarian Law 1996: art. 50-51).

4.2.2.1 Classification of agrarian property

The new agrarian legislation preserves as unalterable the four categories of individual property rights. The only changes introduced were to the two remaining community property regimes, favouring the expectations of the indigenous and peasants (see table 13).

Table 13 Classification of agrarian property

Land Reform Law 1953 (Art. 6-11)	Agrarian Law 1996 (Art. 41)
Rural plot	Rural plot
Small property	Small property
Medium property	Medium property
Agricultural enterprise	Agricultural enterprise
Indigenous community	Indigenous territories (TCO)
Agrarian cooperative property	Community property

Source: Land Reform (1953) and Agrarian Law (1996).

Indigenous territories

Two of the six TCOs sought, requested in 1996, were designated in 2000 (TCO *Multiétnico II* and TCO *Yaminahua-Machineri*). The other four areas seeking designation as TCOs are currently in different administrative stages of execution (*Chacobo-Pacahura, Cavineño, Araona and Tacana* II)[116] (see figure 8). All six locations demanding TCO status are seeking rights for the nine indigenous populations of the region. The indigenous populations can seek access to land through two classes of communal right: the TCO and communal property.

The latter represents a real advantage for many native populations, who are either unable to or simply unwilling to request TCO status. According to De Vries (1998:13), the legal difference between TCO and communal property is minimal. In practice, the TCO has two comparative advantages over the community property instrument: First, TCO designation of certain areas such as protected areas (AP) is allowed (for example: *Isiboro Sécure* Indigenous Territory and National Park; *Pilón Lajas* Indigenous Territory and Biosphere Reserve) (Environment Law 1992: art. 64; Supreme Decree 25906, 22nd September 2000: art. 8); and second, under the TCO designation the area is not limited, nor is a minimum number of families required.

116 The TCO-hopefuls *Chacobo/Pacahuara* and *Cavineño* are not situated entirely within the study area. The TCO *Araona* -hopeful, designated by decree, and the TCO *Tacana* II are located outside of the study area (Municipality of Ixiamas).

Figure 8 Locations of claims over TCOs

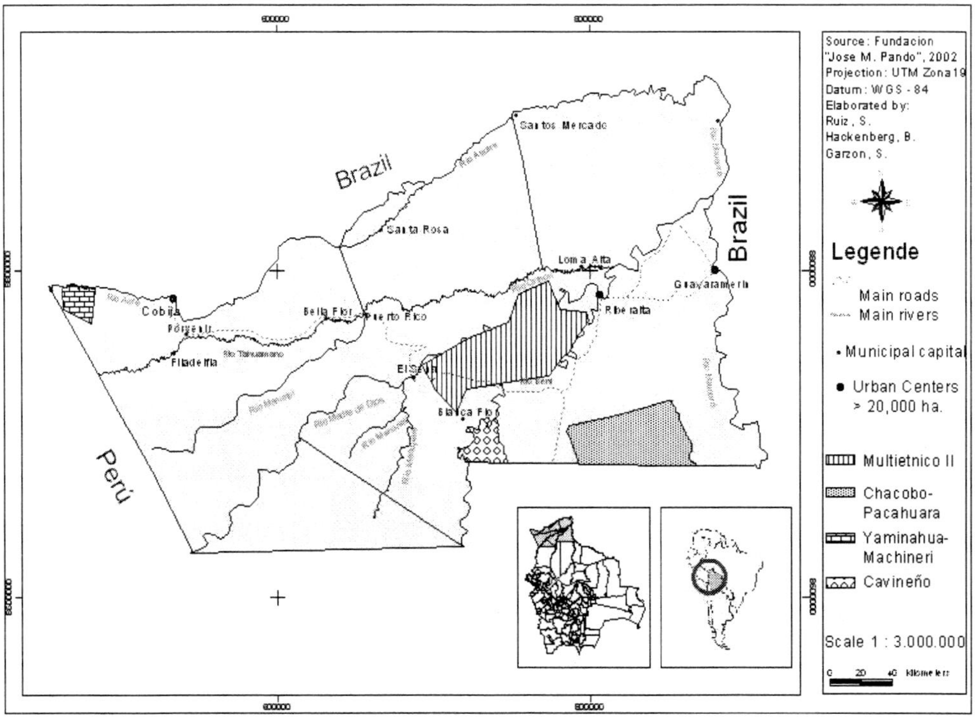

These two advantages are considered relatively insignificant in the case of the study area, however. After almost three years of the land titling process, only two applications have been made for access to land through the communal property instrument (*Mapajo* and *Soberanía*). At the same time, the formation of a TCO inside the *Manuripi* National Reserve (RNVSAM) is not feasible, due to the absence of indigenous populations, which declined during the rubber boom (SALM and MARCONI 1992).

The demographic data collected during the last national census indicates the existence of descendants of nine regional ethnic groups and other domestic ethnic groups within the AP, yet none of the rural communities established there have opted to apply for the designation of land as TCO (MALDONADO 2002). In certain respects, the approval of Decree 25848 has neutralised the applications for TCO status in the area.

Community property (peasant communities)

The most significant institutional change in the history of the northern Bolivian Amazon was the granting of a minimum of 500 hectares to each rural family living in a peasant community (Decree 25848:art. 1). With the land reform of 1953, the *siringuero*[117] families were granted

[117] Rubber and Brazil nut gatherers, who in the past lived in the *barracas*, serving the *patron*.

rubber tree and Brazil nut concessions (maximum of two *estradas*) as well as a small plot of land (50 ha) in a place appropriate for the development of agricultural activities. Estimates for the study area, according to preliminary land titling process data (INRA 2002 a and b), show that 300 rural communities in the study area occupy around three million hectares. Specifically for the Department of Pando these data mean that more than 1.8 million hectares will be granted to the 130 communities registered by the INRA up to December 2003.[118] In the case of the Vaca Diez province, 12% of the rural communities (approximately twenty) would be able to avail of the 500 ha/family during the first phase of the land titling process. In the remaining communities the average area estimated per family, according to the surveys applied during the field study, was between 40 and 70 hectares of forest per family. However, beginning in June 2004 all of the communities could apply for the allocated 500 ha/family, given the possibility of land compensation in state areas, regulating by Decree 27572.

Small property

There is no variation between both agrarian legislations in relation to the category 'small agricultural property'. The extent of the rights remains in 50 ha for 'small agrarian' and 500 ha for 'small cattle'. These two individual forms of agrarian tenure still have a high level of acceptability in the region, due to the freedom of the owners to make decisions over the land use, and for their high transferability. In two more advanced land titling areas[119] in Pando (polygons 3 and 10), 40% of the 58 properties measured have opted for the 'small agricultural property' and 27% for the 'small cattle property'.[120] The small property category is the only alternative for *barraca* holders seeking free entitlement to land.[121]

4.2.2.2 Transfer of agrarian and forest tenures

The transfer of tenures refers the ability of an individual to give up or to transfer the rights entitled to him to a third party. The legislation in force details the possible forms of transfer of rights, to prevent the small properties, in the case of the rural populations, or the accumulation of lands leading to the formation of large estates by the rich. In Latin America, the role that the state should play in protecting or liberating the exchange of goods by communal settlements is quite a controversial topic, related closely to the transfer of property rights. The laws analysed suggest a protective state, presiding over the vested rights of rural communities to protect them against possible attempts on part of other interest groups to occupy their lands.

Broadly speaking, the law allows for four types of transfer:

- The 'rural plot' and the 'small property' are characterised by being slightly limited, in that they may be sold, but cannot be mortgaged or amalgamated;

---

[118] INRA (2004).

[119] So-called polygons by INRA technicians.

[120] INRA-Pando 2002a and b: Polygon Result Reports 3 and 10.

[121] For more information about the enforcement of FES in the region see section 7.2.3.

- The transfer of 'communal property' and TCOs is severely limited as they are inalienable, indivisible, irreversible, imprescriptible and they cannot be merged;
- The third type of transfer relates to 'medium-sized property' and 'agricultural enterprises'. These legal land designations are highly transferable and are oriented towards structuring the land market; and lastly,
- The Forest Law was intended to attend to the requests made by the forest companies to open up the transfer costs of old felling contracts. Nevertheless, the current forest concession holders continue to perceive a limited degree of transferability to their goods, as they are subject to direct restrictions, and cannot be used, for instance, as credit guarantees nor may they be transferred to other persons. Inheritance of the concessions is possible as long as they are considered part of an entrepreneurial heritage (revealed in interviews with several forest entrepreneurs).

In the study area the protective role of the state in preserving the interests of the community members can not always be implemented due to the following reasons: 1) government authorities lack the technical and financial resources to guarantee the effective control of the approved public institutions; 2) high dependence of the peasants and indigenous groups upon the local economic elite for access to resources, and the sale of products on regional markets; and 3) the current economic crisis, which has forced many rural inhabitants to give up their rights and sell the goods acquired.

In practice, the existence of at least four types of black market for goods has been detected, corresponding to *barracas*, the settlements occupied by the Brazilian inhabitants, the plots inside rural communities and to forest concessions (RUIZ 2004a).

4.2.2.3 The socio-economic function' and saneamiento

The 'socio-economic function' (FES) and the *saneamiento* (land titling) are two legal instruments introduced under the reform, allowing the state to apply the proposed categories to the land. The definition of social function in the Land Reform of 1953 was based on the polemic principle "*the land belongs to he who works it*".[122] The definition of FES in the '*Ley INRA*' was rooted in the Bolivian policies of sustainable development.

The main approach to distribution of lands under FES incorporates not only agricultural activities, but also forest activities, conservation, biodiversity protection, research and ecotourism. In practice, it has been demonstrated that the concept of FES has been far from successfully implemented as yet. In the northern Bolivian Amazon, in particular, it has not been possible to establish valid and measurable parameters, relating the work of the extractivist activities with the ownership of the resources. To a certain extent the FMP is the

[122] The work as access to land was upheld mainly by John Locke, who argues that a non-cultivated field is nothing and only becomes valuable through the work of man (GUZMAN 2000:38).

only technical instrument partially recognised by the INRA-Pando agents in the interpretation of the FES-Forestal.[123]

Running parallel to the FES, the *saneamiento* is the legal technical process, dedicated to the regulation and consolidation of the right to agrarian property. According to the law, there are three forms of land titling: 'simple *saneamiento*', 'TCO *saneamiento*'[124] and '*saneamiento* integrated in the land register'. It can be carried out on the initiative of the government (officially) or the property owner. In northern Bolivian Amazon two *saneamiento* methods are applied: 'TCO *saneamiento*' and 'simple official *saneamiento*'.[125] According to estimates relating to the land titling process in Pando two years after it began (2002), 55% of the area of the department is in the initial stage (gathering of field expertise or legal technical evaluation of the properties), 39% in an intermediate stage (public exhibition of results) and only 6% in the process of advanced ownership.[126] *Saneamiento* is without a doubt one of the main instruments to have allowed the state to establish a presence in the region.

However, this process is still in its initial stages. The slow advance is due to the great size of the region, the technical and financial limitations of INRA, the lack of experience and the great number of social conflicts between the regional actors.

4.3 Private institutional change

In this section, institutional change affecting *barracas* since the reform introduction are analysed. In terming them 'extractivist companies', 'commercial organisations', 'rubber properties' or 'productive estates', the tendency is to define the *barracas* as economic organisations (see PACHECO 1992; GAMARRA 1992; DHV 1993b; ASSIES 1997; STOIAN 2000; BOJANIC 2001). However, the *barraca* example also demonstrates the close relationship between an organisation and an institution. On the one hand, the *barraca* is formed by people who manage it (owner and administrator), maintain it (*capataz*) and produce from it (*zafreros* and *fregueces*). Yet at the same time, there exist countless social and economic interrelations required by state rules, facilitating the extraction of resources.

The variability of its internal rules allows us to refer to it as a private 'regime', influencing the social, administrative, economic and environmental dimension (see figure 9). In this

123 For more information, see section 7.2.3.

124 The TCO *saneamiento* is the first land titling process carried out in the region, It was an initiative of the indigenous representatives of the Vaca Diez und Pando. In February 1998 nearly 480,000 ha were designated as TCO *saneamiento* areas, of which 90% corresponded to *Multiétnico II* and 10% to *Yaminahua-Machineri*. Both processes culminated in the granting of ownership titles in February and July 2001 (INRA: Resolución Declaratoria de Área Saneada. 13th July 2001).

125 The official *saneamiento* was instigated by the national government through Decree 25848 on 18th July 2000, because of the countless number of land overlapping, expressed by the regional actors.

126 Telephone interviews with INRA technicians in Pando; 23rd June 2003.

section we will concentrate on analysing the *barracas* as institutions, emphasising the rules that govern forest tenure.

Figure 9 Institutions of 'barraquero regime'

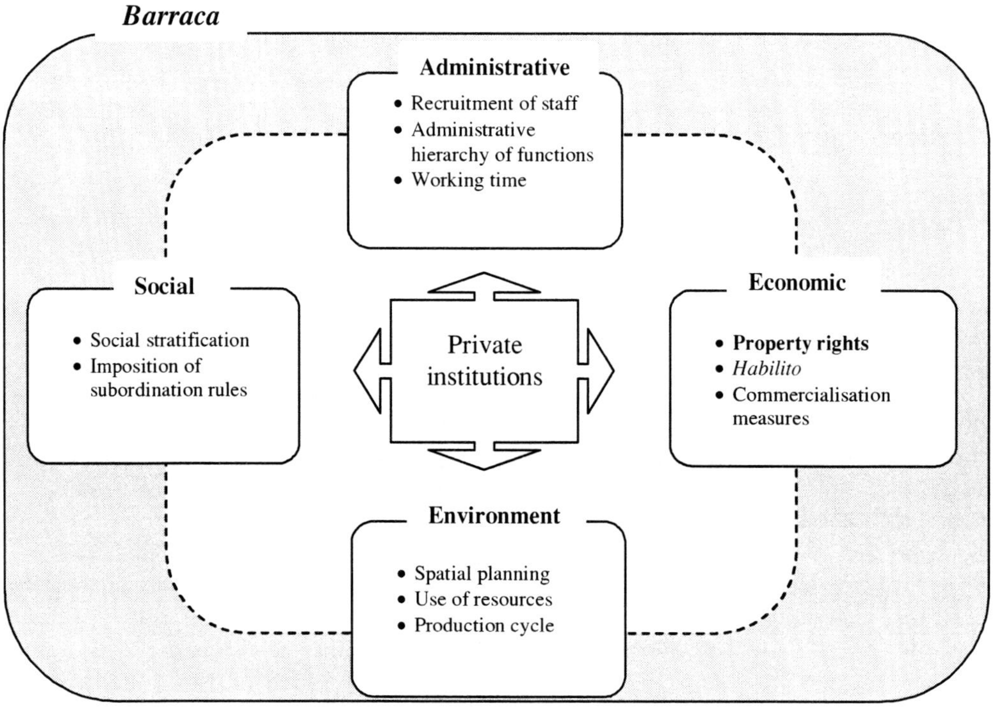

Source: Based on own field study interviews.

4.3.1 Brief description of the '*barraquero* regime'

Give the international rubber boom, the '*barraquero* regime' underwent its greatest development and enjoyed its greatest influence between the end of the 19th century and the beginning of the 20th. Later on, its evolution was more measured due to the rubber crisis, the collapse of the '*Casa Suárez*', and the ratification of Land Reform Law. Despite the institutional complexity, the basis of the '*barraquero* regime' lay in the possession of state land, which granted 'the pioneers' property rights over the natural resources at hand. These rights included access to extensive forest areas, where use was generally not restricted exclusively to the extraction of rubber and Brazil nuts, but also incorporated the use of timber, land for cultivation and wild fauna.

The central person of this regime was the *barraca* holder or *patron,*[127] who enjoyed the power to exclude third parties from the use of 'his resources.'

No single regulatory system existed in the *barracas*. Some *patrones* prohibited greater movement of people into and out of their properties than others. The development of hunting and fishing activities, and the type of agricultural activities carried out by the *fregueces*' families varied among the *barracas*. The more prohibitive the rules, the greater the transition costs incurred by holders to implement the institutions. A effective instrument used by the *patron* in the exclusion process was the *habilito,*[128] because it subjected the *zafreros* and contractors[129] to a state of contractual obligation, renewable at each Brazil nut harvest, removing all intention or expectation of appropriating resources.

In terms of resource allocation, the *patrón* was responsible for deciding where each activity should be carried out and the intensity. He resorted to his knowledge and experience in relation to administration, infrastructure and the availability of natural resources. In general, agriculture was developed around the houses, hunting and fishing in more distant, ecologically diverse places, rubber extraction in the forests, with Brazil nut collection occurring based on the availability of the resource. Only few *barraca* holder*s* established spaces dedicated to conserving the local ecosystem.

The establishment and size of production units shows the close relationship between the rules set down in the *barraca* and the availability of the resources. Starting with the *estrada*, as the basic area unit, the *barracas* demonstrated astonishing territorial planning. The logic behind measuring area in *estradas* and not hectares was based on the daily harvesting work of a *siringuero:* the *estrada* being a circuit, starting and finishing at the home of the gatherer. The union of several *estradas* results in *sub-centros* or *colocaciones*, which when grouped made up production *centros*. As with the *estradas*, their size was determined by the production potential and in direct relationship to the number of families inhabiting it.[130] For instance, PACHECO (1992:190f) estimated that up to forty *siringuero* families lived in the large *centros*. The *barraca* was formed of several *centro*s. This form of territorial and productive planning inside the *barraca*, from top to bottom, was key not only to facilitating rubber extraction, but

---

[127] In the region the term *patrón* is used to identify the *barraca* holder, a name that goes back to the rubber era, when the *patrón* was the person who imposed the rules inside his estate.

[128] *Habilito* can be defined as the set of rules (written and/or verbal) governing an advance cash payment or goods (mainly foodstuffs) for a labour service to be fulfilled in the future, usually going into the forest, collecting Brazil nuts, tap rubber, but it is also employed for palm hearts, harvesting timber and even urban-based activities (BOJANIC 2001:92). Nowadays h*abilito* comes from shell industries to the large or medium *barracas holder* to finance the Brazil nuts harvest. *Barraqueros* employ then, mainly to hire labor force. Usually *barracas holder*s have to repay 'this credit' with the product, which they can obtain inside or outside of the *barracas* (see BOJANIC 2001:88ff).

[129] The contractors were responsible for organising groups of collectors to go into the forests to collect Brazil nuts. The contractor was the intermediary between the *barraquero* and the *zafreros*. He transferred the goods collected to the patron and paid the *zafreros* for their work, according to the *habilito* system, with funds received from the *patron*.

[130] The population distribution revealed two tendencies. On the one hand, a nucleus formed within the settlement, where the *siringueros* lived grouped in camps, normally at the hub of each *centro*. Other families lived away from the hub, scattered all over the area.

also to developing the infrastructure, enabling the transport of products and the effective control of operations on the land.

Barracas were sold, inherited, pledged, exchanged for buildings, rented and even used as mortgage able objects with regional credit organisations (TORREZ 1930:246-249). A concrete example of the high level of transferability of *barracas* was the formation of the '*Casa Suárez*' empire, whose owner went from being a rubber merchant to the largest *barraca* holder in the northern Bolivian Amazon, upon accumulating most of the estates in the region as payment for debts incurred by his clients seeking to transport their products.

Although few *barraca* holders officially owned the lands (see following section), the *barracas* possessed a high degree of security as a result of the recognition afforded them by the rest of the Amazon forest users. The success of '*barraquero* regime' was based on an effective system of control and strong sanctions, directed by *patron*, with the help of a foreman, to ensure against the theft of products and to demand diligence from all of the workers.

4.3.2 Institutional change of '*barraquero* regime'

Private institutions have a 'capacity for obstinacy' greater than that of public institutions (EGER & WEISE 1990:80, cited in SCHMIDT 1999:36). The 'capacity for obstinacy' means that the private institutions enjoy greater persistence and less susceptibility to institutional change, as individuals are better attuned to their contents. However, private institutions are not immune to the transmission of state reforms. The case of the *barraca*s demonstrates that two main processes influence their rules: the fall of international rubber prices, and the approval of public institutions. Under an evolutionary or efficiency perspective, some of the institutions of the '*barraquero* regime' have disappeared, others continue to persist, whereas most of them tend to adapt.

Lost institutions

The possession of state land no longer grants the *barraca* holders tenure over resources. Nowadays no one is interested in colonising new production spaces, not only because of the apparent 'shortage' of land in the most accessible places, but also because their right of possession would be conditional to the land titling process.

On the other hand, the institutions tending to disappear are those that were established in a social and administrative environment that forced the *fregueces* to integrate or to remain in the *barraca*, under the infamous *enganche*[131] institution, a system of sanctions and punishments that in some cases assailed people's physical integrity.

---

131 One of the greatest difficulties for the establishment of *barraquero* regime lay in attaining stable supply of manual labour to extract rubber. Here mechanisms of forced labour based upon *enganche* institution were used, even recruiting from populations outside of the regional borders. *Enganche* required the application of a set of almost compulsive measures to guarantee sufficient manual labour in *barracas* (PACHECO 1992:70). In Santa Cruz, for example, *enganche* was mainly carried out through the establishment of 'houses of *enganche*' that recruited personnel by several means, including through financial advances later discounted from the wages. The recruits received advance payments and other 'favours', all of which were credited to the account of individual, and it was ensured that very few could finish with positive balances. As a consequence none of those contracted managed to return to his place of origin.

The exclusion of third parties, mainly the *fregueces*, from resource use inside the *barracas* is being strongly questioned by the main regional interest groups. This is one of the main origins of the many conflicts taking place. In many cases it is in the main reason for the reduction of the area of the *barracas*, above all in the areas of greater social pressure, where *freguece* families have decided to compete with the *patrón* for forest land, by setting themselves up in rural communities (see chapter 6).

Persistent institutions

The level of internal exclusion exercised by *patrones* over foremen, administrators, contractors, *zafreros* and *fregueces* is still respected and it continues to be effective. For example, in some *barracas* the *fregueces* can only work in agricultural jobs for self-consumption one or two months a year. In other *barracas*, the *patrón* controls hunting and fishing. He limits the amount of ammunition available to each *zafrero*, or prohibits the use of hunting dogs. The aim of this is to preserve the fauna, and also to force the *zafreros* to dedicate more time to Brazil nut gathering and purchase the products sold by the *patrón* in the *barraca* store (meat, noodles, rice, etc.) at prices higher than the market prices. The *patrón* continues to be the central figure inside the *barraca* in terms of the allocation of space and the intensity of the use of resources. He decides the location of the product gathering *centros*, plans the distribution infrastructure, determines the areas for hunting and fishing, etc.

The internal division of the *barraca* into *centros*, *sub-centros* and *estradas* continues to be the territorial base of extractivism. Traditionally, the size of the *centro*s or sub-*centro*s was measured in units of volume (*cajas* or *barricas*)[132], and not in area (hectares). The territorial distribution continues to adhere to the features of the rubber *barraca*s of the last century.

The *habilito*, with some modifications, still serves the *barraca* holder as a means of demonstrating his economic power, or at least reflecting his good contacts with the Brazil nut shelling factories. The *habilito* has become an effective exclusion instrument in relation to the expectations of contractors and more importantly the *zafreros* with respect to the resources of the *barraca*.

Adapted institutions

Finally, adapted private institutions are generally those that tend to be adapted to the new laws of the land, favouring the patrón's attempts to attain access to the forests. For example:

- The latest proposal by the *barraquero* union organisations is aimed at restricting the scope of its tenures towards the use of the NTFPs, excluding its members from the use of timber and land for cultivation. These same organisations also question the name '*barraquero*', which tends to be confused with *patrón*, entrepreneur or large estate holder (*latifundista*). The

---

132 The *caja* (box) is the unit of Brazil nut traded in the country, mainly in the area surrounding Riberalta. The dimensions of the *caja* are 51 x 27 x 35 cm (STOIAN 2000). Depending on the moisture content of the nuts, a *caja* can weigh between 22 and 26 kg (DHV 1993b). In Puerto Rico and the area surrounding Cobija, Brazil nut is traded in *barricas*, which weigh 66 kg, or the equivalent of three *cajas*. The *barrica* better facilitates transport than the *caja*, and as a larger unit reduces the time required for transactions.

barraqueros now call themselves 'traditional rubber/Brazil nut users'. Nevertheless, in the popular language of the region the term *barraquero* continues to be used.

- The fixing of the size of a *barraca* at 15,000 hectares and the assignment unit were established by Decree 27572 of June 2004. From the legal point of view, this is a significant change if it is considered that Decree 25532 did not define the tenures of the *barraqueros*.

- The permanent population distribution within the *barracas* is not based on the productive capacity of the *centros*, but rather it is directly related with securing the *barraquero 's* tenure. It is felt that the reform has led the *barraca* holder*s* to reduce the *freguece* population drastically,[133] in order to prevent the founding of new 'independent communities'.[134] Only the *barraca* holder*s* who carry out extensive agricultural activities, guaranteeing the execution of the FES, opt to maintain a larger number of *fregueces*. MALDONADO (2002) confirmed that in only 11% of the *barracas* where he carried out interviews did the number of *freguece* families exceed ten (n=18 of a total of 27 *barracas* within the AP). A total of 77% of the same interviewees declared that the population did not exceed five families. According to my own estimates based on the fieldwork, the regional average for each *barraca* is less than eight families.

- Given the manpower decrease inside the *barracas*, the supply of *zafreros* during the Brazil nut harvest period is guaranteed by the *contractor*, who is empowered by the *patron*. He assumes responsibility for recruiting personnel and responding for an agreed quantity of product. This contract form allows the *patrón* to reduce his transaction costs and lowers the risk of deception, in the event that a *zafrero* does not fulfil the terms of the agreement.

- The *barraca* transactions are also in the process of adaptation, due to the lack of formal tenures, especially the absence of a legal basis to the commercial agreements between individuals. Whereas in the past many transactions were carried out based on the productive potential of the *centros* and *sub-centros*, today, if a transaction takes place, it is carried out based on the improvements in transport and housing infrastructure. Even economic transactions between *barraca* holder*s* have been altered. The *barracas* no longer serve as insurance against credit or cash advance payments, for example in informal contracts established with the *habilito*.

4.3.3 Influence of '*barraquero* regime' on other institutions

The '*barraquero* regime' is an example of 'path dependence' for all of forest users, in order that its private institutions are chosen contingent of historical circumstances. In the past, the '*barraquero* regime' influenced the formulation of all public laws governing extractivist activities; today, the granting of 500 hectares to each peasant family is seen as

133 STOIAN (2000) mentioned the existence of eight hundred families permanently resident in the *barracas*.

134 The adjective 'independent' served in the past to differentiate between the inhabitants living under the *barraquero* regime and the inhabitants who had managed to organise themselves in communities. At present the adjectives 'farmers' and 'natives' are used to specify each constituted or 'rural' community to generalise the establishments that do not correspond to urban cities.

little more than a derivation of the *patrón's* distribution of the rubber *estradas* to the *siringero* families.[135] At the level of private institutions, the *barraquero* regime has influenced the distribution of space in the remainder of the rural settlements subject to extractivism (private estates, concessions and rural communities), whereas *centros* and *sub-centros* still maintain the same names and dimensions assigned in the rubber era. Even in the case of many rural communities, the population distribution and the ownership of resources by community families are based on the management of space as it was set down in the previous *barracas* (see chapter 6). The '*barraquero* regime' has influenced informally for more than a century the forest activities in the region, and despite the new forest and agrarian legislation enforcement, the '*barraquero* regime' is still in place across almost 1.8 million hectares in the study area.

4.4 Direct consequences of institutional change in the redistribution of forest resources

4.4.1 The agrarian regime enforcement

The analysis of the consequences of the enforcement of the new agrarian regime in the northern Bolivian Amazon is presented in table 14, along with three additional graphs showing land ownership processes from 1957 up to 2001 (see graphs 1, 2 and 3).

The impact of the Land Reform of 1953 in the northern Bolivian Amazon was practically nil (SALM and MARCONI 1992), except that it served to benefit those who were already large landowners prior to 1956 (ORMACHEA 1987). The Agrarian Census of 1984 revealed that 84 large companies in the study area covered more than a million hectares, meaning that several *barracas* exceeded 50,000 hectares. The rural settlements occupied an area of 220,000 hectares (ORMACHEA 1987). The Land Reform Law could not be implemented to favour rural communities in part due to the chaos and corruption in the national administration, but mainly because the '*barraca* regime' was superimposed over the contents of the public institutions. The ownership titles or the 'timber use contracts' required by law did not have any actual value. In reality it was the *patrón* who exercised his control over the land, with or without state approval. According to official statistics, the state granted ownership titles to local actors between 1959 and June 2001, with an estimated 1,119 ownership titles granted. Approximately 63% of all land ownership titles were distributed in the '90s, during Jaime Paz Zamora's government (1989-1993). Most were distributed between 1990-1992, i.e. until shortly before the intervention of the National

135 Although there is no coefficient for the conversion of the unit *estrada* into hectares, it has been deduced that the 500 hectares granted officially to the farmer families are close to the dimensions managed during the rubber era, i.e. almost three *estradas*. Both units derive from the premise that the area granted constitutes the optimum surface area that a rural family can self-administer, produce and survive off under the present infrastructural and market conditions.

Council of Land Reform (CNRA).[136] It has been estimated that, over a period of 44 years, 10% of the study area was granted officially (see table 15).

Table 15 Number of settlements and areas with ownership titles in Pando and Vaca Diez

	Study area				Total	
	Pando		Vaca Diez			
Property class	No. properties	Area (ha) / % of total	No. properties	Area (ha) / % of total	No. properties	Area (ha) / % of total
Agrarian Enterprise	26	200,487.91	21	73,919.33	47	274,407.24
		73.06		26.94		100
Medium	91	52,292.04	198	74,622.65	289	126,914.69
property		41.20		58.80		100
Small property	368	40,359.73	394	38,349.66	762	78,709.39
		51.28		48.72		100
Communal property	10	33,133.91	8	54,936.12	18	88,070,03
		37.62		62.38		100
TCO	2	315,145.97	0	0	2	315,145.97
		100		0		100
Total	497	641,419.56	622	241,827.77	1,118	883,247.33
		72.62		27.38		100

Source: INRA (1958-2001): Registration of agricultural settlement files.

Barracas granted as agrarian enterprises

From the viewpoint of the agrarian legislation, in the Land Reform of 1953 the *barracas* were listed under the category of 'agrarian enterprise'.[137] The first titled *barraca* was '*Conquista*' in Pando in 1968. Approximately 65% of the titled *barracas* in the region were granted between 1990 and 1992. Only in Pando 70% of the titled *barracas* were granted in 1992.[138] Up until early 2001, 61% of the area granted in Pando was in the hands of 26 'entrepreneurs',

136 The CNRA and the INC intervened on 24th November 1992 stoopping the chaos and corruption in the land allocation process (HERNÁIZ & PACHECO 2001:21).

137 The areas stipulated for agrarian enterprises in the tropical region range from 500 to 2,000 ha and from 2,500 to 50,000 ha in the case of cattle enterprises with 10,000 head of older cattle (Law of the Agrarian Reform 1956: art. 17 and art. 21). The INRA Law has assumed these extensions until such a time as the executive authority establishes new dimensions for each enterprise type.

138 The distribution of ownership titles to the large landowners nationally seems to have been a particular vice during the military dictatorships that governed the country. Over a ten-year period (from 1972 to 1982) more than five million hectares were allocated to large landowners (La Razón 12th January 2003). It is assumed that the fraudulent bestowal of land served as a means of returning political favours, or was otherwise related to the corruption of the state's civil servants.

covering an approximate area of 200,000 ha. Given that three million hectares were under *barraquero* control at the beginning of 2000 (ORDUNA 2000:1), one can conclude that nearly 7% of the area occupied by *barracas* possessed an ownership title.

Given the large areas covered by the *barracas*, it is probable that none of the *barraca* holders received titles of ownership for their whole estate. According to the data analysed, one third of the entrepreneurs obtained ownership titles to areas greater than 5,000 ha. Most of *barraca* holders received ownership titles based on the sizes of the rubber *centros*, which on average do not exceed 2,500 ha. To gain access to more land officially, the *barraca* holders were granted several ownership titles for their rubber *centros*, which for legal reasons were assigned to various members of their family under different names (see chapter 6, second case study).

One of the first consequences of the reform enforcement was a drastic decrease in land granted under the 'enterprise' category. During the land titling process, of the 58 settlements measured in polygons 3 and 10 in Pando, three of them corresponded to the medium-sized 'cattle enterprise' category; one 309 ha settlement fell in the medium-sized 'agricultural enterprise' category and another of 21,300 ha in the 'cattle enterprise' category. By June 2004, many of the *barracas* originally granted had over the previous four years become rural communities, the result of a lack of public recognition of their tenures and a consequence of the social conflicts emerging in the region (RUIZ 2004:51b).

Communal property

According to the INRA databases, the first community granted an ownership title in the northern Bolivian Amazon dates back to 1960 (*Libertad*). Fourteen years later, the CNRA granted the second rural community in the region. Until the year of CNRA intervention, this instance granted ten community ownership titles, covering an approximate area of 55,000 ha. However, almost 80% of the area granted up to 1992 corresponded to the community *Alto Ivon* (43,300ha).[139] The distribution of community lands was accelerated considerably with the enforcement of the land titling process (see figure 10). Currently, the INRA administration was limited to the granting of property rights in the form of 'small properties' (25), peasant communities (10) and TCOs (3).[140] By June 2001, the area of community property granted by the INRA covered 441,346 ha. This new policy contributed a raise in the percentage of communal settlements granted to 32%.

Within the community categories, the most favoured group so far is the indigenous group, representing 30% of the total area granted since 1960. However, this situation will change given the number of peasant communities waiting for the granting of property rights in the coming years (see figure 12).

139 www.inra.gov.bo/PortalINRA/DesktopModules.

140 In addition to the two TCOs located in the study area, there is the Araona TCO located in the municipality of Ixiamas.

Figure 10 Area granted in study area according to tenure class and public organisation

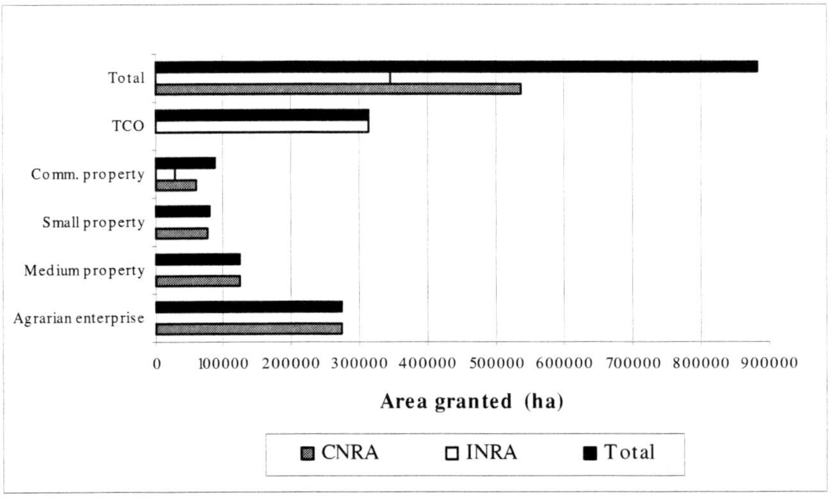

Source: INRA (1958-2001): File of agricultural estate registrations.

Small property

The less privileged category in terms of the land area allocation is the 'small property', covering 86,916 ha, corresponding to 774 granted settlements. Most of the ownership titles distributed under this classification were granted by the CNRA. Since February 2000 the INRA has granted 25 'small settlements', covering 1,560 ha. Of the total area, 80% of the properties distributed correspond to the 'small agrarian property' subcategory; the remaining 20% belong to the category 'small cattle property '.

Land distribution trends

Based on the latest land titling process reports of the INRA's polygons 3 and 10, there is no doubt that the process has contributed to improving access to land by peasants and indigenous communities. During the *saneamiento* carried out in the *Yaminahua-Machineri* TCO, the INRA granted title to one rural community in Bolpebra (*San Pedro de Bolpebra*) and two indigenous communities in the TCO, covering an overall area of 27,766 ha. Up until the end of 2003, eight new ownership titles were given to 'peasant communities', 17 to 'small agrarian properties', 12 to 'small cattle properties' and two were granted title in the 'medium cattle' category. Approximately 50% of the whole municipality area consists of land titled to nine peasant communities and one TCO. Only 3% of the municipal area belongs to individual owners. The remaining 45% is state owned, which depending on its location may be subject to the issuance of forest concessions (see RUIZ 2004b).

4.4.2 The forest regime enforcement

Forest use currently occurs in two ways, as 'forest concession' and 'forest use on private property'. Whereas the area subject to the former is diminishing, forest use on private property is increasing.

Reduction of the forest concession area

The forest area granted to the timber companies has suffered two drastic reductions since 1997. The first resulted from the conversion of areas granted a 'felling authorisation' into 'forest concessions' regulated under the new Forest Law, and the second followed the execution of the land titling process regulated by the Agrarian Law.

In the case of the first reduction, 19 forest areas in the department of Pando were granted 'long-term use contracts' between 1993 and 1995, covering an area of 1,923,896 ha. Approximately 20% of this area was offered up as a form of compensation to forest companies that had made part of their forest area available for the TCO '*chimanes*' in the department of La Paz. Additionally, 215,683 ha of forest were designated 'single exploitation' in 1994 (SIF 1997: Conversion process to the concessions regime; CDF 1994: Registration of forest companies). Under the conversion process, the 19 forest concessions were established on an area of 1,533,967 ha in 1996; the area placed under forest management since 1993 decreased by 30%. This reduction did not affect all of the companies equally, however. The companies presiding over areas designated 'single exploitation', for example, disappeared.

All companies with long-term use contracts opted to transform their use contracts into forest concessions. Some of them held on to their original areas (*Sagusa*), others decided to expand (*Cimagro*) and others decreased in size (*Mineros Pando* and *San Martin*) (SIF 1997: Conversion process to the concessions regime).

The second drastic reduction was directly related to the execution of the land titling process beginning in October 2000, but did not necessarily affect all of the forest concessions. In the municipality of Bolpebra (north west of Pando) this process resulted in a wide overlap of the tenures of private and communal settlements with respect to four forest concessions (*Imapa, Dajer, Don Victor, San Martin*).[141] By early 2002, nearly 65% of the area of the municipality was granted to these companies, accessing nearly 164,059 ha. The territorial overlaps of the concessions resulted in the reduction of the forest area used by three of the companies. This reduction represents approximately 40% of the total area conceded in the municipality of Bolpebra in 1997. Regionally, the second reduction meant a decrease of 45% of the area granted to the forest companies by the SIF in 1997. This reduction of land did not affect the concessions in the same way as the previous reduction. Whereas six concessions maintained the granted area, five gave up their use rights voluntarily, due to the large land overlap, mainly with community settlements.[142] By early 2004, of the remaining 14 concessions, seven were certificated according to international forest norms, five concessions carry out timber logging in scope of domestic law and the two remaining concessions are still attempting to fulfil the requirements of the new law (see figure 11).

[141] The area of *San Martin* in Bolpebra represents only 5% of the whole concession. The rest is located in the municipality of Filadelfia.

[142] Despite the fact that the concession holders are in conflict with peasant communities over land, the holder of 'Mineros Pando' has resigned his right to the land overlapping with numerous *barraca* holders.

Figure 11 Locations of forest concessions

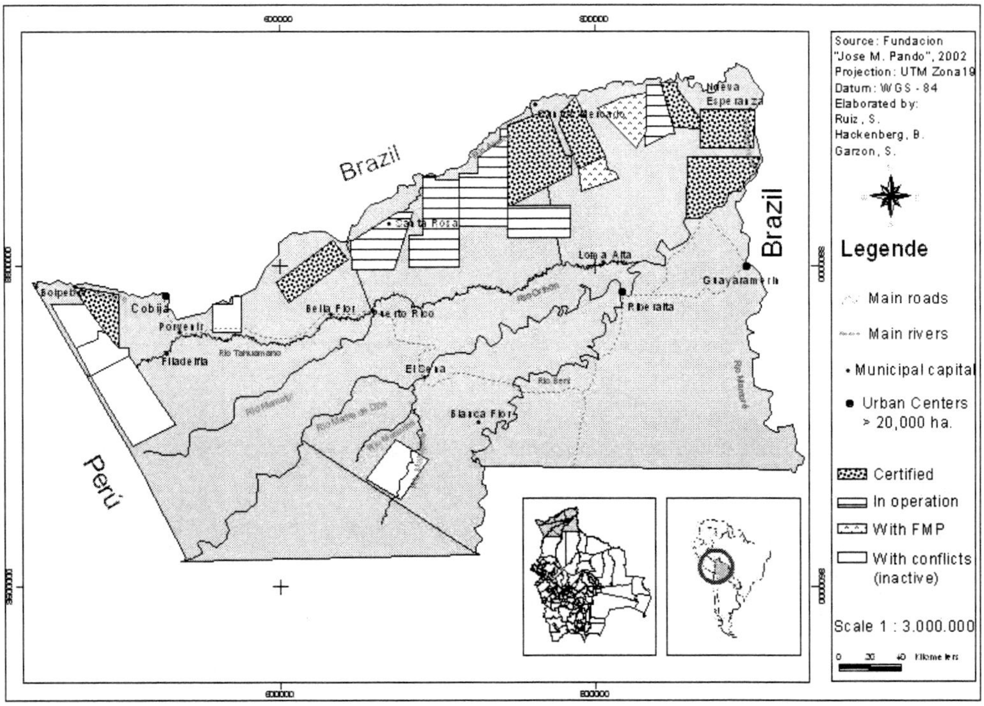

Forest use in 'private properties'

Since 2000, as the area of forest concessions declined, forest use in 'private properties' has increased. The reforms have heightened the expectations of users in relation to forest use on their own properties. Given the lack of progress achieved under the Land Reform Law, the SIF sought to meet these expectations, even granting forest use permits on properties without an official title of ownership. Just as in the rest of Bolivia, the forest companies had to adjust to the new conditions meaning an increase of transaction costs.[143] The SIF agents in the region began their operations with one of the first exceptions to the law. SIF agents allowed the users to extract timber based only on the presentation of POAF (Annual Forestry Operational Plans) for areas smaller than 200 ha, and demanded the future presentation of a FMP for the whole estate.

Since then, for many forest public agents in the region, the exceptions have become the rule, to which they have acceded due either to pressure or negotiation, as part of the exception policy in the new regime (PACHECO 2002).

143 One of the first measures of the 'exception regime' implemented by the SIF was to allow for flexibility in the drawing up of FMPs. Even so, in 1997 only one of the 88 FMPs presented was approved due to the failure in the elaboration of such technical instruments (CONTRERAS & VARGAS 2001:20).

The SIF adopted a flexible forest regime hoping: to increase control over forest management in the region and to increase revenue by payment of forest dues. By 2001 the area of forest in use on private estates was eight times that of 1998. The increase is significant in terms of the number of hectares under forest management and the percentages that these areas represent at the national level (see table 15).

Table 15 shows also the increase in the forest use area on private estates based on the approval of POAF. In the case of Pando, a tendency towards a constant increase in the area approved annually has been observed. The area available in 2002 was 13 times that of the area available in the first year of the study (1998). Until 2002, the proportion of the land area managed as private estate in Pando represented between 23% and 36% of the national area available. In the final year of the study, a slight reduction of the departmental percentage was noted, due to an increase in the number of authorisations in communal estates (TCOs and rural communities) at national level (155 POAFs with a total of 14,019 ha). Nevertheless, this situation may change quickly, if the entitled rural communities in the region decide to become incorporated into forest legislation.

Table 15. Annual Forest Operations Plans (POAF) in Pando under private tenures

Year	Pando		Bolivia	
	POAF approved	Available area (ha) / National %	POAF approved	Available Area (ha)
1998	12	1,418 36.6	20	3,875
1999	60	5,705 32.2	160	17,721
2000	84	8,065 30.5	349	26,443
2001	30	13,458 34.4	440	39,106
2002	36	19,278 23.5	489	82,136
Total	222	47,924 28.3	1458	169,281

Source: SIF (1999-2003): Annual Administration Reports.

When POAFs approved in Riberalta are taken into consideration, the average proportion of area available could correspond to up to 35% of national area. This fact demonstrates the asymmetries existing in terms of resources and personnel within the SIF. Put simply, 14% of the personnel working in SIF (less than 25 regional agents of a total of 173 national agents) are responsible for managing more than a third of the area available on 'private properties'. This situation should be reviewed by the public agents, ultimately leading to the redistribution of the resources, based on the increases in forest activity.

4.4.3 Projections of the use of resources

According to the preliminary land titling results (INRA 2004) and empirical findings, around 6.5 million hectares will be occupied by different users in the near future, corresponding to 75% of the study area.[144] Of this percentage, at least 35% will be under the control of the peasant communities; i.e. about 2.5 million hectares (see figure 12). Furthermore 25% will continue to be managed informally by *barraca* holders (1.8 millions ha) and the remaining 40% will be distributed among forest concessions, TCOs, ARFMs and private owners.

Figure 12 Future land control scenario in Pando and Vaca Diez (estimates)

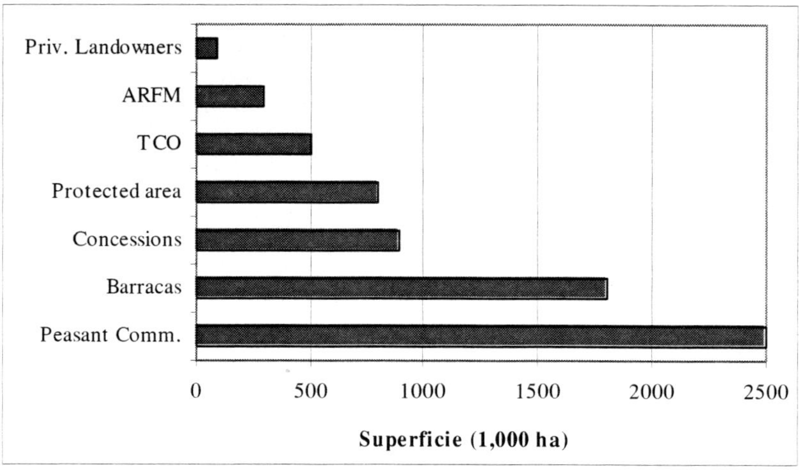

Source: Based on the preliminary *saneamiento* report INRA (2004); Field study interviews.

4.5 Conclusions

The time span of institutional change observed in this study coincided with the statements proposed by WILLIAMSON (2000) (see chapter 2): the Land Reform Law approved in 1953 was altered after four decades, the Forest Decree Law of 1974 after two decades and the traditional institutions of the '*barraca* regime' continue to be in force, with some modifications, after more than one hundred years. Institution changes are identified in two different ways: directly and indirectly. The changes to public institutions mean the direct changes, or as GÖHLER said: 'the visible or spectacular part of

144 The estimated surface area of the study area (Pando and Vaca Diez) is 86,.260 km^2 (for more information see chapter 1).

institutional change'. It is generally characterised by being intentional, planned and oriented towards changing not only the content of the articles, but also the coverage and the concepts of the laws in place. Public agents are one of the main protagonists of direct change, given the functions and responsibilities granted by the state. In case of this study, these changes follow alterations to international policies (modernisation of resource management, decentralisation processes and popular participation), state policies, social pressure exercised by popular groups as well as dynamics of the power relationships between social actors (see chapter 5). The changes of private institutions represent indirect changes and, according to GÖHLER (1997), mean 'the analytical part of institutional change'. Such changes are usually spontaneous or not necessarily planned, obeying the evolution of the power relationships among interest groups, who determine the institutional development.

As the private institutions are not usually documented in writing, the indirect changes do not necessarily involve the alteration of any text, which is why these changes are more difficult to examine, to perceive and to assimilate than the direct changes.

This research has demonstrated a partial influence of the reform on the private institutions. Partial, because not all of the rules disappear; some adapt and others persist. Whether a rule persists, adapts or disappears depends on the degree of compatibility with the system. The more criticism levelled against a particular rule and the greater the damage it causes to social relationships, the greater the possibility that its contents will not be accepted by social actors, and eventually the institution will disappear. This is demonstrated by the extinction of rules previously existing in the *barracas* violating the physical and moral integrity of the *freguece* families.

Of the institutions tending to persist, three types were distinguished: 1) Those validating the *patrón* and confirming his power inside of the *barracas*; 2) those maintaining a direct relationship with the market economy and verifying the strength of the *barraca* holder*s* in this environment; and 3) those maintaining close relationship with the 'natural law', that influences the productive system (territorial planning of the *barracas*, size and distribution of the *estradas*, rules of harvest, etc.). In all cases, the private institutions continue being more efficient than the reform to guide social and economic interactions among forest users.

The institutions that have adapted are closely related with *barraqueros*' desire to preserve their tenures over the forests. In this sense, the adaptation of the institutions can be perceived as a strategy adopted by individuals in order to consolidate their interests. An example encountered is the reduction of the *freguece* population inside the *barraca*, designed to hinder the formation of new rural communities, and at the same time attract a supply of temporary manpower through a contractor, which guarantees the *patrón* his product, but does not pose a risk to his tenures. Given the high capacity for adaptation of private institutions, it is more appropriate to refer to a process of 'institutional transformation' rather than a real change. The rules that survive in the system are those characterised by greater interaction between individuals or those that respond better to the expectations of the beneficiaries.

Having stressed the flexibility of the '*barraquero* regime' prior to the reform enforcement, then it follows that the perception of other authors, who assert the extinction of the *barracas* (HENKEMANS 2002; PACHECO 1992) is debatable. The successful survival by some of the *patrones*, argued from the viewpoint of 'institutional efficiency' and 'institutional evolution', lies in the combination of the following aspects: 1) Inside the *barraca* the rules governing social interaction continue to be 'private institutions'; the *barraca*s constitute 'institutional islands' with their own regulations, where the state still exerts little influence; 2) the '*barraquero* regime' demonstrates a high degree of institutional adaptability, because it nullifies the rules which compromise its future existence and adopts variations which allow it to continue evolving; 3) economically the *barraca* holders still exercise important power relationships and in the *habilito* they have a regulatory instrument to achieve their objectives; and 4) the '*barraquero* regime' remains efficient because of the low transaction costs of forest use. These advantages are even appreciated by the other forest users who during the Brazil nut harvest prefer the informal regime to the reformed system.

Institutional synergy

With the ratification of the Law of Popular Participation in 1994, Bolivia made important steps towards the construction of a decentralised democracy. In addition, this law transformed the public and social actors in the municipalities into the main characters within the development processes. The later sector reforms, above all in the forest sector, sought to grant the local actors new responsibilities in the administration of land and forests. The reform enforcement contributed substantially to the modification of traditional forest systems. The decentralisation of forest duties to the local governments was carried out in a broad context of reforms; this was one of the most important factors facilitating the transition to the current scenario (PACHECO 2002).

The positive effects generated through the public institutions enforcement are called 'institutional synergy'. The synergy effect has been studied in greater detail in the regional sciences, where it is interpreted as the positive result produced by coordinated action between entrepreneurs and other actors (SEINTSCH 2004:32). The effects of 'institutional synergy' originate in narrow bonds between institutional arrangements, and create a qualitatively superior outcome to the enforcement process than would have been obtained with the enforcement of each rule separately. The synergy referred to here is the sum of individual advantages proposed by each regulatory scheme, which multiplies progressively and is reflected over the entire reform process. The essence of 'institutional synergy' lies in the different legal contents, but at the same time in the compatibility of the same towards a common objective. Therefore, the activation of 'institutional synergy' can be considered one of the main conditions propelling the enforcement of the institutional change. Although the synergistic effects are determined by the compatibility of institutions, the reform enforcement also demands a conscious or unconscious cooperation between the social actors. Cooperation is the force that in the final instance activates the 'institutional synergy'. Conversely, without 'synergy' there is no 'social balance' to the reforms and therefore no cooperation.

Figure 13 illustrates graphically the bonds between the institutional contents, and the actions and cooperation required between public authorities during the allocation and control of the forest resources. The previous recognition of rural settlements as 'Local Territorial Organisations'

(OTBs)[145] and the establishment of the communal tenures governed in the agrarian legislation facilitated the awarding of forest tenures to the indigenous groups and peasants.

Figure 13 Institutional synergy in the allocation and control of forest resources

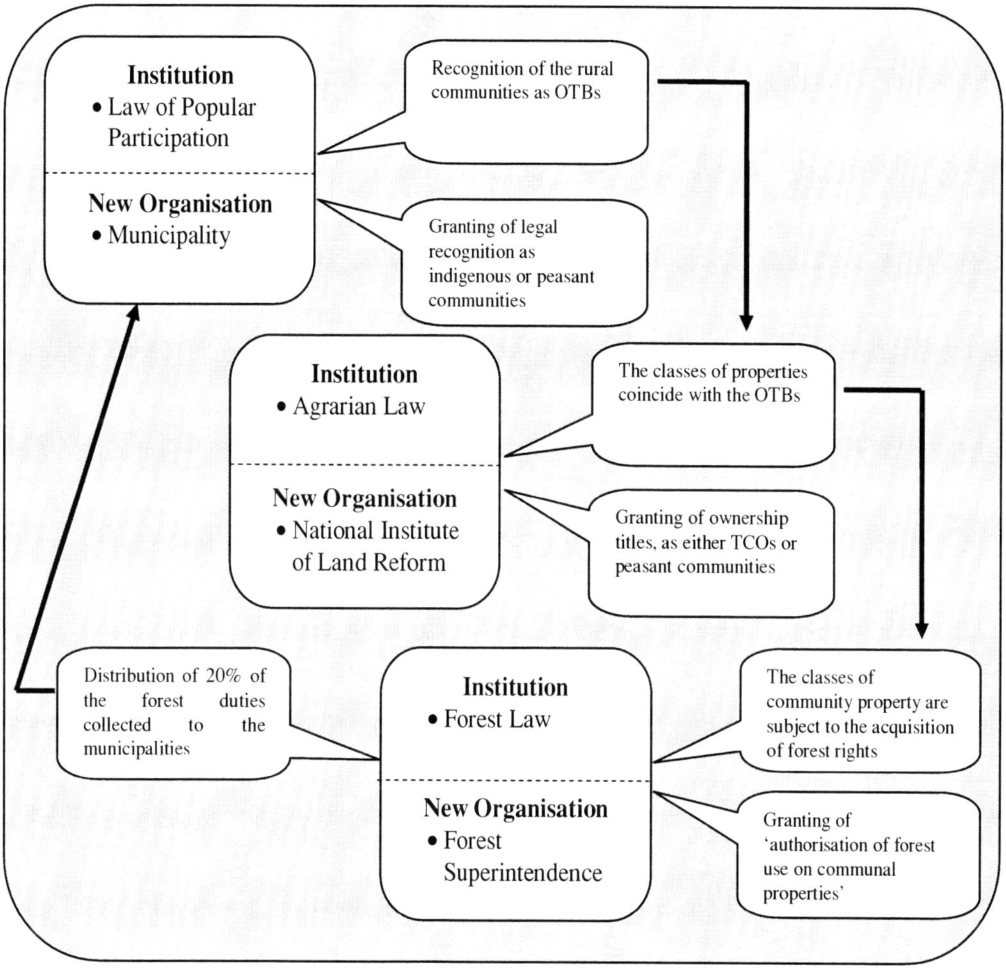

Without the previous work of municipalities, stimulating communal organisation, the INRA would have had problems granting land tenures to the traditional forest users, who in turn would not be able to take advantage of the forest resources made available through the 'authorisation of forest use on private property' instrument. The system feeds into itself. The forest legislation entitles the municipal governments to 20% from the taxes collections made within its jurisdiction, which motivates them to establish their Municipal Forest Unit (UFM),

145 Law of Popular Participation, article 2.

coordinating inspections of the exploitation of the forests with the SIF. 'Institutional synergy' is a reciprocal relationship in favour of interactive laws.

The synergy results not only favour the forest regime, but also agriculture and the administration. The forest regime promotes 'institutional synergy', firstly because it provides the traditional forest users greater access to forests; secondly because it increases direct control over forest activities, and thirdly because it avoids overlaps between agrarian and forest tenures.

The decentralisation regime is favoured for two reasons. Firstly, rural communities are doubly motivated to be organised, not only with the desire to receive social infrastructure projects from the municipality, but also because they have the possibility to access land and forest. Secondly, the collection of forest taxes increases the municipal funds, in many cases making it easy for them to recruit technical staff and to improve their infrastructure.

The design of public institutions, which considers 'institutional synergy', will support successful enforcement. In addition, through this element, the efficiency of public authorities is increased as administrative coordination is stimulated and the transaction costs are distributed during the assignment of the rights and in the control activities. Based on recommendations derived from SEINTSCH (2004:286ff) on the conditions necessary to achieve synergy at a regional level, it can be concluded that the 'institutional synergy' can generate positive effects in the enforcement of the reforms, provided the protagonists of the institutional change, mainly those responsible for the approval of the laws, are aware of the development of certain conditions during the design of the institutions. Such promoting conditions include: 1) macro-political conditions to establish continuous democratic processes that do not discriminate against the participation of any interest group; 2) long-term sector policies able to survive changes of government; 3) key people with the capacity to lead the discussion processes and political negotiation, interested in integrating multi-sector interests necessary to achieve a 'win-win' situation, favourable for all parties; 4) systems to control the institutions enforcement, the responsibility not only of the public authorities but also of civil society; 5) transparency and credibility over formulation and reform enforcement; and 6) public authorities with technical and financial resources, but mainly free of factional influences or influences that respond to the economic interests of third parties.

In this study, 'institutional synergy' was disrupted on two occasions, during the reform process and the adaptation of the laws to the conditions of the study area. In both cases, the main 'guilty parties' were the public entities responsible, insofar as they ignored, consciously or unconsciously, the contents approved in the national legislation. For example:

1) In the reform enforcement:

- the SIF approved FMPs in settlements without ownership titles, and the INRA ignored forest tenures assigned to the forest concessions by the SIF (approved forest plans) during the land titling process;
- public agents were not completely aware of the value the users place upon having the necessary documentation, allowing them to exercise their tenures. Examples of this were

cases where the municipal governments kept secret or delayed the arrival of legal documents for the indigenous communities, or where the INRA agents delayed the *saneamiento*, as was the case in the Vaca Diez province.

2) During the adaptation of the reforms, 'institutional synergy' was also affected when:

- government agents ignored or contradicted legal articles established by reform, substituting them for new institutions in favour of certain power groups. An example of this is article 6 of the *Barraca* Decree (25532), which provided *barraca* holders the option of processing ownership titles over forest;
- another breach of 'institutional synergy' occurred when those responsible for the approval of rules designed the institutions to favour one particular user group at the expense of a third party. An example of this was the approval of Decree 27024, reducing the forest duty charged to the concessionaire companies, thereby reducing the revenues of the local governments affecting the control over forest use.

Changes in forest tenure

Two processes are taking place in study area with respect to forest tenure: as access to forests is being reduced through greater individual land tenures, the expectations over community land are increasing: i.e. over the last 25 years there has been a strong dynamic in the occupation of the Bolivian Amazon forests. In the first period (1980-1990) the forest companies occupied the largest area, whereas in the second period the *barraca* holder*s* were the main forest users. In the future, however, could be the rural communities the group, who would occupy the greatest forest areas. Since the new laws enforcement favours, better than in the past, the distribution of community lands, the tendency towards the commercial use of the forests points to the peak of community forest management, through the legal category 'authorisation of forest use on private property'. This situation will lead to an increase in mixed-use contracts with regional sawmills. However, due to the communal weaknesses and the existence of internal conflicts, these companies may become the main players in the commercial use of the forests.

However, although the enforcement of public reform has improved the legal security of the forest users considerably and facilitated access to rural population over natural resources, this does not guarantee the reduction of social conflicts, nor does it provide for the sustainable use of the forests. Given the strong restrictions on the formal transferability of goods, the high transaction costs, the public rules and the weakness of the state organisations, it should come as no surprise when in the future the traditional institutions continue to regulate the interrelations between individuals, at least in relation to the forest use.

5 Between political opportunism and social pressure: - Adjustment of the reform towards the interests of regional actors -

"Most of the time, the resulting policies (in Bolivia) are more the reflection of the idiosyncrasies of the individuals making the decisions rather than the result of any transparent process involving technical analysis, public discussion or broad consensus"
(TAYLOR, NITTLER & KRALJEVIC 2003:69)

5.1 Introduction

Bolivian reforms analysts and regional interest groups agreed that the reforms ignore the real regional circumstances. Their main argument is that the reform pays scarce attention to the extractivist activities of the northern Bolivian Amazon. The actors interviewed claimed that the new laws only meet with the interests of the Santa Cruz actors, especially the Forest Legislation which concentrates on satisfying the demands of the large entrepreneurs and their desire to exploit timber. This kind of legal marginalisation is not a new phenomenon in the region. In the case of the laws under study it is attributed as much to the lack of political will to incorporate the regional reality in the public legislation and the poor regional knowledge of national agents, as to the self-marginalisation of the regional interest groups, who once again discredited the vigour of the public institutions in the Amazon region.

The reforms incorporated an 'institutional vacuum' in relation to the commercial use of NTFPs. This mobilised the groups of regional actors interested in integrating their rights in the law. In this process one of the first regional initiatives was the organisation of the 'land tenure versus forest rights' meeting held in Puerto Rico in July 1998.[146] From then on each group separately carried out a series of strategies to modify the laws in its favour. For example, immediately after the Puerto Rico workshop the *barraquero* group began an initiative led by the union representatives with the support of parliamentarians belonging to this group. The process of formalising the *barracas* concluded in October 1999, with the approval of Decree 25532. The enforcement of this decree marked the starting point of the implementation of strategies by the indigenous and peasant groups, who organised a regional protest march directed by its main social organisations (peasant federations and indigenous unions). Several decrees were approved by the national government as a result of the march, such as Decree 25538 and Decree 25848 of July 2000. The first repealed the content of the '*Barraca* Decree' and the second granted each peasant family the possibility to attain a land parcel of a minimum of 500 ha.

[146] The work of the regional NGOs was fundamental to this event (SNV, PROMAB, IPHAE and CIPCA-Norte). They summoned 19 groups of actors from all administrative levels of the Republic, including the prefecture of Pando, the sub-prefecture of Manuripi and the municipal government of Puerto Rico.

On the basis of empirical data, this chapter contains an analysis of the mutual influence between the development of public institutions and the interests of regional actors. For this purpose, two theoretical models are proposed. Both models contribute to an understanding of the rent-seeking behaviour of the regional interest groups, both in the re-formulation and enforcement of new public institutions.

This chapter contains the answers to the following research questions:

- How do regional interest groups implementing the reforms react to the 'institutional vacuum'?
- What kinds of strategies do the regional interest groups use when seeking changes to public institutions?

Section 5.3 contains the answers to the questions in relation to the incentives/disincentives the public institutions provide the interest groups and in section 5.4 an analysis of the reactions of the social actors seeking changes to the laws is presented.

5.2 Theoretical framework and delimitation of the analysis

The starting point of this chapter is statements extracted from the literature: "*institutions are the rules of the game and organisations are the players. The interaction between the two shapes institutional change*" (NORTH 1995:15 cited in SCHLÜTER 2001:21); "*the institutions exercise power over the recipients and the recipients exercise power over the institutions*" (GÖHLER 1997:34); "*institutions shape people and people shape institutions*" (HELD & NUTZINGER 1999).

Similar to the social sciences, where interactions are determined between individuals, the 'institutionalists' recognise an 'institutional interaction'. Put simply, the mutual influence between the institutions is considered the stimulus, which causes a reaction in the interest groups. The prospective reciprocity occurs when the answer produced by the individuals serves in turn as a stimulus to transform the institutions. The problem in relation to these statements on 'institutional interaction' is that they lack evidence and context visualisation, which would make possible the identification of the elements and internal factors facilitating change. In this context, this is based on two theoretical models, the first one explaining the 'cycle of the institutional change', or the mutual influence between interest groups and institutions, and the second explaining the social interactions during the process of the institutional design. Despite the fact that the content of both models belong to the classical NIE ideas and that rent-seeking behaviour explains the institutional change, here the theoretical framework has been developed on ideas extracted from regional sciences by HEIDEMANN (1995),[147] which is an uncommon perspective in institutional analysis.

---

[147] CLAUS HEIDEMANN was director of the Institute of Regional Sciences (IFR) at the University of Karlsruhe in Germany. During his academic career he developed his own theory on regional planning, which is well known among academic, political and civil international cooperation employees in Germany. His theory is condensed in graphs that have been used as discussion material in his classes and also as basic scientific documents published by IFR (see http://www.ifr.uni-karlsruhe.de). In spite of the numerous figures prepared, there have been no relevant publications. As a graduate of the IFR (1992-1995), I have adopted two figures prepared by HEIDEMANN in this chapter to contribute to NIE with the visualisation of the interaction processes (see figures 14 and 15).

HEIDEMANN's (1995) original idea was later adapted and supplemented by authors such as KNIGHT (1992/1997), GÖHLER (1997), LEITZEL (1997), HELD & NUTZINGER (1999), SCHARPF (2000), PRITZL (2000), SCHLÜTER (2001) and HANISCH (2003).

5.2.1 Cycle of institutional change

Departing from the basic statement that institutions are the result of human actions (KNIGHT 1992; NORTH 1990), here it is asserted that the constant relationship between both elements produces a cycle of institutional change. According to NORTH (1994), institutional change is an "*incremental process that is a consequence of the choices individual actors and entrepreneurs of organisations are making every day*", [148] unless interrupted by wars, revolutions, and natural disasters, which are the main causes of discontinuous or radical changes to public rules. Actors and organisations make decisions every day and they transform themselves to facilitate the achievement of potential earnings. This fact also bears on the gradual change of the institutions.[149]

Since the institutions are the structures determining the interactions between individuals, it is not possible to separate them from the interest groups. However, as shown in figure 14, both elements can be differentiated in order to analyse and to visualise their mutual influences. Institutions and actors (interest groups) share a common environment, corresponding to a municipality, a region or a nation.

An interest group is made up of the formal or informal union of individuals to defend or to impose their interests in the political arena. In this sense, all interest groups seek to obtain a better collective competitive position or to appropriate collectively the financial revenues generated or withheld by the interventions of the state (PRITZL 2000:49). Starting from the interest groups, as the endogenous variable of analysis,[150] the individuals' perception capacity and their actions are analysed. Such human capacity already received special attention in ancient Greece: our behaviour is not explained by the things in themselves, but rather the perception we have of them.

Actors internalise and are able to understand the institutional agreements through their perceptive capacity. "*The rules not only define the people's obligations and rights, but they also influence their preferences, concept of values, internal rules, intrinsic motivation, status, ideas about justice, legal behaviour, etc.*" (HELD & NUTZINGER 1999:8). In other words, the institutions are part of the 'action resources', making it possible for a protagonist to influence a result in a certain sense and/or to a certain degree (SCHARPF 2000:86).

---

148 NORTH 1994:361 cited in SCHLÜTER 2001:21.

149 Cf. NORTH 1997:5 cited in SCHLÜTER 2001:21.

150 According to NORTH (1990:5), the theoretical institutional analyses should start with the individuals because he recognised that the institutions are the creation of human beings.

The 'action resources' are composed of human abilities,[151] time, and by the available materials and technical resources[152] of interest groups.

Figure 14 Interaction between institutions and interest groups: Cycle of institutional change

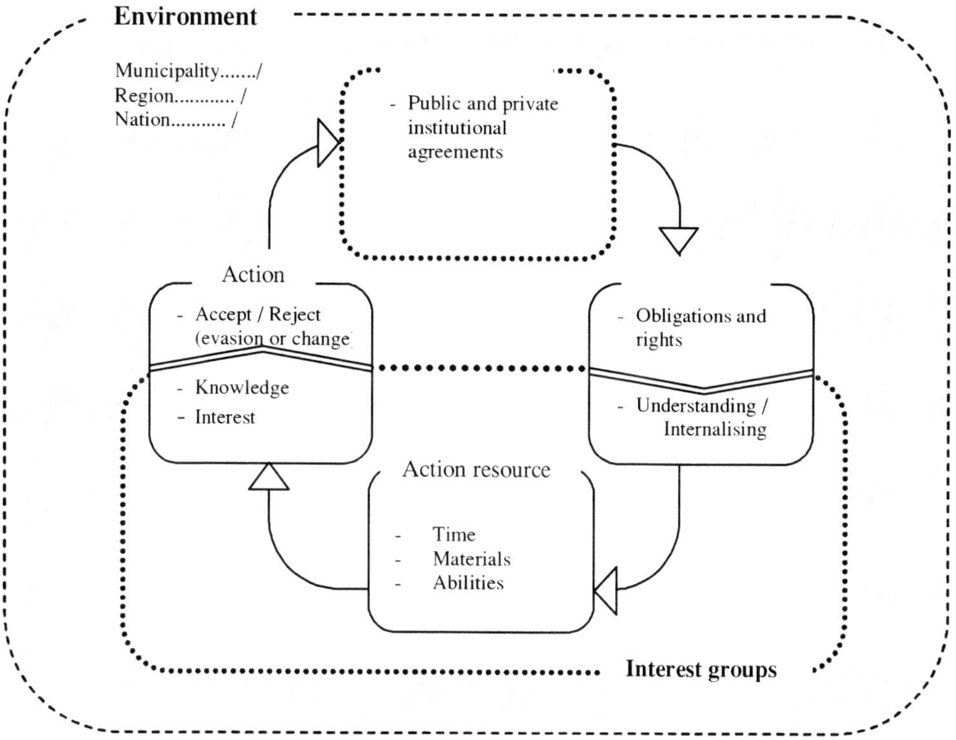

Source: Adapted from HEIDEMANN (1995).

They make up the interaction point between the individuals and the institutions, because during institutional change, institutions can enlarge or restrict the individuals' 'action resources' (SCHARPF 2000:86f), and because the 'action resources' are the main instrument the actors have to change or to adapt the institutions (HEIDEMANN 1995:R-34).[153] Finally, the individuals' actions close the circle of institutional interaction.

The actions of the actors can be explained in relation to their knowledge of the laws and their interest. The knowledge that gives rise to an individual action is always the knowledge of the person who acts, and not the substance of abstract rules: The degree of compliance with,

151 For instance: physical force, education, intelligence, technical training, knowledge, public relationships, political influence, power, social organisation, networks, etc. (see SCHARPF 2000:86)

152 For intance: money, land, forest resources, military power, technological resources, access to information, etc.

153 HEIDEMANN referred to 'budget' instead of 'action resources'.

avoidance and changing of the norms are directly related to the interests, preferences and knowledge of the actors. According to HEIDEMANN (1995), social actors are only in a position to influence the 'determining rules' (also called 'cultural institutions'), or those rules agreed between social actors, that are subject to change.[154] Given the dynamic of the 'institutional interaction', a constant change of rules might be expected, insofar as they change the preferences of the interest groups, or insofar as the actor's rights are not represented in the institutions. However, a primordial condition for the interest groups to influence the design of the institutions is that they become established in the political arena as power agents able to change the laws.

5.2.2 Reactions of interest groups

The knowledge and interests of social actors influence the acceptance or the rejection of institutions. An acceptance of the institutions contributes to the legal enforcement. The enforcement process is eased when the institutions reflect the interests of the actors, or when they incorporate strong enough 'enforcement mechanisms' (sanctions and incentives), which force actors respecting their contents (KNIGHT 1992:2ff). However, the rejection of institutions also forms part of the system, leading either to the avoidance of the institutions or to institutional change. The avoidance of institutions can be attributed to an intentional or unintentional reaction. The non-deliberate evasion of public legislation is supposed to be widespread in the northern Bolivian Amazon, as the regional interest groups do not have the necessary knowledge of the institutional contents. This phenomenon has been detected in rural areas where individuals are not knowledgeable enough to understand the public laws (GOTTWALD 2004:70f). Deliberate evasion has also been much discussed by authors such as SIMAC (1990), PACHECO (1992), DVH (1993b), ASSIES (1995) and BOJANIC (2001), particularly in relation to the attitudes of the *barraca* holders and forest concessionaires, who refused in the past to comply with the public institutions, even though they were aware of the contents. In the past, rule evasion was a strategic behaviour of the elitist groups in the Amazon.

Similar to the characterisation of Russian society as an 'hour-glass society' by ROSE (1995)[155], the *barraca* holders and other forest entrepreneurs were situated at the top half of political and social life and maintained strong informal networks of friends with the bottom half, which allowed them to conserve their well-being. At the same time, they tried to keep the centre of the 'hour-glass' as narrow as possible in order to limit what the state could do to them. In such systems, when deliberate evasion becomes normal behaviour in society, it usually incites changes to the institutions (LEITZEL 1997:118).

Based on empirical findings, individuals are willing to change institutions for four basic reasons: 1) From the administrative point of view, individuals are interested in influencing

---

154 In addition to the determining or cultural institutions, HEIDEMANN (1995) identified a second type of institution, the 'inevitable institutions'. The inevitable institutions are formed by natural laws that only exert influence on the individuals, but are not subject to change, for example, the law of conservation of mass, gravity, the law of entropy, etc. In the context of this study an example of this kind of institution are those that determine the times of the rubber or Brazil nut harvest. These institutions are in direct relation to the prevailing seasons in the study area.

155 Cited in LEITZEL 1997.

'the script, that they have to interpret' with respect to their functions, rights and obligations; 2) from the economic point of view, the rules approved in their favour mean them reducing their transaction costs; 3) from the social point of view, the rules allow them to enlarge their action and negotiation possibilities during the interaction process with other individuals and 4) from the point of view of property rights, the intention of individuals is to increase their legal security and access to the natural resources.

Thus, institutions are a product of bargaining power between the social actors[156] and in consequence they are strongly influenced by their interests. The actors are sufficiently motivated to participate in the political process of the institutional change, even when their 'action resources' are scarce. The widespread interests of the actors results in the participation of many individuals and organisations, the number of which can complicate the research and the understanding by the researcher. With the aim of describing and understanding the role of the actors in institutional change, several academic programmes have directed their efforts towards simplifying the process overview. For instance, in the forest policy debate in tropical countries,[157] the 'countless' participants involved in the drawing up and approval of laws have been classified according to four influential groups (SILVA *et al.* 2002:66ff):

- International actors: the most prominent are the World Bank, the American Agency for International Development (USAID), the Food and Agriculture Organization of the United Nations (FAO) and the northern European governments. These actors assume a strongly protagonistic role when the public and economic powers of the developing countries show signs of weakness;
- State actors: which include the ministries and government agencies responsible for forest policies, and in the case of democratic countries the legislators and political parties. Their focus depends on the government's programmes, the political importance dedicated to the management of natural resources and the technical capacities of their personnel;
- Domestic social groups: are the large-scale timber enterprises, farmers, peasants, indigenous peoples, or the forest users. The potency of these groups depends mainly on their economic and organisational strength;
- Non-governmental organisations: in developing countries, these organisations play an important role in determining the policies of the acting governments. Their power resides in their financial organisation and the technical skills of their personnel.

Similarly, HANISCH (2003:121ff) proposes an other classification assembling the participant actors in the process of changes of the agrarian property rights in Bulgaria as follows:

156 Cf. KNIGHT 1992.

157 SILVA *et al.* (2002) analysed the political development processes in Bolivia, Costa Rica, Cameroon and Indonesia. Their interest groups classification takes into consideration the works of HURRELL and KINGSWORTHY (1992) and PORTER *et al.* (2000).

- At the summit of the process are the politicians influenced by lobby groups, represented by advisors and other leading prominent people, constrained by economic data and elections as well as by mental models and their ideological orientation;
- At mid-level are the bureaucrats in charge of reform enforcement, such as ministries, lawyers and agents of the regional and local administration and
- Finally at the lower level are locals determining how to organise and perform transactions.

While the classification by SILVA *et al.* (2002) differentiated the actors according to their origin, namely between international and domestic actors, the classification by HANISCH (2003) is based on the levels of decision-making. The aim of the classification in this study is to differentiate the interest groups according to the attributes and functions assumed during the process of institutional change and focuses on the analysis of coalition strategies. Therefore the model presented is in direct relationship with the 'action resources' of each interest group, and reflects in a simplified way the countless social interactions between the participants, with the role of the most interested actors standing out. The model presented tries to fill a gap in the NIE, contributing to the theory of institutional change from the rent-seeking perspective. Four interest groups are distinguished in figure 15:[158]

- The promoters fulfil specific roles in organising and leading the process, and are regarded as the 'motors' or 'patrons' of the institutional change. These actors can invest greater action resources in the process of institutional change than the other three groups, measured in terms of the investment of time and skills. They are generally the most visible actors in the process and their interests can be easily identified;
- The providers include all those actors able to supply the inputs requested by the promoters. Among the required inputs are all types of tangible (money, infrastructure, etc.) and intangible resources (knowledge, information, contacts, etc.). The providers or 'suppliers' are generally organisations enjoying technical and political prestige. They are 'international actors' and 'non-governmental organisations' as classified by SILVA *et al.* (2002). The work of these bodies is indispensable in the technical elaboration processes since they can contribute to separating the technical aspects from the political discussions and to advancing the situations and adverse comments, as well as elaborating diverse scenarios to be presented and organised in reports. The providers have strong interests in the process, many of them often difficult to identify.
- The responsible public entities are in charge of approving, promulgating and implementing the institutions, and applying the legislative, executive and judicial powers of the state. According to the theory of public choice and rent-seeking, these actors pursue

158 The same terminology was used by HEIDEMANN (1995), referring to the role that social actors play in regional planning in 'Arena and Agenda' (see figure 28).

personal interests, and in some measure public interests, directed towards the conservation of their political positions and maintaining influence over government decisions;[159]

- The recipients or addressees: are the target groups of the contents of the institutions. A public institution interferes in the lives and activities of the citizens of a state. However, there are groups that perceive greater influence of the legal contents in one way or another. For example, according to the geographical area, the laws can be more important for one region than for another[160], which will ultimately determine the degree of active participation by certain interest groups.

The complexity of the relationships between interest groups is directly related with the hierarchy of the approved institutions. Whereas executive institutions (decrees, resolutions) are characterised as being more flexible und easier to approval, when involving a smaller number of responsible actors (president, ministers, vice-ministers), laws approved by parliament require greater political interaction, increasing the transaction costs. In Bolivia, therefore several institutional initiatives resort to the approval of institutions with a lower hierarchical level (decrees, resolutions, ordinances), even though as a result they become less secure.[161]

Regarding the interactions among interest groups, all of them seek to maintain close relationships with one another, determining the direction and the duration of the process, as well as the content of the institutional agreements, as is shown in figure 15.

Usually the promoters are located at the centre of the institutional change's process, given their diversity of tasks and the access to information: for example, suggestions and observations on the content of the laws are received from the addressee, who also support the promoters of social movements. Promoters get from the providers, usually information, resources, and technical and financial support.

Finally, those responsible supply the promoters with the guidelines and requirements necessary to approve the institutions. Addressees comply with the rules or feed back into the institutional

---

159 In Bolivia, the legislative power is in charge of dictating, countermanding, modifying and interpreting the laws. This power resides in National Congress, made up of two chambers: the deputies (130 members) and the senators (27 members). Generally, the laws originate in the Senate or the House of Representatives and are proposed by one or more of its members. Similarly, the executive authority can propose laws by means of the vice-president of the republic (president of the congress), or by means of a presidential message, on condition that the law is upheld in debate by the minister responsible for the particular sector. In legal matters, the executive authority has the following functions: To sanction the laws approved by the Congress within a maximum of ten days (Political Constitution of the State 1995:art. 76-1 and 96-1). The other administrative bodies of the executive authority contribute to executing and disclosing the contents of the laws; for this they can dictate administrative resolutions.

160 Given the availability of forest resources, Forest Law is much more important for regions like the Amazon region than the Andean region.

161 In Bolivia the national constitution is the institution with the greatest hierarchy, followed by the law, the decree law (approved *de facto* by government), the supreme decree, the supreme resolution, the multi-ministerial resolution, the bi-ministerial resolution, the ministerial resolution, the administrative resolutions issued by technical entities like the SIF and INRA, the prefecture resolutions and municipal ordinances (Statutory law of the Executive Authority 1788: Article 20).

process, making proposals and observations to the promoters; they play the role of 'process catalysts', insofar as they enjoy the option to choose people who represent their political and social interests (in the national parliaments and in the regional associations). While the representatives are restricted by electoral considerations, their behaviour should reflect the preferences of the voters (SAIEGH and TOMMASI 1998:18).

Figure 15 Institutional change: Interactions between the main interest groups

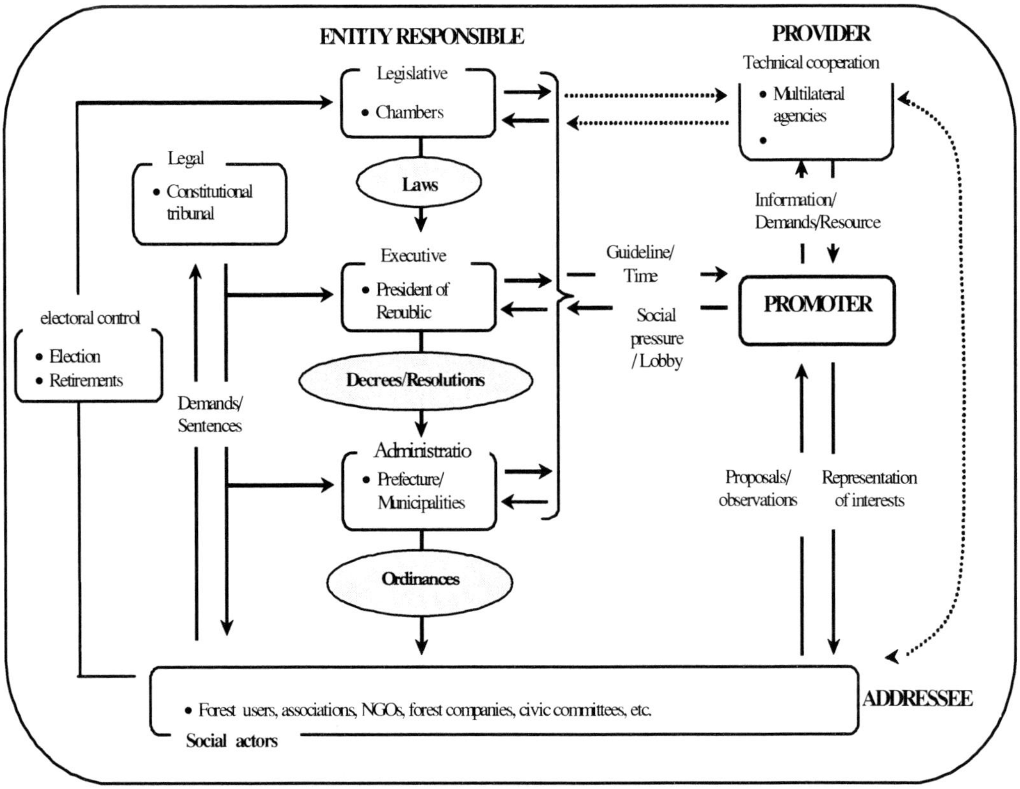

Source: Adapted from HEIDEMANN (1995).

Addressees can also raise requests on the legal contents of the institutions before higher national bodies (executive and judicial powers), should the institutions affect their civic rights. There are direct relationships between those responsible and the providers, and between the addressees and the providers, as shown by the discontinuous arrows in figure 9. However, because the existence of these relationships can raise the transaction costs of the process, these relationships are rarely direct but generally occur through the promoters, who act as intermediaries.

All social interactions depend above all on two factors: first, the level of influence of the actors during the negotiations, and second, on the interests at stake for each participant group. The weaker the bargaining power of the (responsible) public bodies the greater the protagonism of the providers (NGOs and international projects), and/or the greater the possibility that the promoters or recipients achieve their demands. The social relationships between the participants can be explained under different theoretical focuses. HANISCH (2003), for example, explained the behaviour of the politicians based on the 'theory of public choice', the behaviour of the administrators and those responsible for law enforcement (intermediate group) based on the 'agency theory' or 'theory of the bureau', and the behaviour of the local actors based on the theories of the transaction costs, 'distributive bargaining' and 'sociological power analysis'. This study will discuss and explain the opportunist behaviour of the actors involved, applying the approach of rent-seeking behaviour.

5.2.3 Delimitation of the study on the reform enforcement

The study concentrates on analysing the process of institutional change beginning in 1999, when the reforms were adapted to accommodate the expectations of two of the most important user groups in the Bolivian Amazon forests, namely the *barraca* holders and the peasant communities, who together occupy more than 30% of the regional surface area. The public institutions analysed are the Forest and Agrarian Laws, and the Decrees 25532, 25848 and 27572.[162] The information presented has been drawn up based on the data collected during the field phase (August 2001 - July 2002), specifically the personal interviews conducted with the experts from the public (n=20) and private (n=21) organisations.[163] The databases of MALDONADO (2002), ASPROGOLAPA (1998-2000) and STOIAN (2000) were also used, presenting statistical information about the establishment and the categorisations of the rural settlements.

5.3 Cycle of institutional change in the northern Bolivian Amazon

The focus of this section is on answering the first research question, assuming that the dissatisfaction of regional actors motivated the adaptations to the law to better accommodate the real life situations of the inhabitants of the region. To facilitate a better understanding of the law enforcement, the reader will be presented with an ex-ante and ex-post analysis of the reforms, divided into three parts. In the first part a history of peasant and *barraca* settlements is presented, describing the pre-reforms period; the second part deals with the analysis of the Forest Law and the Agrarian Law of 1996, which are here termed the 'institutions of the first period'; and the third part incorporates the analysis of the decrees approved since 1999, referred to here as the 'institutions of the second period'.[164] While the institutions of the first period were centred around

[162] Given the novelty of Decree 27572 approved in June 2004, this chapter concentrates on the analysis of the two previous Decrees: the *barraca* Decree and the 500 ha Decree to the peasant families.

[163] Within the classification of private organizations, one includes only 11 technical organizations and 10 social organisations, excluding the four commercial organisations.

[164] Just as the denomination that the laws receive during the structural reform of Bolivian state, when reforms of first and second generation are identified, here are identified two periods of institutional change, restructuring the forest management in the study area; the first period is given between 1996-1999 and holds the Forest Law and Agrarian Law as the main legal instruments; the second period occurs since October 1999 in which the three complementary decrees are included.

the national policy perspective, where the interests of those governing often took precedence over the interests of the intended addressees, the second package of institutions commenced from an evolutionary perspective or institutional adaptation, seeking to incorporate the interests of the regional actors. To paraphrase HANISCH (2003), the first period illustrates a typical process of "institutional change that goes up-down", whereas the second is characterised more by "institutional change that goes down-up."

5.3.1 Brief history of rural settlements (Pre-reform period)

The analysis of the reform enforcement begins with a history of the elected user groups, from their establishment to the introduction of the Forest Law and the Agrarian Law.

History of the barracas

The first indications of structuring the *barraca* in the Amazon region date from 1860 (BALLIVIÁN 1896:3f). Officially, the 'rubber era' begins in 1863, when Manuel Ugalde received permission to navigate in the region and the privilege of exploiting the rubber (ABECIA 1985:151 cited in STOIAN 2000:57). One year later (1864), Santos Mercados established the first rubber estate in the region at the mouth of the Yata River, affluent of the Mamoré River. Together with the few indigenous groups, who were not involved in the economic production until then, the *barracas* were the only rural settlements in the region (STOIAN 2000). Stimulated with the growth and interest of the markets of Europe and the United States, an increase in the number of *barracas* in the region was evident at the end of the 19th century. There were some 45 *barracas* in the study area by 1894, most of them located along the rivers Madre de Dios and Orthon (BALLIVIAN 1912 cited in GAMARRA 1993:31). In 1893 the 'father of the rubber industry', *don* Antonio Vaca Diez, requested the National Delegation[165] award him more than 2,000 *estradas* under his occupation from 1881.[166] The establishment of the *barracas* followed the fortunes of the rubber markets. Until 1916 only the '*Casa Suárez*', the biggest extractivist company in the region, had obtained the property right of 22 *barracas*,[167] located mainly on the Tahuamanu, Madre de Dios and Abuná rivers. This area comprised nearly 5 million hectares, approximately 12,550 rubber *estradas* (GAMARRA 1993:34), the equivalent of nearly 50% of the area of the region. According to BOJANIC (2001:10), with the incorporation of the Brazil nut on the international markets (1930) the number of *barracas* continued to grow until the fall of '*Casa Suárez*' (1940). In the years after 1940, there was a stabilisation of the *barraca* area, the only notable changes in subsequent years being the increased level of transfer of the established estates. The main cause of the dismemberment of the '*Casa Suárez*' is the increase of sales, ownership changes in the form of compensation, or simple usurpation by third parties, mainly by the administrators and employees of the company. This period is considered the beginning of the current *barraquero* system (CIDOB 1979a: 69). Shortly

---

165 By law of October 28 1890, the National Government of Aniceto Arce creates the National Delegations of Madre de Deus and Purus, to protect the national interests before Brazil and Peru.

166 Letter of Antonio Vaca Diez to the National Delegation, Orthon, 22 December 1893. In October 1890, the Bolivian government creates two national Delegations in the Northern Bolivian Amazon.

167 According to the Law of 1915.

before the definitive plunge of the international rubber market (1985),[168] the *barraca* area covered 1.5 million hectares (ORMACHEA 1987). Based on the public statistics, this figure marks a drastic reduction of the area occupied by the *barraca* holders relative to past decades. By way of conclusion, until 1990 the reduction of the *barraca* area can be attributed more to the fall of the rubber markets, and to the disintegration of the '*Casa Suárez*' than to the effects of the Land Reform of 1953 or the Forest Law of 1974, due to the thin state influence over the tenure and use of the forest.

History of the peasant communities

Contrary to ORMACHEA (1987), the first peasant community in the region does not date from 1920, but rather from 1903, coinciding with the first rubber crisis experienced in the region.[169] Figure 16 presents the foundation by periods of 192 peasant communities in the study area from 1900 up to 1993.

Figure 16 Number of peasant communities founded in northern Bolivian Amazon (1900-1993)

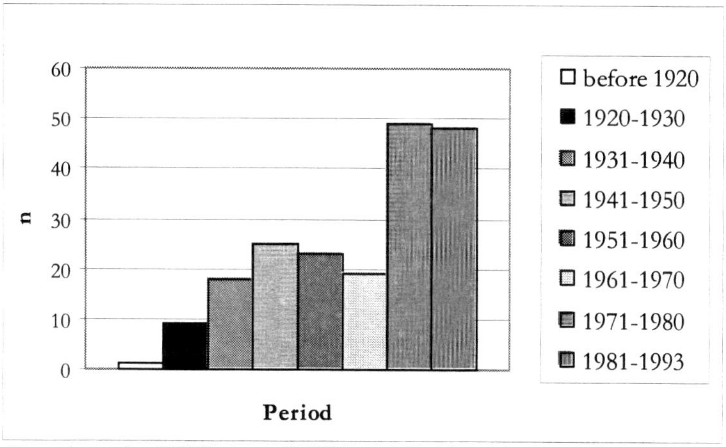

Source: Based on the DHV data (1993) and field study interviews.

The data presented is derived from the databases created during the field study (52 communities) and the research carried out by the DHV consultants (1993, unpublished) (140 communities). As can be seen from figure 16, approximately 5% of the registered communities (10) were founded by 1930, most of them located in Pando. Up to then, the formation of the communities seems to have been sporadic and discontinuous. In the 1930s, the number of communities doubled (18), opening the way for the foundation of the settlements, which today constitute many of the municipal capitals in Pando.[170] With the fall of '*Casa Suárez*' in 1940 and the approval of Land Reform in 1953, approximately fifty new communities were created.

---

168 The last rubber decline on the international market is explained by the introduction of the Bolivian government's neo-liberal policy, which ended Brazilian subsidies for Bolivian rubber production.

169 According to the DHV database 1993, unpublished.

170 El Sena, Bella Flor, Gonzalo Moreno, Humaita, Loma Alta, etc.

Around 25% of all of the communities were founded in a twenty-year period. Until the early '70s, an establishment trend of approximately twenty communities per decade continued. In the two decades from 1971, the number of communities founded per decade more than doubled to approximately fifty.

Between 1970 and early 1990 nearly 50% of peasant communities in the region were founded. This fact can be attributed to the increase in the construction of roads, linking the main rural centres of the region and to the collapse of the international rubber market in 1985. According to the data collected during field study, no peasant communities were established after 1994. From the answers provided by interviewees, this can be attributed to the fact that the agrarian legislation does not recognise establishment on state lands. According to data of the 1984 agricultural census, the area occupied by the rural communities was 220,000 ha (ORMACHEA 1987). In summary, up until 1996 the establishment of the peasant communities can be attributed to the following factors: 1) abandonment of the *barraca* estate; 2) foundation of the main municipal capitals in Pando and 3) the construction of service infrastructures, mainly roads. Figure 17 shows the location of rural communities.

Figure 17 Locations of rural communities

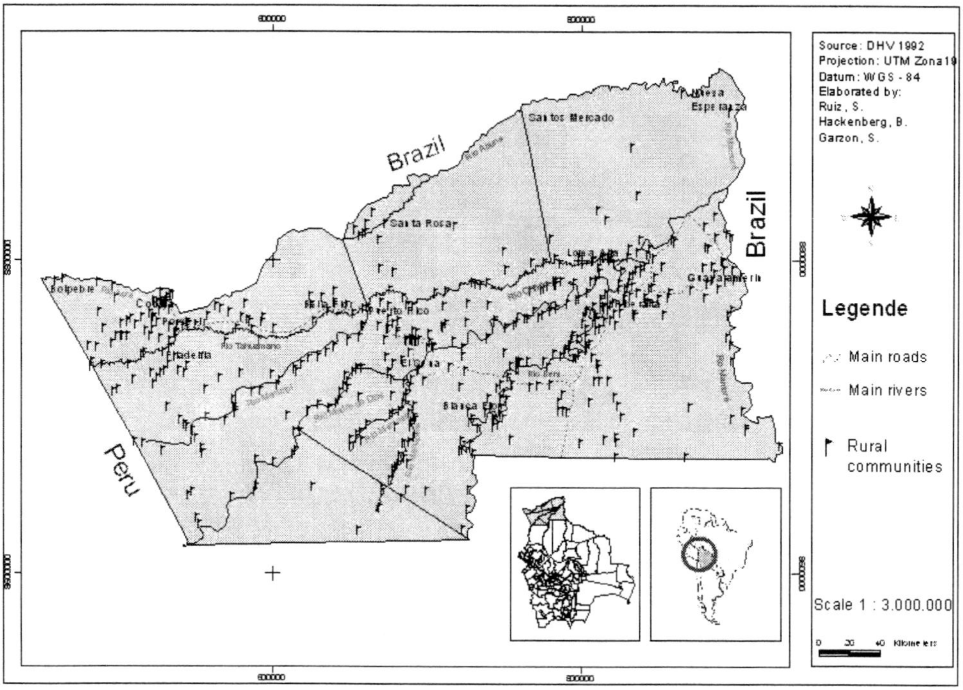

5.3.2 Incentives, enforcement and evasion of the institutions of the first period

As mentioned in chapter 4, in the first four years the forest concessionaires remained the group most favoured by reforms, with gradual incorporation of the indigenous groups; firstly when awarded approximately 1.5 million hectares and secondly through the consolidation of two indigenous territories (TCOs), covering approximately 300,000 ha. Like peasant people, *barraca* holders did not appear to be sufficiently motivated to comply with the new laws (see table 16).

The '*barraca* regime' was again placed above public law. Put simply, up until the early part of the new millennium no *barraca* holder had requested the conversion of his estate to forest concession. However, the *saneamiento* in TCO *Multiétnico* II, carried out after 1998, was a first indication of the dwindling security of the *barraquero* system in the face of indigenous interests over the land. Nearly 91 individual properties, between 1 and 70,000 ha, were threatened with the loss of their rights.

The five largest *barraca* holders who possessed around 50% of the area requested by indigenous groups (approx. 440,000 ha) lost a great part of their *barracas* (see ARAMAYO 2000:198). The social conflicts and the legal security of the *barraca* affected the emergence of new private settlements on 'open land'; according to field study information only two of the interviewed barraca holders (n=36) declared to have been founded between 1995-2000. The location of the new *barracas* coincides with the peripheral areas, characterized as having little service infrastructure and low population density. Comparing the data of the three case studies with the information received by the 36 interviewed *barraca* holders, the reforms drastically reduced the transferability of *barracas*. Starting from 1996 very few holders resorted to buying or selling *barracas*, changing them for other fixed estate, receiving as part payment for assumed debts, or using them as credit guarantee to finance the Brazil nut harvest. A similar reaction to that of the *barraca* holders could be observed amongst the peasant communities, who until 2000 showed little motivation to formalise their tenures.

The few examples of consolidation of their lands are framed in the *Multiétnico* II *saneamiento* process, where in 2001 ten peasant communities neighbouring the TCO were titled an approximate area of 36,000 hectares (INRA database 2001). According to field study results, however, most of peasant communities were not satisfied with the granted surface, which is why their leaders proceeded in many cases to question the failure of the INRA before the National Agrarian Tribunal.

The perception by the *barraca* holders and peasants of not being sufficiently included in the Law leads to the organisation of several regional meetings, with the purpose of concerting the best form of incorporating their expectations into the national legislation. The regional workshop held in July 1998 was the most important of these regional meetings.[171]

Up to here, one cannot necessarily speak about a division between both parties. On the contrary, a certain 'alliance' rather is observed between both groups against the territorial indigenous expansion. This situation changes quickly when the *barraca* holders achieve the approval of Decree 25532, but above all when this institution begins to be implemented. With this decree, the *barraca* holders hoped to control nearly three million hectares, ignoring the presence of the several peasant communities (see figure 18).

[171] Here the main agreed points were: To demand from the forest authorities the preference of the traditional inhabitants of the region in future concessions; Re-formulation of Agrarian Legislation, incorporating an article that recognizes as basic unit of communal endowment an area equal to or bigger than 500 hectares for rural families; to urgently demand the INRA, starting the land titling in the region.

Table 16 Public incentives and real impact of the enforcement of institutions of the first period (1996-1999)

Forest users	Instruments/Public Incentives	Real impact	Strategies groups and other approved institutions
Barraca holders	The Forest Law does not provide the *barraca* holders the opportunity to formalise their rights to NTFP use. The Agrarian Law eliminates the possibility of granting the lands occupied by the *barracas*, as these settlements do not fulfil the established criteria of the FES.	Until 2000, there was no known of intention on the part of any *barraca* holder to formalise his rights under the possibilities offered by the reform. In reality, the '*barraquero* regime' remains the rule, giving legitimacy to NTFP use. Nevertheless, under the land titling process of indigenous lands, the *barracas* officially become rural communities. The low legal security provided reduces the transferability of *barracas*, which was common in the past.	Starting in 1998, on the initiative of some national parliamentary representatives, the administrative authorities of the government (SIF and Ministry of Sustainable Development) began to include the *barracas* in the forest legislation. These actions concluded with the approval of Decree 25532 in October 1999.
Peasant communities	Through the communal property legal instrument regulated by the Agrarian Law, a maximum of 50 ha is allocated to each extractivist peasant family. The Forest Law allows them to take advantage of the forests once the land has been granted and a FMP drafted.	In general, they have shown little interest in formalising their rights, a factor attributed to the peasants' poor knowledge of the rules, the high transaction costs involved in meeting the legal requirements, and most importantly because the 50 ha/family is, in many cases, not enough to consolidate the traditional extractivist properties. The few communal titles distributed after 1996 were the result of the *saneamiento* process in the two regional TCOs.	Initially the activities of this group concentrated the defence of the rights of communities affected by the *saneamiento* of indigenous lands. The quest to consolidate their rights is a reaction to the approval of the *Barraca* Decree, as this rule is contrary to their interests. A popular protest march was organised in response, called 'Land, Territory and Natural Resources'. Moved by the protest, the government approved Decree 25848, granting a minimum of 500 ha to each peasant extractivist family living in a community.

Source: Based on field study interviews.

Figure 18 Locations claims over barracas

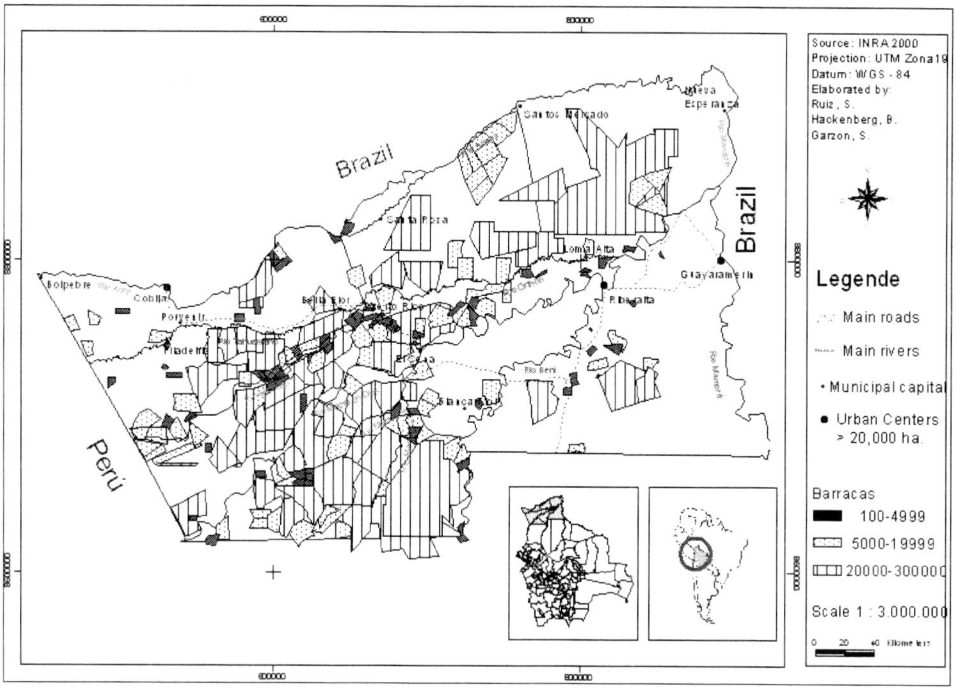

5.3.3 Incentives and enforcement of the second period institutions

The approval of the Decrees 25532 and 25848 marks a new era in the reform enforcement in the Amazon region introducing rules closer to the reality of regional interest groups (see table 17).

Decree 25532

Decree 25532, commonly known as '*Barraca* Decree', was approved on October 5th 1999 as a complementary institution to the forest legislation, during the constitutional government of Hugo Banzer. The decree is based on the interpretation and legal regulation of Article 29 of the Forest Law: "*Being areas where non timber resources are predominant from the commercial or traditional point of view, the concession will be granted for this primordial purpose, their holders enjoying the exclusive right of the timber product use.*"[172]

The traditional right of *barraca* is formalised through transforming it into NTFP forest concessions (Article 1). In addition, the decree regulates the payment of forest taxes for Brazil nuts on the basis of volume (Article 3). However, one of its more controversial articles states that the *barraca* holders have the right to maintain their claims over their large estates (Article 6).

[172] Art. 29 Parenthesis II, Forest Law.

Table 17. Public incentives and real impact of the enforcement of the institutions of the second period (1999-2004)

Forest users	Instruments/Public Incentives	Real impact	Strategies groups and other approved institutions
Barraca holders	Decree 25532 regulates the establishment of forest concessions for NTFP for the northern Bolivian Amazon with the aim of integrating the *barraca* in the national legislation.	In the study area alone (Pando and Vaca Diez), 221 *barracas* demanded more than three million hectares. If granted, forty percent of the requested area would have been in the hands of 12 *barraca* holders. The largest registered *barraca* encompassed nearly 400,000 ha (ASPROGOAL 2000).	With the demise of Decree 25532 and the distribution of the lands to the peasant communities, the expectations of the *barraca* holders with respect to the size of their entitlements decreased substantially. One of the later proposals presented to the executive recognised an area of up to a maximum of 25,000 ha/*barraca*. Due to the political weakness of the group and to the constant change of the national authorities these proposals took four years to be considered. In June 2004, the government approved Decree 27572 limiting the area of the *barraca* to 15,000 hectares.
Peasants Communities	Decree 25848 confers a minimum area of 500 ha to each peasant family living in a community. This decree takes into consideration extractivist activities engaged in across large forest areas.	Great interest in the formalisation of their community property rights. As with the *barraca* holder group, the decree increases the expectations held by the peasants. Of the 54 peasant communities interviewed, 20% declared land exceeding the average of 500 ha/family, in some cases the averages were in excess of 1,500 ha per family, with a range of between 541 and 2,500 ha per family.	As a group, the peasant communities are strong and together with the indigenous group fight to neutralise the demands of the *barraca* holders. Due to the increasing expectations in relation to access to the land, a multisector commission in the region decided to put a limit to the granting of land to rural families, set at a maximum of 540 ha/family.[173] Decree 27572 defines the right of the rural communities at 500 to 1,000 hectares.

Source: Based on field study interviews.

Because the legal technical process of conversion of the *barraca* exceeded the time set out in the decree (April 2000), in May 2000 a second decree was approved (25783) which extends the conversion term by three months until July 2000. Both decrees were repealed with the promulgation of Decree 25848, July 10th 2000, a response to one of the first measures of pressure exerted by the rural communities during the Third Indigenous-Peasant March.

173 Personal interview with the technician responsible for the INRA-Pando *saneamiento*; May 3rd 2002.

Decree 25848 (500 hectares Decree)

Decree 25848 was approved on July 18 2000, also under the presidency of Banzer. This ruling modifies the general regulation of the Agrarian Legislation, initially approved in May of the same year. Of the five approved articles, the following content stands out:

> *"In the Pando department, the Vaca Diez province of Beni [....] the minimum unit of endowment per family in rural and indigenous communities is set at 500 hectares"*[174]

The barracas Decree enforcement

Until its repeal, the enforcement of *barraca* Decree was speeded up thanks to the work of the representatives of the *barraquero* associations with technical support of BOLFOR office in Riberalta. Until its repeal, the enforcement of the According to database of their representative organisations, in the study area (Pando and Vaca Diez) 221 *barracas* were registered during the conversion process to NTFP concessions that covered an area close to three million hectares (see Table 18).

Table 18 Registration of barracas in the conversion process to NTFP concessions

Category	Size (ha)	*Barracas* (n)	Total surface (1,000 ha)	Surface (%)
Large *barracas*[175]	> 20,000	44	2,194	71
Medium *barracas*[176]	5,000 < 20,000	83	696	23
Small *barracas*[177]	500 < 5,000	94	188	6
Total		221	3,078	100

Source: ASPROGOAL (Database 1998-2000 without publication): Registrations of *barracas* for conversion to forest concessions.

Seventy percent of the area was demanded by nearly thirty *barraca* holders, who declared possession of 44 *barracas*. Twenty three percent of the surface demanded

[174] Article 1: complementary to article 238 of the general regulation of the Agrarian Law on the execution of the FES.

[175] The majority of large *barraqueros* live in Riberalta and 85% of them are affiliated to ASPROGOAL; the other 15% are distributed between ASPROGOALPA (Cobija) and AARENARMAPA (Puerto Rico). Of the 2 million hectares that these *barracas* include, approximately 75% belong to 12 *barraca* holders. Approximately 90% of the area occupied by the large *barracas* is concentrated in Pando. The biggest estate registered has more than 390,000 has. Altogether it has the greatest direct relationship with the regional forest industry, both Brazil nut factories and sawmills.

[176] The holders of medium *barracas* also inhabit the urban centres (Cobija, Riberalta, Puerto Rico), although one knows medium barraqueros who live permanently in their production centres, as is the case of the AARENARMAPA members. This group has 38% of the total of registered medium *barracas*. ASPROGOAL is also the association of *barraqueros* with the greatest number of medium establishments registered (66%), followed by ASPROGOALPA of Cobija (19%) and the other 15% is in AARENARMAPA. The medium *barracas* constituted 23% of the area covered by these establishments.

[177] The small *barraqueros* live generally in their centres of production. 35% of small *barracas* do not exceed 1.500 ha. AARENARMAPA is the association with the greatest percentage of members with small *barracas* (63%). In number, 40% of the registered *barraqueros* belonged to this category. The smallest *barracas* of the registry have 150 hectares and the average of the group comes to 2000 ha/*barraca*.

corresponds the medium size *barraca* holders and 6% of the total demand corresponds the small *barracas* holders.

Comparing with other available registrations of the same associations,[178] or with the 1984 agricultural census results, the attitude of the *barraca* holders was guided to expanding not only the number of *barracas*, but also the surface occupied by their settlements. The presence of rural communities and the situation of many of the *barracas* in transition were ignored.[179] Only the surface of the *barraca* in transition, according to field data gathered by STOIAN (2000), represents around 30% of the total of demanded settlements.

The 500 ha Decree enforcement

The enforcement of Decree 25848 was almost immediate, due to the provision of public funds according to Article 5. The activities developed by peasants in consolidating their lands, coincide with this field study (August 2001 to June 2002), when a strong dynamism and interest in better organising their communities was observed, marking out their communal limits, keeping contact with the regional organisations, etc. Just like the land expansion of the *barraca* holders with the Decree 25532, several rural communities seek to occupy larger areas, because the Decree 25848 does not limit the maximum of size per family. According to the database prepared during the field study, of the 54 peasant communities interviewed, 20% of them declared to exceed the average of 500 ha/family. This situation is more frequent in Pando, especially in places with smaller population density and less pressure on the forests (northeast area of the department). The area occupied, on average, exceeds 1,500 ha/family, with variations between 541 and 2,500 ha/family. However, not all the peasant communities will be able to consolidate the 500 ha/family. Mainly in Vaca Diez province the average land per community is 200 ha/family, where 10 communities that do not end up having more than 100 ha/family (field study findings). All empirical findings coincide with the preliminary data of the land titling presented by the INRA–Pando in 2004, where the approximately 130 rural communities claim 33% more area than they is allowed by law. According to the available data of nine polygons,[180] in seven of them the demands of the peasant communities are higher than 500 ha, the area recognised by INRA for peasant members (so called FES) (see figure 19).[181]

---

178 The data presented in chart 18 was compared with the database collected by ASPROGOALPA in 1998 and with the data collected during the field phase of the present research, as well as with the databases of STOIAN (2000) and MALDONADO (2002).

179 According to STOIAN (2000), the *barracas* in transition are establishments in process of conversion to rural communities, where the *patrón* continues controlling Brazil nut extraction, while he loses political power by the foundation of an '*Organización Territorial de Base*' (OTB) by the residents, or patrones are being pressured to distribute the land in plots to *fregueces*.

180 In the case of polygon 4, corresponding to municipalities of Cobija and Porvenir, only there are data about number of communities, and not about the occupied surface.

181 Due to Decree 25848 not put limit to the peasants claims, the INRA agents together with representatives of other regional social organization agreed to put a limit of 540 ha per peasants family (more information see section 5.4.3). The greatest differences found occur in the polygons with smaller pressure of the population to the resources, that is to say of the municipalities of Nueva Esperanza, Villa Nueva, Santos Mercado, Santa Rosa, Ingavi and Bella Flor. Here the percentage of the demands exceeds the FES by 40%.

Figure 19 Differences between claimed surface and FES[182] in the peasant communities of Pando (1,000 ha)

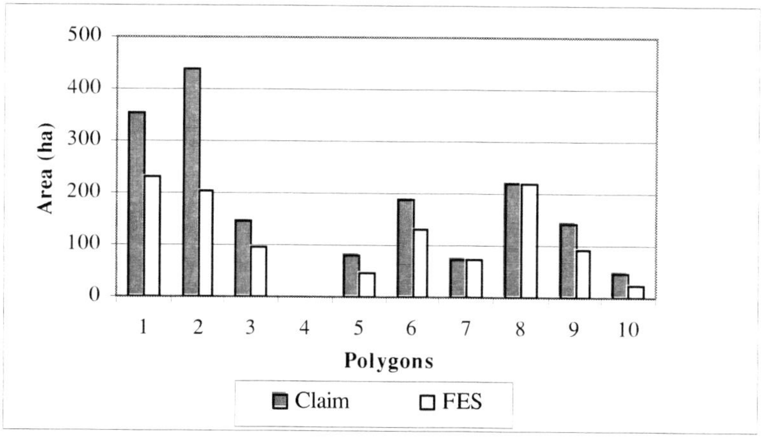

Source: INRA (2004) Preliminary *saneamiento* data for Pando.

Given the novelty of Decree 27572 from June 2004, its impact on the *barracas* and on the rural communities must be ignored here.

5.4 Influence of interest groups in institutional change

In the previous section it was demonstrated that the 'institutional vacuum' contained in the reforms produces few incentives for regional actors to implement the laws. However, when the laws are adapted to meet the interests of regional actors, they in turn become motivated to fulfil the public institutions. This section concentrates on the analysis of group strategies of regional actors to adapt the legislation in their favour through the drawing up and approval of Decrees 25532 and 25848.

5.4.1 *Barracas* Decree

The formulation initiatives of Decree 25532 began in 1998, shortly after the workshop on land tenure was organised in Puerto Rico. The second national senator for Beni department and representative of the Vaca Diez province, taking advantage of his constitutional mandate, requested technical support from the SIF to incorporate the demands of the *barraca* holders in the national legislation. Beni's senator belongs to the group of large *barraca* holders, and he was interested in consolidating nearly to 300,000 ha, proposed for NTFP concessions. The proposal was accepted by the SIF agents, who believed that a large forest area was used outside of Law 1700 (Technical agent of the SIF, Interview; August 12th 2003).

Parallel to SIF support, the *barraqueros*' representatives appealed for technical support from private organisations, such as BOLFOR and PROMAB, whose technicians prepared the outlines for the formulation of 'Brazil nut Management Plan' in 1998, to be considered as the

182 For more information on FES see section 4.2.2.3 and 7.2.3

technical and ideological base of Decree 25532.[183] Both technical organisations have been characterized for supporting the expectations of national entrepreneurs, since their foundations. Parallel to the Beni senator's initiative, the three *barraquero* associations began lobbying inside the region, getting support and resources by the local association members (see figure 20).

Figure 20 Preparation and approval process of Presidential Decree 25532: Key actors and interactions

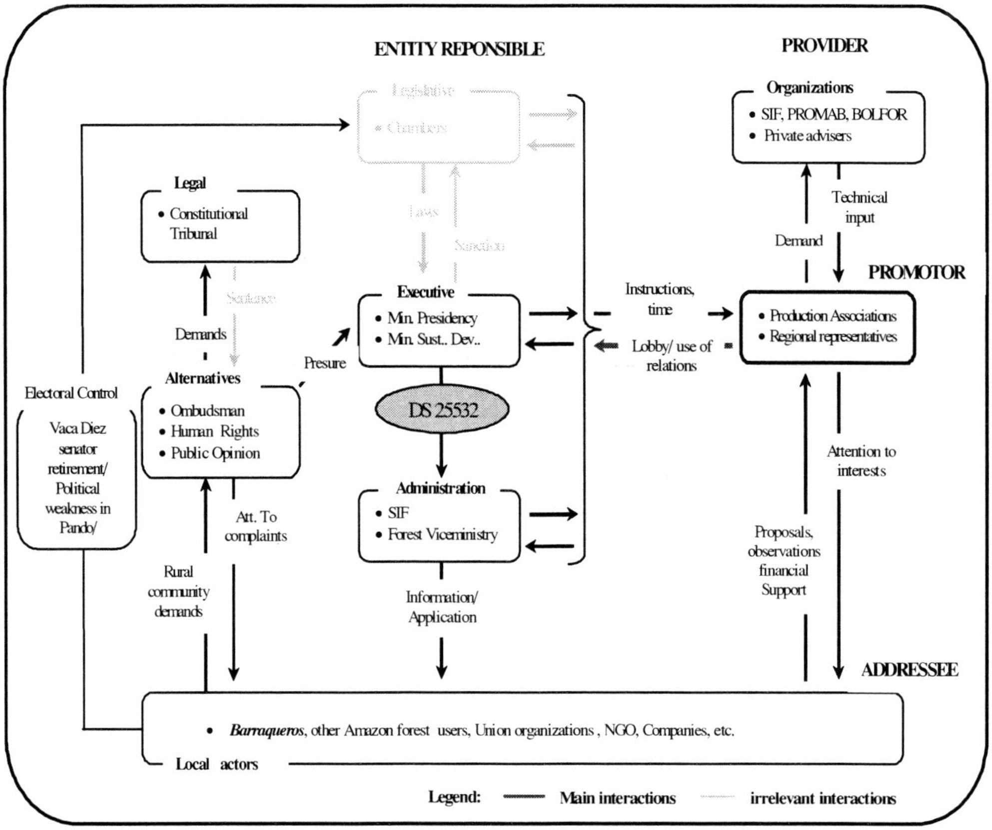

Source: Adapted from HEIDEMANN (1995) and based on field study interviews.

The diffusion of decree inside the executive authorities lasted around one year. "*For the majority of the political decision-makers, topic about the barracas was not known.*"[184] Here the tactics applied were to convince in the first instance the Minister of Sustainable Development, authority in charge of taking the forest politics ahead. Once the idea had been approved in this ministry, the Minister himself took the proposal to the National

183 Personal interviews with Ex- BOLFOR technician from Riberalta; August 13th 2003.

184 Personal interview with Ex-National Senator of Beni; June 5th 2002.

Council of Economic Policy (CONAPE), the highest authority of interministerial coordination formed by six of the 14 ministries.[185] In the final stage of the process the project was strengthened by the incorporation of the first Pando Senator who exercised the functions of Senate President in 1999.[186]

When the decree reached the office of the Ministry of the Presidency the process had already gained form and votes, the Minister himself assuming the coordination and diffusion role with the other ministries.[187] While the promoter's actions have been guided to reach consensus in the executive spheres, regional experts agreed that at local level not all *barraca* holders participated in the same way. The main backing of the recipients came from large *barraca* holders, who assisted the project with important economic and logistical contributions. They paid the travel costs of the regional representatives to the Government's headquarters, held discussion meetings with the members of the associations, and hired the professional services of experts in legal and forest matters.

According to data collected during the field study, small *barraca* holders declared they knew and understood the institution only after its approval.

Errors attributed to Decree 25532

According to regional expert interviewees (n=41), the following three legal flaws led to the repeal of the decree:

- First: the *barraca* holders made high demands on temporal enforcement of decree. The decree accelerates the conversion process, specifying a minimum term, first of six months, later extended to nine months, favouring their exclusive interests, to the detriment of the land claims of other traditional forest users[188] (50% of interviewees);

- Second: it regulates the conversion of the *barraca* without a process of national or at least regional bidding, ignoring the rule of land titling process. The arguments of regional experts are 70% in agreement that Article 1 contradicts the Forest and Agrarian Legislations; and

- Third: it states that the *barraca* holders converted to forest legislation did not give up the claims for ownership of lands, thus contradicting the spirit of the Agrarian Law against large land owners (Article 6) (90% of interviewees).

Additional to its 'legal flaws', Decree 25532 is also attributed with a weak participation and agreement with other regional interest groups, mainly with the members and representatives of the rural communities (75% of interviewees). According to the indigenous and peasant leaders the decree enforcement generated more dissatisfaction than its approval, due to the fact that in a

185 The CONAPE was a ministerial body created during the Banzer presidency to assess and propose regulations and policies directed towards strengthening the national economy.

186 The president of senate chamber in Bolivia, formally is the third most influential person in national politics after the President and Vice-President of the Republic.

187 Personal Interview with ex-National Senator from Beni; June 5th 2002.

188 Since the process of *barraca* conversion exceeded the first limit of time established until April 2000, the *barraquero* representatives again achieved the approval of a second decree (25783) that extended the conversion period until 31 July 2000. Decree 25783 was approved on 19 May 2000.

period of five months (January – May 2000) the *barraca* holders tried to occupy one third of the whole regional surface, ignoring the presence of several rural communities.[189]

The approval of the *Barraca* Decree led the rural population to question its constitutionality. Indigenous and peasants unions, supported by regional NGOs and the Catholic Church, took their protests to the national authorities and faced the public opinion, by writing letters and press releases. Initially, the executive did not react to these requests. However the complaints were backed by other organisations like the '*Defensoría del Pueblo*' (ombudsman)[190] and the Permanent Assembly of Human Rights,[191] bodies that became links to go with the requests to the Constitutional Tribunal itself.[192]

Until the repeal of Decree 25532, no sentence issued by the Constitutional Tribunal against the requested ruling is known. The repeal of decree occurs with a reaction of the Third Indigenous - Peasant March, pressing the national government to annul the July 10th 2000 ruling. The rural population also resorted to other measures such as the 'punishment vote' against the two political representatives who promoted the decree. The representative of the Vaca Diez province was not re-elected as a senator and the political weight of the Pando senator declined throughout the region (see figure 20).

5.4.2 '500 hectare Decree'

For lack of parliamentary representation of the group in charge of defending their interests at national level, the action taken by the regional leaders was to pressure the government through the execution of Third National March, called '*Land, Territory and Natural Resources*'.[193] Although all indigenous and peasant organisations supported this decision,[194] the unions of the northern Bolivian Amazon were fundamental in its organisation, mainly CIRABO and the Peasant Federations- Pando,[195] Vaca Diez and Guayaramerín (see figure 21). The demonstration took force with the incorporation of more than 600 peasants, indigenous persons and settlers of which more than 80% came from the region. As political platform, the march had national demands considered in 31 points, among which were the community endowment of 500 hectares to all peasant families and the annulment of the *Barraca* Decree (CEJIS 2000).

---

189 Personal interviews with main indigenous and peasant leaders in the region (n=5).

190 The Town Ombudsman is a public authority ordered to look after the fulfilment of the rights and guarantees of the people in relation to the administrative activity of all the public sector (Law 1818 1997; art. 127). The Town Ombudsman receives its operating budget from the Legislative power.

191 In Bolivia, both these bodies are characterised by looking after the basic needs of the social groups with the least political representation, acting as legal link between the civil population and the public bodies.

192 Press release La Razón, July 14th 2000.

193 The march started on June 28th in the Pando, from where several hundred peasants and indigenous inhabitants went from their communities to the city of Riberalta http://www.angelfire.com/ok3/lfcreativa/separata.html.

194 Among several of its protagonists one mentions the Coordinator of Ethnic Towns of Santa Cruz (CPESC), the peasants and settlers Federations of Beni, Santa Cruz and the Province of Gran Chaco and the representatives of several indigenous territories of the Department of Beni.

195 It refers to the Peasant Federation at the time led by Fermín Terraces.

Figure 21 Preparation and approval process of Presidential Decree 25848: Key actors and interactions

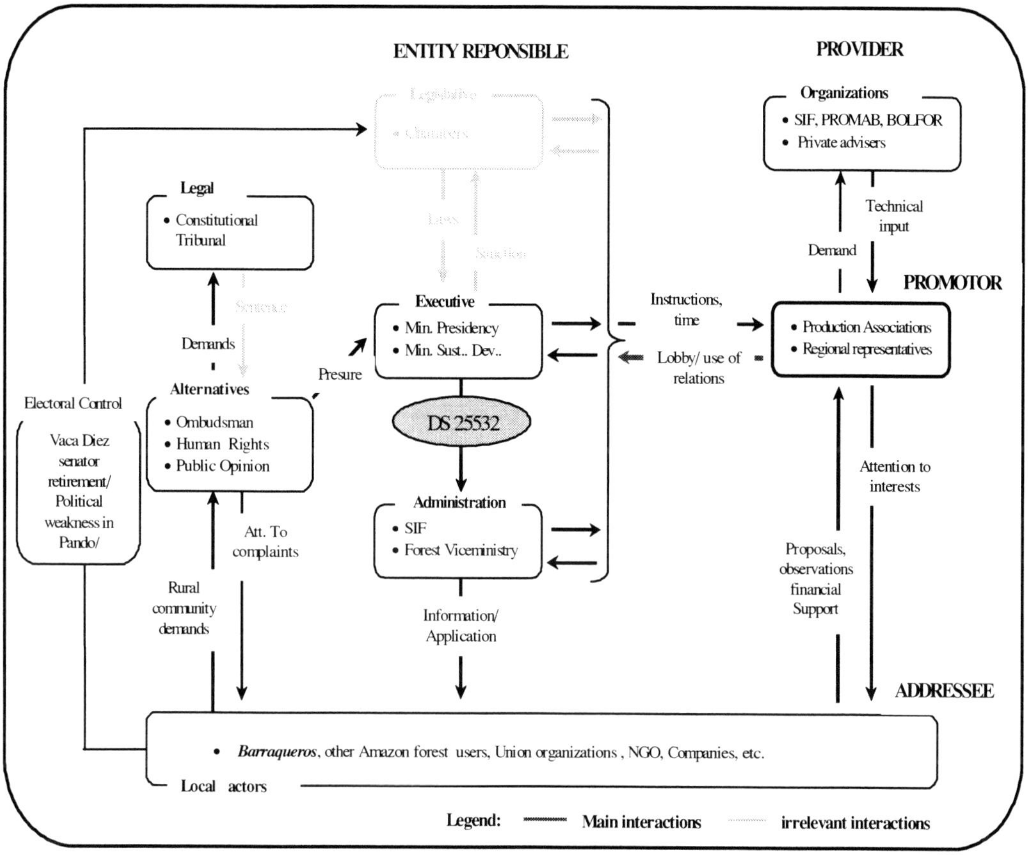

Source: Adapted from HEIDEMANN (1995) and based on field study interviews

As much in preparation of peasants' claims as in organisation and financing of the march, the work of some regional NGOs, which traditionally support the demands of rural groups, was important (CEJIS, CIPCA-Norte, Caritas, ACRA and IPHAE).

Their technical contribution consisted in editing documents, that support the position of peasants and their claims on 500 ha[196] and in formulation of decree's draft version, presented to national authorities for consideration. Another substantial contribution of NGOs was the advice to communal leaders at the time of negotiations with government authorities.

196 The proposal was based on considering the annual economic income by family, under the systems of subsistence agriculture, dependence on the extractivism as main source of financing and the unfavourable circumstances present for the commercialisation of the timber. With 500 hectares an average family of six members could reach an average annual income of Bs. 7,750 (approximately US$ 1,000).

Providers supporting the social movements are Catholic Church, Ombudsman and Assembly of Human Rights; their mission was to act as guarantors and to exercise a kind of control system to look after execution of signed agreements.

The march coincided with a high social tension in the country. The national authorities were occupied solving other very important issues of social strife, such as protests by policemen in the city of La Paz, who were demanding a wage increase, or the 'fight for water' campaign by the inhabitants of Cochabamba. This meant finding a politically weak government to negotiate with, motivated in solving social conflicts as quickly as possible. Thus the almost immediate reaction on the part of the executive power is seen, interested in slowing the demonstrators down so that they do not find the government giving in, where the government would have supported greater social pressure from other groups, that would even have meant the President's resignation.

The executive power conformed a negotiation commission, led by Minister of Presidency, three other ministers (Agriculture, Sustainable Development and Housing), two vice ministers (Environment and Indigenous Matters) and National Director of INRA. The negotiations between demonstrators and government were intensified, when the march got to Montero, a town located 45 km from Santa Cruz city. The negotiation culminated on July 16th at 4:30 in the morning, with the signature of the act of conformity in the negotiations of which the most important results are the approval of several public institutions: four presidential decrees,[197] a ministerial resolution (035/200)[198] and an administrative resolution of INRA (088/200).[199] Most of the 31 demands presented by peasants and indigenous people were successfully considered.

Regarding the formulation of Article 238 in the decree, 500 hectares are determined the minimum area to which each peasant family is entitled. In this respect the promoters of decree were astonished by the 'benevolence' of the national authorities, since the original draft was limited to consolidate an area no greater than 500 ha.[200] The *barraca* holders protested against the annulment of Decree 25532 through a public official statement to the national Government, demanded for the increase of land insecurity, that limiting the investments of regional forest. Following measures of pressure concentrated on declaring the region in a state of emergency and giving a term to national government, assisting the union claims.[201]

---

197 Apart from the Supreme decrees 25838 and 25848, decree 25847 was approved. It establishes that indigenous communities, peasants and individual colonizers must not present a *saneamiento* plan or a deforest plan in case of indigenous people, when the area is less than five hundred hectares and Decree 25849 authorizes the Central Bank to open development lines up to US$ 10,000 from General Treasury of the Nation, to take care of the emergency needs of small rural producers throughout Bolivia.

198 The Ministerial Resolution corresponds to the Ministry of the Presidency to guarantee the rights of the rural communities to the proceeding of its legal personality (July 14th 2000).

199 The administrative resolution of INRA cancels another similar resolution that approved the 'procedure for the certification of certain fiscal land availability for forest concessions, conservation of biodiversity, research and ecotourism'.

200 Personal interview with three participant members (NGO Technicians) in the government negotiations, on different dates.

201 Official statement of ASPROGOAL, July 18th 2000.

5.4.3 Other institutions

The Decree 25848 enforcement lead to a territorial expansion of peasant communities, influencing the emergence of social conflicts, mainly with the traditional land holders, like barraqueros and forest concessionaires. For that reason the National Director of INRA jointly with members of regional '*Saneamiento* Committee'[202] agreed to define temporarily the claims of peasant communities at 540 hectares in February 2002.[203] This institution and the approval of Ministerial Resolution 164, at the end of 2002, regulating the execution of the 'Brazil nut management plans', helped the *barraca* holders to maintain their demands over land. Later in June 2004, another decree was approved (27572) allowing the *barraca* holders to transform again their productive states into NTFP concessions, however this time up to a limit of 15,000 ha. The new Decree 27572 is a result of the constant pressure exercised by the barraca holders through the organisation of popular protest,[204] negotiations with the regional authorities, taking of public offices, meetings with the presence of national authorities in the region, blockade of the main regional access routes (rivers and roads), etc. Until June 2004 at least five versions of decree drafts were known, that warned of a gradual reduction of expectations and attenuation of *barraquero* group. The proposals contained significant changes, compared to Decree 25532, for example: The term '*barraqueros*' (*barraca* holders) used before as synonym of patrones or large entrepreneurs was substituted by "traditional users of non consuming use of the northern Amazon". Equally, the legal proposals fell during the negotiation period (2000-2004) from 100,000 ha as maximum area to 15,000 ha. Decree 27572 as approved even mentions as new addressees of forest concessions, all individual or collective people using NTFPs since early 1990; i.e., it does not close the possibility of awarding concessions to indigenous or peasants communities. The decree also recognizes the land titling process and lastly it concentrates on granting only 'forest concession', leaving aside the possibility to give the barraca holders land ownerships titles.

Decree 27572 also defines the size of peasant communities, between 500 and 1,000 ha/family. Furthermore, for all those communities which are not able to receive the 500 ha, for example in the Vaca Diez province, the decree allows them to request lands near to the community or in bordering areas, complementing the size deficit. Immediately after the approval of Decree 27572, the indigenous representatives protested through their national and regional organisations (CIDOB, CIRABO and CIPOAP) that did not accept the Decree until late August 2004.[205]

The territorial restriction of the *barracas* to an area of 15,000 ha as well as the recognition of the rights of rural communities denotes the partial attenuation of political bargaining power of the *barraca* group, and can be attributed to the following factors:

---

202 The *saneamiento* Committee is formed by regional NGOs like IPHAE, CIPCA, SNV, Caritas-Cobija and ACRA, as well as by Peasants Federation of Pando and Vaca Diez (personal interview with the President of '*Saneamiento* Committee ', March 02th 2002.

203 Personal interview with the technician in charge of *saneamiento* of INRA-Pando; May 3rd 2002.

204 The '*Gran marcha barraquera* ' took place on 5 October 2001in the city of Cobija, with more than 300 people taking part.

- The political weakness in national spheres, due to the loss of parliamentary representation as their main promoters; i.e. the *barraca* holders renounced on their lobby group, with the corresponding rupture of political relationships with decision-makers in executive power, in a period characterized by constant changes of government cabinet. This situation increased the transaction costs of political bargaining, not only by assuming communication cost between both regional and national levels, but also because many of arrived agreements were ignored by successors authorities.;
- the internal division of the three regional unions, representing divergent interests among large *barraca* holders (ASPROGOAL), medium and small *barraca* holders (AARENARMAPA and ASPROGOALPA) and
- the gradual growth of the political and social power of peasant and indigenous groups at regional level, in addition to other factors, brought with them the technical and financial support of the NGOs, helping them to oppose the interests of the powerful elite groups.

5.5 Conclusions

The experiences from the study area are helpful for understanding the strategies employed by the interest groups to change the laws, as well as for distinguishing the circumstances that the social actors avail of to negotiate with the responsible public groups, depending on the action resources that they hold. While the *barraca* holders utilise their contacts with those in charge at political level, the peasants and indigenous groups organise massive public events, taking advantage of the force of their numerous members. The *barraquero* strategies were successful in favourable political situations, when their sector representatives assumed important public positions. However they also require strategies for application in other unfavourable situations. The rural groups, on the other hand, take advantage of political and social crises, and use the opportunities to make demands of the government. When referring to the strategies employed by the peasants, SCOTT (1985) spoke of '*non conventional weapons*', not necessarily less efficient than those applied by the elite power groups. The experiences from the study area also shed light on the participation of the recipients, firstly in the drafting of public institutions and secondly in their enforcement.

But if both *barraca* holders and peasants have effective strategies to change the laws, the question remains: Why did institutional change happen newly at the beginning of century? A possible answer can be seen according to BUCHANAN (1999) who analyses the change of the fiscal policies between the 80s and 90s in the United States, asserting that the differences lies by the 'temperature of the taxpayers'. At the end of the 70s years of taxpayer rebellion are seen, and starting from the 90s apathy sets in. Although the tax burdens remain, their incomes increase along with a relatively lower inflation that does not harm their interests.

Something similar happens in the Northern Amazon region. In the *barraquero* case, in the previous regime nobody dared to request the change of the laws, because quite simply their

205 Press article La Razón 24th August 2004.

interests were not affected. The '*barraca* regime' undertook responsibility to regulate the use of the forest, and its influence even caused the public agents to adapt themselves to it. This way the apathy of most of the regional interest groups is explained at the time to discuss the reaches of the reform, which meant the emergence of the 'institutional vacuum'. Nevertheless, at the beginning of the 90s and up to 2000, the '*barraquero* regime' began to show its first weaknesses before the demands of the forest companies and the indigenous groups. This situation forces the *barraca* holder*s* to activate their lobby groups, through their parliamentary representatives that succeed in promulgating Decree 25532 in a little more than one year.

In the peasant case, not having any lobby groups or parliamentary representation, the road towards change is more complicated. In the early 80s, that is to say after the military dictatorships, the regional initiatives concentrated on re-organising their associations (in the case of indigenous) or strengthening them (in the case of peasants).[206] One of the first major results of the organisation happens in 1990, during the 'First Peasant March' that served the rural groups to accumulate experience and to verify bargaining power with the political actors (see table 20). The first march and those that follow contribute to increasing the self-identification of rural groups, strengthening the bonds between indigenous groups and peasants of other Bolivian' regions. Through those 'new' contacts run the knowledge and acquired experience of important national leaders, and national professionals (sociologists, political scientists, and anthropologists) interested in contributing to the process of the social changes with their knowledge.

At local level it is difficult to predict how the rural communities prepare for the change. Until 1994 at least in Pando, the history of the *barraca* still influenced communal organisation and leadership.[207] The research carried out by CARMEN GOTTWALD (forthcoming) will provide more information on this topic; for instance that the degree of organisation of rural settlements also depends on the education of its members.

With the approval of the Popular Participation Law, the state begins to establish its presence in the area. The number of municipal governments grows from four to seventeen,[208] the state recognises the community organisation and grants them legal personality, the local population chooses its municipal representatives, etc. One of the most important contributions in the Popular Participation Law for the communities of the study area is the development to local organisation and the grant of 'legal personality'. Neither process at the outset was even considered as important by the inhabitants of rural areas themselves, for example: at the start of the law enforcement the local elite promoted 'legal personality'. The municipal mayors distributed these documents to the communities for favours of the rural population 's electoral votes, in order to gain more sympathy with the execution of public investment projects, financed by the funds of 'tributary co-partnership'. The *barraca* holder*s* too, appealed to set

[206] The Vaca Diez Peasants Federation was founded in 1953, that of Pando in 1974 and the first Indigenous Centre (CIRABO) in 1989.

[207] In Riberalta, where the influence of the *barraca* was less, the communal establishment was better organised.

[208] Until1994 only the municipalities of Cobija, Puerto Rico, Riberalta and Guayaramerín existed.

up OTBs with the members of permanent families, with the purpose of being favoured by these public funds.

However, the communal organisation takes on greater importance with the approval of the Agrarian Law, specifically with Decree 25848 that regulates the access to the land for rural communities and it carries out the process of land titling. Once the members of the community complete this procedure, they will be able to receive land and forests.

Despite the effort of peasants and indigenous groups, the changes would have been slower without the support of NGOs. At the beginning of the 90s there were only two NGOs that took charge of providing productive advice to rural inhabitants.[209] However, by 1994 the most important NGOs providing support in relation to land tenure issues were founded (CEJIS, ACCRA, IPHAE and CIPCA-North). In addition, during the land titling process at initiative of the Catholic Church, the '*Saneamiento* Committee' was formed. This organisation groups together the main NGOs of the rural sector and takes charge of following up the actions of the INRA and forming the rural leaders to meet the requirements of the Agrarian Law. Due to their national and even international relationships, the NGOs are the organisations that prepare the best technical and legal knowledge in the region. Thus NGOs give excellent advice to the rural leaders during the political negotiations, assist the communal leaders in current topics and even finance important peasant or indigenous initiatives.

Beside of this regional context, other aspects contributed strongly to the institutional change, for instance: the return to democracy in Bolivia after almost ten years of military governments; the international policies of sustainable development and poverty alleviation promoting the use of the resources for the local traditional users; the changing in the form of policy making in Bolivia integrating civil initiatives more and more; the partial removal of the national elite group power, as well as incorporating new rural representatives in national politics and at the time of the approval of Decree 25848, partially removing the political weakness of the national government.

Dynamics of institutional change

Institutional change as a dynamic process can be understood as a cycle of interrelations between interest groups and institutions. Human acts will, in general, be oriented towards increasing one's own rights and reducing one's obligations. Depending on the political weakness of the public agents, the beneficiaries will achieve their ideals and force the state to adjust the laws. These ideas coincide with BUCHANAN (2002), who stated that politics is never in a state of balance, or rather that balance does not appropriately describe what the political actors seek to achieve. The institutional level will always be inclined, however slightly, toward the group demonstrating greater political influence. The political actors always have a reason to be active, defending the institutions achieved, or requesting changes to those institutions that harm their interests.

---

[209] CARITAS-Guayaramerín (1987) and ACRA (1993).

However, in the arena of political decision-making often the defence of existing rights is easier than obtaining new rights. Those recipients can deduce directly their privileged position from their current situation, while those seeking advantages usually have vague ideas about the potential impact of a given state measure. In addition, those affected generally find it more difficult to become organised, because they do not know with certainty the exact benefit of their claims, nor the moment and their personal participation (see PRITZL 2000:252).

Although institutional dynamics is not a typical characteristic of public property rights (WILLIAMSON 2000), a high rate of institutional change has been observed in the use of the forests of the Bolivian Amazon. Since the beginning of the research at least eight crucial institutions determining forest tenure are known to have changed either partially or entirely. The high rate of institutional dynamics is influenced by the fact that the legislation continually favours certain forest users and excludes others. Initially *barraca* holders and peasants were excluded (1996-1999), before the *barraca* holders then obtained recognition of their claims, surpassing those of the peasants (1999), and finally the wishes of the peasants were incorporated into national legislation, at the expense of the *barraca* holders (2000). This 'back and forth' in forest tenure in the case of the study area is caused by:

- The public agents' poor understanding of the forest management system in the northern Bolivian Amazon, particularly in relation to extractivist activities, seen in the actions of several national decision-makers in executive spheres (ministries, vice-ministries, general directorates). The Agrarian Law and the Forest Law include general issues about land and forest use, which apply to other regions of Bolivia, such as the highlands, valleys and southern Amazon region, but not necessarily the northern Bolivian Amazon;
- The broadly opportunist behaviour of the regional power groups during the formulation and enforcement of public institutions in attempting to garner favourable outcomes for their members, thereby inhibiting opposition groups from consolidating their aims.

The high rate of institutional change delayed the research schedule, as certain activities required more time than originally planned, such as data collection, the literature review and even coming to terms with and gaining insights into the relationships in Bolivia's political system. However, the process of institutional change in the northern Bolivian Amazon presents an excellent opportunity to analyse the numerous strategies employed by regional interest groups in such a climate.

Comparison of the two institutional change processes analysed

A similarity between the two processes of institutional change is that both groups strive for the approval of decrees. The decree is currently a popular form of institution in Bolivia. It is a legal instrument employed both by the government when the executive power lacks influence in parliament and by those governed when they seek to reduce their transaction costs, as to initiate or to change a decree is easier than changing a law.

In both processes the role of the social organisations stands out, particularly the *barraquero* associations and the Peasant Federation, whose functions are summoning their allies in the defence of the claims of each group. OLSON (1968), BUCHANAN (1965)[210] and HEIDEMANN (1995) stated that the advantage of the representation of common interests through associations, as compared to the representation of individual interests, is that organisations, due to the collective action of their members, are able to invest greater 'action resources' in order to influence social and political process . Even the work and initiative of those separate leaders or political representatives who constantly request the reformulation of the rules, rarely exceed the results achieved by associations because political representatives are too preoccupied with other problems, or are only interested in immediate results to strengthen their own position, instead of trying to carry out any legal change (BUCHANAN 2002).

Despite their importance, the protagonism of the regional associations when lobbying is limited to the sphere of those responsible at national level, and when defending their claims using technical arguments. Under such circumstances the associations' representatives resort to forming coalitions with other actors reinforcing their interests with the required information. Therefore, the providers are also fundamental actors, as they provide information, resources and technical advice, necessary for the formulation of the institutions and for scripting technical arguments in support of a particular legal proposal. Similar to the experiences of the rest of Latin America, in Bolivia the providers comprise international cooperation organisations and NGOs whose influence increases in relation to the weakness of the responsible groups or promoters (see SILVA *et al* 2002:67). Providers contribute to the reduction of the transaction costs of associations, through their facilitation of access to information and their support of political negotiation.

A third similarity is the way in which both processes developed. Both are characterised as being closed processes, integrating only the groups affected, that is either the *barraca* holders or the rural communities, excluding participation of the regional and national population. The partial orientation of each decree in favour of a certain power group reflects the closed negotiations between the state and target groups involved.

The successful exclusion of rivals in the formulation of public institutions trying to improve their own interest can be interpreted as rent-seeking behaviour. Furthermore, according to empirical findings rent-seeking can also be used to explain the behaviour of political actors during the law enforcement. For instance, the approval of Decree 25532 meant an increase in the area to which *barraca* holders are entitled from 1.8 million hectares in 1984 to 3.5 million hectares in 2000, without population growth in the rural areas. Also the demands of several peasant communities were increased after the approval of Decree 25848: according to ASSIES (2002), the average peasant plot in the region ranged from 20 to 80 ha prior to 2000. According to empirical data collected during the course of this study approximately 20% of the peasant communities interviewed possessed land in excess of the average entitlement of 500 ha/family, with a size range varying from 541 to 2,500 ha per family. From this perspective some of the protagonists and leaders of institutional changes can to different degrees be considered rent-seekers. Exactly rent-seekers are:

---

210 Cited in SANDMO 1990:52

- Some public agents, especially the main decision-makers, by taking part in closed negotiations, approving decrees and granting comparative advantages to pressure groups do harm to the remaining forest users. The possible rents they pursue relate to maintaining their public positions and the power to make political decisions. By reducing social pressure and increasing the collection of forest taxes, they guarantee the continuity of their work.

- Some promoters, such as representatives of *barraca* holders and peasant communities, demand the approval of institutions, which do not define exactly the exercise of their rights. Their rents are the consolidation of large expanses of land, through taking advantage of their contacts and the information on national policy available to them (in the case of the *barraca* holders), or through maintaining their positions as representatives, which provides them a link to regional and national organisations, and the possibility of more financially rewarding work in the future, in case of the peasants.

- Some providers support legal proposals despite being aware that their allies' claims exceed their legal entitlements. The managers of NGOs and development projects are interested in attaining any available economic funds for the law enforcement, or simply looking for the recognition of their organisations, receiving credit for the work they have done in the presence of their donors.

- Some forest users interpret the contents of the law in their favour, discriminating against the legitimate rights of their neighbours, without regard for the possible emergence of conflict. Clearly, the main rent pursued is the formal consolidation, sometimes exaggerated, of land.

Although it is clear that each group pursues different rents, it would not be fair to generalise and say that all of those involved are merely rent-seeking. In many cases, their work is equally motivated by strong ideals and convictions. An alternative means of explaining the behaviour of some political actors could be 'Advocacy Coalition Framework', proposed by SABATIER & JENKINS-SMITH (1999).[211]

In terms of the differences between both processes, the participation of the addressees stands out: Few members of this group actively participated in the *barraca* Decree, mainly supporting the project financially. In the case of the 500 Hectares Decree, the key was the participation of at least 600 community groups, exerting pressure on the government directly. However, in both cases the role of the members of both associations in the writing of technical proposals was restricted. A second difference between the two processes is the strategy applied by both groups: The elite groups have direct access to the centre of political power and take advantage of their contacts and knowledge, whereas the rural groups exert pressure on the responsible state entities by harnessing the force of social movements.

The interest groups choose their strategies and actions on the basis of their 'action resources' and interests. Table 19 contains a summary of the strategies used by the groups studied that are

---

[211] Within a political subsystem, the 'Advocacy Coalition Framework' assumes that actors can be aggregated into a number (usually one to four) of 'advocacy coalitions' each composed of people from various governmental and private organisations that both (1) share a set of normative and causal beliefs and (2) engage in a non-trivial degree of coordinated activity over time (SABATIER & JENKINS-SMITH 1999).

also representative of other past regulatory approval processes in the scheme of the global process of institutional change.

Table 19 Strategies of elite and rural groups in the process of institutional change

***Barraca* holders**	**Peasants**
- Form small working groups, consisting of members with good access to information and high level of economic and political influence. - Ignore the interests and proposals of the opposing interest groups, avoid processes of popular agreement as much as possible. - Activate contacts and influences at the highest levels of political decision-making (ministries and parliament). - Strive to win over the will of the decisions-makers, through lobbying their ideas. - Use the force of *clientelism*[212] and political nepotism working on the basis of a system of political favours.	- Activate the participation of the local members during the whole process. - Conduct protest marches of long duration, as well as blockading roads along the main regional access routes. - Draft public demands and pass them on to alternative organisations such as the Permanent Assembly of Human rights and the Office of the Ombudsman. - Pressurise the government with claims related to other social topics also affecting the group. - Form alliances with other social groups with the same interests (settlers and landless people). - Negotiate with the government at critical political moments. - Delay negotiation sessions until they achieve their objectives. - Use the Church and the Town Ombudsman as guarantor organisations ensuring the execution of the agreements made.

Source: Based on field study interviews.

In the case of the elite groups, the *barraquero* strategy is similar to the strategy used by the forest entrepreneurs in the process of formulating the '*Plan Soberanía*' of 1993,[213] which signalled the intention of national forest entrepreneurs to control nearly two million hectares of forest in Pando (RUIZ, 2004b). In the case of the rural groups, social movements are the main strategy used to influence the contents of the reforms. In the contemporary history of Bolivian democracy, these movements go back to the early nineties, and the First Indigenous March. In each case, the promoters of the social movements were the representative associations, such as the 'Peasant Confederation of Bolivia' (CSUTCB) and the 'Indigenous

212 Political clientelism is a type of political bond between a socio-economic person of high status that protects and/or supports another person of lower status who in return offers general support and loyalty. Political clientelism is based on asymmetric transactions although mutually beneficial and open for both sides (FARINETTI 2000).

213 The promotion of this ruling has been attributed to the President of the Bolivian Forest Chamber, a person with economic and political influence who was awarded 4 of the 19 concessions granted (Press article, Primera Plana 14th September 1994). The political power and influence that Santa Cruz entrepreneurs had in those times even prompted the government to ignore the contents of the 'Ecological Pause Decree', which prohibited the granting of new forest contracts throughout the country for a period of five years. On the other hand, the forest entrepreneur leaders obtained support of the directorate of CDF of Pando, in spite of the social demands of the Pando population. With the '*Plan Soberanía*', Santa Cruz entrepreneurs awarded themselves about 80% of the total area of the concessions in the region.

Confederation of Bolivia' (CIDOB). The national strategies have also frequently been backed by regional and national NGOs.

As illustrated in table 20, in the three popular marches that took place since 1990 there was a close relationship between the social movements and the approval of laws, strengthening the position of the peasants and indigenous groups in their quest to access natural resources.[214]

Although each group exhibits typical behavioural patterns, when the applied strategies do not achieve the desired effect, the actors often resort to imitating the successful tactics of the opposition groups. For example, the loss of the *barraqueros*' political influence in congress forced them to copy some of the peasants' methods, such as road blockades, popular marches and assuming public offices (INRA and SIF).

Often a successful strategy is the result of combination of both adopted and traditional strategies as shown by the approval of Decree 27572 in June 2004. Strategy imitation is not easy, however. The *barraca* holders have shown themselves to be far less effective than the peasants when they apply their pressure measures. The experience and technical advice of external organisations are often decisive factors in the implementation of successful strategies. In their absence, the imitating group is not able to handle key aspects, such as negotiation. For instance, the *barraca* holders are less consistent with their threats of strikes or road blockades than the peasants, and they frequently tend to lessen the pressure on authorities without having achieved their objectives.

214 The social movements also promoted the integration of marginalised regions into the national political context. The origin of the first two marches in the east of the country served to integrate the regions of Beni and Chaco. The same can be argued in the case of the third march, which originated in the northern Bolivian Amazon region, making it possible to present to the government the reality and the needs of this part of the country.

Table 20 Relationship between the main social movements and institutional change

Event	Approval of new public institutions	Main institutional change
First Indigenous March for Territory and Dignity (Aug. - Sept. 1990)	- Decree 22609 TI Sirionó (Sep. 1990) - Decree 22610 Isiboro-Sécure (Sep. 1990) - Decree 22611 TI Chimane and Multiétnico (Sep. 1990)	- As a result the government approved in principle three Presidential Decrees recognising the first four Indigenous Territories (TI)
After the march a National Commission was formed to draw up the preliminary draft of the Indigenous Law, which was also decisive in the re-formulation of the national constitution of 1994	- Law 1257 Ratification of agreement 169 ILO (Jul. 1991) - Decree 23110 TI Pilon Lajas (April 1992) - Decree 23111 ILO Pilon Lajas (April 1992) - Decree 23112 TI Chiquitano I (April 1992) - Decree 23500 TI Weenhayek - (April 1993) - Law 1551 Popular Participation (April 1994) - Law 1615 National Constitution (February 1995) - Law 1700 Forest (July 1996)	- Later four more decrees were enacted recognising a total of eight TIs up to 1993 - The Law of Popular Participation incorporated the indigenous communities and peasants in the legal, political and economic life of the country, through the recognition of Base Territorial Organisations (OTB) (art. 1-3) - The new constitution of the state recognised Bolivia as a pluri-cultural and multilingual country (art. 1) and established the TCO (art. 171) - Involvement of peasants, indigenous communities and other traditional user groups, previously marginal groups, in forest management
Second Peasants and Indigenous March for Territory, Rights of Political Participation and Development (Sep.-Oct. 1996)	- INRA Law (October 1996)	- Recognition of the property rights of the indigenous communities, peasants and TCO - Incorporation of 16 new indigenous claims, making a total of 24 TCOs with deadline be titled
Third Peasants-Indigenous March for Territory and Resources (Jun. - Jul. 2000)	- Decree 25838 Abrogation of Decree 25532 (July 2000) - Decree 25848 Modification of the Regulation of the Agrarian Law (July 2000)	- Abrogation of Decree 25532, which converted the barracas into NTFP forest concessions - Granting of 500 ha as the minimum unit of endowment per family inside rural communities in the northern Bolivian Amazon - Declaration of land titling process in the northern Bolivian Amazon

Source: Based on the regulatory scheme in force and other bibliographical sources.

6 Between gossip, boycotts and alliances: - The social conflicts over forest use -

"Before the reforms began, peace reigned in these places.
Nobody doubted the rights granted to us, the *barraqueros*.
Our properties were so well defined that if a *siringa* (*Hevea*) tree
fell on the border between two estates, its produce was distributed between both owners."
(Personal interview with a *barraca* holder, Río Beni, February 2002)

6.1 Introduction

The starting point of this chapter is the approval of the decrees benefiting the *barraca* holders and peasants, referred to in chapter 5. The enactment of both decrees divided the regional interest groups into two groups: those who criticised the formulation of these institutions, generally consisting of the *barraca* holders and forest concessionaires and the rural communities who were in favour. Many interviewees considered this division a new social phenomenon, but conflicts over forest use are a constant in the history of the northern Bolivian Amazon. The roots of many of them go back to the period of colonisation by the rubber companies (1870), and they have always been characterised by the involvement of a wide range of actors. The conflicts varied between local conflicts occurring inside the rural communities and *barracas*, and intergroup conflicts between regional social associations, even taking on international overtones, as was the case during the warlike conflict between Bolivians and Brazilians over the extraction of rubber.[215] By way of summary, four periods in the history of the conflicts over forest use can be distinguished: 1) the colonisation period (1870-1900); 2) the rubber crises (1900-1913; 1940-1960 and after 1986);[216] 3) the period beginning with the onset of commercial timber exploitation (from 1980); and 4) the enactment of the reforms (from 1996). During the colonisation period, the Amazon Basin was populated by ethnic groups whose social, economic and political lives were characterised by a high degree of mobility over a wide territory (PACHECO 1992). The emergence of the rubber economy in the north of the country awakened the interest of a great many entrepreneurs, who went in search of Bolivia's 'black gold'. These 'pioneers' explored the rivers in search of

---

[215] The emergence of rubber as a product of interest on the worldwide markets, and the great natural deposits stored in the Acre region brought back the old territorial problems between Spain and Portugal, inherited by the new Latin American states, such Brazil and Bolivia. The beginnings of rubber exploitation resulted in the birth of towns, particularly Brazilian towns, in uninhabited zones within the Bolivian forests, many of them sponsored by the Brazilian government itself. The national policies of both countries implemented after 1890 acquired the overtone of an international conflict after 1903, when Brazil annexed Acre, after a warlike confrontation that ended with the signing of the Treaty of Petrópolis, on 17th November 1903 (KNOLL 1993).

[216] STOIAN 2000.

siringales, leaving records of their presence when marking the rubber trees and declaring the ownerless areas[217] part of their property (ASSIES 2002). The assumption of the possession of the indigenous territories was carried out *de facto*, and in many cases endorsed by the national authorities (GAMARRA 1992:42ff; PACHECO 1992:63).[218] Due to the resistance provided by the indigenous populations defending their territory, the forests of the region became a kind of battlefield. The forest entrepreneurs with greater economic resources and a large number of *peones* frequently prevailed, resulting in the establishment of *barracas* (GAMARRA & KENT 1992:197ff).

Between 1890 and 1900 the highest levels of large concentrated areas of land were registered to big merchant-farmers (GAMARRA & KENT 1992:212f). Approximately 75% of the forest areas were controlled by the '*Casa Suárez*', the biggest extractivist company of all time (FIFER 1970). However, in many *barracas*, the *patrón* lost control over the productive area he controlled following the rubber crisis and the fall of the *Suárez* empire (1940). The fall of prices on the international markets forced many *barraca* holders to abandon their lands, with the *fregueces* subsequently occupying the abandoned estates. In this way, new types of rural settlements were born: the '*independent communities*' on the one hand, and small and medium *barracas* on the other (ASSIES 2002; STOIAN 2000, PACHECO 1998; ORMACHEA & FERNADEZ 1989). Although this process was peaceful, it still brought with it new lawsuits amongst the new forest owners seeking the re-definition of property limits. The commercial exploitation of timber in the early eighties led to increased social dissent amongst the forest users, because many felling permits were granted in favour of the new forest entrepreneurs based on political and economic interests.[219] In 1994, the entrepreneurial interest was consolidated when big forest areas bordering the international frontiers were granted under the '*Plan Soberanía*'. This policy gave rise to new conflicts, initially involving the regional entrepreneurs:

> "*... we (the regional entrepreneurs) had the biggest problem with the approval of the 'Plan Soberanía', because Santa Cruz's strong forest companies divided the department of Pando according to their interests. It was painful to see that all our lands had been redistributed.*"[220]

Until mid 1996, peasants and indigenous people participated more as spectators than protagonists of the conflicts. In recognising their traditional rights, the new laws forced the forest companies and the *barracas* to accept the presence of the rural communities.

---

217 The term *baldío* means state land or land without any owner.

218 Thus, the indigenous Amazonian population was 'exterminated'. The surviving indigenous people became labourers in the '*barraca* regime', moving away from their original social organisations and annulling their right to forest property. The second process endorsed by the state authorities, was the evacuation of the populated territories, and the consequent concession of the land to the interested explorers (PACHECO 1992:66-67; GAMARRA 1992:45; Law of 23rd February 1878).

219 "*Thus is my country, Bolivia. The national laws are made to suit the interests of business*" (SIMAC 1990:345f).

220 Personal interview with a Riberalta entrepreneur, May 13th 2002.

> *"The recognition of the existence of the rural communities is neither a dream nor an illusion."*[221]

Almost a decade after the introduction of the reforms, the social conflicts expanded across the whole regional area. The conflicts affected the ten forest user groups in different ways and to different degrees. However, the main protagonists of the current conflicts are the *barraca* holders, the large private owners and the forest concessionaires on one side, up against the communal interests of the indigenous, the peasants and the ASLs. Most of these conflicts occurred in the years after 1999, following the approval of the decrees pertaining to the *barracas* and peasant communities (ASSIES 2002).[222]

The aim of this study is to examine the role of the reforms in the current social conflicts, as well as to analyse the strategic behaviour of the local users in their quest to control the forests. In short, answers to the following research questions are needed:

- To what extent did the reforms contribute to the current conflict situation?
- What kinds of strategies do the protagonists use to assure their tenure or access to the forest in conflict situations?

The first question was answered through the analysis of interviews with forest user groups (n=164) and the analysis of primary data provided by the SIF and INRA. The second was based on an analysis of three case studies involving the six forest user types with greater access to the markets.[223]

6.2 Theoretical elements of the conflicts

6.2.1 Conflict definition

At the end of the seventies, interest in the study of social conflicts increased. This situation has given rise to an inflation in the definitions of the term 'conflict' (GLASL 1999:11), a fact that has caused many authors to arrive at the conclusion that the theory is undergoing a period of conflict, disabling and restricting its development (LUHMANN 1994, cited in THIEL 2003:6). The various definitions differ in terms of the diversity of the aspects they incorporate, as well as by their scope and focus (see table 21).

In the most general definitions, for example, conflict is given, "*when a divergence exists between individuals*" (BERLEW 1997, cited in GLASL 1999:12). This definition is incomplete, as much in practice as in theory, because a conflict situation can rarely be considered in such simple terms.

---

221 Personal interview with the president of the Peasant Federation of Pando, October 5th 2001.

222 For more information see chapter 5.

223 Chapter 3 contains a description of the methods, providing more information on the groups interviewed, as well as the criteria for choosing the three case studies (see chart 12).

Table 21 Variability in the definitions of conflicts and key attributes

Definition	Author	Key attributes
Social conflict is a struggle of values and aspirations to enjoy a position, power and resources, in which the objectives of the opposition consist in neutralising, hurting or eliminating their rivals.	COSER (1956)	Struggle of values and aspirations; resources; elimination of rivals
'Manifested conflicts' are characterised as having different 'subjective interests' aimed at a particular territory, illustrating competition situations in relation to the resources use and territorial conflicts.	OSSENBRÜGGE (1983:49ff)	Territorial conflicts; Competition over land use
Conflict is expressed as struggle between at least two interdependent parties pursuing incompatible goals, access to scarce resources, and subject to interference from the rival party in achieving those goals. The conflicting actors frequently find themselves in positions of both opposition and cooperation.	HOCKER & WILMOT (1995:21f)	Struggle; Incompatible goals; Opposition and cooperation
Conflict is the 'motor' of social change on the one hand, but it also appears as a figure threatening the destruction of the social order, both outcomes being the two sides of the same coin.	BONAKER (1996:16)	Social change; Destruction
Social conflict is a realty in which at least two parties participate (individuals, groups or states). Each pursues different goals or aspires to a common objective, which can only be achieved by one of them, and/or resort to the use of different incompatible means to achieve their goals.	WASMUHT, (1996:180f)	Aspiration towards same goal; Incompatible means; At least two parties
Conflict is an inevitable part of human interaction, occurring in every arena and setting of human endeavour. Parties may experience conflict over 'rules' that guide their interactions, including how decisions are made.	WALKER & DANIELS (1997:13ff)	Human interaction; Rules and decisions as cause of conflict
Social conflict is an interaction between actors (individuals, groups, organisations, etc.), where at least one actor experiences disagreements in thought, ideas or perceptions with other actors, and through its execution a loss to one of the actors occurs.	GLASL (1999:14f)	Interaction; Disagreements; Perceptions; Damage.
Conflict is perceived as an artefact of human needs that have been denied (BURTON 1990), a result of resource competition between different actors (HIRSCH *et al*, cited in BUCKLES 1999), and as a perception of a lack of equality, justice and fairness (KANT & COOKE, cited in BUCKLES 1999).	HELD (2002:78)	Denied necessities; Competition; Inequality and injustice
Conflicts involving forests can generally be divided into two types. In the first, the timber or other forest products are harvested and sold specifically to finance armed conflicts, resulting in both loss of lives and displaced populations.[224] In the second type, conflict over forest resources, and in particular timber, erupts between or among stakeholders with rival claims to control or ownership.[225]	THOMSON & KANAAN (2003:1)	Warlike collisions associated with timber use; Opposed demands of the local users

224 Although this particular definition is not relevant to the study area, it is interesting to see the close relationship between timber conflicts and armed struggle. Examples include the governments of Liberia and Burma.

225 The second group of conflicts can take several forms. For example, conflicts over resource ownership or access can occur between a village and government bodies (e.g., the military or the forest service), between a village and a private actor (e.g., a logging company/concessionaire), or between two villages (THOMSON & KANAAN 2003:1).

Often conflicts involve many elements and actors, and sometimes finish up being the most dramatic and traumatic events in the life of the individuals involved (FOLGER *et al.* 1997:12, cited in WALKER & DANIELS 1997:14). Conflict is perceived as struggle, competition, rivalry, warlike clashes and fights. At the same time, a few authors associate contrary attributes with conflict such as cooperation, with some even considering it the main motor of social change.

A working definition was developed for the purposes of this study, based on an idea developed by OSSENBRÜGGE (1983):

> Land conflict equates to an incompatibility of 'subjective interests' in a specific territorial area between at least two interdependent parties, each trying to prevent the other party from achieving their goals, in a context characterised by competition over land use.

The definition highlights conflicts, as struggles over land use localised in productive areas. According to OSSENBRÜGGE (1983), such conflicts can be analysed on basis of 'subjective interests'; these are the only interests of which the negotiating parties are aware DAHRENDORF (1955:27; 41, cited in OSSENBRÜGGE 1983). DAHRENDORF also identified 'objective interests', which only have a value under the analysis of a theoretical structure. Later on OSSENBRÜGGE associated 'subjective interests' with 'manifest conflicts' that are open to be interpreted and analysed by social researcher, and 'objective interests' with 'latent conflicts', originating from highly complex contradictions (e.g., the problem of regionalism that is approached by the conflict of functional and territorial organisation of a society), requiring a theoretical foundation. In addition to the numerous definitions of conflict in the literature the following functions are also mentioned :[226] A contribution to the development of society;[227] the spread of disagreement among opposed forces; the promotion of the identity and unity of a group; the generation of a dynamic interaction process, including competition and collaboration; the driving force behind social change and the role played in achieving a new balance of power.

6.2.2 Levels of conflict escalation

An understanding of the development of conflicts and the identification of their different stages help the social researcher to differentiate conflict and non-conflict situations in practice. The escalation of conflicts has been illustrated and discussed by several authors, such as KAHN, LEDERACH, GLASL and THIEL, who concurred that conflicts develop in steps. GLASL's (1999) model is discussed here. This model projects an escalation of the conflict process, running contrary to other models, which demonstrate an uninterrupted escalation of up-down or 'going with the stream'.[228]

---

226 See IMBUSCH & ZOLL 1996; BONACKER & IMBUSCH 1996:71f; PANIAGUA *et al.* 2000:11.

227 According to MAX WEBER, cited in BONACKER & IMBUSCH 1996:64

228 The GLASL model largely contradicts the model proposed by KAHN, who talked about a process of conflict escalation similar to a stairway, where parties ascend the steps, illustrating the increasing levels of violence. Another different means of illustrating the development of conflicts was proposed by LEDERACH (1992:31), who claimed that conflicts develop in a spiral form and follow certain typical changes, moving from its centre towards the periphery over the course of time.

Figure 22 illustrates the escalation of conflict in nine steps or phases, divided into three stages that at the same time illustrate the increased turbulence of social relationships. While in the first stage a situation may arise where the two parties can be considered winners (win-win situation), in the second stage there is a winner and a loser (win-lose situation). In the third stage, both parties are considered losers (lose-lose situation); this is the point where the dimensions of the conflict may ultimately mean the destruction of the social system. At each step the actors can act in certain ways. Therefore, each step taken determines both the behaviour of the individuals and their competitors, and the possibility for each party to either win or lose.

Figure 22 Escalation of conflict: stages and steps

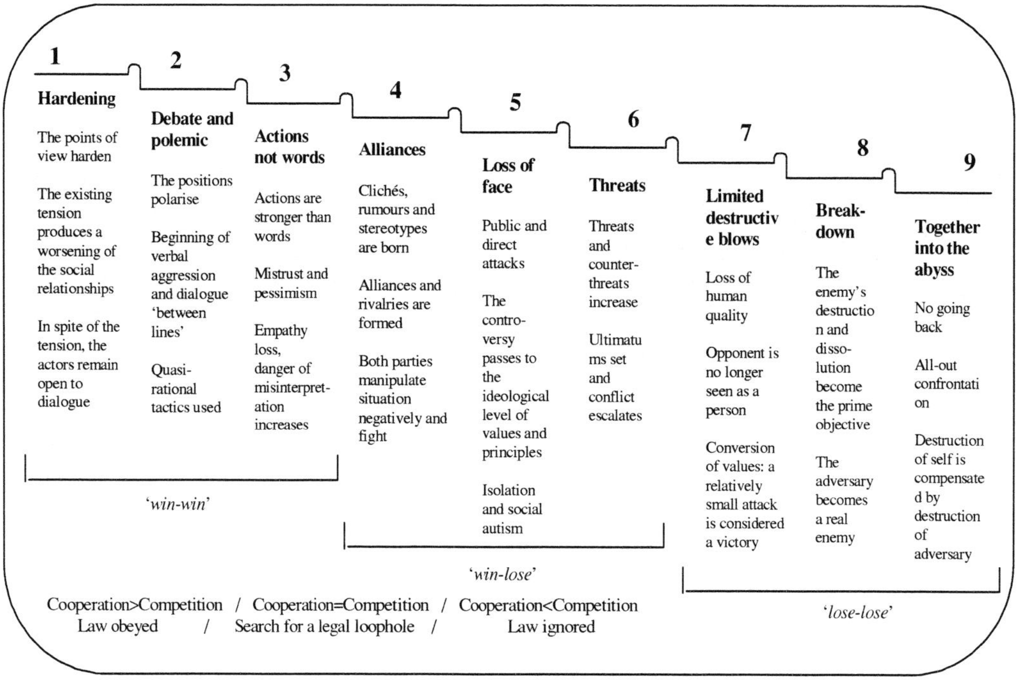

Source: Adapted from GLASL (1999:218f).

At each moment, the process happens step by step, represented as the slip from a higher level of regression to a lower level of regression. At each step the parties behave according to their mentality, their feelings and spirits, as well as for the reasons and aims pursued (HOFSTAETTER 1957: 215, cited in GLASL 1999:216). Figure 22 also illustrates the relationship between cooperation and competition variables cited in the definition.

Whereas during the 'win-win' stage there is a bias towards cooperation, the second stage reveals a balance between both variables, and in the last stage, the lose-lose stage, the bias towards competition increases (GLASL 1999:279ff). Similar to the cooperation and competition relationships, the attitude of the parties towards the law alters according to the development stage of the conflict. At the beginning, the individuals fully recognise the existing rules and take great care not to break the institutions.

Later, in steps 4-6, the parties take pains to find loopholes in the rules to use them against their opponents, without necessarily breaking the institutions. In the last stage, the parties care little for the observance of rules, and are even willing to break them if they are an impediment to the achievement of their aims (GLASL 1999:280).

The advantage of GLASL's model (1999) is that it depicts conflict development in several steps, dividing them into stages representing the level of seriousness of the struggle. It is also interesting because it relates the conflict to several theoretical elements, such as the readiness to compete, to cooperate, and to comply with or to ignore rules. However, some criticisms of the model can also be made, including: 1) The nine steps proposed are possibly not adapted to every cultural context; 2) the 'win-win', 'win-lose' and 'lose-lose' situations depend only on the stage of development of conflict; 3) the escalation of the conflict is rigid and happens without varying the order of the levels; and 4) the relationships between cooperation and competition are influenced by the development of each stage.

Another important issue to highlight is the difference between problems and conflicts. 'Problem' is a commonly used term in popular language, and has even been used as synonym for conflict. However, even though all conflicts derive from the existence of one or more problems, not every problem necessarily develops into conflict.[229] One of the most important problems in relation to the issue of forest use in the study area derives from the territorial or land overlap between rural settlements (see figure 24). An example to illustrate the difference between conflicts and problems is provided by the 'Manuripi protected area', where only three of the 38 *barracas* declared themselves to be in conflict with the administration of the reserve. However, in other cases examined during the field study, the 'territorial overlaps' were an important source of conflict, especially when these involved forest users belonging to different groups. This study revealed that seven of the 102 reported conflicts were not solely attributed to territorial overlaps (n=164). In more than 90% of the conflict situations recorded the source was a territorial overlap.[230]

From this perspective, the analysis of the 'territorial overlaps' takes on special importance, as the main reason lies in the overlap of institutions, i.e., the overlap of two or more tenures on one territory. Such an overlap can take on three forms: 1) Among public institutions, for

---

229 To illustrate this difference I will resort to taking an example from daily life: A family possessing just one vehicle, with two or more of its members seeking its use may be considered a problem. The interested parties can reach an agreement in relation to the times and frequency of use, in which case the problem continues, without giving rise to conflict. The problem could end in conflict if the individuals seek to use the vehicle at the same time, or breach the agreements made.

230 Studies of territorial overlaps in Bolivia (in Santa Cruz) determined that a single territory can be used by two different interest groups without giving rise to conflict. This is conditional to the actors having divergent interests in the natural resources, such as in the case of the peasant communities and the oil companies in the Choré region. The interest of the first group lies in the use of the land, whereas the second group wishes to take advantage of the subsoil resources. Despite not entirely dismissing the possible emergence of conflicts, these do not necessarily arise as a result of the competitive use of the same resource, but rather as a result of discord arising between users when faced with the contamination of plots, the opening of roads, etc. (RUIZ 1996).

example between property rights of peasant communities and forest concessions; 2) Among public and private institutions, for example between property rights of TCOs and *barracas*; and 3) Among private institutions, for example between the traditional property rights of the *barraca*.

The focus of this study is directed at examining the first two types of 'institutional overlap'[231] because in the case of an overlap of private property rights the reform maintains little influence, and because the overlap of *barracas* does not generally lead to the emergence of conflicts.[232]

6.3 The reforms as source of conflict

"When the state becomes the focal point of the conflict on institutional change, the state institutions become a new source of conflict" (KNIGHT 1992:193).

Conflicts over natural resources such as land, water and forests are present everywhere: people are competing for resources that they need or they want to assure or to improve their subsistence (BUKLES & RUSNAK 2000). The more common sources of conflict are: the exclusion of a specific user group from the management of the resources; the divergent interests competing for the same resource; the recognition of NTFPs as a source of wealth; the overlapping of agricultural with forest interests; the contradiction or lack of clarity in laws and policy; the unequal distribution of resources; the lack of clarity on territorial limits; the generality of the national laws, which do not always coincide with the local provisions, etc. (FAO 2001:2; BUKLES & RUSNAK 2000; ASHBY 1998, cited in HELD 2001:78; GTZ 1997:13; PENDZICH *et al.* 1994:20f). Institutions are an important source of conflict, but they are not the only cause.

Compared to the old forest and agrarian legislation, the Bolivian reforms seek to solve the issue of 'institutional overlap', at least between agrarian and forest interests, as the number of public bodies in charge of granting rights to land (INRA) and forests (SIF) has declined, also decreasing the administrative chaos in the distribution of natural resources.[233] At the same time, the reforms propose a system of forest concessions based on defined areas, and prioritises forest use on titled agrarian estates. Nevertheless, in the northern Bolivian Amazon the reforms cannot ignore the link between the existing laws and the current conflicts.

231 Here the terms territorial overlap and institutional overlap are synonymous. Usually the main cause of territorial overlap in the study area is the overlap of institutions.

232 During the conversion process to 'PFNM concessions' in 2000, 50% of the '*barraca* holders' declared an overlap with other users. The most serious cases involved the 'enterprise-run *barracas*', some of which registered up to ten overlaps in a single state. This common problem among the *barraqueros* ends in conflict in less than 1% of all cases (ASPROGOAL 2000; field study).

233 Under the previous regime the rights to land were granted by two organisations (CNRA and INC) and the rights to the use of forest by different levels of public administration (approval of the departmental representatives of the CDF for short term contracts; Ministerial Resolution for medium term contracts; and Presidential Decree for long term contracts) (RUIZ 2004a). The numerous alternatives to get an official land titling without coordinating of administrative functions led to state chaos, since a same plot was given to two or more forest users.

Indicators of the fact that the laws have increased the likelihood that forest users will enter into conflicts are the following: 1) the traditional power groups loss of control over the forests , like that of the *barraca* holders, as well as concessionaries; 2) the rise in the expectations of the forest users in relation to controlling forest areas after the approval of public institutions, and 3) the rise in the 'territorial overlap' between the main groups of forest users.

The traditional power groups' loss of control over the forests

Comparing with the past, the *barraqueros*' and forest concessionaires' loss of control over the forests corresponded to a simultaneous rise in the control exercised by the community based forest users. As is presented in figure 23, the communal land held by the peasants and indigenous will have increased from 200,000 hectares in 1984 to approximately three million hectares in the year 2010. At the same time, the individual land tenure of the *barraca* holders will decline to approximately 50%of the area held in 1984, as will also be the case for the concessionaires from 2000. Figure 23 illustrates the breakdown of the historic monopoly over the forests of the traditional power groups, which only became possible through the emergence of conflicts with the new communal landowners.

Figure 23 Forest tenure dynamics in the northern Bolivian Amazon (1980-2010)

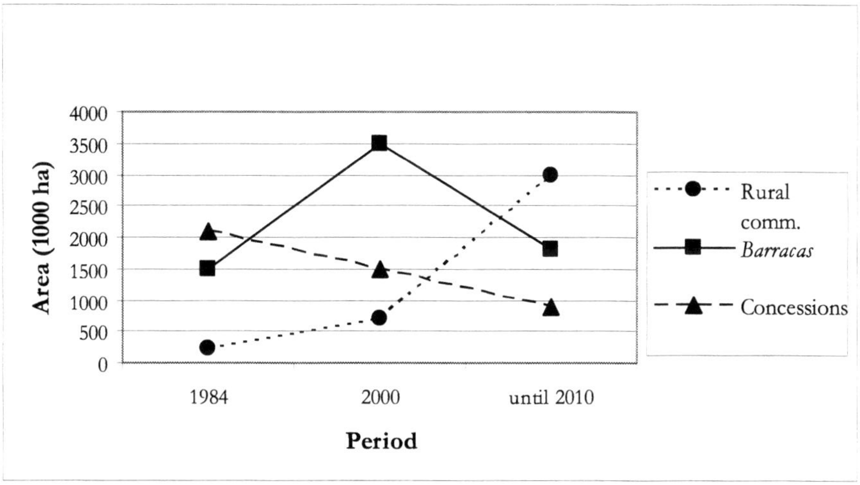

Source: Based on the Agricultural Census of 1984, cited in ORMACHEA 1997; ASPROGOAL database (1998-2000, unpublished); SIF (2002); INRA (2004); own estimates for 2010.

The rise in the expectations of the forest users

Immediately after of the approval of each decree a rise in the expectations of the forest users could be observed. The strategies employed included an indirect strategy, namely increasing the number of rural settlements within each productive sector (see table 22), as well as a direct strategy involving the assumption of possession of large forest areas (see table 23).

Table 22 Divergences in the number of forest users according to different sources

Sources	Region (Pando, Vaca Diez and Ixiamas)				Study area (Pando and Vaca Diez)		
Forest user type	**Unions (2002)**[234]	**CIPCA (2002)**[235]	**FSUTCP *et al.* (2000)**[236]	**STOIAN (2000)**	**DHV, (1993)**[237]	**INE (2002 a/b)**[238]	**Author's estimate**[239]
Peasant communities (A)	400	551	725				300
Indigenous communities (B)	100						50
Total (A)+(B) rural communities	500		725	400	460		350
Barracas (C)	350			300			200
Total (A)+(B)+(C) rural settlements	850			700		555	550

Source: Based on several sources of secondary information and on field study interviews.

According to the information gathered by private organisations, there are apparently at least 850 rural settlements in the region, that is to say, 150 settlements more than were estimated by STOIAN (2000) before the approval of both decrees, or 250 settlements more than the number registered in the population census of 2001 by the national statistics institute (INE).[240]

---

234 Data derived from interviews with the social organisations (three peasant federations, two indigenous unions and three *barraquero* associations) during the field study, and corroborated by their registries of members.

235 URAPOTINA (2002), using data available in the CIPCA-North, declared 551 peasant communities in the region, consisting of more than 12,206 families. The CIPCA-North data for the study areas included 468 peasant communities, distributed in 176 communities in the Vaca Diez province (2,416 families) and 292 communities in the department of Pando (6,800 families). Report available on the internet: http://www.ftierra.org/Tierra%20a%20Debate/Pulso/02-01-11.htm

236 Technical report produced by the peasant federations of Pando, Vaca Diez and Guayaramerín, under the framework of the national 'fight against poverty' policy.

237 Database compiled during the analysis of the Amazonian region, consisting of eight volumes (DHV 1993). The database also includes the approximate registry of forty *barracas*, identified by those responsible for the study.

238 Database of the National Census of Population and Housing, also available on the internet: http://www.ine.gov.bo/beyond/ReportFolders/

239 Data derived from interviews with 164 forest users, in addition to the *saneamiento* reports by the INRA and the statistics of the last national census (INE 2002 a, b).

240 According to the census data of 2000, there are nearly 55 rural settlements in the entire Ixiamas municipality. Due to the cartographic deficiencies mentioned in chapter 1, it is not possible to determine the exact number of settlements in the northern part of the municipality. According to my own estimations, there are about 25 rural settlements in the northern part of Ixiamas, both *barracas* and peasant communities, making an approximate total of 575 rural settlements in the whole region.

The differences presented in table 22 are a response to the strategies used by the main social organisations, used to justify the rights and the expectations of their members when facing the national authorities and to weaken the position of their opponents. The assumption of possession of bigger productive forest areas is one of the main sources of 'territorial overlaps'. Its roots may lie in the imprecise formulation of many articles of the public institutions that do not comply with the basic institutional principle "*the institutions should lead the expectations of the individuals*". The laws do not assume the responsibility for limiting the maximum demands of the users. For example: 1) the Forest Law does not determine the maximum size of the concessions; 2) the Agrarian Law leaves open the size a TCO may occupy; 3) Decree 25532 does not limit the *barraca settlements* and lastly 4) Decree 25848 is only limited to regulating the minimum distribution of 500 hectares to the peasant families. As a resulting this imprecise formulation, the four greatest user groups have increased their claims over the forests, as presented in table 23.

Table 23 Expectations of the regional interest groups and consolidation of their rights to the forests

Forest user	Right/Expectation (Public institution)	Year	Source
Forest (timber) companies	Nine forest companies consolidated an area of 1.5 million hectares in concessions (Forest Law).	1997	SIF (1997)
TCOs	725 indigenous families demanded approximately 500,000 hectares (Agrarian Law).	1998-1999	MANZANEDA (2003) CIRABO (2000)
Barraca holders	350 *barraca* holders claimed rights to a total area of three million hectares[241] (Decree 25532).	2000	ASSIES (2002) Pulso: (21.07.00)
Peasant communities	300 peasant communities will consolidate 2.5 million hectares of land by 2010. (Decree 25848).	2000-2010	ASSIES (2002) ORMACHEA (1987) INRA (2004)

Had all of the demands made been met, only in Pando 70% of the area of department would have been occupied (approx. 4.5 million hectares). [242] In effect, only 30% of the departmental area was redistributed (two million hectares) to the forest users in order to fulfil the FES established by law.

Rise in the 'territorial overlap'

The increase in the number of members by sector (table 22) as well as the territorial expansion of the settlements (chart 23) occur more frequently in Pando, the Bolivian department with the lowest demographic indexes. Both indicators are responsible for a high degree of territorial overlap in the region. At national level, the magnitude of overlapping is reflected in examples where there are more than five 'levels of different rights' over a single territory, and it is estimated that between 30-60% of

---

241 Prior to the last rubber crisis, the approximate area that the *barracas* covered was 1.5 million hectares (Agrarian Census of 1984, cited by ORMACHEA 1987).

242 Preliminary *saneamiento* data for Pando (INRA, 2004) revealed that the 129 registered peasant communities and the 761 estates cover an approximate surface area of 4.5 million hectares.

the national territory is subject to some degree of overlap, generally leading to interminable legal processes, and even physical confrontation (URIOSTE & BALDOMAR 1998:10). According to empirical data a total of 65% of all rural settlements in the study area are affected by 'territorial overlap' (see figure 24).

Figure 24 Overlapping claims

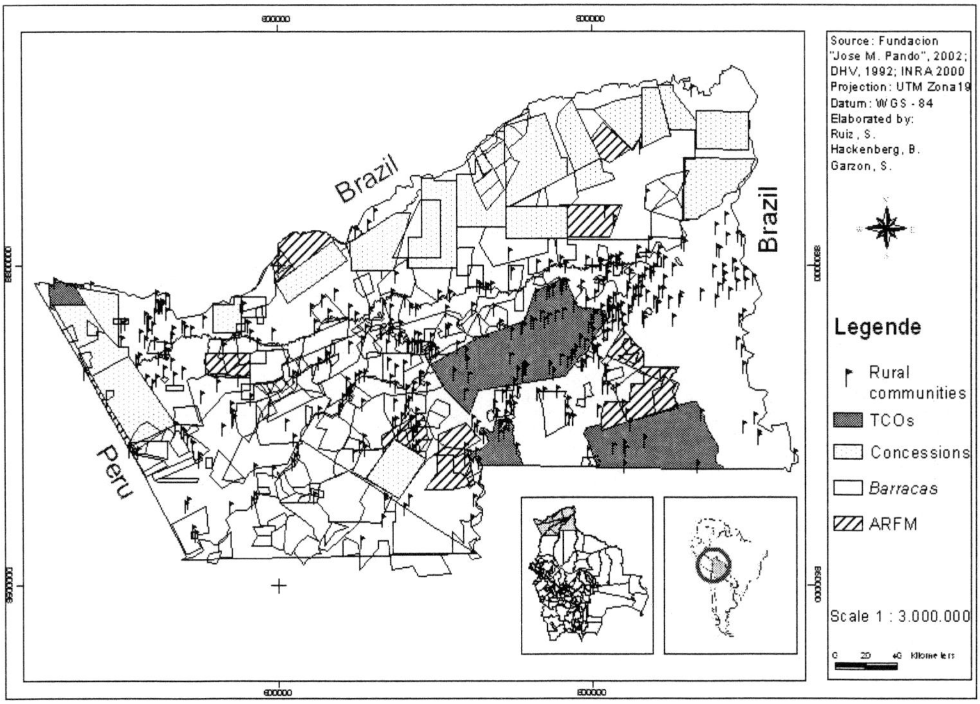

The content of figure 24 is further elaborated upon in figure 25 showing the ten identified conflict zones. These data are corroborated by empirical information collected during the field study involving 164 forest users and from the preliminary results of the *saneamiento*, presented by INRA in early 2004. All ten zones represent conflicts manifested at different escalation levels. They are described in table 24 and presented in figure 25 with different colours, which vary depending on the forest user groups present and on the demographic density.

As to the north east, the zones of conflict are large but not necessarily actively in conflict (zones 1 and 2). The most important conflict zones lie along the main transport routes and in the region centre. The majority of the regional conflicts (30%) are located in zone 5, involving either *barraca* holders and indigenous communities or peasants communities and indigenous communities. This zone can be considered the 'cradle' of the current land conflicts. This has been the case 1998 when the indigenous demand for the establishment of a TCO meant an overlap in the interests of powerful *barraqueros* and peasants.

Figure 25 Locations of real and potential ten zones of conflicts

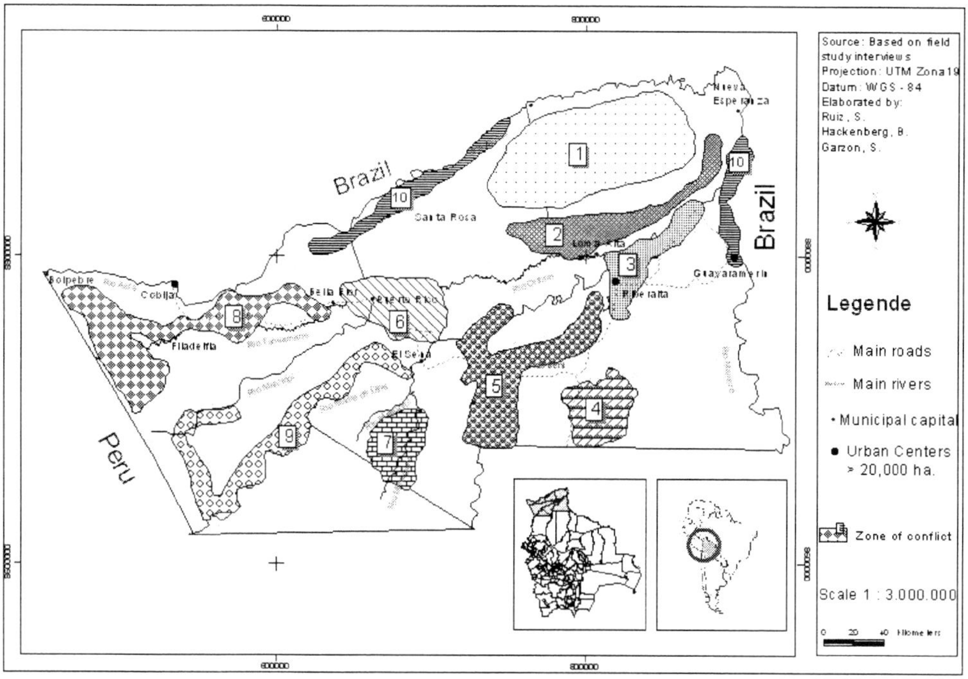

Table 24 Description of the ten zones of manifested and potential conflicts

Zone	Users	Characteristics	Source of conflict
1	Large *barraca* holders, forest concessionaires and Brazilian inhabitants	Relevant across a great area to the north western end of the region, with the emergence of few, but burning conflicts (6% of the registered total) mainly between large *barraca* holders and rural communities.[243] Jointly with zone 2, this district exhibited the smallest indexes of population density (between 0.2 and 0.4 hab/km²).	Monopolising of large areas of land for Brazil nut collection and timber exploitation.[244]
2	Forest companies and large peasant communities	Until 2001 only the superimposed forest concessions were considered, with few and dispersed rural settlements. After the land titling process began peasant communities were established resulting in the loss of up to 50,000 ha by two forest companies.[245]	Similar to zone 1.

243 In 2000 the main problems confronting the *barraca* owners were the establishment of forest concessions, the boundary of the AFRMs and the overlapping between their estates. According to ASPROGOAL registries, a total of ten territorial overlapping were declared. None of them took into account the new protagonists of the conflict, the peasant communities.

244 The potential annual timber harvest exceeded 60 m³/ha in the zone (ZONISIG 1997).

245 According to preliminary *saneamiento* results (INRA 2004).

3	Peasant comm., private land-owners, military settlements and *barraca* holders.	Accounts for 13% of the total conflicts recorded, and pertains to the northern part of the Vaca Diez province, where pressure on the land was relatively strong. The peasant communities were in conflict with each other, and the holders of private and/or military settlements.	55% of the conflicts referred to land, and 30% to Brazil nuts.
4	ASLs, private landowners, *barraca* holders and indigenous communities	In the south of Vaca Diez, with little population pressure but with a relatively high pool of timber. It was the area with the second highest number of conflicts (20%) and the most dynamic in relation to the change of the protagonists' legal statuses: In 1998 until 2000 all conflicts were between private landowners; from 2000 until 2002 between the ASLs and *barraqueros*; since 2002 after foundation of new peasant communities they themselves became protagonists of conflicts. The southern end was characterised by conflicts between indigenous people and *barraca* holders. The first case study is located here.	60% of the conflicts referred to timber. Other causes of lesser importance were Brazil nuts and the occupation of land.
5	Indigenous communities, peasant commu-nities, *barraca* holders and priva-te landowners	The area with the greatest number of registered conflicts (30%) and location of the second case study. It coincided with the territorial demands of the indigenous towns. The main opponents were the *barraca* holders and the indigenous communities (50% of the conflicts inside the area), but conflicts also existed between indigenous communities and peasants (20%).	The usurpation of the land from the *patrones* was the cause of 35% of the conflicts; Brazil nut collection 35%[246] and timber 20%.
6	Peasant communities and *barraca* holders	The location of states coincided with the central tract of highway "Cobija-El Sena". It was the fourth most important area in terms of frequency of conflicts (10%), and second in terms of the diminished area of *barracas*.	Litigation over land and Brazil nut extraction.
7	*Barraca* holders, forest companies and peasant comm.	Many *barracas* in conflict with the allocation of forest concessions. Due to the pressure exerted by peasant communities, distribution of concessions has stopped here.	100% of the conflicts were based on forest use (Brazil nuts and timber).
8	Forest concessions, peasant commu-nities, indigenous communities and *barraca* holders	Here six forest concessions were established, four of which were inactive due to the pressure exerted by the peasant communities. It was the area with the third highest incidence of conflict (15%), and the location of the third case study.	50% of the conflicts based on timber exploitation. Other important source is the access to land by pea-sant communities (35%).
9	Protected areas, *barraca* holders and peasant communities	A reserve was established in Manuripi. Conflicts were few but violent (3% of total). The main protagonists were the *barraca* holders and the AP seeking use of timber, and the peasant communities demanding access to land.	Timber exploitation, access to land and the restrictions on hunting and fishing during Brazil nut harvest.
10	Brazilian settlements, forest concessions, and peasant communities.	Border with Brazil, where most of the concessions are located. The conflicts were accentuated by the absence of control of national agents. This area resembled other border areas, such as the Abuná province, Federico Román and the municipality of Guayaramerín.	Illicit exploitation of all types of natural resources, mainly timber and fauna.

Source: Based on field study interviews; INRA (2004) preliminary results of *saneamiento*

246 This zone had an abundance of Brazil nut trees (5-9 trees/ha) (ZONISIG 1997).

Of the 164 interviewed forest user, this study registered 102 conflict situations. I.e. that around 62% all forest user in the study area are involved at lest in a land conflict.

Contrary to the conflicts over natural resource use in other Bolivian regions, where the users were interested in land for the purpose of developing agrarian activities, in the northern Bolivian Amazon the main reason given in 50% of the registered conflicts (n=102) pertained to forest use (see figure 26).

Figure 26 Main reasons for the regional conflicts

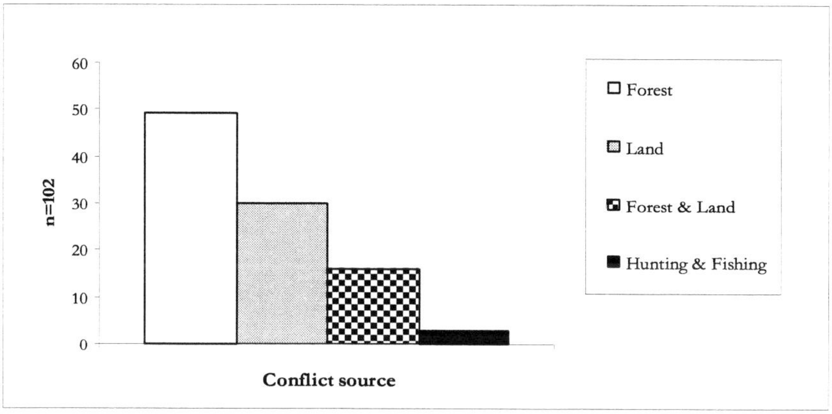

Source: Based on field study interviews.

The second greatest source of conflict surrounded the occupation of the land, at 30%. This related mainly to areas with greater population densities. The third most common cause, at 17%, was the mixed interest in controlling both resources (forest and land). The final source of conflict related to hunting and fishing interests, accounting for 3% of the total conflicts.

The principle category, 'forest use', was comprised primarily of conflicts over timber exploitation (41% of the registered cases), followed by Brazil nuts (37%) and finally interests in mixed forest use (timber and Brazil nuts) (22%). In the ten conflict areas, the *barraca* holders participated in 30% of all registered conflicts (102 of 164 interviews), followed by the peasant communities (23%), the forest concessionaires (17%) and the indigenous communities (12%) (figure 27).

When compared with the data presented in table 24, it becomes clear that the groups with the greatest expectations in relation to forest use are also those with the greatest participation in the conflicts. Although the data presented show the influence of the reforms on the conflicts, the public institutions are not the only causes of conflict. Apart from the failings of the reforms, the attitudes of the regional (social unions and NGOs) and the national (government bodies) interest groups are central to the current conflict situation (more detail see section 6.6).

Figure 27 Participation of forest users in the regional conflicts

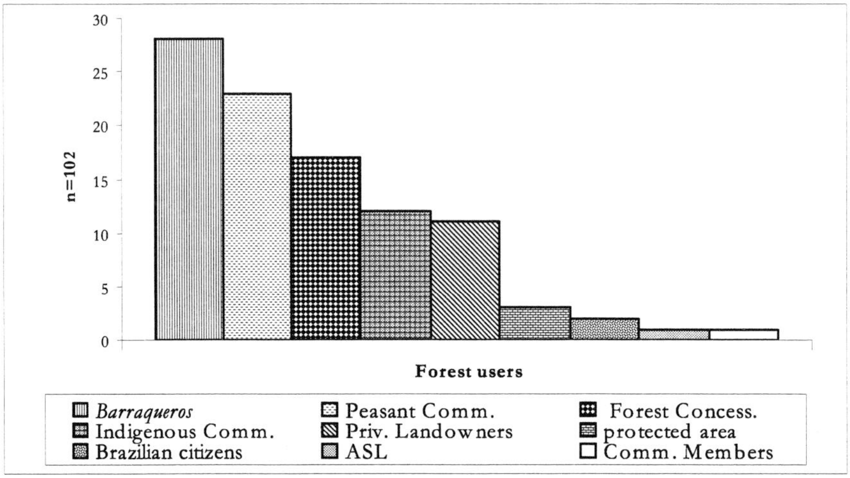

Source: Based on field study interviews.

6.4 The case studies

This section details the examination of the strategic behaviour of six user groups in conflict and their desire to regulate the commercial use of the resources, based on three case studies:

1) A local community association (ASL) and a '*barraca* holder'

2) An indigenous community and a 'private landowner' and

3) A peasant community and a forest concessionaire.

The term 'private landowner' refers to formal property right categories, including the large '*barraca* holders' who have managed to retain a part of their settlements. Due to the large dimensions of the *barracas*, these settlements are generally managed in the same way as the entrepreneurial *barracas*, i.e., through an external administrator, with strong links to the forest industry (see table 26). Despite the emphasis of the study on the local actors, it is impossible to exclude the rest of the regional participants from the analysis, due to the close interaction between the protagonists and other actors. To facilitate the description of the case studies, the focus on 'arena and agenda', as proposed by HEIDEMANN (1995:P-.21), is presented next. This approach also served as a methodological instrument for data collection in the fieldwork phase (see figure 28). The term 'arena' represents the 'location of the facts', where the interest groups are identified according to their duties and rights, and assume four different roles (protagonists, providers, those responsible and promoters). Here the protagonists are the forest users with incompatible interests. The providers are usually regional private organisations, mainly NGOs and social unions. As mentioned in chapter 5, they provide technical and economic support to the protagonists and are, therefore, considered the main allies of the coalitions. Those responsible are usually the public authorities in charge of preparing and executing the laws.

Figure 28 Arena and agenda

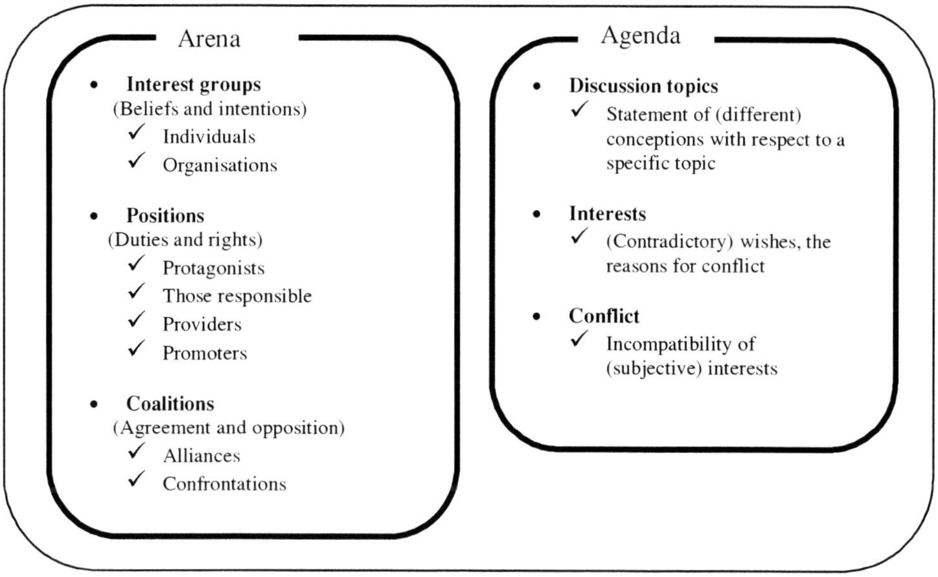

Source: Adapted from HEIDEMANN (1995:P-21).

Although this group claims to possess an interest in the conflicts and their outcomes, they are not directly affected by the conflicts. The last characters in relation to conflicts are the promoters, understood as the motors or initiators of the process. The promoters may belong to any of the three previously mentioned categories, because each participant is in a position to influence the origin and development of the conflict. Therefore, the term 'protagonist' should not give the impression that these are the only actors able to determine the course of the conflict. The agreement and opposition among the interest groups makes it possible to enter into alliances and confrontations, a widely used strategy in conflict situations.

Agenda' represents 'what should be done'. The discussion topics proposed by the interest groups are distinguished, representing past difficulties, acquiring validity through conflict.

The topics are not solely characteristic of the protagonists, but can also be introduced by the groups of allies. The interests influence the acts of individuals and groups, and they are the reasons moving the parties to sit down together and talk. 'The interests are usually associated with desires, needs, concerns, personal convenience and the attractiveness of a particular product. Unsurprisingly, the participants identify more than one single interest as the definitive reason behind any conflict. 'Agenda' is the analysis and bargaining room within a conflict.

'Arena and Agenda' concept makes it possible to collect data and present the results systematically. It also distinguishes between the differences in the meaning of the discussion topics, the interests and the conflicts. Both elements are often confused in the conflict analysis. Despite the figure presented, it is not adequate to identify other strategies executed by protagonists, that do not represent the coalitions. On the other hand, the terminology used to denominate the interest groups may give the erroneous impression that the 'protagonists' are the only actors able to decide the course of the conflict.

6.4.1 First case study: Conflict between ASL and *barraca* holder

The '*barraca* holder' arrived in the vicinity in the late sixties and was the original occupant of the conflict area. His establishment as a *barraca* followed the purchase of several small untitled properties and the later accrual of unclaimed land, until eventually assuming an area of over 30,000 ha in the early eighties. The same property holder managed the *barraca* from its inception, and inhabited the estate with a part of his family. The economic activities borne out were directed mainly towards forest use – previously rubber, and more recently Brazil nuts and timber, as well as semi-intensive agriculture and extensive cattle rearing (see table 25). At the time of the rubber boom, more than 100 families worked the *barraca*, diminishing to eight *freguece* families in the early 2000s. Up to 2001, three FMPs were enacted by the SIF, allowing the '*barraca* holder' to utilise nearly 535 ha. Due to the high social pressure of forest use characterising this conflict zone (no. 4 in table 24), by mid 2002 the property holder had decided to transform his settlement into a peasant community. His decision was formalised in December 2003 with the granting of 'legal personality' by the municipality of Riberalta.

In contrast, the establishment of the ASL, as a legal feature introduced under the Forest Law, was subject to the approval of a municipal ordinance (July 1999). This ruling defined an area of 147,200 ha as Municipal Forest Reserve (ARFM). Immediately afterwards the municipality technicians proceeded to designate two ASLs in order to award them part of the concession area. The ASL analysed here is made up of chainsaw workers (*motosierristas*) and timber retailers from Riberalta who received 30,000 ha from the municipal government in 2001 subject to approval by the Ministry of Sustainable Development and the SIF. This process was not concluded until September 2002, due to the existence of conflicts and the extensive land titling process. The SIF approved approximately 1,000 ha for commercial timber use.

Characteristics of the first case study

Characters	Description
Resource use before the reforms	Area managed by the '*barraca* holder' dedicated mainly to the extraction of NTFPs and semi-intensive agriculture.
Conflict situation before the reforms	Conflict between the '*barraca* holder' and other traditional users (indigenous and several private landowners).
Events instigating the conflict	- The territory of the ARFM delimited by the municipal council of Riberalta in July 1999 overlapped with the area of the *barraca*. - The approval by the SIF of four technical instruments allowing the '*barraca* holder' to extract timber (between 1999 and 2000) on territory overlapping with the ARFM.
Beginning of the conflict	In July 2001, a multisector commission confirmed that a proportion of the timber granted the '*barraca* holder' originated from inside the ARFM. In spite of the recommendations that timber use be stopped, the removal of the timber was officially sanctioned.

Strategies	- The '*barraca* holder' sought a change of legal status (see figure 29), in order to obtain technical and legal advice, and to establish links with companies (sawmills) for the purposes of selling timber. - The members of the ASL exhibited a high capacity for resistance and perseverance, and publicly questioned the attitude of the regional authorities.	
Overlapping area	An area of approximately 20,000 ha with commercial timber species was demanded by both parties, corresponding to more than 65% of the total area.	
Attitude of the responsible authorities	- Contradictory actions executed by the UFM – great effort demonstrated in the delimitation of the ARFM on the one hand, yet subsequently 'establishment certificates' were issued to third parties for areas overlapping with the ASL. This situation can be attributed to the temporary changes of personnel in charge of the UFM in Riberalta in some cases. - The SIF authorised the extraction of timber from places well-known for the high frequency of conflicts. - The redistribution of the land in Riberalta by the INRA was well behind schedule in Riberalta	
Others characters	***Barraca* holder**	**ASL**
Principal ally(ies)	At the beginning of the conflict, a regional sawmill was fundamental to forest use. Following the formation of the community, the support of the Peasant Federation took precedence.	Initially technical and financial support provided to the association by NGOs. Later the partners acted almost alone.
Strengths	Great capacity for reaction to the institutional changes and the increased social pressure.	Remained organised in spite of the difficulties faced.
Weaknesses	Signed informal short-term agreements with the new peasants to guarantee access to the forests.	Deficiencies in the system of community administration of resources.
Participation in other regional conflicts	Conflict with two other peasant communities, as well as internal conflicts among the members of the new community over the ownership of timber.	Conflict with some peasant communities in September 2003 over timber extraction, and with three peasant communities over access to the forests.
Main interest in relation to resource use	Controlling the forests, mainly for the commercial timber use.	
Status of the conflict according to GLASL's model (1999)	In the second stage (win-lose), between the levels 4 (alliances) and 5 (loss of face), although the damage caused to the opponent was relatively slight, concentrated mainly on the prevention of the use of timber.	
Outcome of the conflict by the end of 2003	The *barraca* holder founded a peasant community jointly with the members of the *freguece* families. The ASL received approval for the use of approximately 1,000 ha.	

Alliances and confrontations

As is detailed in figure 29 both groups formed alliances to strengthen their positions.

The *barraquero's* main allies were those responsible for the sawmills run with the technical and legal costs approved in the FMP. The sawmill was also in charge of building the infrastructure necessary for the extraction and marketing of timber. A second support group comprised attorneys-at-law (lawyers) and technicians (forest engineers) who assisted the '*barraca* holder' in the continued exercising of his rights. Some of these professionals were hired by the *barraca* holder, whereas others belonged to his family.

Figure 29 Arena and agenda: first case study

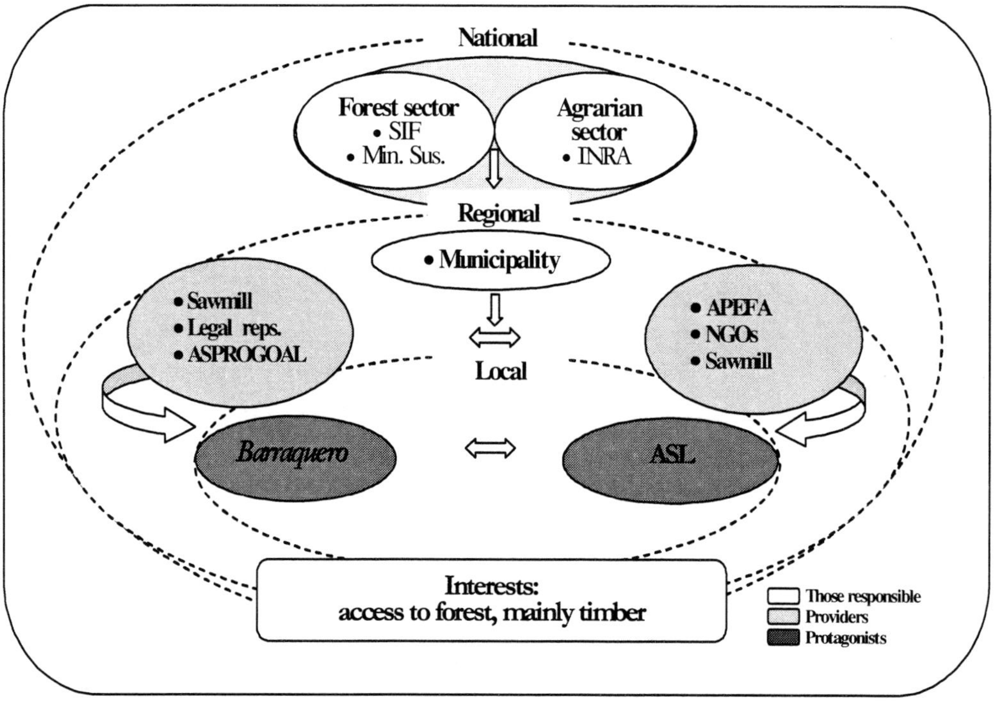

Source: Based on field study interviews.

The degree of participation of the association of *barraqueros* (ASPROGOAL) in the conflict was not clear. With the status change, the Peasant Federation of Vaca Diez reinforced the position of the group. The new community was to receive the support and experience of the federation during the *saneamiento* process planned for June 2004.

The ASL members received the technical and economic support of a local NGO in Riberalta. It contributed to the completion of the requirements for the formation of the ASL, then to financing the association offices, the creation of the FMP and to looking for the contacts required to market the timber. Despite the support of the NGO, which declined over time, the members of the ASL assumed most of the work themselves from mid 2003. In August 2003, an agreement of sale for the timber harvested was signed with a regional sawmill, on the basis of a POAF approved by the 2002 administration. From the category 'those responsible', the

SIF and the Ministry of Sustainable Development stand out amongst the national organisations. The SIF-Riberalta approved four technical instruments for the '*barraca* holder', allowing him to extract timber in 2001. Likewise, a POAF of 1,000 ha was approved for the ASL, which allowed them to extract timber at the end of 2003. At the time of writing, the ASL had not yet received the legal recognition of the Ministry. This process will not occur until the INRA completes the *saneamiento*s, which have been delayed by more than two years. At local level, the UFM technicians of the municipality of Riberalta played a predominant role in the conflict.

On the one hand the municipal agents are officially the strongest allies of the ASL, as they obtained the approval of the municipal council for the establishment of the ARFM (1999), and fomented the organisation of the association. At the same time, however, they granted 'establishment certificates' to the groups opposing the ASL; to several individual users without ownership titles in 1999, and later on (2003) to the inhabitants of the *barraca* then organised as members of a peasant community. The discussion topics broached in this conflict are representative for the rest of the study area with respect to the following points:

- Delimitation of the ARFM in off site, ignoring the traditional settlements boasting the technical support of private (NGO) and government organisations;
- Extended approval of negotiated 'establishment certificates' by the municipal technicians without proper documentation to prove ownership of the land; and
- Approval of FMPs in settlements without ownership titles, and non-compliance with sustainable forest management (SFM) criteria, as many forest users only concentrate on stretches of forest containing commercial species.

Tenure of the protagonists

The first case study represents the institutional overlap between a traditional property right (*barraca*) and a property right granted by the state (ASL). Table 25 reveals the comparison between the tenure of both groups in conflict. As both groups sought control over timber, the main strategies applied by both parties were aimed at receiving official recognition of their claims from the public regulatory scheme. However, the illegal use of the forests in order to capitalise upon the resources before the opposing group continued.

6.4.2 Second case study: Conflict between indigenous community and 'private landowner'

The histories of both settlements have a common root in the time of the rubber boom, when the district studied made up part of the assets of the *Casa Suarez*. In 1984, after changing hands approximately five times, an important forest company from the region acquired the ownership title in exchange for a property (housing) located in Riberalta. As was tradition, the transaction included the *freguece* labour force that worked for the previous *patron*. At the beginning of the nineties the new owners successfully claimed title to more than 6,800 ha, divided into three ownership titles granted under different names.

Table 25 Comparison of the property rights of the 'barraca holder' and the ASL: (case study 1)

Type Character	*Barraca* holder	Local community association (ASL)
Generalities (rights)	- Traditional: The *barraca* is the most important type of informal property right in the northern Bolivian Amazon. This form of resource tenure persists almost exclusively through traditional institutions.	- Legal: ASL is the newest tenure type. The implementation degree in the study area was low. Only one ASL was granted partial operating rights. Due to the social conflicts and the slow saneamiento process, the ASL was legitimised only by order of the municipality, through the approval of a Municipal Ordinance.
Comprehensi-veness	- According to traditional rights, 30,000 ha belonged to the *barraca* holder, including the use of the forests (mainly Brazil nuts), as well as the land and wild fauna. - With the approval of the FMP, the rights to the use of timber on approximately 535 ha were formalised. Another 12,400 ha remained informal.	- The main rights were oriented towards timber utilisation, with the assignment of 30,000 ha by the municipality (April 2002), but not yet approved as concession by the SIF. - By early 2004, only 1,000 ha had been recognised following the approval of POAF-2002. - NTFP extraction also permitted, subject to prior application and adaptation of the FMP. - Agricultural activities were not carried out. - Hunting and fishing almost non-existent amongst the settlements.
Exclusion	- High level of exclusion internally. The *fregueces* worked on a contract basis. - The right to agriculture and cattle rearing were reserved for the *patrón* (80 ha in rice production and 60 ha grass) - The forests were the exclusive property of the *patrón*. - Hunting and fishing were open to third parties. - Exclusion problems with regard to other peasant communities and third parties.	- Serious third party exclusion problems, because the ARFM affected the rights established before the reforms. - The approval of POAF-2002 resulted in the exclusion of third parties (sawmills) from timber use across an area of approximately 1,000 ha.
Use Designation	- The holder had the right to choose the location and type of activity to be developed for all the resources.	- The use designation governed by law, impeding any non-forest activities, as well as any activities not detailed in the FMP.
Duration	- Traditionally, Brazil nut areas maintained their perpetual right. However, with the reforms it became questionable. - The formal right to < 200 ha timber use in the FMP was restricted to a single use (one year).	- Legally, the forest concession granted to the ASL was based on a minimum felling cycle of 20 years. - The right to timber use was limited to the single use of the POAF-2002 (one year).
Allotment type and size	- Traditionally based on the rubber or Brazil nut production volume, which determined the size of the production *centros*. - The reforms influenced the use of the hectare as the main unit of area.	- Allotment type of the concession based on hectares. - The approval of the FMP required the inclusion of timber volume estimates. - There isn't size limit of the concessions. Nevertheless the municipalities can only grant 20% of their forest area.

Transferability	- In the past, the transfer of resources was open (the holder bought his land). Currently, there is a drastic decrease in the informal land market of the *barraca*. - The *centros* remain transferable, usually without the flow of money (inherited or given to confidants).	- Felling contracts agreed with sawmills, regulating the gross sale of the forest trees, or the transfer of the usufruct rights of the specific goods.
Payment of taxes	- The *barraca* holder did not pay any tax directly. The owners of the shelling factories assumed the Brazil nut patent. - The sawmill assumed the timber tax.	- According to law, the patent calculated based on the area of the AAA (profitable annual area) established in the POAF; the members of the ASL negated this
Operational requirements and operational control	- The *habilito* excluded third parties from the benefits of the forests, by binding them with a limited contract. - Control over the forests was intensified during the Brazil nut harvest, reducing theft and the invasion of property. - Control over the timber was intensified after the conflict began.	- Control over timber is increasing given the interest of the ASL members - State control could potentially increase through the improved formality of the rights.
Security	- High degree of insecurity with respect to all resources, due to lack of public laws. - Conflicts with different forest users (ASLs, private landowners and peasant communities).	- Their rights were conditional to the execution of the land titling process and the local population's expectations. - Of the three communal tenure types, the ASL was the weakest of all, due to the low hierarchy of public law. - Conflicts with several forest users (barraca holders, private landowners, peasant communities).

Source: Based on own field study interviews.

With the fall of the price of the rubber, the *freguece* population dropped to a minimum of seven families in 1996.[247] Despite the fact that the *freguece* families formalised their rights as a rural community in 1995, the settlement continued to function as a traditional *barraca* (administered by a third party) until the end of the Brazil nut harvest of 1998. The formation attempts of the community took on greater force at the end of 1999, when the community members received legal recognition (legal personality) from the municipality four years after the first application was made.[248] The foundation of the community coincided with the *saneamiento* executed in the '*Multiétnico* II' TCO. Given the facilities and advantages in terms of access to the forests, the land titling process motivated the community members to transform their settlement into an indigenous community in 2000. In June 2001, jointly with other communities within the TCO, the members received a community title over the land they occupied. Currently, 25 families inhabit the community, some of which were invited to become part of the settlement. Others returned to the old *barraca*, where they previously lived as *fregueces*.

[247] There is no concrete data on the number of *freguece* families at the time of the transaction in 1984.

[248] According to Law of Popular Participation, the process of obtaining legal recognition as a rural community should not last more than three months from the time the first application is made.

Characteristics of the second case study

Characters	Description	
Resource use before the reforms	*Extractivism* was the main activity, and was under the control of the administrator. The history of the settlement dates back to the time of the '*Casa Suarez*'.	
Conflicting situation before the reforms	Conflicts existed with the two neighbouring communities, whose beginnings, according to the interviewees, stemmed from the sale of the *barraca* in 1984 and the failure to delimit clearly the borders of the settlement. Several *freguece* families abandoned the settlement, which can be interpreted as a *freguece* strategy employed against the *patrón's* traditional rights and power.[249]	
Events instigating the conflict	The receipt of 'legal personality' as a peasant community in August 1995.[250] Three attempts by the INRA between 1999 and 2000 to verify the area demanded by the *patrón* were unsuccessful.	
Beginning of the conflict	'Legal personality' in November 1999 resulted in (re)organisation of the community. This provided the members of *barraca* with an incentive to emancipate themselves from the *patrón*.	
Strategies	Both groups resorted to the use of radical strategies against their opponent. Little negotiation took place between parties. Dialogue and communication broke off, press articles were published, both groups resorted to the use of emotional rhetoric against their opponents. This conflict can be considered one of the most conspicuous in the region, as its discussion topics captured the attention of the regional and national media.	
Overlapping area	27,000 hectares, corresponding to 100% of the original area of the *barraca*.	
Attitude of the responsible authorities	- The municipalities were to retain the legal status of the area as 'peasant community' for four years; - The INRA could not meet the private landowner's demands, due to the pressure exercised by the indigenous population, and annulled the three ownership titles; - The National Agrarian Tribunal failed to find in favour of the objections raised by the 'private landowner' against the decision of the INRA; - Given the conflict situation and the lack of documentation concerning the ownership of the property, the SIF did not approve two FMPs presented by the administrator of the private estate.	
Others characters	**'Private landowner'**	**Indigenous community**
Principal ally(ies)	The administrator.	Both indigenous union and NGO.
Strengths	Contacts with the political spheres at regional and national level.	Solid alliance with other interest groups also competing for receipt of the lands included in the indigenous claim.
Weaknesses	At the decisive moments they were not present on the estate, leaving all responsibility to the administrator.	Deficiency in the internal organisation of the community and conflicts among communal leaders.

249 SCHNEIDER (2001:380ff) referred to 'emigration' as a possible strategy for informal indigenous and mining groups to show their discontent with the attitudes of the mining companies in Venezuela

250 Officially, the community belonged to the municipality of San Lorenzo, but it received its 'legal personality' from the municipality of Gonzalo Moreno. The initiative was then taken up by the local professor and the technicians of the municipality of Gonzalo Moreno, with the objective of receiving public funds in order to improve the education and health infrastructure.

Participation in other regional conflicts	Conflict with two other indigenous communities over unclear borders between settlements.	Conflict with the same two indigenous communities demanding the right to the property of two Brazil nut *centros*.
Main interest in relation to resource use	Possession of the land and use of the forests for Brazil nut and timber extraction.	
Status of the conflict according to GLASL's model (1999)	At the second stage (win-lose), between levels 4 (alliances), 5 (loss of face), 6 (threats) and 7 (limited destructive blows), with significant property damage caused to the opponent, to the extent that the 'private landowner' was robbed entirely of his traditional right and hostages were taken to force the government authorities to consolidate the indigenous demands.	
Outcome of the conflict by February 2004	A large part of the settlement was titled in favour of the indigenous community under the legal feature TCO. Nevertheless, the productive *centros* titled were refuted and won by the 'private landowner' before the National Agrarian Tribunal. In effect, the indigenous right has been consolidated across the whole area and, therefore, the disputed area is currently occupied by the indigenous group.	

Alliances and confrontations

The membership of the 'private landowner' in the *barraquero* association provided him a position of strength when carrying out actions pertaining to the conversion process of the *barraca* (December 1999 and July 2000). Later on, in 2001, the landowner and the same association, including other *barraca* holders affected by the TCO, took their objections jointly to the National Agrarian Tribunal[251] (see figure 30). Their greatest ally locally was the administrator, who occupied the settlement until April 2001. The administrator played a fundamental role during the last two years, by receiving from the tenure holder the right to timber use in exchange for payment for his work. In some cases, the administrator became the focus of the conflict through his actions (see table 30 for details of the FMP). In terms of support for the indigenous group, the Peasant Federation of the Madre de Dios province in Pando, later replaced by the Indigenous Union of Riberalta, stood out due to the decision in favour of belonging to the *Tacana* ethnic group. First contact with the Indigenous Union dated back to late 1998, and coincided with the beginning of the Multiétnico II TCO *saneamiento* process.[252] The role of this NGO was decisive in gaining access to the forests. During the land titling process its support was concentrated on the technical and legal *saneamiento* assessment, and on the internal organisation of the community. The alliance of the indigenous group with the Indigenous Union and the NGO allowed them to maintain a rigid position in the face of public attacks. Another advantage provided by the Indigenous Union was the coordination of activities with other social organisations, such as the 'ombudsman',[253] 'human rights' groups and the 'Union of Indigenous Communities of Bolivia'.

[251] The National Agrarian Tribunal was the only jurisdictional authority in place to mediate in cases where there is opposition to the resolutions dictated by the INRA.

[252] The fieldwork phase began in August 1998 and concluded in May 2000.

[253] The ombudsman was the public authority ordered to guard the fulfilment of the rights and guarantees granted the people in relation to the administrative activities of the public sector (Law 1818 1997; art. 127). The town ombudsman's operating budget was provided by the legislative power.

Figure 30 Arena and agenda: second case study

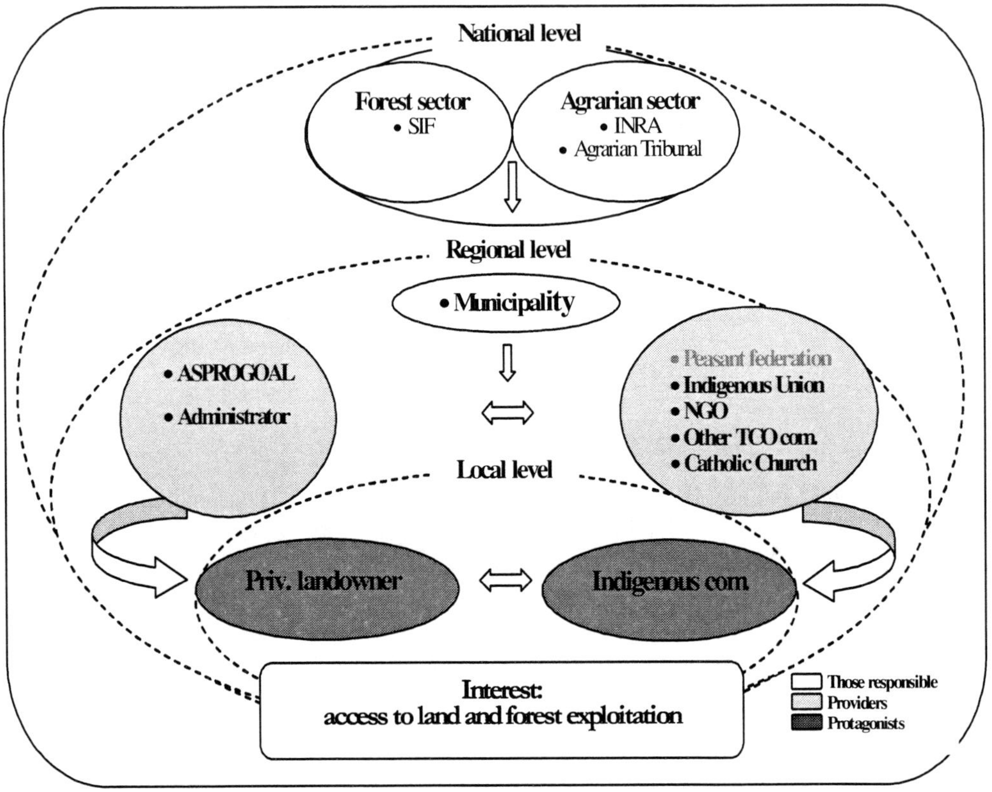

Source: Based on field study interviews.

The change from peasant to indigenous communities made possible the receipt of support from other member communities within the TCO, mainly at the time of occupying the lands, and in preventing the INRA from proceeding to evaluate the claims made by their opponent. Lastly, the Catholic Church was shown to be committed through the '*Saneamiento* Committee' (1999), working with NGOs and social unions from the region, thereby allowing it to provide good technical and legal advice to the rural communities in conflict with the *latifundistas*.[254]

The INRA and the National Agrarian Tribunal were notable amongst those responsible for the agrarian sector. The actions of the INRA were decisive in the development of the conflict for three reasons. It was proved incapable of meeting the demands of the landowner during the *saneamiento*, it revoked the land ownership titles, arguing on the basis of the abandonment of the settlement and the related corruption,[255] and by granting ownership titles to the indigenous. Given this situation, those affected negatively by the actions of the INRA called into question the

254 Personal interview with Monsignor of Pando and Vaca Diez, president of the Saneamiento Committee 2nd March 2002.

255 Three final resolutions of the *saneamiento* of 12th and 14th December 2000, as well as of 5th January 2001.

technical and legal procedures executed by the INRA before the National Agrarian Tribunal, whose judgement was made in favour of the private landowner in September 2001.[256] Legally this situation requires the revision of the outcomes of the *saneamiento* process.

The SIF acted cautiously in the conflict. Firstly, the FMP presented by the administrator in 1999 was rejected, based on the false ownership claims and the existence of conflict between the indigenous groups and the *barraca* holders. The contents of the FMP were made valid again in 2003, this time in favour of the indigenous groups. By early 2004 an area of 200 ha was in an advanced state of approval.

An impartial role of the municipal authorities in the conflict was difficult to identify, given that the members of the community received 'legal status' four years after their approval. This situation can be attributed to the following motives: 1) Initially the 'legal status' tool was used by the political parties as an instrument 'to buy votes' in the municipality; 2) the lack of communication between technicians of the first municipality (*Gonzalo Moreno*), where this document was erroneously processed in 1995, and the technicians of the municipality responsible (*San Lorenzo*) or 3) the possible collusion between the authorities and the 'private landowner'.

The main discussion topics added by this conflict to the regional 'agenda' were criticism on the part of the 'private landowner' of:

- the criteria to assign the label 'indigenous' to the descendents of the *freguece* families;[257]
- the original number of families required to organise a community;[258]
- the short sightedness of INRA in not recognising the FES-*extractivista* in a region rich in NTFPs and
- the role of other interest groups such as the NGO, the union associations and the Catholic Church.[259]

Criticism on the part of the members of the indigenous community concerned:

- suggestions of administrative fraud in the titling of large land areas;
- the greed of the *barraqueros* who occupied extensive forest areas without paying any taxes to the state and

256 Three National Agrarian Tribunal decisions, Sala Primera No. 13/2001, 14/2001 and 15/2001 and a telephone interview with private estate holder, January 22nd 2004.

257 The proprietor argued that the people on his territory could not be termed indigenous because they did not speak the language, nor did they adhere to the customs of the *Tacana* ethnic group.

258 The *barraca* was inhabited by a maximum of five *freguece* families.

259 "*The use of the forest means money, and what interests all NGOs is its control. Supporting the interests of the indigenous and the peasants is not of any direct interest to them. The local population is being used as flags of their financial interests*" (interview with the private estate holder, 5th June 2002).

- the conditions of the *freguece* families living inside the *barraca* under systems similar to slavery.

Tenure of the protagonists

The second case study represents the 'institutional overlap' between two demands, one supported by a 'public-private' mixed institution (private landowner) and another by a public institution (indigenous community). Table 26 compares the property rights of both conflicting groups.

Table 26 Comparison of the tenure characteristics between a 'private landowner' and an indigenous community: (case study 2)

Type Character	'Private landowner'	Indigenous community (Inside a TCO)
Generalities (rights)	Legal: 'Private landowner' is a class of right over land assigned by state, so its rules are strongly influenced by public institutions. Given the weak enforcement of the Land Reform, two different types of 'private landowner' appeared in the region. According to forest statistics and 'exception regime' applied by the SIF, under the first type, the users can formalise their timber use, even if their settlements have not been titled;[260] and under the second, the partial titling of the large *barracas* is granted, a mixed form of traditional and public right, as was demonstrated in the second case study.	Legal: The Popular Participation Law integrates the rural communities in the structure of the state through their recognition as Local Territorial Organisations (OTB) and the granting of 'legal status'. Designation requires presentation of regulations, the establishment of directives and the presence of at least ten families. The formal tenure of the indigenous communities over the land are determined by the Agrarian Law, through the TCO, or community property.
Comprehensi-veness	The landowner possessed two forms of right over his property: - Formal ownership titles to three *centros* of 2350 ha, 2300 ha and 2170 ha, assigned under three different names to members of his family, all of which were annulled by the INRA at the end of 2000 - Informally, the land exceeded 20,000 ha. Until 2000, the landowner was entitled to use land (subsistence agriculture), forests (mainly Brazil nut) and fauna (hunting and fishing).	- Formally the property right over land was shared with other members of the TCO (a single ownership title of 290,000 ha shared between approximately thirty communities). - The right to commercial timber was exclusive. The approval of a FMP for 200 ha was expected in 2004. - The law recognised traditional rights to subsistence use, incorporating all of the available natural resources, including fauna and the water.
Exclusion	- Legally the ownership title incorporates a high third party exclusion level. In practice, this right was been ignored by the indigenous community and annulled by the INRA - In adjacent areas managed as *barraca*, third party exclusion tended to diminish with the enforcement of the reforms.	- The level of exclusion of third parties to resource use is high. - Problems of internal exclusion among community members and/or other communities of TCO, mainly in relation to Brazil nut use, but also hunting and fishing.

260 They must present 'only' the 'establishment certificate', and a confirmation of the existence of a conflict free locale. This situation meant that, at least up to 2002, most of the so-called 'private landowners' formalised their rights under Law 1700, a ruling lacking the legal mandate for such an effect.

Use Designation	- Similar to the *barraquero* model, where the *patrón* or administrator decides the place, the form and the type of the productive activities.	- Brazil nut *centros* were distributed on basis of the level of production for each family. - Timber belonged to all members. - Agriculture was carried out along the rivers, but no restriction existed in this respect. In 2002 a community *chaco* was carried out among all members.
Duration	- Legally the ownership title grants unrestricted tenure over the land. - Brazil nuts and limitless fauna, according to traditional rights.	- Perpetual right over all the resources used as subsistence. - Tenure over timber use, with prior approval of the FMP<200 ha, for one year.
Allotment type and size	- Formally the INRA assigns the agricultural land in hectares. - Traditionally NTFPs are assigned based on production potential.	- The allotment model and sizes formerly used in the *barraca* have been adopted; i.e. volume units (*cajas*) prevail over units of area (hectare).
Transferability	- Legally the ownership title allows a high transfer level (sale, mortgage, inheritance, rent, etc.). - In the past there was a high level of informal transfer of the Brazil nut *centros* (sale, exchange, inheritance, etc.). For example, the lands were traded in 1984 for a property located in Riberalta.	- As a community or TCO transfer is severely restricted by law. - Transfer of rights among community members; temporary leases of the Brazil nut *centros* are common. - The transfer of rights among TCO members is not ruled out.
Payment of taxes	- It was not possible to check the payment of taxes made on land held as 'agrarian'. - The holder does not incur the expense of the Brazil nut tax.	- Free of all taxes on the land. - In the case of commercial forest use, the taxes are cancelled according to the percent of the volumes extracted assumed by the sawmills. - The Brazil nut tax is also assumed by the shelling companies.
Operational requirements and operational control	- Until 2000, effective operational control was applied by the administrator, mainly in the places nearest to the household.	- It is compulsory that the family members inhabit the community, mainly parents and children of school age. - Harvesting the Brazil nut with the help of third parties is not permitted (contractors or *zafreros*). - The time of Brazil nut harvest is agreed between all members. - The territorial control is permanent, through establishment of the 'land and territory brigade', formed by two community members. - Control over the Brazil nut is intensified at harvest time.
Security	- Legally it is the class of individual tenure with the highest degree of security on land. - In practice, the social pressure has asked questions of the genuineness of the rights, as they have largely been 'usurped' from the proprietors.	- High degree of security over almost all resources thanks to the recognition of their common laws in the public institutions.

Source: Based on field study interviews.

6.4.3 Third case study: Conflict between peasant community and forest concessionaire

The establishment of the peasant community dates from the early eighties, when members of one family decided to occupy the land of an abandoned *barraca* to form a community.

This was facilitated by the opening of the trunk road, providing a link with the city of Cobija. However, the official foundation only occurred in 1994, at the initiative of the rural schoolteacher, with the objective of accessing the funds proposed by the Popular Participation Law.

From the inception of the settlement the occupied area increased continuously, due to the qualification of new lands and the purchase of some of the neighbouring *barracas*. Thus, until the mid-nineties the community members occupied an area of 25,000 ha, with a declared population of 33 families. The history of the forest company also dates from the eighties, then under the form of a *barraca* estate belonging to the same company. In 1993 the '*Chimanes* Indigenous Territory' and the '*Refugio de Vida Silvestre El Dorado*' were established in the north of La Paz, on the land where the logging company was located. Since that time, the state has compensated the company with a long term contract for timber use within the perimeter of the former *barraca*.[261] With the approval of the new Forest Law, the 70,000 ha granted in 1993 were converted to forest concession.

Characteristics of the third case study

Characters	Description
Resource use before the reforms	Although both parties claim to have been established in the region in the early '80s, it is not clear which group first occupied the area in conflict. At the beginning of 1993 the forest company received official permission to use the forests, without the opposition of the peasant community.[262] According to the concession holder, the interest of the community in the forests began when they sold the forest resources to a regional sawmill informally (1999), and escalated with the approval of 500 ha Decree (2000). According to the peasant leaders, the permission granted in 1993 incorporated an area overlapping with part of the area initially occupied by the peasants.[263]
Conflict situation before the reforms	- As the area is adjacent to the border with Brazil, the main conflicts involved Brazilian inhabitants using the natural resources on the Bolivian side of the border.
Events instigating the conflict	- The forest concession approved under the POAF-2000 in 1999 overlapped with the land demanded by the community. - All of the community's timber resources were sold to a regional sawmill by the community authorities in 1999.

261 In this respect, the concession presented here differed from other regional concessions, in that it was not part of the '*Plan Soberanía*' (for more information see chapter 4).

262 Personal interview with the forest concession holder, 13th May 2002.

263 "*From the beginning, our settlement included the old limits of an abandoned barraca, occupying the space currently in conflict. To our astonishment the state granted the concessionaire the right to forest use inside our settlement in the early nineties.*" (Personal interview with the community vice president and secretary 28th April 2002).

Beginning of the conflict	June 2000, after the community members demanded the SIF and the municipality resolve the issue of the overlap of their traditionally held land and use rights with that of the forest company. In October 2000 the community members prevented the fieldwork necessary for the update of the POAF-2000.
Strategies	The strategies adopted were not based on the formation of alliances. The opponents sought continually to use dialogue and negotiation. At the same time, the peasant group resorted to emotional rhetoric; the confiscation of materials, preventing the company from working; openly denouncing the company to the public authorities as corrupt; addressing letters to the regional authorities in order to request a halt to the extraction of resources and blackmailing officeholders when the accusations were ignored. The community members also actively participated in demonstration marches.
Overlapping area	3,200 ha inside the POAF-2000, corresponding to 13% of the area demanded by the peasant community and to 5% of the area occupied by the company.
Attitude of the responsible authorities	- In 1999 the SIF approved a FMP<200 hectares in favour of the peasant community, directly adjacent to the land held by the forest company. - The technician responsible for the UFM detected anomalies in the extraction of timber from the approved 200 ha. - Preliminary *saneamiento* results of the INRA were in favour of the peasant community.

Others characters	**Forest concessionaire**	**Peasant community**
Principal ally(ies)	The technical professionals hired by the company.	The sawmill was a beneficial indirect partner of the community, justifying the demands for access to the forests.
Strengths	Always sought dialogue with the opponents, and at the same time strengthened their own position by adhering to other international rules (forest certification).	Their success resided in their persistence in seeking to achieve their objectives, using 'current weapons' against the system as a whole. [264]
Weaknesses	It was not possible to identify any weaknesses.	Internal divisions within the group, which strengthened the position of their opponents.
Participation in other regional conflicts	Conflict with Brazilian inhabitants situated on Bolivian territory.	Conflict with the regional sawmill, and between community members and leaders.
Main interest in relation to resource use	Forest use, mainly timber use.	
Status of the conflict according to GLASL's (1999)	The conflict was at the first (win-win) and second (win-lose) stages, between levels 3 (actions not words), 4 (alliances) and 5 (loss of face), with minimum damage caused to the opponent.	

264 All of this cited strategies were referred to by SCOTT (1985) as the 'current weapons' used by the 'weak groups'.

Outcomes of the conflict up to February 2004	According to the preliminary outcomes of the *saneamiento*, the INRA recognised the right of the community over 15,000 ha, including the 3,200 ha in conflict. At the same time, the SIF granted 66,000 ha in favour of the forest company after the successful completion of the forest certification process. There remained a possibility that both parties might use the timber within the conflicted territory, ignoring the agreement made between the community and the sawmill.

Alliances and rivalries

The alliances and rivalries were not the main characteristic of this particular conflict. In the case of the forest company, the technical support provided by the professionals (two forest engineers and two administrators) working for the entrepreneur stood out. Their activities allowed the company to meet the requirements dictated by law.[265] During the conflict the technicians played an important role in negotiations with the community members, as well as completing the technical requirements outlined by the certification body. Forest certification contributed to the open demeanour of the company personal, improving the relationship with their opponents. The concessionaire also received general technical support from PANFOR. This included development of the forest inventories, the POAF maps, the establishment of the permanent sampling plots, etc. Through an external consultant, PANFOR contributed to facilitating the negotiation process between both parties at the initial stage of the conflict (see figure 31).

The peasant community received less external support during the conflict. Their power resided in the application of non-conventional strategies and in having learned how to live with the conflict. The conflict became a useful instrument that allowed them to be heard by the regional authorities and other interest groups. However, the sporadic presence of external assessors was also noticed by the peasants, mainly at the time of writing protest letters directed at the municipalities, the SIF and the INRA. The contractual relationship with the regional sawmill provided potential support, as it also had an interest in seeing the community awarded the disputed area.

The participation of the Peasant Federation of Pando was minimal and basically formal. Support for the peasants was limited because the federation was divided as a result of the private and political interests of its leaders.[266]

265 These people are responsible for fulfilling the demands imposed by the SIF, that is to say, they develop the POAF, pay forest duties, control the management of the timber on site, make socio-economic studies of the settlements within the concession, etc.

266 Personal interview with the vice president and secretary of the community 28th April 2002.

Figure 31 Arena and agenda: third case study

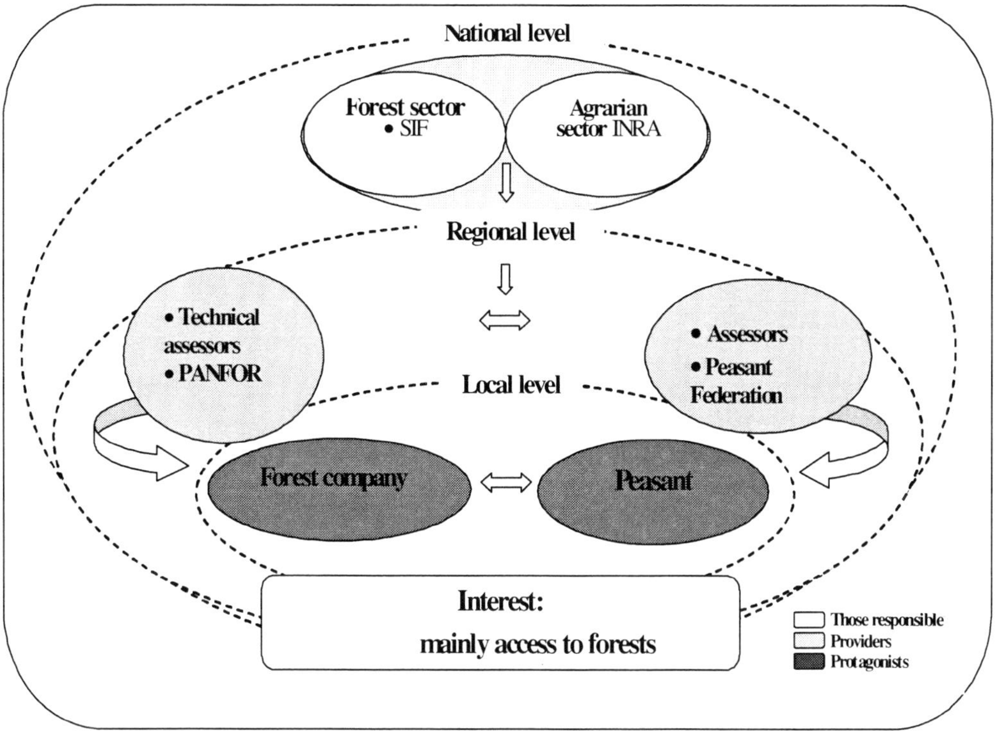

Source: Based on field study interviews.

The main topics contributed by this conflict to the regional agenda were:

- criticism of demands exceeding the 500 ha apportioned to each peasant family, and
- criticism of the influence of the regional entrepreneurs over the regional and national authorities, which allowed them gain access to extensive areas as forest concessions.

Tenure of the protagonists

This case study compared the institutional overlap between two public institutions (forest concessionaire and peasant community), characteristics of both of which are presented in table 27.

Table 27 Comparison of the tenure characteristics between forest concessionaires and peasant communities: (case study 3)

Type / Character	Forest concessionaire	Peasant community
Generalities (rights)	- Legal: Forest concession is a class of tenure granted by state, therefore, its management is highly influenced by forest legislation - The history of the forest concession goes back to the early '90s (1992). As compensation for forest companies in the north of La Paz affected by establishment of AP '*El Dorado*' long term contracts were granted in accordance with Forest Decree of 1974.	- Legal: The formal right to the land is contained in DS 25848, a supplement to the Agrarian Law, and provides for the allocation of 500 ha per family. - At the same time, the Forest Law grants the right to the use of the forests, mainly timber and Brazil nut, with prior approval of a FMP.
Comprehensiveness	- The original area granted in July 1997 covered 70,000 ha, with MFP approved in June 1998, and three POAFs up to 2002. - The FMP included the use of a reference to NTFP use. - Completely restricted agricultural activities. - Hunting and fishing excluded.	- Their original claim was for 25,000 ha. - Officially they are entitled to 15,000 ha (thirty families were registered in the *saneamiento*). - In 1999 a FMP<200 ha was approved and five 'authorisations to deforest' smaller than five ha.
Exclusion	- After *saneamiento*, formal right guaranteed a great capacity for the exclusion of third parties from the utilisation of timber. - In practice, the exclusion of Brazilian inhabitants from all types of resources is problematic. The neighbouring communities also extracted Brazil nuts. Beginning in 2004, the company hired *zafreros*, gathering around 10% of estimated production.	- Similar to the indigenous communities. High level of external exclusion with serious exclusion problems for members, especially during the Brazil nut harvest.
Use Designation	- Use is regulated by law and uses other than that of the forests are not provided for. - Minimum felling cycle of twenty years, determining the division of production according to annual compartments (AAA) - Nearly 10% of the area is dedicated to forest protection, for the establishment of 'permanent sampling plots' and the building of a production infrastructure. - An intensity of use of 80% of the available volume is allowed.	- Each family is allocated a plot of 500 ha. - Timber in each plot is property of the family. - The Brazil nuts are available to all. - Agriculture is practised around the homes, coinciding with the places with greater access. - Hunting and fishing are open to community members only and not third parties. No one may make commercial use of these resources.
Duration	- Forty years, renewable successively by the approval of forest audits executed every five years. - As a consequence of the successful certification of the company under international parameters the right will be renewed automatically, without need of audits.	- Perpetual right to the land, passed on from one generation of community members to the next. - Right to timber use, with prior approval of a FMP<200 ha (1 year).

Allotment type and size	- The concession is assigned in hectares. - The approval of the management instruments requires units of volume for the transport of timber. - In the case of the Brazil nut, use is similar to the situation of the *barracas*.	- The rights to the use of resources (land, timber and Brazil nuts) are distributed based on the division of plots of 500 ha per family. - It cannot be ruled out that certain community members possess more than 500 ha.
Transferability	- Rights are transferable, where the SIF assumes the control of the contracts. - In effect, the rights pertaining to the collection of Brazil nuts have been transferred to the local populations.	- Transfer of the rights greatly restricted by law. - In a contract executed by a lawyer the commercial timber was sold indefinitely to a sawmill in Cobija,. - There were four families living in Cobija renting their plots to third party 'carers' (*cuidantes*), without recognising any property rights for them. - Private rules allow the transfer of plots and use among community members.
Payment of taxes	- According to law, every year a forest tax by hectare is cancelled of US$ 1.00 on the total of the concession. With the approval of Decree 27024 (2004), concessions holder must to cancel US$ 4.00 per year per production's hectare only. - According to certification requirements there should be no delay in the payment of taxes.	- No tax on the land. - In the case of commercial forest use, the taxes are cancelled according to the percent of the volumes extracted assumed by the sawmills. - The Brazil nut tax is shared equally with the shelling companies.
Operational requirements and operational control	- Operational control is supporting by the SIF and by wardens hired by the company. - In conflict situations demands are made of the SIF and/or dialogue is entered into with the opponents.	- It is not compulsory for the community members to inhabit the community. Nearly 20% lived in Cobija. - For the Brazil nut harvest, each community member can employ a *zafrero* whose work is restricted to a specific plot. - Effective control of the forests by all members was disputed, especially in relation to timber.
Security	- After the saneamiento 90% of the area was made available to the concession holder. This right category is an alternative for the large *barraca* holders to improve their legal security.	- High degree of legal security over the land and use of the forests.

Source: Based on field study interviews.

6.4.4 Outcome of the case studies

In order to summarise section 6.4, table 28 highlights the results obtained from the study of the three conflicts, based on the data available up to February 2004.

Table 28 Results of the three case studies according to the percentage of the demands consolidated

Study	Protagonist	Initial demand (ha)	Consolidated demand		Results [267]
			(ha)	(%)	
Case 1	*Barraca* holder	30,000	500[268]	1.6	'Loser'
	ASL	31,000	1,000	3.2	'Loser'
Case 2	Private landowner	27,000	50[269]	0.18	'Loser'
	Indigenous community	27,000	21,000	77	'Winner'
Case 3	Forest concessionaire	70,000	66,000	94	'Winner'
	Peasant community	25,000	15,000	60	'Winner'

Source: Based on field study interviews.

According to case studies, the parties most affected by the enforcement of the reforms were the 'private landowner', the *barraca* holder and the ASL members. They were able to consolidate less than 5% of their demands. The 'victorious' the parties, consolidating more than 60% of their claims, were the forest concessionaire, the indigenous, and the peasant community. In all three cases, land titling process was fundamental to deciding access to the forests, as well as to influencing the strategies of the users. However land titling process did not guarantee the solution of the conflicts.

As a result of the strategic behaviour of forest users, the conflicts always moved to other levels. For instance, in the first case study the external conflict between *barraca* holder and ASL moved into the new peasant community, where the '*barraca* holder' demanded the exclusive rights to timber use, contrary to the interests of the community. In the event that the peasants' demands were to be met, the ASL members would then have demanded compensation for the land lost, a situation that could continue to generate conflicts with other forest users.

In the second case study, although the settlement was still occupied by the indigenous members, the 'private landowner' did not give up his legal right. His position was reinforced by the judgement of the National Agrarian Tribunal in his favour, although a softening of his

267 All parties managing to consolidate a minimum 50% of their initial demands were categorised as winners. Those below 50% were the losers.

268 As a member of the new peasant community, the *barraca* holder was officially entitled to a maximum area of only 500 ha.

269 By 2004 the INRA had officially recognised 50 ha in favour of the 'private landowner'. Another 6,000 ha were won by the 'private landowner' unofficially. However, the situation remained uncertain for both parties, even though in reality the indigenous groups occupied this area.

original stance was evident. In this case, the most important current conflicts were those occurring between members of neighbouring indigenous communities (inside the TCO), mainly during the Brazil nut harvest.

Lastly, the conflict observed in the third case study moved to the level of the social relationships between peasants and the sawmill. The sawmill claimed the right to the community forest resources based on a contract of sale. Here, the peasants either had to comply with the agreement made with the sawmill, or use the forest jointly with the forest concessionaire. However, the outcome as either a 'loser' or a 'winner' is not necessarily representative for all forest users in the study area, mainly for the individual user the *barraca* holders and the concessionaires. In the northern Bolivian Amazon there exist *barraca* holders who maintain productive estates 50% above their traditional demands, especially in zones with lower population densities. In the case of the forest concessionaires, several companies have lost 100% of their concessions due to the territorial overlap with rural communities, especially in the north western part of Pando.

In the case of the community users, the results of the research could be generalised for a great part of the study area: the ASLs continue to be the loser within the community group, since none of them have been able to consolidate more than 5% of their initial demands. Since the land titling process began the indigenous and peasant communities, on the other hand, have prioritised their claims over land, and subsequently they have good chances of consolidating their initial demands, especially in the department of Pando.

The denomination 'loser' or 'winner' can be relative depending on the strategy used by the parties. For example, if the *barraca holder* decided to consolidate his right as a 'private landowner', he should get between 50 and 200 ha. If he decided to become a member of a new peasant community, his land entitlement is doubled, consolidating 500 hectares.

Lastly, in several cases a so-called 'winner' of the reforms would appear to be the Bolivian state itself, because many users don't fulfil the FES, with the result that a large part of their claims become state property.

6.5 The strategies of conflicting parties to gain access to the forests

In this section the behaviour of the protagonist groups with respect acquiring access to forest use is analysed. The definition of 'strategy' used in this study was similar to that proposed by SCHNEIDER (2002:380), including both the conscious and unconscious behaviour of individuals, directed towards the realisation of their goals.[270] The actors proceeded to execute their strategies under diverse circumstances. In some situations the individuals may or may not have taken into consideration the rest of their environment, including the action of their opponents. The actors may also have carried out their strategies optimising the restrictions provided by fixed parameters, just as managing the logic of market behaviour in the

[270] SCHNEIDER (2002) avoided the division between conscious and unconscious behaviour in the sense that these cannot be demonstrated empirically and that *de facto* both alternatives are always given.

neoclassical economy (KNIGHT 1992:17). One way or another, the actors were obliged to confront situations characterised by interdependence between individuals.[271]

This study is focused on the analysis of the protagonists' strategies under the perspective of the institutional and economic spheres. The first sphere emphasises the use of the public rules, considered as the available means of the actors to ensure the formal tenure of their resources. Therefore, the goal outlined was to enforce what was established by law. In the economic sphere the means used were financial and the goal of the protagonists was to obtain economic benefits from the forests, even when their tenure over the forests was uncertain. In both spheres the individuals demonstrated opportunist behaviour to strengthen their position, such as rent-seeking.

The strategies analysed were divided into two groups, according to the differences and similarities between the forest users: those with communal property rights (ASL, indigenous community and peasant community) and those with individual property rights (*barraca* holder, private landowner, and forest concessionaire) (see figure 32). The strategy employed by the protagonists was a mixture of the means available, both of the institutional sphere and of the economic sphere. However, each group maintained a certain sphere of power or influence over its opponents, resulting in individual preference in the choice of strategy. As the formal tenure of the communal users (rural communities and ASLs) have improved with the introduction of the reforms, these groups tended to base their strategies on the use of institutional means. The individual users, mainly *barraca* holders and 'private landowners', by the effort that the formalisation of their tenure represented, generally resorted to the use of means available in the economic sphere.

Figure 32 illustrates this situation based on the differences of colours, where the dark colour (grey) represents a greater level of influence than the light colour (white). Adapting the concepts on strategies proposed in the literature on 'livelihood strategies',[272] in conflict situations the protagonists have two strategies. In the institutional sphere one has the so-called '*adaptive strategies*', which are no more than an answer to the structural changes, such as the introduction of new rules or state policies. It was evident that all the interviewed actors made an effort to choose these strategies with the aim of formalising their tenure, as far as possible. In the economic sphere, they are the so-called '*survival strategies*'. These are the strategies the protagonists resorted to in cases of emergency, and were often the last resort of the individuals to achieve access to the forests, especially when the execution of the 'adapted' strategies failed.

---

271 According to ELSTER (1986 cited in KNIGHT 1992), this interdependence can be of three types: 1) the gains made by each actor depend on the gains made by all; 2) the gains made by each actor depend on the choices made by all; and 3) each actor's choices depended on the choices made by all.

272 See DE HAAN 2000:19, cited in HENKEMANS 2001:26.

Figure 32 Strategic behaviour of the forest users in conflict

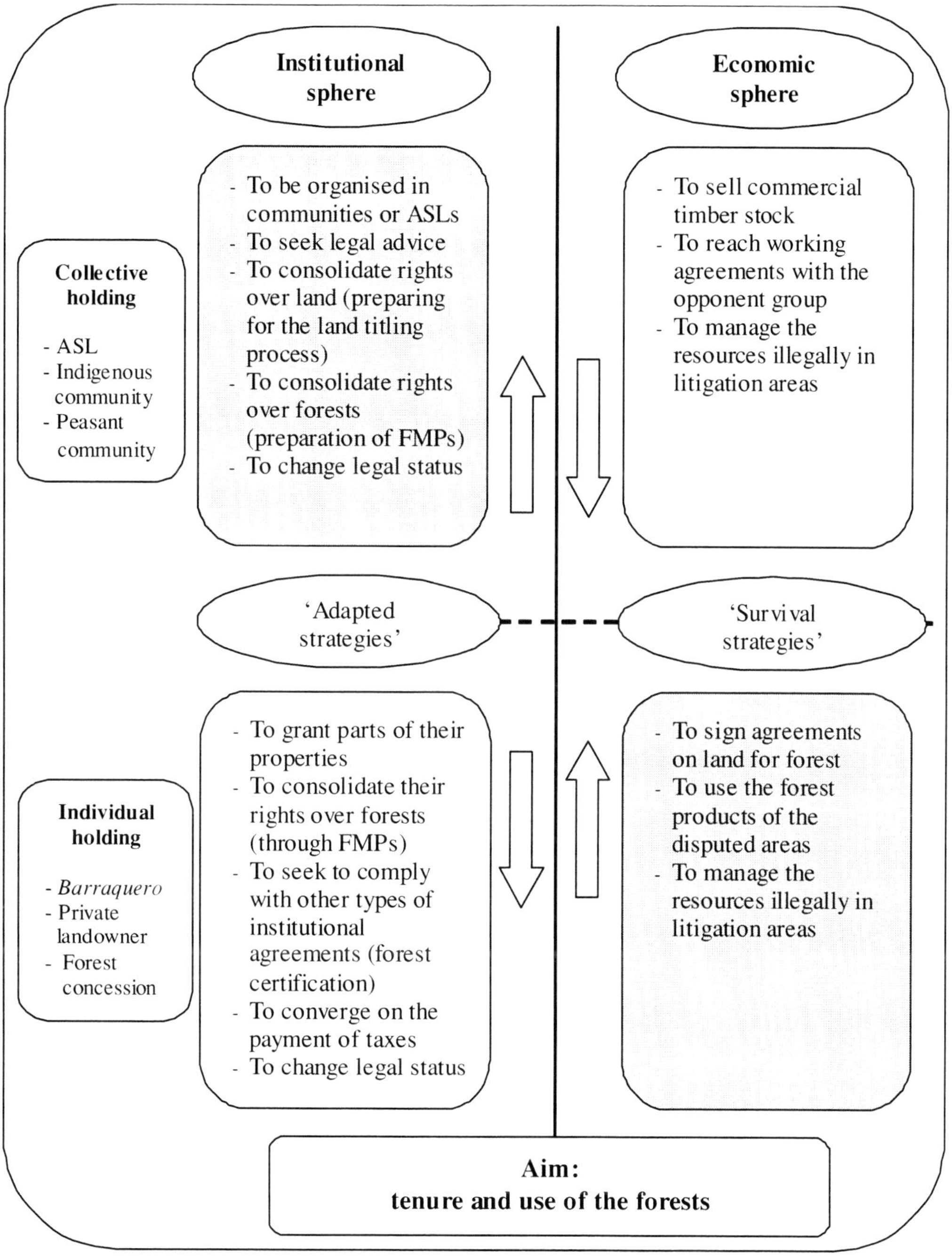

Source: Based on own field study interviews.

The terminology adopted on 'adapted' and 'survival' strategies makes more sense if the general context of analysis is considered, oriented towards examining the influence of the reforms on conflict emergence. Here the actors tended to adapt to the new public institutions to control the forests, or they should be able 'to survive' or using the forest 'at any price', even infringing the rules provided. Contrary to the focus of 'livelihood strategies',[273] where the '*adapted strategies*' were carried out based on deliberate behaviour and the '*survival strategies*' are carried out based on non deliberate behaviour, in the conflicts analysed, following the recommendations of SCHNEIDER (2000), the possibility that both strategies involved the two behaviour types was not discarded.

The arrows in the figure 32 represent the competition relationships (diverging darts) and cooperation (converging darts) between individuals. Thus, in the institutional sphere, the parties generally pursued antagonistic objectives, reflected in the legal logic that only one of the protagonists could consolidate his right to a territory.

This situation motivated the individuals to compete and often to escalate the level of conflict. Without discarding the possibility that forest use 'at any price' increased the level of conflict, in the economic sphere it was observed that the parties often pursued needs or complementary interests, allowing them to carry out actions in common. This situation often stimulated a certain level of collaboration and balance in the disputes, and helped to improve the social relationships between the protagonists. However, the '*survival strategy*' usually caused conflict, particularly when executed jointly with third parties.

6.5.1 Institutional sphere in communal holding regimes

The strategies used by the communal actors were: 1) to be organised in groups; 2) to seek legal advice; 3) to consolidate formal tenure and 4) to change their legal status.

Organisation

Organisation was a basic requirement to access the resources in any of the three types of communal holding. In the case of the rural communities, without organisation one was not entitled to the land, and without land the forests could not be used legally. Organisation was a complicated process demanding time and effort on the part of the members. The first step was to found the community or association, later to choose its representatives, carry out a census of its members, become affiliated with a social union, edit articles of association, as well as document the history of the settlement, process the establishment certificate in the municipality, the legal status, etc. Leadership and group organisation were challenges to communities who had worked within an extractivist culture. Many extractivist communities in Brazil looked to outsiders as leaders since historically they looked to rubber barons for resources. Other communities were settled on their land by the federal government and

---

273 The concept of 'Sustainable Livelihood' was developed by the British organisation DFID (Department For International Development) as a normative concept with the aim to improve the lives of poor people and to strengthen their sustainability. This is a holistic framework, which includes and conceptualises both the internal and external components of livelihoods in a dynamic model (HENKEMANS 2001:10-18).

subsequently looked to the government to make major decisions (JONES, in prep.). According to the results of the study, in the best of cases, the time that lapsed from foundation until obtaining legal recognition (legal personality) was 16 months (case 1), with a possible duration of four years, as the case of the indigenous community showed.

The communal organisation provided support to the social and technical organisations such as the indigenous unions, peasant federations and the regional NGO. The reforms fomented the process of communal organisation, initially with the approval of the Popular Participation Law (1994) and more recently with the execution of the *saneamiento* (2000). Both events impelled many communities to upgrade their legal steps and even other private settlements decided to be organised in communities,[274] because under the forms of community right, forest use was guaranteed, and access to the forests was speeded up.

Seeking technical-legal advice

The conditions of poverty and marginalisation within the region forced the rural communities to look for actors that could provide the regulatory information necessary, and in many cases they ran with the transaction costs that represented the step of the requirements established by law. Research carried out by HENTSCHEL (2004) demonstrated that the members of a peasant community visited these organisations 46 times with the purpose of being informed on the technical and formal requirements for the creation of FMPs. The users visited both public and private organisations. The most sought after public organisations were the INRA, the SIF, and the municipal government. At the same time, the demand for the support of the NGOs and the social unions from the communities was growing given their efficient work.

According to the primary data collection, the three communal parties interviewed sought support mainly in relation to the following items:

- information on the general contents of the laws, specifically on their rights;
- advice on founding and organising communities, specifically in relation to the legal requirements;
- technical advice for the creation of FMPs or other technical instruments and
- support to face the opponents in conflict situations.

The case studies revealed the comparative advantage of the rural communities and ASL near Riberalta, in relation to the access to technical information. Contrary to the organisations based in Cobija, the organisations that provided technical services in Riberalta had greater experience, maintained better coordination, and they had more technical personnel to attend to community claims.

274 The communal organisation of the private settlements, mainly *barracas*, occurred most frequently in zones where the arrival of the INRA technicians was delayed, as for example the province Federico Roman in Pando and the Ivón *Cantón* of the municipality of Riberalta.

Consolidating the formal land and forests tenures

Considering that in the past the traditional institutions took charge of governing forest use, the population's interest in fulfilling the public rules can be considered as a new form of behaviour in the region. In order to consolidate the right to the land, the rural communities usually prepared for the *saneamiento*, informed themselves of the date when the INRA technicians were to visit, demarcated their property borders and established markers at the intersection points with their neighbours. However, if these actions were not enough to guarantee access to the resources, the protagonists were prepared to carry out more violent actions, as was the case of the members of the indigenous community who on three occasions successfully hindered the calculation of the entitlement to demands made by their opponents when taking the working teams and the members of the INRA *saneamiento* commission hostage.[275]

Regarding the execution of the forest tenure, the three community groups prepared FMPs, but due to the presence of conflicts in most of the cases, the plans were not entirely approved (table 29).

Table 29 Drafting of FMPs according to forest users in conflict

User	Initiation (year)	Support organisation	Initial demand (Area)	Current status of approval	Main difficulties and conflicts
ASL	2002[276]	IPHAE	The whole concession area (31,400 ha)	1,000 ha approved in September 2002.	Overlaps; low timber prices; the ASL partners failed to agree on the division of the forest taxes.
Indigenous community	2003	Sawmill	200 ha	Process of approval in advanced stages by November 2003.	Initially the rights over timber inside the TCO were not clear. Uncertain whether it belonged to all the ethnic groups or each community separately.
Peasant community	1998	Sawmill	Nearly 15,000 ha	In 1998 a FMP<200 ha was approved and five 'authorisations to deforest' with a total of 15 ha	Overlaps; conflicts with the sawmill owner; conflicts inside the community.

Source: Based on SIF reports.

[275] "*The national director of the INRA announced that he will resort to police troops, not only to recover the teams that were taken by the indigenous groups in the northern Amazon, but also to free the technicians being held hostage*." (La Razón, February 23rd 2000).

[276] The fieldwork started in 2000.

At regional level, the drawing up of community FMPs was in its initial stages. It was estimated that by the end of 2003 only 1% of the rural communities presented FMPs to the SIF, with a total of 2,700 ha approved. In the case of the indigenous communities this process was even more complicated, due to the previous agreement that all the members of the TCO should be included. A common alternative was the approval of a FMP corresponding to less than 200 ha processed individually in the name of a community plot holder, as was observed in the third case study.

Change of legal status

The second case study revealed a change of the legal status of a community initially founded as a peasant community, which then became indigenous, resulting in a number of advantages for the members in terms of access to the land:

> "... *a while before the saneamiento commission passed, contact was made with the Indigenous Union. Previously we worked with the Peasant Federation and our legal status was originally that of a peasant community. We received better advice from the Indigenous Union and their support NGO. They had more experience in saneamiento topics. The neighbouring communities, also affiliated to the Indigenous Union, guided us and they supported our making this decision. We were the last indigenous community incorporated into the TCO. Inside the community there were only two people who initially opposed our becoming indigenous. Now all are convinced that it was the best decision we could have taken*".[277]

The legal change from peasant status to indigenous was one of the most hotly debated discussion topics at regional level, not only criticised by the *barracas* holders, but also by many peasant leaders who lost land during the *saneamiento* in the TCO. Those opposed to the indigenous groups argued that the 'self-proclaimed indigenous' did not meet the requirements necessary for incorporation into the traditional ethnic groups of the region (they did not speak the language, or adhere to the traditions). Their decision was based entirely on the access to resources.[278] However, from the point of view of the public institutions, the legal change did not contradict any law. The granting of rights to the natural resources was based on the self-determination of the people.

6.5.2 Institutional sphere in regimes of individual holding

The individual actors employed the following strategies: 1) sought ownership titles to parts of the large occupied areas of land; 2) attempted to consolidate their rights to forest use; 3) adhered to international rules and standards; 4) paid the forest taxes and 5) as with the communities, they sought to change their legal status.

---

[277] Personal interview with the vice president of the indigenous community, January 18th 2002.

[278] Summary of several interviews carried out mainly with *barraqueros* and peasant leaders, neighbouring the *Multiétnico* II TCO.

Granting parts of settlements

In the past, due to the large size of the *barraca* estates, no single ownership title embraced the total area of these settlements. To make official their ownership of the land, the *barraca* holders used to negotiate ownership titles for each of their production *centros*. In order to comply with the law, the *centros* were assigned to different members of their family, just as the private landowner studied, who had three ownership titles covering almost 6,800 ha assigned to three different people. Considering the analysis of the ownership titles delivered to the regional companies presented in chapter 4, the strategy of granting land is not representative for all of the *barracas*, but mainly for the medium and the small. The '*barraquero* regime' offered enough legal security to the 'entrepreneurs'. Only those with better information and bigger public contacts at national level formalised their tenure. It is estimated that nearly 10% of the area claimed in 2000 was granted title under the category 'agrarian enterprise' (see table 14).

Consolidating the forest tenures

As with communal settlements, the three forest users with individual tenure drew up FMPs. In the first two examples (*barraca* holder, private landowner), both protagonists drew up more than one FMP, processed under different names, the same as the ownership titles to the land (see table 30).

Table 30 Drafting of FMPs for individual holdings

User	Initial area	Approval state	Observation (agreement)
Barraca holder	Almost 535 ha divided into two FMP<200 ha and two applications to extract felled timber.[279]	All of the plans were approved between 1999 and 2001.	Three forest documents were produced in the name of the property holder and the fourth under an employee's name, according to the terms of the 'wood for the *barraca* holder, land for the accomplice' agreement.
Private landowner (administrator)	Almost 400 ha divided into two FMP<200 ha.	The FMPs were not approved because the ownership rights were unclear.	One FMP was drawn up under the name of the administrator of the *barraca*,[280] and the second under the name of a *freguece*, under the agreement of economic remuneration for the timber sold.

Source: Based on SIF reports.

279 In the process of enforcement of the Forest Law, many social actors demonstrated strong resistance to obeying the new law. Thus, the SIF approved 'exception regimes' that condoned the forest users taking advantage of the timber subject to specific times and clauses. One of them was the IOP-527/2000, which authorised actors to remove all the timber cut under the previous regime (1974). Nevertheless, some actors consider that under this normative was cut new tress, that were registered falsely to 'exception regimes' (illegal logging).

280 The land was rented to the administrator in 1999, a time of crisis for the barraca holder, because the 'company' could not perform its duties. The rent contract provided the administrator usufruct rights to the forests (timber and Brazil nuts).

However, the 'accomplices' were not always family of the property holder, but rather people close to the '*patrón*' (generally *fregueces*), with a certain level of influence inside the settlement. They entered into agreements, usually verbal, in exchange for economic remuneration, or the granting of rights to some of the resources (land for cultivation).[281] This strategy was one of the main reasons for the conflict in the first case study: The creation of FMPs was related to the pursuit of four concrete objectives: 1) to set down precedents of settlement; 2) to try fulfilling the FES-forest, during the land titling; 3) to use the timber without risk of seizure; and 4) to obtain business profits from the forest.

Resorting to compliance with international rules (forest certification)

Forest certification helped the users in several ways. Besides meeting demands for forest products on national and international markets (JONES, in prep.), it was an excellent tool for managing conflicts (ELLIOTT 1997:97), insofar as it reduced the social tension between forest companies and local communities (QUEVEDO 2004). At the same time, forest certification also proved an outstanding measure towards securing forest conservation (Cámara forestal 2004).

Two additional advantages in Bolivia were: the national government rewarded voluntary certification, with the automatic renewal for twenty years of forest tenure without the need to carry out the five-year technical audit required by law. The forest duty required of the certified company was also reduced, specifically the reduction of the Rate of Forest Regulation established by Decree 27024. As a result, at the time of writing Bolivia boasted 1.5 million hectares of certificated forest, distributed among 12 private concessions and a TCO (Cámara forestal 2004). In Pando, five forest companies were certified, with a total of 590,000 ha, corresponding to 40% of the whole domestic area.

With an estimated one million hectares under the control of forest companies, concessionaires viewed forest certification as an important strategy for legitimising their tenure in the eyes of the rural communities. This was demonstrated in the third case study, where the forest concessionaire not only consolidated his right to forest use, but also called upon technical advice to solve the conflicts, improving the image of his company in the eyes of the regional and national forest authorities.[282]

The payment of taxes

The payment of forest taxes can be viewed as a strategy, since it eliminated the risk of seizure and sanctions that could legally be more drastic than the costs of complying with the law.

---

281 "*The ARFM of the municipality of Riberalta [...] is largely managed by the famous FMP smaller than 200 ha, prepared with documents that seemingly clarify the ownership of property [...], making agreements between neighbours appear etc., in order to approve their plans.*" (Letter from the Director of the NGO to the National Forest Technical Intendant, June 26th 2001)

282 "*At the end of 2003 we officially received the certification document covering almost 100% of the forest concession. The area in conflict with the community, which represents less than 5% of the total, is subject to the decision made by the INRA, whether in favour of or against the company. We make an effort to maintain good relationships with all our neighbours. This is a condition of the certifying authority.*" Telephone interview with the forest concession technician, January 13th 2004.

Regardless of whether the payments of taxes were carried out as a forest concessionaire, a private landowner or the owner of a forest company (shelling factories and sawmills), the Forest Law improved the state revenues through the implementation of the concept of the payment of forest patents (see chapter 7, figure 37). At national level, the concessionaires of the northern Bolivian Amazon were considered exemplary in relation to the payment of forest taxes.[283] The fulfilment of their obligations was a deliberate strategy, as it allowed the forest users to demand state support to maintain their property rights in a region where the interests in the forests had increased significantly. However, the mere payment of the forest taxes does not necessarily mean that the actors were not involved in illegal forest management.

Changing legal status

As was the case with the communities, the individual users continuously sought greater legal security over their settlements. The 'less expensive' change, and subsequently more common, was that of the *barraca* holder to private landowner, within the framework of the 'exception regime' proposed by the SIF.[284] However, the individual users, mainly *barraca* holders revealed a willingness to belong to any legal group in order to preserve their access to the forests. For example, the *barraca* holders claimed forest concessions, ownership titles, drew up management plans, transformed their settlements into peasant communities and even called themselves indigenous.

> "*... my father was in the region for more than thirty years, then he had his barraca and marketed rubber. Now we are spread out in the area with different rights. Two of my siblings and I decided to become indigenous; another of my siblings is a member of the peasant community, and finally, the fifth son decided to remain a barraca* holder."[285]

Figure 33 illustrates the changes of legal status undergone by the protagonist in the first case study. For almost thirty years the landholder managed his estate under the private rules of the '*barraca* regime'. Due to the increased pressure on forest use and the lack of legal security, he resorted to drawing up two FMPs to guarantee his access to the timber. Thus, he passed over to the category of 'private landowner', at least in the official statistics of the SIF.[286] This new legal situation did not guarantee total access to the rest of his settlement, however. Only to 2% of the area claimed was granted, due to his decision to form a peasant community inside the *barraca*.

---

283 Declarations of the Forest Superintendent, when comparing the situation of the study area with the rest of the country (telephone interview, 13th March 2004).

284 See chapters 4 and 7 for more detail.

285 Personal interview, director of an indigenous community, January 14th 2002.

286 The Agrarian Law is the only ruling granting the unrestricted entitlement to property use. Nevertheless, the adjustment of the Forest Law to accommodate the conditions in the study area meant many users without ownership titles were entitled to use the forests under the 'authorisation of forest use on private property' category (see chapter 4, and chart 19).

Figure 33 Changes to the barraca holder's legal status

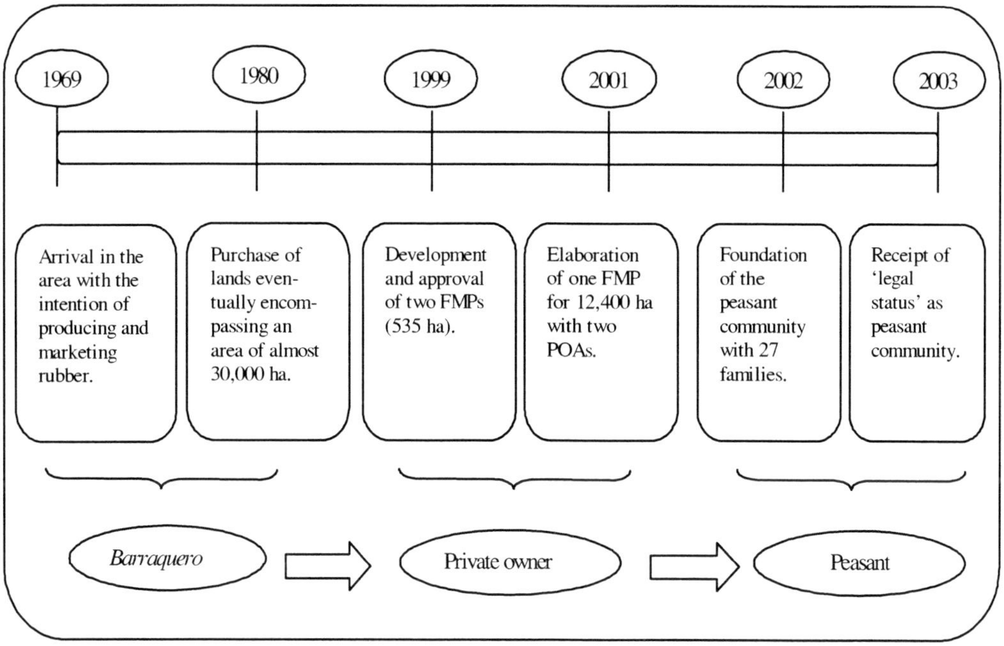

Source: Based on own field study interviews.

At the time of writing, the peasant community was legally recognised as such and had good chances of consolidating at least half of the property claimed originally (14,000 ha). Officially, the *barraca* holder possessed a plot of only 500 ha. The legal change did not imply changes in resource use, however. From the outset the property holder used the forests as much as the land. The main aim of his strategy was, therefore, to increase his legal security, or at least to assure the commercial use of the forest products.

6.5.3 Economic sphere

Given the similarity of the strategies and the interdependence exhibited by both groups, this sphere is presented for both holding types concurrently.

Service agreements with the opposing group

The shortage of work and the difficult economic situation were conditions favouring the establishment of a high level of interdependence between the community members and the entrepreneurs of the region. Two of the three case studies demonstrated that between opponents it was possible to sign service agreements, at the initiative of any of the groups. For instance, during the 2002 harvest two members of the ASL were engaged by the '*barraca* holder' to gather Brazil nuts in the disputed area. The produce was later sold to the *barraca* holder at market price.[287] In the second case study, the forest concession technicians also reported that after the certification process, which included a recommendation to improve the social relationships with the groups in conflict, the company proceeded to sign service agreements with ten members of the opposition peasant community to carry out work in the sawmill and to work as wardens in the concession area.[288]

The cooperation in relation to work tended to lead to an improvement in the relationships between the opponents. A precondition for this was the opponent's perception that he was not an enemy, but rather a person with similar interests. The agreement of services generally strengthened the position of the individual groups, and they in turn strengthened the *clientelismo* relationship. The undersigning of private agreements was a good means for the more economically powerful groups to enjoy the benefits of the forests in an indirect way.

Agreements on land and forest

Two types of private agreements relating to land and forest existed: those signed between protagonists, and those executed with third parties.

Real examples of agreements signed between protagonists in the northern Bolivian Amazon included:

- An agreement between the administrator and the indigenous community for the Brazil nut harvest of 2000, which comprised the following clauses: 1) the biggest 'centros ' were to be controlled by the administrator; 2) the community members were to sell the Brazil nuts to the administrator, receiving a price determined by the market in Riberalta and 3) the administrator was not to hire external Brazil nut gatherers for future harvests.[289]
- An offer made by the controllers of the forest company to the peasants to purchase at market price the trees in the disputed areas.

  "We have to be interested in doing business with the community, because this area is near our workspace, and we have drawn up a 2,500 ha POAF. The timber has already been offered and paid for. We have signed an agreement with the community, where we have undertaken to pay for the timber standing in the conflict area. The problem is that they have other conflicts with the Cobija sawmill and we all are waiting for the decision of the INRA."[290]

Examples of agreements between protagonists and third parties from the northern Bolivian Amazon included:

---

287 Personal interview with an ASL member, February 12th 2002.

288 Telephone interview with the forest concession technician, January 13th 2004.

289 Acta de Buen Acuerdo, January 27th 2000.

290 Personal interview with the concession holder, May 13th 2002.

- The sale and perpetual transfer of the existing trees in the peasant community to a second forest company (sawmill), comprising all tree species, ages, positions (growing and/or cut), particularly the species with high commercial values.[291]
- In the first case study, a 'land for timber' agreement was reached between the *barraca* holder and the families of the new community. Under this agreement the property holder granted the land to the members of the community in exchange for the rights to the commercial exploitation of the timber and for preference above other possible merchants with respect to the sale of Brazil nuts.[292]

Conflicts continued subsequent to aforementioned agreements in three of the four cases, mainly because certain individuals, after having achieved their objectives, refused to meet their own responsibilities. Agreement with third parties often resulted in increased conflict, although in some cases it was a useful strategy to move the opponent away from the benefits of the forest.

Agreements between protagonists generally occurred during the second stage of conflict escalation (win-lose), i.e., when they were still speaking. Agreement with a third party was possible at any of the three stages and even before the beginning of the conflict.

Illegal management of the resources in disputed areas

The three case studies revealed commercial forest use with the partial or total absence of felling authorisations and timber transport.

In the first case, the members of the commission responsible for the inspection of timber harvesting and the FMP for the area overlapping with the territory of the ARFM reported:[293]

- The apparent inflation of the profitable volume of a FMP for cedar (*Cedrela odorata*) to ten times the average volume found in the area[294] and
- The doubtful origins of old timber allegedly cut during the previous regime, that was in many cases new trees, felled to complete the quotas approved by the SIF.

The second case study revealed:

- The demand made by the indigenous people to the forest authorities for the felling and transport of timber, carried out by the administrator, a few months after the reorganisation of the community.[295] However, this activity seems to have been executed with a certain

---

291 Private purchase/sale contract, March 25th 1998. The FMP and removal plan were executed within the framework of the current contract between 1998 and 1999.

292 Personal interview with the *barraca* holder, May 15th 2002.

293 Technical report on the inspection made into harvested timber in the ARFM-Riberalta (letter to the President of the Committee of Support for the forest regime, August 22nd 2001).

294 The inventory of 400 ha within the ARFM revealed an average volume per hectare of 1 m^3 compared to 11.5 m^3 declared in the FMP.

295 Letter to head of the Operative Forest Unit of Puerto Rico (November 25th 1999).

level of complicity on the part of some community members, who received money to facilitate the process.

- The president of the community also authorised all community members to sell up to three trees per family, justified on the basis of the economic necessity of the households.[296]
- On another opportunity, the community members decided to cut five cedar trees (*Cedrela odorata*) inside of one of the refuted Brazil nut *centros*, in rejection to the failure of the National Agrarian Tribunal against the community. After felling the timber, the same community members proceeded to denounce the felling of the trees to the SIF, in order to receive approval for the transport and the sale of the products (records of special community meeting, September 23rd 2001).

The illegal management of the resources observed in the third case study was more complex, as two other groups in conflict with the peasant community and the forest company were involved as well as the protagonists themselves.

Examples of illegal logging involving the peasant community and the sawmill: The SIF approved 84% of the area originally proposed in the FMP<200 ha. The remainder was omitted due to the overlap with the area claimed by the forest company. However, the inspection report by the office manager of the Bella Flor UFM declared that in excess of 168 ha were actively being utilised.[297]

Illegal use involving the forest company and Brazilian inhabitants: "*In order to avoid conflicts with the Brazilian settlements inside the area the concession holder resorts to buying the timber cut by these people. This solution to the situation may potentially be harmful to the interests of the company, in the case that illegal logging practices would be generalised*"[298]

All of the conflicting protagonists exhibited a tendency towards illegal logging, a tendency accentuated in situations where the tenure of resources was less certain. Illegal logging also increased where third parties showed an interest in the utilisation of the forests, especially if these third parties were sawmills or people without property rights over the forests, yet who were powerful in economic terms. The species most susceptible to illegal logging were the valuable species, previously *mara* (*Swietenia macrophylla*) and now cedar (*Cedrela odorata*). The

---

296 "*The community president made it known that we are authorised to sell timber in order to meet the current needs of the community [...] It was agreed that each family could use up to three trees*" (records of special community meeting, August 26th 2000).

297 UFM Report, Municipality of Bella Flor, September 12th 1999. Other evidence of illegal logging included: 1) "*The SIF carried out its work. However, in practice one can argue that the sawmill did not respect the limits of the concession.*" (Interviews with the forest concession holder, May 13th 2002); 2) "*Under the timber contract with the sawmill, wood from all over the community was extracted in order to meet the authorised quotas. We do not even know how much timber the sawmill took out, we only saw the trucks leave.*" (Personal interviews with a member of the peasant community, April 29th 2002); 3) "*R..., the 'cubicación' (measuring in cubic meters) of the timber that I am sending you will have to be done jointly with G.... since it is not exact. We made it coincide with the number of 'cubes' authorised by the forest authority [...]. Please do it well. Thank you, S....*" (Note written by those responsible for the sawmill, undated).

298 PANFOR 2000: technical report on conflict mediation, unpublished.

increased poverty of the rural households also intensified the tendency towards illegal logging, as the individuals depended on the natural resources to improve their family revenues. This was more pronounced in years where the price of the Brazil nut was lower, as the rural inhabitants supplemented their revenues with the sale of timber from their plots. Finally, another two aspects promoting illegal logging were the technical and financial shortcomings of the SIF, and the weaknesses of the system of sanctions applied to the offenders (see chapter 7).

6.6 Conclusions

The focus of the research on individual case studies facilitated the garnering of insights into the circumstances of the local actors, making it possible to understand their interests, needs and the strategies employed to consolidate their rights to forest use. The three case studies were representative in relation to the following points: 1) typifying the areas of greatest conflict in the region; 2) the topics of discussion on the regional agenda for all of the interest groups; 3) the interests of the forest users with respect to Brazil nuts, but increasingly towards timber use and the occupation of land and lastly 4) the participation of other regional and national groups interested in forest use and in the law enforcement.

Despite the fact that the case studies did not reflect the situation of medium and small *barraca* holders, the studies revealed that they were able to survive the effects of the reforms, and that although they remained in conflict with other local actors, they often counted amongst the winners. The study of a small *barraca holder* involved in a conflict would have provided more definite conclusions concerning the strategies they employed to preserve their tenure. Other topics remaining open after the conclusion of the case studies include: illegal logging and the conflicts inside the communities, potentially decisive issues with respect to the sustainable management and conservation of the forests.

Other sources of conflict

Up to now, the analysis has concentrated on revealing the emergence of the conflicts as a result of the unsuitable public institutions. Nevertheless, the current conflict situation must be argued under consideration of three additional variables: 1) the behaviour of the actors responsible for implementing the laws (public bodies); 2) the aims of other regional actors with respect to forest use and 3) the history of the social relationships between the various forest users. Whereas the first two points derive from a political/economic perspective and can be analysed under the theoretical approach of rent-seeking, the third one involves a significant social component.

Behaviour of public agents

The behaviour of public agents favouring the private interests of certain interest groups, has been a major topic of discussion in several publications (see SIMAC 1990; URIOSTE & BALDOMAR 1998; HERNÁIZ & PACHECO 2001). In the case of the northern Bolivian Amazon the national authorities have been seen to contribute to the emergence of conflicts, either during the formulation of the institutions, or at the moment of their enforcement. The formulation of institutions can cause conflicts when the rules favour certain users or are restricted to regulating the tenure of one group in particular. This is potentially the case with decrees pertaining to the *barraca* holders and the peasants when: 1) the responsible actors propagate institutions under strong social pressure; 2) the national governments reveal weakness during negotiations; 3) agents ignore legislation; 4) agents return political favours and 5) the authorities responsible are themselves directly interested in the approval of the institutions. In the process of institutional enforcement, the government authorities were in the main responsible for the territorial overlaps. They tended to grant rights to a single territory to different parties,[299] approved legal instruments based on documents that could not guarantee the traditional right of the claimants[300] and they ignored the claims of traditional users. Often, the origin of the overlaps was a lack of coordination between public agents, and at other times the constant change of officeholders, mainly inside the municipal governments and at national level.[301] The attitude of the public authorities may have been involuntary behaviour beyond the reach of the technical and financial possibilities of those responsible, but may also have been intentional behaviour, motivated by favouritism toward one group of beneficiaries and in some cases even blatant corruption.

Interests of the regional actors

In terms of the interests at stake for other regional actors, the reforms created ideal conditions for new regional organisations to assume important tasks. Among the indirectly favoured groups, the NGOs, forest sawmills and social unions stood out as those who pursued concrete interests and could directly influence the development of the conflicts.

With respect to the NGOs, it was assessed that 11 of approximately twenty technical organisations working in the region were interested in supporting the enforcement of the Agrarian Law and the Forest Law. Although 50% of the NGOs were founded before the reforms, only one of them (CEJIS) was in charge of land tenure issues and social conflicts since 1996. Altogether 90% of the analysed organisations adapted their activities to the demands and expectations generated by the new regulatory scheme, mainly toward *saneamiento* and the elaboration of FMPs. The results of this study revealed the leading role of the NGOs in the emergence, development and solution of the conflicts, based on: 1) availability of technical and financial resources; 2) availability of information on the topics concerning forest users and 3) the specialisation of their activities, concentrated on supporting specific demands of the groups.

---

299 One example was provided by the boundary of the ARFM and the certificate of establishment granted by the municipal technicians.

300 For example, the approval of FMPs in untitled settlements and where there were clear conflict situations over the use of the forests.

301 Since the beginning of the study (October 2000) the president of Bolivia changed three times and there were at least six ministers for sustainable development. At the municipal level the change of the head of the UFM of Riberalta aggravated the conflict between the *barraquero* and the ASL, as the new authority furnished the *barraca* holder with an establishment certificate for the area previously declared ARFM by the municipality.

A second decisive group in the development of conflicts was the social organisations conformed by peasant federations, indigenous unions or producer associations whose main working goal in almost all cases was to fight in favour of the demands of their members in relation to forest access. Often a working symbiosis was established between social organisations and NGOs, where the peasant federations receiving the support of 80% of the interviewed NGOs (n=11) were the organisations most helped, followed by the indigenous unions, receiving the support of 50% of the NGOs and finally the producer associations (20%). The second case study revealed that the Indigenous Union - NGO 'symbiosis' was fundamental in determining the outcome of conflict in favour of the rural community.

Lastly, the reforms served as an incentive for the establishment of new regional sawmills. It was estimated that 25% of the sawmills active at the time of writing were set up after 2000.[302] Their presence was due to the flexibility of the rules for FMP execution on private settlements and the increased area of the rural communities. Their interest in timber use led them to sign agreements with the right-holders, as was demonstrated in two of the three case studies, and ultimately led to conflict (first and third case study).

Much of the behaviour demonstrated by the various interest groups could be explained by rent-seeking, where the most influential groups received rents, not necessarily in cash, for a certain political intervention that favoured certain individuals at the expense of the rights of others. Thus, the 'rent seekers' were the public agents and politicians whose unpredictable and contradictory behaviour were the result of the subjective lack of will to fulfil their tasks appropriately. They were not necessarily committed to reducing social uncertainty or improving legal security. The prevailing public functioned, most often, to their own benefit or the benefit of the social elites above those who should really have been the source of their interests.[303] Not only the Public agents were 'rent seekers', however. They included almost all the social groups with any kind of power in the forest sector, for instance, local actors, including all forest users, and timber and Brazil nut entrepreneurs who bribed the public authorities in return for benefits under the enacted institutions. Without bribes many local actors would not have been awarded their claims, or at least not at that time, or in that form or precise way.[304] At the local level, 'rent seekers' are all those peasants, indigenous people, concessionaires and *barraca* holders who sought to obtain large forest areas at their neighbours' expense and resorted to relationships in the upper spheres of administration or social representation. 'Rent seekers' also included the entrepreneurs (sawmills) who encouraged the forest users 'to comply with the law', falsifying, lying or hiding information at the moment of the approval of legal instruments. The list of 'rent seeker' groups continued at regional level, incorporating the social organisations and mainly the NGOs that 'advised' or pressurised the governments to change the regulations so that they might benefit from the

302 Fundación José Manuel Pando 2002.

303 Cf PRITZL 2000:90.

304 Cf PRITZL 2000:117.

resulting institutions. This situation occurred mainly when the governments were unable to respond the social demands or did not enjoy enough social or political support.

History of the social relationships

While rent-seeking was a factor of the analysis of the conflicts from a political perspective, the reasons for many of the conflicts also lay in the histories of the social relationships between forest users dating back to the rubber era. At that time, the *patrón* controlled the rights, privileges and even the private lives of the individuals who served him.[305]

To ignore the history of the social relationships would mean to ignore the history of many of the current conflicts. The three case studies revealed historical social relationships, characterised by asymmetrical power relationships in favour of the social elite. The first case study illustrated the desire of the *barraca* residents to prevent the *patrón* gaining control over the forests. When the *fregueces* achieved their independence and obtained rights to land, the *barraquero*'s traditional tenure was called into question, reducing the scope of his interests, mainly in relation to timber use. The conflict between the peasant community and the forest concessionaire (third case) may have had its origins in the imprecisely defined borders of the settlements in the early eighties. Then the supremacy of the individual landowner group could explain their prolific expansion over the areas occupied by the community group. In this situation the reforms may have been the instrument instigating the conflicts, insofar as the peasants received the support of the state in the defence of their traditional rights. Nevertheless, the second case study, which involved the confrontation of the 'private landowner' with the indigenous communities, better reflected not only the tense historical relationships between both users, but also the rebelliousness assumed by the old *fregueces* formerly subjugated by the *patrones*. Similar to the behaviour adopted by the subjugated classes during the Spanish colonisation, when many of the institutions were enacted in the faraway Europe, the *barraca* residents had no other alternative than "*to accept the institutions imposed upon them, but not to comply with them*".[306]

With the reforms the protagonists received other labels, the *patrón* became a 'private landowner' and the *fregueces* became 'indigenous'. Nevertheless, the objectives of the conflicts remained the same: the control of the forests and the suppression of the opposition. Therefore, depriving the *patrón* of his land and dominating the infrastructure of the property could be viewed as one of the main objectives of the indigenous, and the actual occupation of the lands one of the main achievements of the conflict.

Escalation of the conflicts in the northern Bolivian Amazon

Being well aware of my academic limitations as a social scientist and at the risk of making a mistake, in this section I will present the conflict escalation model applied to the study

305 GAMARRA 1992:131.

306 Cf PRITZL 2000:83.

area.[307] I will begin the discussion citing JUAN PABLO LEDERACH, one of the most important Latin American academics in this field.

> *"Conflict is an academic term. In the daily language of Latin America this word is associated with a warlike confrontation."*[308]

This statement prompts one to expect a certain cultural difference in the handling of conflicts. In western culture, through the influence of the media, each political or social disagreement tends to be presented as a great dispute (BECK & SCHWARZ 1995:13f). In the daily language of the northern Bolivian Amazon, the local population expressed their different interests using synonyms such as '*pleitos*' (litigation), '*malentendidos*' (misunderstandings), '*lios*' (mess) and '*chiveríos*' (trouble).

The first problem arose in the application of the theoretical model developed by GLASL (1999), mainly with respect to the first stages (1-2). At this point of a conflict the parties tended to avoid any reference to the existence of problems with their opponents, developing certain almost hidden forms of behaviour, which made the exposure of the existence of conflicts difficult. These statements were based on primary data collected during the field study, where more than 80% of the interviewees (n=164) answered 'no' to the existence of conflicts, and 'yes' to the existence of '*malentendidos*' in relation to forest use. The refusal to recognise the existence of conflicts could be explained by the following factors in the case study area:

- Through rebuffing the existence of conflicts, the regional elites were able to oppress the rural population's opinion and to subordinate themselves to the imposed institutional system;
- The lack of experience and the faulty development of traditional mechanisms to manage or regulate conflicts had a negative impact upon the social environment, and ultimately eroded trust between the opposing groups;
- The distrust of the state authorities and especially the national legal system, the procedures of which were rarely transparent and were an inadequate means of facilitating the resolution of conflict[309]
- The intimate interdependence of the forest users, also referred to as '*traditional clientelism*',[310] whereby the client submitted to the *patrón*'s decisions and he to the support of his 'clients'. In many cases this resulted in ongoing common benefits, which led to a kind of 'path dependence' in the socio-economic relationships of both contenders.

---

307 The model presented for the study area was based on the analysis of the three case studies complemented by the participation in three further conflicts involving indigenous groups, partly as spectator and partly as mediator (for more information see chapter 3), as well as interviews with the 164 forest users.

308 Cf. LEDERACH 1992:23.

309 According to PRITZL (2000:85) the judicial power in many Latin American countries is limited to the conferral of a cloak of legality to the political and bureaucratic instruments, and consequently the citizenry considers it corrupt, inefficient and subject to manipulation by the political elites.

310 For more information see chapter 1.

The conflict escalation model adapted to the northern Bolivian Amazon recognised eight levels, divided into three stages (see figure 34). Not all stages were symmetrical in terms of the number of levels. The longest lasting stage was the second, at which point the parties invested more time and resources in solving their differences. Between levels, the possibility of the conflict escalating was smaller than between stages. A conflict does not necessarily increase in a single step from one level to another, but rather when the threshold between two stages is passed.

Figure 34 Conflict escalation in forest use in the northern Bolivian Amazon

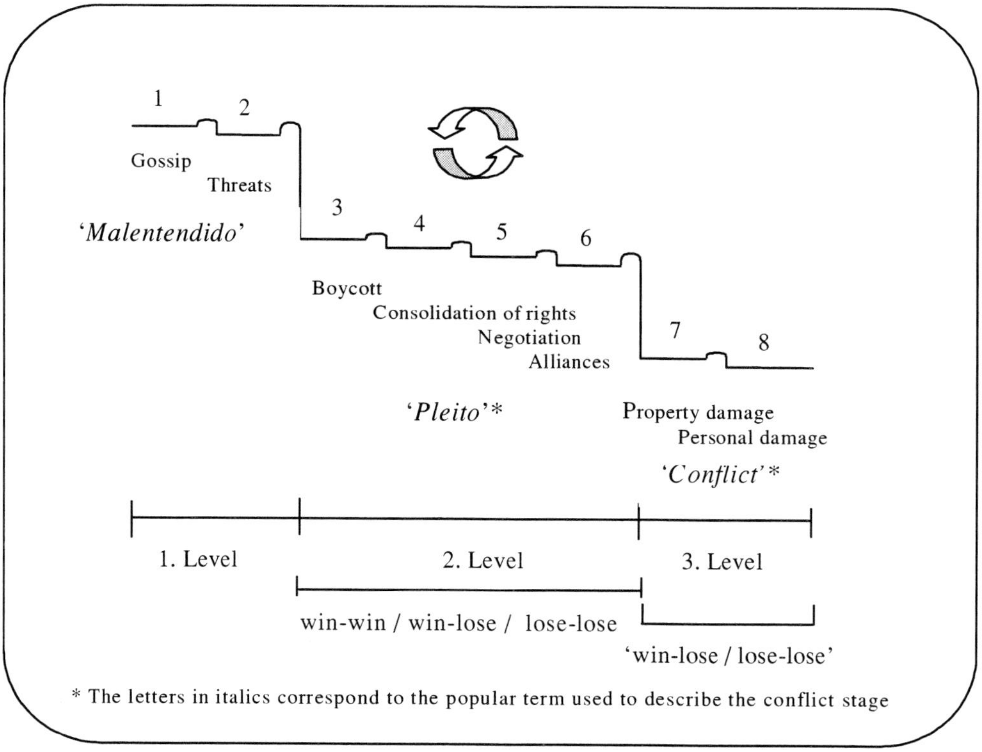

Source: Based on own field study interviews

First stage

The most appropriate popular term used to describe the first stage of conflict was 'misunderstanding' or 'disagreement', made up by two levels: rumour, commonly referred to as 'gossip', and threats. Both elements were 'traditional weapons' to which the competitors resorted, and despite them representing an increase in the nuisances and the social tensions, their practice did not imply greater transaction costs in relation to other levels. The emergence of gossip meant a hardening of the position between parties. Therefore, its identification by the researcher served as an indication of the existence of tense relationships between individuals. According to the 'temperature' of the protagonists, the threats (second level) were made in the form of offence, verbal insults, escalating to the point of oaths threatening the eradication of the opposition. The objective was to establish one's own power and to intimidate the opposition.

In GLASL's model, gossip and threats arose in the second stage, more specifically at the fourth and sixth levels, respectively. However, in the study area both elements arose at the beginning of the disputes, seemingly due to the lingering oral culture of the population and the low costs represented for the protagonists. Neither the gossip nor the moderate threats necessarily erode the social relationships. On the contrary, they functioned as pressure valves, easing the social tension accumulated between the participants, making dialogue or the initiation of negotiations a possibility. Due to the oral culture in the study region, both levels often accompanied the development of the conflict until the end of the second stage. In the first stage one can hardly speak of winners or losers, because the parties did not risk much. According to the protagonists it is a preliminary stage to the negotiations and debates, which require the investment of greater resources, or where the ownership of the goods at issue is usually decided.

Second stage

The boycott level may be viewed as the initial step of the second stage, where the individuals demonstrated a more open acceptance of the conflict situation when trying to impede, in different ways, the development of the opponent's activities. The boycott was manifested in different ways, sometimes through the seizure of materials and workers, other times through the blockade of the production areas, presenting demands to the regional authorities seeking to paralyse the granting of rights, etc. One of the main characteristics of this stage was that the order of its levels was not significant. Despite the fact that the boycott was distinguished in many conflicts as the first level, the possibility could not be discarded that other conflicts began with bargaining, the formation of alliances or with the quest to consolidate rights.

Another characteristic of this stage was its amplitude. Many parties invested a lot of time in consolidating their rights or in negotiating with the opponents. Therefore, it was often possible that the four levels ran in parallel. In the quest to consolidate rights alliances were formed, and at the same time boycotts and bargaining took place.

The '*pleito*' and/or '*chiverío*' were the most appropriate terms to describe the popular interpretations of this stage of a conflict. They provided an image of confusion, dispute, mess and disorderly conduct to which the protagonists should submit. It was observed that from this point the individuals were increasingly interested in reaching an agreement to solve their differences, made evident by the investment of time, knowledge and other resources by the participants in order to strengthen their position. The case studies demonstrated that at this stage it was possible for both parties to win (third case study), to lose (first case study) or for one party to win and the other to lose (second case study). The winner/loser relationship made more sense if we analysed the inclination of the actors to cooperate or to compete from the development perspective of the three stages, just as GLASL's model suggests (1999).

Because this stage can be predominant in terms of its duration, contrary to the concept put forward by GLASL, I do not agree with his view that conflict escalation always ends with the destruction or fall of the social system. Many parties made an effort to remain in conflict, at a 'bearable' level, in order to help them strengthen their position against their rival, and the rest of society as a whole. Therefore, the participation in conflicts can be considered a strategy, contributing to an increase in the bargaining power of the main actors, as was demonstrated in the second and third case studies.

Third stage

Violence, first in the form of property damage and later on as damage to the opponent's personal integrity, was not always employed by the groups as a means to solve their differences. According to the interviewees, the use of the seventh and eighth levels indicated a real conflict situation, so that the most appropriate popular term for this phase was 'conflict'. An analysis of the popular sentence, "*Our land is so noble that there is enough land for all...*", may lead one to the conclusion that violence was, to a given extent, restricted due to the low dimension of the conflicts, developed in a context characterised by low population pressure and large areas of forest.

The parties did not necessarily fight over the shortage of resources. In most of the conflicts analysed, the interviewees declared that they had not reached the seventh level. However, the possibility of encountering conflicts in the third stage of development was not discarded, principally in the Manuripi protected area and the municipality of Ixiamas.[311] Due to the low intensity of the disputes, the conflict situations could yet end as 'win-lose' situations at this stage, and only in some extreme cases as 'lose-lose'.

The outcomes of the conflicts were strongly influenced by the intensity of the confrontations and the degree of social interaction between the main actors. Conflicts with strong *clientelismo* relationships were often less violent than the conflicts between independent parties.

The protagonists' conflict strategies

The strategies employed by the conflicting parties in the three case studies are presented in table 31.

[311] During the field phase a series of violent conflicts was reported, for example, between peasants and *barraqueros* in the protected area, where the production infrastructure and private goods were destroyed. Other cases of violence were reported between *barraqueros* and the indigenous support groups, where according to CEJIS data (2003), between 1996 and 2003 14 people including indigenous people, NGO advisers and leaders of the Indigenous Union were attacked. It is also known that illegal timber activity produced a few victims, mainly during the Forest Law adjustment process in the region.

Table 31 Strategies used by the protagonists in conflict

Parties / **Strategies**	**ASL**	***Barraca* holder**	**Indigenous comm.**	**Private landowner**	**Peasant comm.**	**Concessio naire**
Effort to fulfil the law						
Change of legal status	*Motosierris-tas* → ASL members	*Barraquero* → landowner → peasant	*Fregueces*→ peasants → indigenous	*Barraquero*→ landowner		*Barraquero* → conce-ssionnaire
Interest to enforce of legal instruments						
Use of contacts at political level						
Communication breakdown						
Formation of coalitions with	NGO	Sawmill	NGO and indig. union			
Compliance with other standards						Certification
Agreements with the opponents						
Snubbing of signed agreements						
Boycott of activities of opponents						
Use of emotional rhetoric						
Illegal logging in litigation area						
Seizure of posse-ssions and/or kidnapping of the opponent						
Public questioning of anomalous handling on the part of the authorities						
Tendency to cooperate						

Source: Based on field study interviews and on SCHNEIDER (2002).

Level of importance in table 31

High
Medium
Low

The environment of the conflict situations examined was characterised by the asymmetry of information and rights. Upon comparison of the six protagonist groups one can conclude that all were making an effort to improve their legal security through compliance with the law.

Most of the protagonists (5 out of 6) resorted to changing their legal status and only the most privileged, like the regional entrepreneurs, maintained close relationships with the government authorities, be it through formal or informal channels. These are the most successful rent-seeking strategies, as the forest users are able to capture more public resources, favouring their own interests. The formation of coalitions was not a strategy commonly used by the protagonists. Of the six groups examined, the example of the indigenous community was the most successful, where the alliance formed with the NGO and the Indigenous Union were fundamental to access to the resources. This case was representative for the other indigenous communities whose area of influence was the city of Riberalta. The indigenous representatives took advantage of the available contacts and the experience of both support organisations. The case study with the fewest alliances was the third, where the rural community worked 'alone'. Or rather, it resorted sporadically to external support, according to the needs of its members. Insofar as the formation of alliances was important to reinforce the position of the protagonists, to compensate for this situation the peasants resorted to the use of other means of pressure, like boycotting the regular activities of their opponents, the use of emotional rhetoric to raise public awareness of the activities of the regional authorities, the illegal use of the resources, etc. These results coincided partly with the strategies observed by SCHNEIDER (2002) and the situation of the mine workers in Venezuela, who resorted to the use of unconventional strategies to weaken their opponents, such as emotional rhetoric, espionage, robberies, sabotage, etc. The formation of alliances depended on two aspects: the first was the influence that each party had to overturn the results in its favour; the less influence a party had, the greater the possibility of finding allies to strengthen its position. The second was the actual means of solving the conflicts.

The individual groups resorted to forming closer alliances with people close to the protagonist. Whereas the indigenous communities cooperated with the Catholic Church, NGOs, human rights groups and their social unions, the individual groups were often strengthened internally by the presence of technical and legal advisers belonging to the family or hired for the purpose of exercising these functions.

A similarity was observed between the strategies executed by the indigenous and the rural populations, mainly in the use of the non-conventional weapons (last third of table 31) and in their efforts to comply with the law. Finally, the use of strategies had a direct relationship with the outcome of the conflicts. In general, the parties that implemented a diversified strategy were able to consolidate more than 60% of their expectations and were consequently considered winners in this study.

Relating the outcomes of the tree case studies (see table 28) with the strategies executed by the parties (see table 31), whether an actor becomes a winner or a loser depends on the following aspects:

- the capacity to adapt to the contents of the reforms and international requirements (forest certification). One of the most polemic, but at the same time effective strategies in this respect, was the change of legal status.
- the diversity of the strategy, not restricted to the use of only one instrument, but using several alternatives, depending on the development stage of the conflict. For example, the initially employed violent actions, such as boycotts of the activities of the concessionaire, the seizure of materials, public questioning of the work of public agents, yet at the same time maintaining dialogue and a willingness to cooperate with the opponent.
- the technical and moral support received by the allies, as demonstrated by the indigenous community in the second case study.

Another important strategy at regional level, distinguishing winning from losing, was the capacity to reconcile sector interests with the national legislation. During the research the most efficient groups were the peasants and the indigenous, which pressurised the public agents, defended their rights and prevented the opposing groups (*barraca* holders and forest entrepreneurs) from exploiting institutions favouring their position.

Cooperation in conflict situations

On the basis of the empirical findings presented in this study, a widening of the definition of conflict is proposed to include not only competition but also the alternative of cooperation between conflicting parties. Such ideas are not new in the social sciences (see COSER, WEBER, SIMMEL, LEDERACH) but differs from the logical point of view, which would suggest that actors with incompatible interests are unable to cooperate. Here a paradox emerges in the interaction between the opponents, who must cooperate to achieve their goals. That is to say that cooperation in conflicts may be understood as a strategic behaviour on the part of the parties in order to maximise their benefits.[312]

If the conflict is considered a competition situation, we should accept that cooperation in certain circumstances is restricted. However, in each conflict cooperation, as little as it may be, is an important factor, since without it, the risk of the destruction of the social system is much greater. The most important thing is then to recognise that cooperation in certain circumstances does not necessarily acquire the conventional forms. In conflict situations cooperation is expressed in the parties maintaining communication, in the inclination toward negotiation, in not adopting uncompromising positions, etc. In the case of this study, the widespread *clientelismo* relationship between the social casts engendered cooperation. The wide social, economic and political dependence between the *patrón* and the client forced these groups to cooperate, even increasing the social tensions. Thus, the *clientelistelim* relationship constituted a kind of path dependence for both groups, at least during the period

312 According to AULINGER (1996:30, cited in SEINTSCH 2004:127), cooperation situations are, "[...] *situations where each of the participants reaches his objectives as much as the others.*"

of legal transition and while the actors were not aware of other alternatives. The bias of the protagonists towards cooperation also increased, especially in peripheral regions, when:

- there was great uncertainty over the actor's legal entitlement to the desired forest utilisation rights;
- there was little state support in the solving of conflicts, and when the public mechanisms put in place to manage conflicts were inefficient (poor sanction mechanisms, corruption justice system);
- the costs of negotiation were high.

The three case studies varied in terms of the cooperation and competition levels. The most extreme cases were represented by the second and third case. While in the second case the opponents decided to compete openly for the occupation of the forest, in the third case greater attempts at collaboration in order to solve their differences were observed between both groups. Neither protagonist broke off the dialogue, they tried to negotiate their differences, and they demonstrated an ability to work together in other environments not related to the conflict. In the third case, the inclination to collaborate may have been influenced by the following factors: both protagonists valued the relationship with the opponent; competition over the resources was not significant in the context of their overall expectations and the balance of power was more or less even, both parties could draw upon institutions supporting their claims.

The inclination to cooperate was decisive in achieving the desired results. Whereas the second case was a typical 'win-lose' conflict, the third was identified as a 'win-win' conflict.

Cooperation should also be analysed in relation to the balance of power between opponents. In conflicts with asymmetric relationships, the party with the greatest influence tended to push out or eliminate the rival, without considering the possible cooperation alternatives seriously. In conflict situations competitive behaviour was accentuated in the individuals more readily than cooperative behaviour. Cooperation often served as a 'double edged sword' to weaken a rival's position, for example when one proceeded to sign 'temporary agreements'[313] that were not necessarily enforced and the objective of which was to increase the costs of the opponent's transactions, a situation that could mean his financial downfall in many cases and in consequence the definite abandonment of his rights.

Functions of social conflicts

The enforcement of reforms is not possible without the emergence of social conflicts, above all in peripheral regions where the traditional elites have taken charge of distributing arbitrarily the tenure of land and forest. Nowadays, they are forced to submit to other rules that do not necessarily correspond to their interests. Social conflicts can favour or impede the reforms enforcement according to the circumstances. This characteristic obeys the well-

313 'Temporary agreements' in conflict situations were often agreements reached between the protagonists to strengthen their own position temporarily, but were subsequently broken, mainly by those groups with the greater legal backing (for a more detailed explanation see section 7.3.1).

known dichotomy attributed to the conflicts that represents both functionality and dysfunctionality in a social system (BONACKER & IMBUSCH 1996:71).[314]

Similar to the ideas developed in social sciences, in the institutional sphere one also sees the characteristic of dysfunctional and functional dichotomy in relation to the law enforcement. Conflict is considered a nuisance or interference in the reforms enforcement, when through it, the recipients refuse to comply with the laws, and in the worst cases, when they resort to replacing the public institutions by other private institutional arrangements, enjoying greater recognition and enforcement. In the study area institutional dysfunctionality caused by conflicts was more common prior to the reforms, where the individual landholders exercised enough pressure through their private institutions, which prevented the rural communities from imposing their officially recognised right.

In the dysfunctional dimension, the conflicts overturn the principles of the reforms and they diminish its genuineness. The institutional dysfunctionality caused by the conflicts is directly related to three aspects: 1) the magnitude of the violence of the conflicts; 2) the degree of power and the available alternatives of the (legally) excluded groups; and 3) the available social and state enforcement mechanisms for conflict resolution.

Interpreting GLASL's model of the escalation of conflicts (1999), violence in conflicts increases the institutional dysfunction, since the affected individuals' trust in the enforcement of private or public arrangements, and because the individuals tend to radicalise their positions without any regard for the institutions, as was occasionally found in the study area. Therefore, the greater the power of the affected groups, the greater the threat to the law enforcement. Power makes it possible for the affected individuals to ignore or to adapt the public institutions, sometimes replacing the reforms with imposed institutional agreements.

The strategies employed by those affected influence institutional functionality. For example, in rent-seeking cultures, where a high frequency of rent-seeking could devalue the importance attributed to all of the population complying with the law. Lastly, the institutional function is affected when the state institutions cause conflicts without being able to provide the tools or necessary enforcement mechanisms to resolve them. The creation of the 'Reconciliation, Arbitration and Conflict Resolution Commission' in Decree 27572 could represent an important advance in reducing institutional dysfunctionality, provided the regional interest groups are interested in conflict resolution, or simply accept this mechanism.

Social functionality[315] is intimately related to the functionality in the institutional sphere. Conflicts are also credited with the function of propelling institutional change. The recognition of conflict as an agent of change is summed up in the paradox: "*conflicts, crisis, confrontations, etc. lead to social*

---

[314] Two perspectives attributed to the conflicts that predominate particularly in conservative societies evaluate the functions of social conflicts solely from a negative point of view. On the one hand, conflict represents a phenomenon or pathological event that threatens the social order and that must, therefore, be fought. On the other hand, conflict is a negative element because it represents an 'irritating' deviation from an ideal condition (BONACKER & IMBUSCH 1996:71f).

[315] "*The conflict as instigator of social changes*" (COSER, SIMMEL, MARX and ENGELS, cited in BONACKER & IMBUSCH 1996:72) stresses the functionality in the social sphere.

order, consent, integration of the system and freedom" (BONACKER & IMBUSCH 1996:72). In the northern Bolivian Amazon, the elitist groups have been aware of the functionality of the conflicts to conserve their dominion in the system; they have always been concerned with oppressing and denying the existence of social dispute in their relationships with the other groups. The introduction of reforms in peripheral regions must cause conflicts for their enforcement to succeed; the new laws would not have fitted in without the removal of the traditional institutions; the territorial expansion of the communal groups would not have been possible without 'taking' the lands from the forest entrepreneurs and *barraca* holders.

At national level, the conflicts have also served to reinforce the position and strategies of the peasants and indigenous demanding from the state the incorporation of their claims over land in the public institutions. At local actor level, the conflicts mean winning important areas in the social and political dimensions, especially for many community leaders who through conflict are being integrated in the technical spheres and making political decisions, and in some cases taking jobs that improve their overall living conditions. In this context, the inhabitants of the rural areas are learning how to coexist with the conflicts. Although this means an increase of their emotional load, not all the people are interested in an immediate solution, mainly those that have been able to improve their own social and economic situations. This increase in the bargaining power of the community groups must be considered in relation to the past. It does not mean the write-off of the power of the *barraca* holders or forest entrepreneurs; their power is still confirmed through the exercise of private institutions forcing the peasants and indigenous people to use their community area only under established economic conditions.

About the variability of the property regimes

The eleven characteristics distinguishing resource tenure between protagonists, were useful tools to detect overlaps between the rights in conflict. At the same time, the characteristics are an effective means to identify the variability of property regimes found in reality. In other words, the four property regimes over natural capital proposed by BROMLEY (1991) are not enough to describe the different tenure types in the study area. In other words, the four property regimes over natural capital proposed by BROMLEY (1991) are not enough to describe the different tenure types in the study area.

For instance, a regime ignored in the typology by BROMLEY (1991) is the 'traditional property', which is important in a region such as the northern Bolivian Amazon where there is little state influence. Although the attributes of 'traditional property' can be similar to 'private' or even 'common' properties, the difference lies in the enforcement mechanisms applied by social control. The distinction of 'traditional property' helps also to identify other typical regimes in the study area that usually originated from a mixture of private and public tenures. Even in the more formal tenures (private landowner, forest concessions, ASLs, and rural communities) the 'traditional property' strongly influences the resource use.

This situation is even clearer in the extractivist activities, where the characteristics were mainly regulated by private institutions. In order to show the variability of property regimes found in the field study, three tenure types in communal regimes are presented (see figure 35).

Figure 35 Types of tenure regimes in rural communities

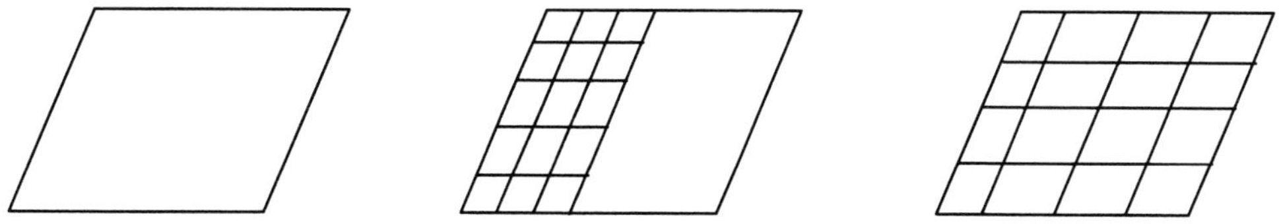

1) Collective community 2) Mixed community 3) Individual community

1) Collective community model: Basically all the existing resources belong to each member of the community. This was common in the indigenous communities (*Esse ejjas, Machineris, Yaminahuas* and *Pacahuaras*), but also in recently formed peasant communities and in peasant communities where there was a strong relationship between the members. This model also applied to the *Yaminahua-Machineri* TCO. The rules were flexible and the members could use the resources at their discretion. The community authorities usually governed the use of the commercial timber. The *chacos* were generally located around the house and each individual could have any space necessary to establish one. This model was more common in the department of Pando than in Vaca Diez. The leniency of the rules provided good conditions for 'free-loaders' or individuals who took greater advantage of the community goods than others. Nevertheless, this model allowed the individuals to develop their activities in the production sector, providing the family greater advantages and preferences.

2) Mixed community model: Each family is assigned the exclusive use of land through the distribution of plots, generally between 50 and 100 hectares, while the forest is managed in a combined way. This model was efficient in terms of planning the community's productive areas, according to the forest or agrarian nature of the resources. It was frequently observed in intermediate communities, founded before the rubber crash and could be found across the whole region. A variation of this model provided for the distribution to each family of productive areas inside the community forest, as was observed in the indigenous community featured in the second case study. Generally, the size of the plots and the associated resources were not all equal.

3) Individual community model: Each family is assigned a plot excluding other community members from the land and the forests on it. This alternative was found in old communities, mainly on the borders of the central highway and was frequent in Vaca Diez. In theory, this model is the one that presents fewest externalities, because each member knew what goods corresponded to him and was willing to exercise greater control over the utilisation of the resources. Asymmetries were also observed in relation to the size of the plots and the number of plots distributed to each family member. This model is practised in the peasant community featured in the third case study.

In the three models, the assignment units of the resources may vary. On the one hand they were open to the influence of the reforms, with the resources distributed in hectares, or in the case of the extractivist communities or *barracas in transition*, the distribution units were often still be *cajas* or *barricas*, distributed according to the *centros*. Given the importance of the extraction of NTFPs, the traditional units influenced the distribution of the resources strongly. Even in the 'individual community' model, the size of the plots assigned to each family may maintain a direct relationship with the production of the *centros*, where the most influential families accessed the most productive sites. The apparent physical delimitation shown in figure 35 does not represent the real situation. The utilised areas were generally continuous, and it was unusual to find demarcations dividing the community plots inside the communities. The same occurred with the external demarcations of all of the rural settlements, which were defined only on maps. However, with the *saneamiento* enforcement, there was an advance in the physical demarcation of the land, frequently in those places with greater numbers of disputes. Variability in individual regimes is more complicated, since it depends on the size and its geographical location of the settlement. While agricultural and cattle settlements, commonly located close to urban centres, are influenced more by models proposed in the reforms, extractivist settlements retain *barraca* characteristics. However, as presented in tables 25 and 26, even the extractivist settlements vary in their features depending on their legal status.

7 Discussion and conclusions

"The success of the purposes of the reform varies considerably
depending on the informal restrictions that prevail.
However, the most decisive thing for success is the rent-seeking environment."
(FISCHER 2004:563 adapted from DOUGLAS NORTH)

7.1 Introduction

Several Bolivian analysts agree that the reforms have contributed to modernising the public administration and to the sustained management of the natural resources. They also agree on the political and social efforts carried out by the state to implement laws consistent with international policies, thus transforming Bolivia into one of the model countries of the American continent in terms of issues such as decentralisation and resource conservation.[316]

However, after almost ten years of the reforms, the main criticism is centred on the fact that they have not changed the Bolivian reality. There continues to be an unequal distribution of resources. The public administration is still unable to control the allocation of the resources; year after year the state incomes derived from forest taxes decrease; illegal logging continues to affect the sustainability of the forests; many traditional users have not been able to formalise their rights; etc. Added to this is the slow enforcement of many aspects of the reforms, as for example the *saneamiento* process, which four years after its initiation has been successfully concluded in only one of the ten polygons making up Pando (Municipality of Bolpebra).[317] In other aspects, the reform enforcement has exceeded the expectations even of the state entities in charge, for example in the approval of management plans for private properties.

The example of the study area is important to demonstrate how big the breach between the enforcement progress and the legal challenges yet to be overcome still is. The aim of this chapter is to draw up a balance on the reform enforcement, based on empirical results and the interpretation of available technical documents (see section 7.2). Subsequently, conclusions will be discussed with reference to the two main theoretical elements presented in chapter 2: rent-seeking and the functions of the institutions (see section 7.3).

316 PAVEZ & BOJANIC 1998; ANTELO 2000; CRESPO 2000; PACHECO 2000; CONTRERAS & VARGAS 2001; BOSCOLO & VARGAS 2001; HERNÁIZ & PACHECO 2001.

317 According to official plans, the *saneamiento* in the region should have been concluded after no more than two years.

7.2 The reform enforcement: Balance a decade after approval

This section is based on the available publications, basically describing the enforcement of the laws at national level, such as the works by ANDERSSON (2004), BOSCOLO & VARGAS (2001), CONTRERAS & VARGAS (2001), FUNDACIÓN JOSÉ MANUEL PANDO (2002), HERNÁIZ & PACHECO (2001), NITTLER (1999; 2000), STOIAN (2000), BOJANIC (2001), PACHECO (2000; 2002), PAVEZ & BOJANIC (2002) and PRISMA (2000; 2001). Several reports published by the CDF, SIF, INRA and Ministry of Sustainable Development are also reviewed, presenting statistical data for the last ten years, pertaining to the reform enforcement from the perspective of the public agents.

All of the secondary information reviewed represents the more important publications from Bolivia discussing the enforcement of the agrarian and forest legislation. However, the majority of these documents have been developed according to either technical or political criteria, not necessarily scientific, to satisfy both the requirements of the Bolivian public administration and certain international organisations (USAID, CIFOR, BOLFOR, FAO, etc.). In addition, the results of field interviews are also taken into consideration, although they were not originally designed to accommodate the wide analysis spectrum presented here (administrative, economic, environmental and social). The field study concentrated on the collection of data mainly in relation to the administrative and the social issues. However, the intention behind the addition of an economic and environmental dimension is to present a broad evaluation of the reform enforcement, as the objectives are rooted in the development of a comprehensive national sustainable development policy. Additionally, within the confines of the limitations referred to, the purpose of this section is also to compare the impact of the reforms in the context of each of the four dimensions and to establish projections for the near future.

Arguments outlining both the positives and the negatives of the laws enforcement are presented; and consequences for the study area derived from the available publications, and also to a large extent on the basis of personal observations made during the field study. The formulation of the reform objectives (see table 32) are interpreted in relation to the main stated principles and impacts of the agrarian and forest legislation (including laws and decrees). Note that the conclusions concentrate on the evaluation of the nine objectives highlighted in figure 2.

Given the importance of administrative dimension in the overall context of the reforms and in the context of this study, the relevant analysis will be presented based on four indicators. The availability of primary and secondary sources of information facilitated the analysis of the administrative dimension of the reforms using the selected indicators.

Table 32 The reforms in the northern Bolivian Amazon: selected objectives and evaluation parameters

Dimension	Selected objective	Regulatory instruments	Indicators
Administrative	- Decentralization of the administrative management of the natural resources - Transparency in the assignation of tenure	- Public organisations with new attributes - Forest concessions - Land titling - Public audiences and management reports to the National Congress	- The number of public authorities with new attributes - Administrative coordination - Transparent assignment of rights - Public audience at regional and national level of the SIF
Economic	- To facilitate the local population's access to use of the resources - To improve government finance through the forest taxes	- New agrarian and forest ownership classes - Obligation to pay forest taxes and redistribution of the income to regional and local organisations	- Tenure characteristics in the laws studied - Distribution of benefit among the principal regional actors - Annual incomes of the regional organisations (municipalities and prefecture of Pando)
Environmental	- To promote a sustainable non-selective use of the forests - Protection and conservation of the natural resources	- Forest management plans - Establishment of the agrarian and forest FES	- Management plans approved by the administration - Control of stocks and forest operations implemented - Criteria for the enforcement of the agrarian and forest FES
Social	- To put an end to inequalities in land tenure and use of forests - To integrate the traditional users in the legal use of the forest - To reduce the incidence of conflicts arising from land distribution	- New classes of forest right - Bond between agrarian and forest rights - Recognition of rights of the traditional users to the Amazon forest - Creation of the 'Reconciliation and Arbitration Commission'	- Area occupied by the forest entrepreneurs and the rural communities - Formal or informal status of the traditional user group - Incidence of conflicts between forest users

The economic dimension, on the other hand, due to the focus of the reforms on the use and distribution of the natural resources, as well as the lack of secondary information, is treated only narrowly and ambivalent. The indirect influence of Forest Law and Agrarian Law on important economic aspects and indicators, such as increased job creation, increased export values, household incomes, rural poverty, etc., had to be categorically excluded. An increase or decrease of such indicators is also directly related to other domestics laws (Economic development), international agreements, state policies and even depends on the price variations of forest products on international markets. On the other hand, the economic analysis includes the generation of public incomes, based on the payment of forest taxes, as a fiscal policy included in the reforms. However, as the use and employment of forest taxes are relevant for public organisations, its analysis could have been incorporated in the same way in the administrative dimension.

In spite of the importance of the environmental dimension for the northern Amazon region, this is the most difficult to analyse, because the reforms have not developed the tools necessary for the enforcement of the environmental objectives of the reforms. At the same time, it is also the aspect least studied, and therefore there is little secondary information. Again the indicators selected are closely related to the available information and are in direct relationship with the main public activities currently executed by the INRA and SIF.

Finally, in the social dimension, the selected indicators could only represent a small part of selected objectives. The available data show only the legal enforcement at regional level, ignoring other important indicators at local level, such as the distribution of forest inside rural communities; aspects which may lead one to arrive at quite different conclusions.

In addition to the four dimensions, it is also necessary to consider time as an important factor of the enforcement. After a decade of the reforms, establishing a state presence has proved easier than contributing to the economic development of the regions or to improving the sustainability of forest use.

7.2.1 Administrative dimension

The administrative dimension includes all those tasks that guide the work of the public agents in enforcing the reforms; these tasks range from state representation, the formulation of policy, design of institutions, administrative coordination, technical advice, assignment of property rights to control over the natural resources.

The Law of Popular Participation is considered the most important institution of the whole public administration system, as it details the new governance concept: a bottom up administrative process, where the role of local government (municipalities) stands out, accompanied by other instances of social control (municipal unions, so called *Mancomunidades*, OTBs and vigilance committees).

Success of and progress in the reform enforcement

One of the biggest successes credited to the reforms in the study area is the achievement of a greater state presence, for example, with the establishment of new public organisations in charge of forest administration. There has been an increase in the number of authorities and public agents, but also of the responsibilities and functions that they exercise at local level. Although in some cases this could lead to the poor coordination of activities, at least the control over forest use has improved in relation to the past. The control functions previously delegated to two regional authorities (CDF Regional Direction Pando and CDF Sub-regional Direction Riberalta), are now exercised through 19 local authorities, established by the SIF itself (Operative Forest Units - UOB), and by the Municipal Forest Units UFM of the local governments (see figure 36).[318]

Figure 36 Institutional changes in the public authorities of the forest sector

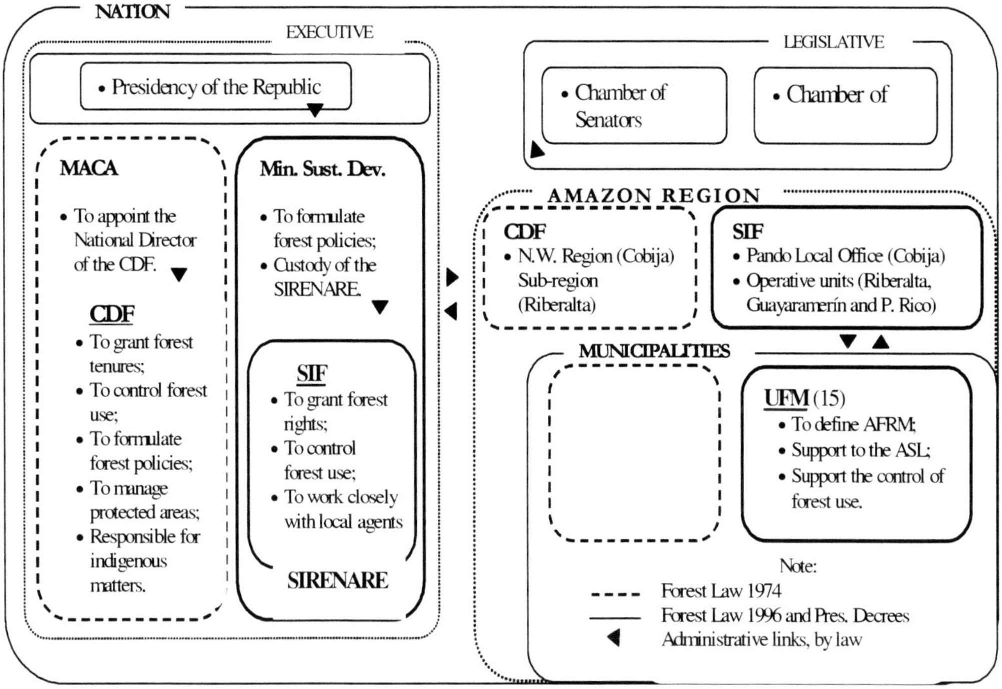

Source: Based on Forest Law (1974); Forest Law (1996); Decree 25158 and Decree 25956.

Not only were the tasks of the CDF in relation to the forest sector reassigned to three different national authorities,[319] but new public agents have also come into play, such as the municipalities and the prefectures that acquired responsibilities in the area of forest use, thus becoming protagonists of the new regime enforcement (PACHECO 2002a). Especially the establishment of the municipal governments, as local organisations near to the forest users, has accelerated the enforcement of the reforms at forest level. This topic is important in the region, given its territorial dimension and the poorly developed communication infrastructures.

[318] On the basis of field study interviews with 12 responsible municipalities and at least five regional people in charge of the SIF and INRA.

[319] The CDF was in charge of many technical and political issues, not only in the forest sector but also in the management of protected areas and in indigenous matters (see figure 36). With Law 1700, the responsibility for the development of forest policy was given to the Ministry of Sustainable Development, the control and inspection of the resources to the SIF and the National Forest Development Fund (FONABOSQUE) was placed in charge of forest conservation.

In fact, the incorporation of municipal governments in the control of the forests is one of the most lauded aspects of the Forest Law. They are also able to propose to the Ministry of Sustainable Development the delimitation of up to 20% of their total forest area, as well as establish ARFMs and offer technical support to the ASLs. According to ANDERSSON (2004), the municipal governments play an important role in facilitating the formal access of small forest users to timber use. This could become important in the region when all of the municipalities proceed to demarcate 20% of their state forests, meaning that 2 million hectares could become 'municipal forest areas' under the direct administration of the local governments.

The reforms have also contributed to reducing the political dependence between public organisations (SIF and INRA) and the national parties. Under the old regime, the head of the public forestry administration served at the discretion of the Minister, and the stability of the position and of his subordinates depended on the direction of uncertain political winds (CONTRERAS & VARGAS 2001:5). Since 1996 the President of the Republic names the forest superintendent based on a short list presented by the Congress, a position then held for six years (see figure 36). This more competitive process provides for the selection of personnel subject to technical and not purely political criteria, both at the decision-making and the technical level.

Additionally, the increased wages paid to such professionals, and a position of longer duration than that of the executive power (5 years), help to attract more qualified technical personnel, improving the technical advice provided to the forest users. At the same time, the new legislations increase the public's trust in the state services and the public organisations have greater prestige.[320]

The same aspects could be used to explain the progress in the administration of the agrarian sector. Here the reforms have also contributed to eliminating politics in the appointment of the technicians, to improve access to technical personnel for those requiring assistance, to provide technical advice to the public, to establish a greater state presence in the region, etc. The delegation of responsibilities to the municipal governments is the most pronounced difference between the two regimes: the INRA Law grants less responsibility to the municipal governments than the Forest Law.

There have also been changes with regard to the level of transparency in the assignment of rights. Under the previous regime, people with political influence were at a great advantage where the awarding of forest rights was concerned (CONTRERAS & VARGAS 2001:4; PACHECO 2002b).[321] Their direct relationships with the public decision-makers were enough to exclude the other users from all types of information and rights. At the same time the forest rights granted were not clear; for instance, a study carried out before the approval of the reforms cited the existence of at least three different forest felling rights covering one area. In

---

[320] According to the findings by NITTLER (1999), 69% of 88 interviewed forest users (concessionaries, land owners, TCO representatives, and public agents at local, regional and national level) declared that the SIF enjoys greater prestige than the earlier CDF organisation.

[321] For example, fifty enterprises managed 185 concessions on an area that comprised more than 22 million hectares, equivalent to 40% of the forests in Bolivia (CONTRERAS & VARGAS 2001:4).

the Choré region (Santa Cruz), not even the forest holders knew the exact extent of their possession (RUIZ 1996). This led to several overlaps, both with agrarian and forest tenures. The new forest concessions, based on area rather than volume, have the advantage that the social actors know more clearly the territorial extent of their tenures, on maps and on the ground. This also makes it possible for them to distinguish between the areas dedicated to commercial production and the protected areas dedicated to conservation, as well as the state lands. In short, the new system of concessions has not only improved government control, but it also encourages the social control over forest use, forcing the concessionaires to use only the forest areas granted them.

The transparency in public decision-making is also increased because the new system makes it possible for the forest users to access the documentation and information available in the SIF, participate in the annual public audiences or to submit claims directly to the regional forest agents (NITTLER 1999).

The reforms establish greater state control in the work of the public organisations. For instance, Article 22-II of the Forest Law forces the Superintendent to surrender accounts to the 'Controllership of the Republic' in a biannual report. This report details: the forest rights granted, the collection and the distribution of the forest taxes, the approval of management plans, the raw material supply, the inspections and forest audits, as well as other outstanding information on the real and effective enforcement of the forest legislation. The superintendent has to present the same information to the President of the Republic, in the form of an annual report from the forest administration, with a copy also presented to the National Congress. So far seven administration reports exist. The full reports are also open to the public, either through the annual publications of the SIF or by visiting their web page.[322]

The *saneamiento* has also increased transparency in the granting of agrarian rights in comparison to the Land Reform of 1953. The process of land distribution works under the execution of the FES, the criterion used to check the ownership of the properties and to evaluate the activities carried out (mainly agricultural, but also forestry or conservation).[323] The process is also structured in such a way that the INRA leaves the possibility open to the public to access the available information, in any of the *saneamiento* stages, as well as to hold local public audiences before the definitive granting of the ownership titles.

Failures of and challenges facing the reform enforcement

In spite of the advances experienced in the administrative dimension, one of the main impediments to the public institutions enforcement is the poor technical and financial capacity of the public organisations in relation to their responsibilities and the dimensions of the areas they control. Of all public agents, the prefectures (departmental administrations) are the authorities functioning least effectively. According to empirical findings, only two of the 15 regional and local public organisations (municipal governments, agencies of the INRA and

---

322 See www.superforestal.gov.bo.

323 For more information about FES see section 7.2.3.

SIF) consider the prefectures to be important partners cooperating in the laws enforcement. The prefectures continue to fail in their role as the link between the local demands of municipalities and the national policies. The reasons for this are both institutional and geographical. Firstly, the reforms process itself is not sufficiently clear to grant control of the use of natural resources to the departmental agents; and secondly, the prefectures are usually located far from the local population, as was observed in department of Beni and the cities of Trinidad (department capital) and Riberalta; a situation that limits communication and the coordination of regional policies. Therefore, many of the department decisions in Beni are aimed mainly at supporting local cattle rearing and tourism activities in the areas surrounding Trinidad, neglecting the extractivist activities of northern Amazon region.

The lack of forest policies is not only a characteristic of the departmental administration. There are no incentives at national level encouraging economic or conservation activities in the region. In the last four years this situation has become worse, due to the political uncertainty of the executive power. During this period, four presidents who changed their minister of sustainable development at least seven times governed the country. The non-prioritisation of the forest sector in the national policies retards the reform enforcement and does not guarantee solutions to the conflicts over the distribution of resources.[324] This situation can also be attributed to the lack of parliamentary support for the governments and the social crisis that Bolivia is going through. Public agents prefer to solve broader social and economic problems that compromise the stability of their mandate.

At the regional level, although the authorities have qualified technical personnel, there are not enough of them, nor are the logistical and financial means available. The local agents, responsible for several administrative duties, neglect the control and field inspection of the forest resources. Those responsible for the UFM, who are often the only available professionals in the municipal governments, are obliged to meet other types of social demands not necessarily related to forest use. In many cases, especially in the smallest municipalities the professionals of the UFM become technical and legal advisors of the mayor and assume administration and finance duties. To give an idea of the lack of technical personnel and capital resources at the disposal of the forest administration in the region; on average each public agent, SIF and UFM technician, is responsible for nearly 250,000 ha, with a budget that fluctuates between US$ 0.04 and US$0.06 per hectare in the best cases.

The efforts at decentralisation have been affected by the poor administrative coordination between public authorities and local actors.[325] For example, during the *saneamiento* in Pando, the INRA only sporadically coordinates its activities with the SIF or the municipal

---

[324] One indicator to measure the lack of political will of the executive at national level is the delay of at least a year in the official appointment of the staff in charge of the SIF and the INRA. Up to June 2004 both authorities had temporary directors, subject to serious technical, political and financial restrictions.

[325] Cf. SMOKE 2003 cited in ANDERSSON 2004.

governments (horizontal coordination).[326] One result of this is that INRA does not recognise the rights approved by the forest administration (for instance FMPs for forest concessions) at the time of land allocation, or ignores national forest policies, such as the 'national forest plan', which identifies areas with forest suited for either conservation or production, but not for agrarian purposes. The coordination has also proved ineffective in cases where the SIF approves FMPs in settlements without ownership titles, ignoring the *saneamiento* process.

This lack of horizontal coordination is reflected at all administrative levels, from the lower levels, including the technical offices in charge of the laws enforcement, up to the higher levels of the ministries and the national superintendence, responsible for dictating national policies and supervising resource use. Both the agrarian and the forest sectors have not only coordination problems, but they also compete openly for the administration and control of the natural resources.[327]

The faulty horizontal coordination may have its roots in the legislation itself, which prioritises the use and distribution of land over forest use and conservation. The introduction of the FES-*forestal* in the Agrarian Law provides new criteria for land distribution, but these are ignored in the enforcement, due to the lack of experience or the negligence of the agrarian agents. The lack of horizontal coordination influences the behaviour of the local users (agrarian and forest) who adopt those policies or institutions best suited to their interests, which leads to an increase in the emergence of social conflicts.

The lack of coordination is also observed between organisations at different administrative levels (vertical coordination). The increased number of local organisations (municipalities) hinders coordination. The coordination of activities between the SIF and the UFMs is observed occasionally, in forest control and especially in resource allocation.

This situation is also considered one of the main reasons behind the conflicts taking place. The municipalities demarcate their ARFMs ignoring the duties of the regional agents, and at the same time regional SIF agents approve forest plans in areas identified as ARFMs (see chapter 6, first case study). These acts contribute to the emergence of social conflicts, as was mentioned in the first case study in chapter 6.

---

[326] Eighty percent of the municipalities interviewed (n=12) declared sporadic coordination with the INRA in the land titling process. The coordination between municipal governments and the SIF improves to 60% through the work of the UFM. Despite of this increasing, 90% of all interviewees have been considered that even in forest issues, administrative coordination must improve.

[327] According to BOSCOLO & VARGAS (2001:7) the forest sector suffers unfair competition from the agrarian sector, because forest use is not perceived as having the same 'dignity' as agriculture and cattle rearing. The 'agrarian-forest' sector competition is a complex subject that arises as an outcome of policies governing access to and use of land according to the concept "*the land belongs to the one who works it*", promoted by the Law of Agrarian Reform of 1953 and strengthened by the Law of Colonisation. Both laws provided direct and indirect incentives aimed at advancing land distribution and promoting farming. These differences of vision are compounded by the respective tax regimes. For example, in the agriculture sector the payment of the tax occurs subsequent to the use of the resource, whereas in the forest sector the payment must be made prior to the use of the resource. In addition, the agrarian landowner is entitled to define the value of his property by means of self-assessment, with tax based on this value. The tax is rarely paid, however, because a public registry of rural properties does not exist (see BOSCOLO & VARGAS 2001:7f).

The lack of coordination represents a challenge to the development of an efficient national forest programme that involves the various interest groups (forest users, government agencies, NGOs and private enterprises) in the control and use of the forests.[328] The political weakness of the forest administration has led to changes to the reforms. In the study area, at least eight crucial forest use regulations have been partially or totally changed in the last five years (1999-2004). Of these, five are the most important decrees that directly influence the changes to the characteristics of the property rights.[329] In the process of 'reform adaptation', not only have decrees been enacted, but also countless resolutions of the SIF enacted under the 'exception regime'. The 'exception regime' opened the possibility for the forest users to extract timber, for example based on the execution of annual forestry operational plans (POAF)[330] with the commitment to draft an FMP in the future.[331] For many forest operators in the north, such exceptions to the law became the rule (PACHECO 2002b).[332]

In the northern Bolivian Amazon the option to use timber on private properties upon the approval of the POAF has encouraged many forest users to formalise their activities. However, part and parcel of this is the receipt of favours from public agents, the making of false declarations, negotiations with neighbours involving the exertion of pressure and the exploitation of resources in areas where tenure is unresolved. Consequently, the 'adaptation' of the reforms has diminished transparency in the allocation of resources.

Another aspect that affects transparency in the assignment of tenure is the non-fulfilment of Article 30 of the Forest Law, which stipulates that the granting of forest concessions be subject to a public bidding process. The 19 forest concessions granted in Pando were the result of the voluntary conversion of long-term felling authorisations granted under the previous regime. Therefore, national forest agents formalise the political power of the forest entrepreneurs who were able to approve the '*Plan Soberanía*' in 1993, infringing several public institutions, such as the 'Ecological Pause Decree' of 1990.

The municipal level has the lowest administrative transparency. As in the past, the local public agents continue to grant tenures to the local actors under conditions contrary to those established by law. They proceed to approve 'settlement certificates' in highly conflicted areas, they designate as ARFM areas occupied by third parties and they illegally delay the delivery for 'legal personality' made by rural communities, thereby hindering access to forests, etc.

---

328 Cf. ANDERSSON 2004.

329 The *Barraca* Decree (25532); decree cancelling the *Barracas* Decree (25838); 500 ha Decree establishing the minimum land entitlement for rural families (25848); decree reducing the forest tax (27024); and the decree approved in June 2004 limiting the rights of the farming communities (500 to 1,000 ha) and recognising a maximum of 15,000 ha for the *barraqueros* (27572).

330 *Plan operativo anual forestal*

331 SIF Resolution 019/97, later modified by resolution 44/2000.

332 A 'short list' of the approved exceptions includes: 1) the sworn declaration to remove all the 'old' wood felled under the old regime; 2) the permission for timber utilisation in properties smaller than 200 ha, without titling; 3) the

The Agrarian Law establishes the *saneamiento* as the main tool for the redistribution of land. The INRA has not been able to develop more specific parameters to apply the FES-*forestal*, and most of the settlements under the traditional institutions continue working in an informal way. Here the most affected group are the *barraca* holders, who until June 2004 were unable to claim their traditional rights over the forests. However, this situation could change with the enforcement of Decree 27572, allowing them to keep up to 15,000 ha. Other forest users are also affected, mainly those that inhabit the most marginal areas in the region (*fregueces*, Brazilians of Bolivian descent, small peasants, etc.). In this dimension, the emergence of many conflicts, especially in the most remote areas, means the reaction of the affected actors against the state, in the search for greater transparency and government impartiality in the enforcement of the institutions.

The objectives of the administrative elements of the reforms were well implemented initially. The subsequent lack of state policies, coordination between public institutions, the political uncertainty of the executive and the 'adaptation' of the reforms place a question mark over the reform enforcement, however. When the current situation is compared with that of the old regime, the reforms have contributed: 1) to increase state control over resource allocation and the inspection of forest production activities; 2) to clarify the functions of the public institutions; 3) to decentralise administrative decision-making, giving the local public agents greater responsibilities and financial resources; 4) to reduce the political dependence of the public organisations, improving the technical advice available to the local actors.

7.2.2 Economic dimension

The economic dimension includes those rules established in the reforms to foment: 1) the development of regional economic activities,[333] 2) the generation of public and private incomes based on forest utilisation and 3) greater access to natural resources, reducing the transaction costs incurred by forest users complying with the law. Although the reforms concentrate on improving the management of natural resources, their impact on the regional economy occurs only indirectly. For example, the development of economic activities is subject to the clarity of the characteristics of tenure; the improvement of the local population's incomes is facilitated by the traditional user groups' access to the forests, resulting in more forest products; the financial contribution to the state is manifest in the increased forest taxes, reducing the burden on the National Treasury's budget; and the reduction of the transaction costs occurs through facilitating the local population's access to legal information, or through clarifying tenures, reducing the need for control activities, such as in the case of the emergence of social conflict.

authorisation of forest use on lands smaller than 3 ha; 4) the permission for the ASL of timber resources with the presentation of a single POAF, with a commitment to present a FMP in the future (PACHECO 2002b).

333 There are three main regional economic activities: Brazil nut extraction, exploitation of timber and extensive cattle ranching (BOJANIC 2001).

Success of and progress in the reform enforcement

The physical delimitation of forest concessions has increased the legal security of the timber sector. In the same way, the *saneamiento* will help to reduce the levels of informal regional activities, particularly in the communal holdings. In order to facilitate access to the forests, a greater number of tenure classes are differentiated under the reforms. These classes are clearly defined, particularly as refers to the characteristics regulating transferability, duration, allocation type, payment of taxes and comprehensiveness of tenure.[334] In the case of the northern Bolivian Amazon, the characteristics regulated by the law have gradually been adjusting to the reality of Brazil nut extraction. The first step was the temporary formalisation of the traditional rights of the *barraca* (1999-2000) through Decree 25532,[335] subsequently the minimum assignment of 500 ha of land per member family of a peasant community (2000) through Decree 25848. The incorporation of the extractivist activities in the national legislation means differences in the distribution of resources between the northern Bolivian Amazon and the remaining regions of Bolivia.

The laws being examined demonstrate greater compatibility in terms of the granting and delimitation of tenure. On the one hand, the right of concession is conditional to the execution of the *saneamiento*, and on the other, the 'authorisation of forest use in private property' category allows landowners to manage forest within their settlements. Both the Agrarian and Forest Laws contribute to reducing the overlap of tenures, avoiding cases of double interests in a same area. At the same time, the historical dichotomy between forest use and land use is also solved, it being determined that only the use of the forest resources is allowed within the concessions, and even for the extraction of the NTFPs the law demands the consent of the concession holder (CONTRERAS & VARGAS 2001). The delimitation of the forest tenures motivated the forest entrepreneurs to take on new challenges, such as the forest certification of their concessions, seeking to open alternative markets for their products abroad.[336]

However, the reform did little to foment the increase of private investment. One of the few examples is the establishment of new sawmills, which doubled in number after 1996, from approximately 15 to 31 enterprises.[337] These new actors are generating employment in rural areas and they are in a position to sign service contracts with the rural communities to exploit their raw materials. One of the main reasons for the increase in the number of sawmills, without forest tenures, is apparently that the new forest entrepreneurs are interested in exploiting the community forests, controlled by the indigenous and peasants. Relative to the distribution of the incomes among forest users, it is assumed that the 'democratisation' of forest use will contribute to reducing the economic breach between the forest enterprises and the communal users. The rural communities have increased their participation in the regional

[334] For more information on the characteristics of the property rights see chart 3 in chapter 2.

[335] Decree 25532 approved in 1999 was later countermanded in July 2000, due to the social pressure exerted on the government by the rural communities.

[336] Bolivia is the tropical country with the highest area of certified forest, at more than 1.5 million hectares (QUEVEDO 2004).

[337] Fundación José Manuel Pando (2002).

production of Brazil nuts from 20-32% in 1992 to 34% in 1997.[338] According to STOIAN (2000:139) the main benefit of the 'democratisation' process are the higher returns on the part of independent collectors: in the Brazil nut season 1996/97, communal members received US$6.6 per box, as compared to US$3.9 paid to an average *zafrero* on a *barraca*. However, until 2000, the shelling factory owners (25%) together with the *barraca* holders (7%) received almost 20% more of the exported stocks of Brazil nuts than the rural communities (11%) (BOJANIC 2001).

The income distribution does not necessarily depend on the redistribution of resources, but rather on the changes that could be made to other types of private arrangement institutions governing the Brazil nut trade, such as the *habilito*. However, the population's incomes could increase significantly if the communities begin to manage their forest areas in a complimentary manner, integrating the production of NTFPs with timber exploitation, and even entering the markets by producing environmental services, such as carbon sequestration.

The reforms could also improve the economic situation of rural households; they can generate greater incomes from forest use than was the case prior to receipt of tenure, as they can demand higher prices from the regional traders for their own products.

One income that has increased noticeably since 1996 is that of the public organisations due to the establishment of a new system of forest taxes. While the Forest Decree of 1974 demanded the payment of the tax on the volumes extracted, based on the declarations made by the tenure holders, the new law obliges the concessionaires to pay an annual tax on the total area assigned to them. The introduction of the new tax has reduced the wide scale tax evasion that occurred under the previous regime. It represents an efficient form of collection and the mechanism applied to distribute the revenues to the public authorities that cooperate in the control of the forests is also a vast improvement (NITTLER 1999).

With respect to the incomes received by the regional organisations within Pando (municipalities and prefecture), in the first year of the reforms (1997), the incomes received were eight times that of the five previous years by the CDF-Pando (1990-1994) were multiplied by eight.[339] In 1998 the tax revenues amounted to one million dollars, which fell to US$ 800,000 in 1999 (see figure 37). In these first three years the public agents who benefited most were the nine municipalities with forest concessions within their jurisdictions; in four of the municipalities the duties collected even exceeded the incomes of the tributary co-partnership established by the Law of Popular Participation.[340] The revenues were used to pay the technical personnel's wages, to provide materials and infrastructure for the UFM, and for many small municipalities the taxes provided the only means to invest in social projects, such as

---

338 STOIAN 2000:138

339 Revenues increased from US$9,000 to US$72,000 (see figure 37).

340 When comparing the municipal income generated by the Law of Popular Participation and the Forest Law in 1999, municipalities like Bolpebra, Nueva Esperanza, Santos Mercado and Ingavi received more revenue from forest tax than through tributary co-participation.

the renovation of schools, health centres, local roads, etc. The success achieved in the administrative dimension in the first years (see figure 40) is directly related to the increased state income, which made it possible for the local organisations to exert greater control over forest use.

From the perspective of the CFD and SIF, the reforms also improved their economic situation. Under the previous regime the CFD had to fulfil more duties not only in the forest sector with lower financial resources (see figure 36). The SIF also receives more money, and is required to concentrate solely on the Forest Law enforcement.

Administrative decentralisation has helped to facilitate the rural population's access to information, and consequently the transaction costs arising from the public institutions enforcement have tended to decrease in comparison with the old regime. One important example is the granting of *personeria juridical*, 'legal personality', to the rural communities, a step that was quite bureaucratic and slow in the past, and that was carried out in the seat of government (La Paz). Since the reforms, this step is initiated in the municipalities, and any final appeals are heard by the departmental prefectures. This procedure should not take more than three months from the moment the documents are received by the municipal government.

The reforms have also accelerated the process of granting forest tenures, particularly to the forest entrepreneurs, considering that in the past long-term contracts required the passing of a Presidential Decree carrying the signatures of all the ministers and of the President of the Republic himself. The new law grants this authority to the Forest Superintendent, through the approval of administrative resolutions. Decentralisation has also contributed to the regional SIF and INRA organisations assuming greater responsibility in the assignment of tenures. For example, in the regional offices of the SIF, the POAF applications of those forest enterprises with a FMP approved by the national office can be granted, as is the case with POAFs less than 200 ha and 'logging plans' for less than 5 ha. Under the Agrarian Law, the whole *saneamiento* process, including the definition of the agrarian property rights, is the direct responsibility of the departmental authorities. This situation favours all who use the regional forests to access resources, especially the excluded groups, with smaller economic resources and poor access to information.

Failures of and challenges facing the reform enforcement

Property rights remain unclear, as the reforms leave many of the details of the tenure types open to the interpretation of the forest users, specifically the property sizes. There is no maximum area associated with the forest concessions, ASLs and TCOs; and other tenures such as those of the peasant communities, although they have been defined, have quite broad ranges (between 500 and 1,000 ha per family). The area of the *barracas* was not limited until mid 2004. The imprecise delimitation of property rights is also one of the main reasons for conflict, a situation that reduces the security to invest in or to conserve the forests.

Other poorly regulated characteristics are: 1) the use designation of rights, especially of those activities relating to forest conservation; 2) the operational control, through a stricter and more transparent establishment of penalties and sanctions for the offenders; and 3) exclusion inside the rural communities, where strong imbalances in resource distribution are still evident, favouring the groups with greater economic and/or social power. The lack of clarity of the property rights weakens the legal security of the holders. Most affected are the concessionaire companies, where the entrepreneurs also claim additional problems, such as restrictions in the transferability of their rights, mainly for sale or mortgage, and are now demanding the denationalisation of the forest tenures. According to NITTLER (2000), the transfer restrictions present another of the great challenges of the concessions model, namely the establishment of a market for forest rights permitting the trade of goods acquired through the creation of a private/state mechanism that guarantees the use of the concessions with mortgage purposes and that defines a minimum value for these.

BOSCOLO & VARGAS (2001:8) also contributed to the discussion of the forests as 'state property'. They asserted that the forest rights face technical and legal disadvantages not encountered at the same level in the case of other property rights, such as 'agrarian property'. According to the authors, this disadvantage promotes the permanent binding of the state lands under the concept of '*that which belongs to all, belongs to none*'. Interpreting the statements made by BOSCOLO & VARGAS (2001) for the study area, they question the vigour of the state control mechanisms, responsible for implementing the forest legislation. In the absence of certain mechanisms the confusion between 'state property' and 'open access' increases. In addition, the current national fiscal policy does not favour the forest holders; the state demands the enforcement of legal instruments by the companies (such as the forest plans and the payment of forest taxes) without guaranteeing the security of their tenures. Frequently forest holders suffer the reduction of their areas to meet the demands of agricultural users. Nevertheless, the discussion on the binding of the forest tenures is quite a complicated topic, and it is probable that often the source of the problem is the state's granting of forest rights on areas overlapping with land occupied by rural groups. At the same time, the forest entrepreneurs are also interested in maintaining 'open access' to the forests, as long as this allows them to take advantage of illegal logging, often providing greater incomes than the legal exploitation of the forests, due to the low transaction costs.

Despite the problems evident in the timber sector, in the northern Bolivian Amazon the greatest shortcoming of the reforms remains the delimitation of the NTFP tenure for all forest users. This area of forest use is still governed by informal rules, which regulate the use of the forests in the communal and individual properties. Until mid 2004, only two of the 11 tenure characteristics, namely size and allocation type were regulated properly. The collection of the NTFP taxes is still not completely clear, nor are other characteristics such as the operational control, the exclusion form of the rights inside of rural communities, the relationship between timber use and NTFP extraction, the conservation activities, the agricultural expansion allowed in extractivist areas, the level of transferability granted to the extractivist right, the duration of the tenures, and most particularly the comprehensiveness in relation to other NTFPs including hunting and fishing activities.

The increased revenue accrued by the state during the first three years of the reforms (1997-1999) fell considerably after 2000. This was supposedly due to the national economic crisis that affected the forest administration, and resulted in the insolvency of forest enterprises. The dimension of national debt accrued by the forest companies at national level reached US$10 million in 2003, a fact that forced the state to annul more than sixty concessions with paid quotas until April 2003 (BOLFOR 2003). LLANQUE *et al.* (2003) called into question the insolvency of the concessionaire enterprises before the payment of their obligations, given the increases in the values of forest product exports after 2000. Therefore, it is not clear whether the debt assumed by the forest enterprises is the product: 1) of the national economic crisis, 2) or whether it corresponds to the widespread behaviour of the entrepreneurs in the past of not paying debts, or 3) whether it was a strategy employed by the entrepreneurs to pressurise the Government into reducing taxes.

In any case, the possible annulment of the concessions was perceived by those responsible at the SIF as a threat to the system, because it meant a reduction of the organisation's finances. Given this risk, those in charge of the SIF, together with other private organisations (National Forest Chamber and BOLFOR) proposed to the Government the adaptation of Law 1700 to accommodate the reality of debt and the capacity of entrepreneurs to pay.[341] This resulted in the approval of Presidential Decree 27024 allowing the concessionaires to pay a dollar per hectare on the area used annually (according to the POAF), plus an extra forest regulation tariff used to finance the SIF.[342] A year after the Decree 27024 enforcement, the annual incomes for the department of Pando appear to have been standardised at an amount slightly above US$ 200,000, similar to the amounts received for the year 2000 (see figure 37). The approval of Decree 27024 will allow the SIF to 'survive' the coming years, but in no way does it guarantee the effectiveness of the control and inspection of the resources. It compromises the efficiency of the originally conceived model seriously, insofar as it restricts the investments of material and the staff of the competent authority, and limits the on site control of the illegal and selective use of the forests (see figure 39). The reduction of the transaction costs proposed in the reforms should be considered as relative, since it is in direct relationship with the context of the social actors; despite the state making an effort to bring its services close to the rural areas, the inhabitants of the peripheral regions continue to face serious difficulties when obeying the laws. The problem resides in the long neglect of the region by the state. As a result, most of the rural communities do not fulfil the basic requirements to access the forests, such as the communal organisation and the procedure to grant 'legal personality'.

---

341 At the beginning of 2003 it was estimated that the debt flow increased at a rate of US$4 million/year, with the enterprises' capacity for payment only US$1.5 million/year (BOLFOR 2003).

342 Decree 27024 was approved on 6th May 2003 during the government of Sanchez de Lozada. The main objective of the decree was to avoid the annulment of the forest concessions and to finance the SIF, through the reprogramming of the enterprise debt and a new system of payment of forest taxes. Specifically, the decree ends the determination of forest tax on the basis of 'annual harvesting areas' (*area anual de aprovechamiento*) (AAA) and the total area of the granted concession (Article 3). In addition, the forest concessionaires have to pay a 'Forest Regulation Tariff' (*tarifa de regulación forestal*) (TRF) of around US$ 4,00 per hectare managed each year (Article 4). The state does not reduce the debt of the forest enterprises, but allows them to meet their obligations through a payment plan of 100 months. The percentage of distribution of the tax has not been modified for the prefectures and municipalities, but it establishes that the income from the TRF favours the SIF exclusively.

Figure 37 Departmental revenues from forest taxes in Pando: Administration 1990-2003

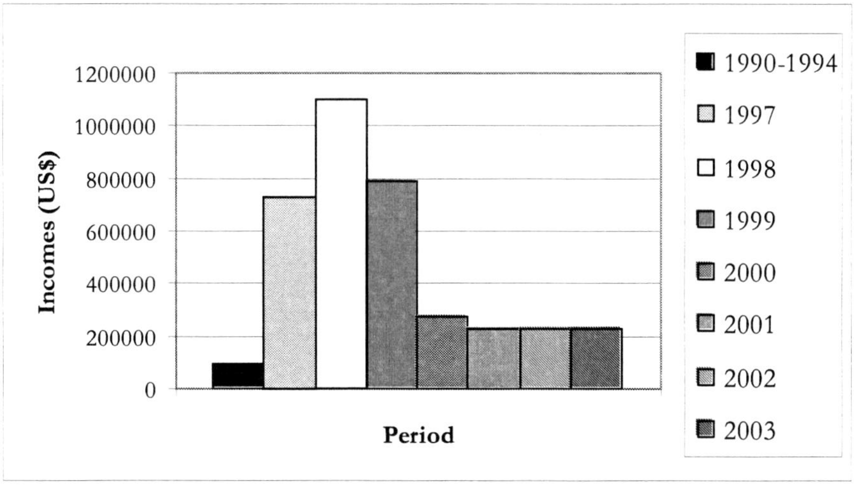

Source: SIF (2004): Effective collection of forest taxes according to DS 27024; SIF (2002b): Area tax debt on 31/12/01; CORDEPANDO (1990-1994): Departmental incomes from forest concessions.

According to HENTSCHEL (2004:83ff), to access the forests the communities must be aware of the institutional contents of at least three laws: the Law of Popular Participation, granting them the recognition as OTB; the INRA Law, governing the *saneamiento* process; and the Forest Law, forcing them to draft a FMP as a prerequisite for legal forest use. This means having to complete at least 12 formal steps, between communal organisation, subjection to the *saneamiento*, contacts with sawmill's technicians, drawing up of the FMP, timber felling, payment of the forest taxes, etc. In accordance with the declarations of the members of the community interviewed by HENTSCHEL (2004:84), the main legal cost that the community members incur in the organisation process is the compilation of the personal documents of the community members, because most of the population in the region does not have a personal identification document (GOTTWALD 2004). Another point that represents time and effort is the need to demonstrate the communal organisation, which includes having a democratically elected leader and a system of several charges regulated by the community that is responsible for the important matters of its members.

The technical organisations (NGOs) and the forest companies (sawmills) play an important role in the reduction of transaction costs. For example, it was demonstrated in two of the three case studies that during the land titling process[343] the forest users tend to change their legal status in order to access the resources; '*barraca* holders' become 'peasants', 'peasants' become 'indigenous', depending on the availability of information, finance and legal support

[343] According to regional experience, the *saneamiento* can last between two to three years, starting from the INRA's first contact with the community and lasting until the granting of the executory deed.

provided by the regional private organisations and companies. However, the alliances between forest users and regional organisations do not always entirely favour the local actors; the financing of forest plans by the regional companies increases the dependence of forest users when it comes to the processing of raw materials and in the trading of the products.

In short, the partial integration of extractivism has improved the tenure of resources, particularly of the communal users and, since June 2004, of the *barraca* holders. However, the vagueness of property rights, reducing the security of tenures and giving rise to social conflicts decreases the incentives for private investment in rural areas.[344] At the same time, the reforms alone will not improve the rural population's incomes. This situation depends on changes to other traditional institutions used in the trade of forest products, such as the *habilito*, or even the change of international institutions, such as the EU guideline 98/58, which requires that the aflatoxine[345] levels in Brazil nuts are less than 4 ppb (parts pro billion).[346]

Furthermore, an increase of local incomes also depends on other external aspects of the institutions, such as the price of timber or Brazil nuts on international markets, as well as the rural communities options for and interest in utilising their forest areas, and the possibility to seek other alternatives. This type of comparative analysis is complicated by the lack of available information in relation to the local population's incomes at household level under the previous regime, and the diversity of job types in the study area, characteristic of livelihood systems that vary from year to year and even between harvests.

Positive aspects of the reforms in comparison to the previous regime include: 1) the increase of the public revenues, freeing the state from financing the control and inspection of the forests and 2) the relative decrease of the transaction costs incurred in the quest for formal forest access, insofar as the administrative decentralisation brings the state apparatus closer to the regional actors.

7.2.3 Environmental dimension

The environmental dimension of the reforms includes all actions intended to contribute to guaranteeing the sustainability of resource use to slow down the degradation of the ecosystems, to reduce deforestation and to conserve the fauna and flora.

Contrary to the administrative dimension, where in the last years a series of technical and scientific documents have been drawn up aimed at evaluating the advances of the reforms, research work in the environmental dimension has been scarce. The problem resides in the complexity of environmental research work, which requires greater periods of observation

---

344 According to KAPMEYER (2004:155), 'Security of tenure' enters any decision to invest, as it affects the discount rate for investment that the household calculates on the future benefits.

345 Aflatoxine is a carcinogenic toxin produced by a fungus (*Aspergillus flavus*). It infects Brazil nuts in high humidity, and is characteristic of bad storage or problems in the drying of the nuts.

346 This international institution could influence the NTFP economy of the region more significantly than any Bolivian institutions, because it means a high sales risk on export markets and a great threat for the whole regional industry given the lack of proper technology and funds to meet the requirements.

and specifies a wide range of criteria to determine the impact on the environmental sustainability of the natural system. The evaluation of the environmental dimension becomes even more complicated if one considers the generality of the institutional objectives, and especially the lack of necessary tools and enforcement mechanisms for law enforcement. The laws under study seek to achieve their objectives indirectly, through the enforcement of few mechanisms that are not sufficiently linked to the environmental legislation in force. Acknowledging these restrictions, it remains to try to evaluate the enforcement of the two most important technical tools regulated by law: first, the drawing up and enforcement of the 'management plans', and second that of the 'socio-economic function' (*función economica-social,* FES) applied in the redistribution of the land.

The management plans, as technical tools, are central to the Forest Law, intended to foment sustainable forest management (SFM). However, SFM is not a novelty in the reforms, since the previous legislation did not ignore it completely. Indeed Law 1700 imposed these tools as a requirement to access forest use. The FMP rules incorporate minimum rotation periods (20 years), the protection of juvenile trees (20%), the diameters of trees felled are determined, they include considerations on the extent of the area to be protected inside the concessions (up to 30%), and they even detail the measures dedicated to reforestation. To achieve these objectives forest professionals accredited by the SIF who assume civil and/or penal liability for the proposed contents draw up the management plans. The FMP enforcement is made viable through the POAF, and in both cases the SIF is responsible for its approval and control.[347]

On the other hand, the FES is the criterion that determines the granting of access to land, based on the production activities carried out, and it is the basic tool of the *saneamiento*. The FES is assessed on site according to the data given by the property holders. Thus the cattle farmers are evaluated on the basis of the quantity of existing livestock, and production infrastructure such as corrals, sheds, silos and pasture land; the peasants on the cultivated hectares of land, the forest users on the hectares of forest in production, etc. The FES also includes conservation, research and ecotourism activities.[348]

Success of and progress in the reform enforcement

At national level, one of the most highly eulogised achievements of the reforms is the reduction of the area officially granted for forest use from approximately 22 million hectares in 1995 to 7.5 million hectares in the 2002 (SIF 2003). At regional level, the reduction of the area for forest use was from in excess of 2 million hectares to a million hectares.[349] From the point of view of forest conservation, several Bolivian environmental analysts agree that the decrease of the area has served not only to slow down the uncontrolled use of the forests but also to promote their conservation (CONTRERAS & VARGAS 2001). Under the new regime the controlled use of the forests, based on the area of the approved POAFs, applied to 200,000

[347] Cf. CONTRERAS & VARGAS 2001:12f.

[348] INRA Law 1996: Article 2.

[349] For more information see chapter 4.

hectares nationally in 2002, of which around 35% belongs to the study area (70,000 ha). In spite of the transaction costs incurred in the drawing up and approval of management plans, the forest users in the northern Bolivian Amazon were more understanding than other Bolivian regions.[350] The approval of POAFs for 'private properties', in particular, has constantly increased from administration to administration in the last five years (see figure 38).

Figure 38 Increase of the POAF area approved in Pando (1998-2002)

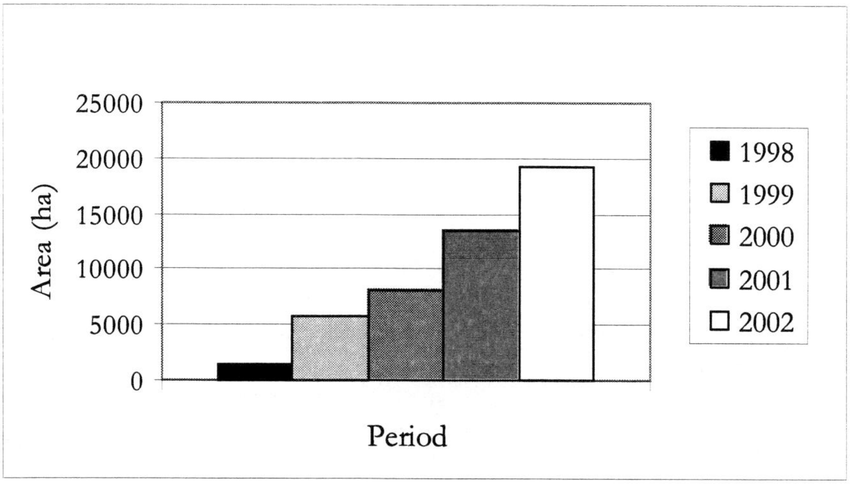

Source: SIF (1999-2003) Several administration reports.

In 2002, for example, nearly 20,000 ha were only approved for use under the 'authorisation of forest use in private property' instrument, and more than twice as much under the tenure of forest concessions (47,000 ha) (SIF 2003). Under the previous regime the execution of the management plans was null (CONTRERAS & VARGAS 2001:20), and those in charge of the SIF in Pando argue that the acceptance of the POAFs has contributed to reducing the informality of the use of the timber. It has also allowed the SIF to establish better control in the places where there is higher pressure on the resources. Regarding the protection of the resources, the FMP should identify the areas dedicated to the conservation of resources like 'servitudes and ecological reserves', considered legally as susceptible areas of use inside the forest concessions or private estates.

Usually the servitudes or ecological reserves are located on the banks of rivers (gallery forests), flood plains (*curichis*), hillsides with marked slopes, or in places of high biological diversity, where the law forbids the holders to carry out any type of commercial use.

The legal incentive for the users is freedom from the payment of forest taxes inside these areas, which can represent up to a maximum of 30% of the total assigned concession.[351] Until

350 Telephone interview with Forest Superintendent;

351 Forest Law 1996: article 29.

early 2000, when the concessions in the region remained unaffected, the percentage of the protected area in the concessions represented 14% of the negotiated area (200,000 ha). However, inside each one of the concessions the percentages of conservation areas vary between 37.5% down to 1.3% of the total area assigned.[352]

The enforcement of the management plans is directly related to the forest control activities of the SIF. In the past, two control mechanisms were applied most frequently by the regional agents (CDF-Pando and CORDEPANDO): 1) sporadic inspections of the *barraca*, for the collection of NTFP taxes aimed at improving government revenues and 2) the 'surveillance' of timber movement over land through control posts or *trancas*. Both mechanisms were ineffective, the first due to the total absence of registrations of the tenure of resources, and the second because the process was plagued by corruption (PACHECO 2002b); the volumes and declared values were suspicious and the collected incomes unaccountably low (ROPER 2000 cited in PACHECO 2002b).

As figure 39 shows, with the increase of personnel and of public authority financing, the control operations in Pando reported a constant rise in the first three years of law enforcement (1998-2000). Of all the control activities in Pando, three inspection types stand out: illegal logging, the transport of products and the pre-approval of management plans including POAFs.[353] Until 2000 these three activities represented up to 70% of the total of inspections executed in the department (SIF 1999-2001). The possibility of corruption at the control posts and other types of illegal logging should be restricted by the introduction of the 'Forest Certificates of Origin' (*certificado forestal de origen*, CFO), as the CFOs approve the exploitation, the transport of the products and they guarantee the origin of the timber.

In order to increase the effectiveness of control, the CFOs are granted in direct relationship with the production values specified in the FMP, they may only be used once and their validity is only temporary (in general three months). Officially all control activities are bound to a system of penalties and seizures that include the payment of cash, the confiscation of products and/or materials and even the closing of forest enterprises.

In relation to the establishment of the FES, although this topic is not a novelty in the new agrarian legislation, the INRA Law broadens the narrow concept of "*the land belongs to the one who works it*" (specified in the Land Reform). In the old agrarian legislation, 'work' is synonymous with production on the land, oriented towards the development of agricultural and/or cattle activities, discriminating against other activities like ecotourism, forestry, research and the sale of environmental services that contribute to the conservation of the ecosystems. The new FES-concept recognises these activities as legitimate grounds for

352 See www.superforestal.gov.bo/atlas/pando/concesiones_pando.htm.

353 Among other activities cited are: inspection of the *saneamiento*, inspection of the processing industries and the supply of products, control of burning, post FMP and POAF-approval inspections, etc.

landownership, and the land register reveals important settlement information, collected during the field visits.[354]

In the study area the FES-concept has been partially adapted to accommodate the fact that the forest, and not the land, is the main resource used by the Amazon inhabitants. Here, the two most important achievements with respect to the granting of land are: 1) the establishment of the peasant communities based on 500 has per family, without having to demonstrate any activity type besides *extractivism*, and 2) the granting of lands to the forest users who have managed the forests since at least 2000, with management plans approved by the SIF. In this last point, during the *saneamiento* the INRA recognised the demands of around twenty individual users for between 300 and 4,000 hectares, located mainly in the municipalities of Bella Flor and Puerto Rico.[355]

Failures of and challenges facing the reform enforcement

Given the breadth of the definition of sustainable management, the reform enforcement in the environmental dimension is the most polemic and highly criticised. While some authors maintain that the effects of the laws have been positive steps towards the sustainable use of the forests, others maintain a critical perspective on the (positive) results of the institutional changes pertaining to the environment.

Critics of the reforms claim that even though most of the forest concessions in the region have a FMP, and although POAFs have been accepted on private properties, these tools are merely a bureaucratic requirement for forest access; that in reality few holders consider the management plans to be documents detailing their planning and production (PRISMA 2000; CONTRERAS & VARGAS 2001; PACHECO 2002b).

Based on interviews with 23 forest concessions at national level, BOSCOLO *et al.* (2002, cited in SNOOK *et al.* 2003:5) stated that the practices of forest management adopted by the forest users are significantly influenced by the forest regulatory scheme and by the SIF's regulation activities. The practices most widespread among the interviewed enterprises are the primary forestry activities, including forest inventory, the delimitation of the annual harvesting areas, the design of forest road networks and extraction routes, etc. Other activities include the cutting of climber plants, the control of hunting, the planning of tree felling etc., practices contributing to the overall conservation of the ecosystem. In other words, the forest regulations and the SIF controls have a great impact on the prescription of the production operations, but they neglect the environmental objectives declared in the law, such as protecting the species composition, structures and ecological functions of the forests.[356]

---

354 Field visits are the fourth stage of the *saneamiento*, which includes the collection of data for the land registry and the surveying of the settling of the land.

355 Telephone interview with the technician responsible for the *saneamiento* in Pando (April 29th 2004).

356 Cf. BOSCOLO & VARGAS 2001:13.

The examples of the POAFs in the three case studies demonstrate that the forest users do not necessarily resort to drawing up management plans simply to comply with the SFM rules. The main reasons behind their decision are: 1) to set down a physical marker of their establishment, complying with the 'FES-*forestal*' concept and thereby formalising their use rights; 2) to derive economic benefits from the areas in conflict at the expense of their opponents; and 3) to take advantage of the offers made by the forest enterprises interested in exploiting their timber, and in many cases assuming all of the transaction costs. In the research by HENTSCHEL (2004), the drawing up of one community 50,000 ha FMP had to do with the leaders' speculation over land, as he sought to occupy an area greater than that already held (6,800 ha).[357]

The growing number of POAFs, presented in figure 38 is attributed more to the effect of the 'legal adaptation' of the forest regime proposed by the SIF than to the forest users desire to practice SFM.[358] For the forest concessionaires it is more profitable to establish contracts with the supposed landowners than to use the areas granted them.[359] The adaptation of Law 1700 should not necessarily be considered a measure designed to consolidate the environmental objectives of the reforms, as an analysis of the POAFs in three case studies revealed:

- The POAFs identify forest stretches with greater numbers of commercial forest species, contrary to the objective of integral and non-selective forest use;
- The contents of the POAFs are short-sighted; generally referring to the harvesting of a product that will devalue the forest in the long-term;[360] and
- The POAFs do not necessarily reveal an assumption of responsibility for the protection of the resources; the commitment to conserve the ecosystems is being ignored.

The evaluation of resource conservation becomes even more complicated when one takes into consideration that from 2000 the SIF reduced its control activities in the forests substantially due to the reduction of its budget. As can be seen from figure 39, the levels of inspection in the last two years of analysis (2001-2002) have declined in some aspects (illegal logging and the evaluation carried out prior to approval of the management plan) when compared to the operations carried out in the first years following the introduction of the reforms.

---

357 Based on Decree 25848, which does not delimit the community area, the 87 families making up the community aspire to consolidate more than 100,000 ha (HENTSCHEL 2004:84).

358 for more information about 'legal adaptation' see section 4.4.1.2 (Forest use in private properties)

359 For example, a company from Pando applied for and obtained use rights on 27 properties of less than 200 hectares each, and the volume extracted is greater than that from its own forest concession (CONTRERAS & VARGAS 2001:31).

360 In the third case study, the peasant community, the holders abandoned the plots used by the forest company and nobody wants them any more because all of the community members consider the value of the forests to have declined.

Figure 39 Main inspections carried out in Pando by the local SIF offices

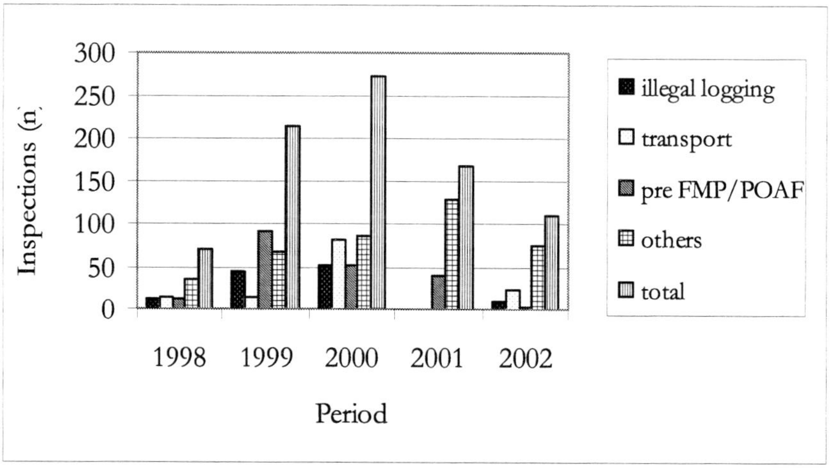

Source: SIF (1999-2003): Several administration reports.

In Riberalta the more frequent control operations are, for example, the pre-authorisation of the management plans and the transport of products. The purpose of the former is to evaluate the production data presented in the forest inventory, and the controls are rarely continued during and after logging. Controls of the transport of products occur periodically, although realistically the technical and financial means for effective control are lacking. The controls on transport over land are executed by two posts (*trancas)* located on the main access roads to the city of Riberalta, which are easily avoided.

The SIF-Riberalta has four technicians, one vehicle and one motorcycle, responsible for controlling an area in excess of 40,000 km^2 (municipality of Riberalta, the province of Federico Román and part of the Madre de Dios province of Pando).[361]

The control system is belittled by the weak system of sanctions and penalties applied to offenders. Analysts point out that the costs of obtaining a legal extraction license are greater than the penalties for illegal logging, and that these penalties can be avoided, too[362] (CONTRERAS & VARGAS 2001:32). According to information provided by the person responsible for the SIF in Riberalta, in the event of abnormalities observed in the production of timber, the most frequent 'penalty' is to contact the offenders in writing. As the SIF does

---

361 Telephone interview with the technician responsible from the SIF-Riberalta (May 26th 2004).

362 In order to obtain a logging permit it is necessary to submit an ownership title, a land use plan of the settlement (POP), and a 'logging plan'. However, in most cases users do not have the documents needed to prove property rights, which is the main barrier to proceeding with the rest of the paperwork. On the other hand, a POP is expensive and many small-scale producers are not able to cover the costs. Given these difficulties, the government agreed to draw up POPs for the poorest local actors for free (Decree 25847), a promise the result of political pressure, and one which the government has not been able to live up to the present day (CONTRERAS & VARGAS 2001:32).

not as yet have a list of sanctions to apply in the case of serious infractions (the felling of juvenile trees or trees inside the protected areas) it requires the offenders to pay the cost of the tree at market price plus a 'small' penalty applied, based on the public agent's judgement. In the event that products are seized, *"the materials confiscated by the SIF are returned indirectly to the offenders through public sales, where the buyers are probably the same actors responsible for the illegal logging in the first place."*[363]

Forest certification carried out in accordance with international norms contributes to covering the technical and legal vacuum in the national forest administration. The forest users opting for certification, accepting more rigorous examinations and controls, are closer to achieving the objectives of SFM.

Regarding the *saneamiento* and the enforcement of the agrarian FES-concept, the example of the northern Bolivian Amazon typifies the breach that exists between the 'sound proposals' contained in the public institutions and their enforcement in practice. Given the INRA's lack of experience in the Amazon region, the criteria used to verify the FES are derived from the practices applied in other Bolivian regions, where agricultural activities prevail. Although the INRA land registry includes questions on forest use, generally there are no parameters to verify the right of extractivist activities, especially of individual claims. Therefore, in the first four years of the *saneamiento* (2000-2004) the extraction of NTFPs in the *barracas* was considered illegal. MALDONADO (2004:129ff) criticised the enforcement of the 'FES-*agraria*' in forest regions. According to his observations in a protected area (Manuripi National Reserve), more land is distributed to those *barraca* holders who clear the forests in order to establish livestock than to those who adapt to the environmental regulatory scheme and only intervene in the forest four months a year during the Brazil nut harvest.

Despite the efforts to recognise the 'FES-*forestal*' concept, the reforms continue to fail to accommodate for the regulation of NTFP extraction. The following have yet to be regulated:

- Hunting and fishing during the Brazil nut harvest; year after year the animal population, mainly mammals, birds and reptiles, is seriously affected, as the *zafrero* families are supplied with meat;
- The incentive for the forest users to use the forest as a whole, i.e., to use the timber and to extract other NTFPs; in the case of the study area the FMP should include both aspects automatically;
- The impact on the ecosystem of the commercial extraction of NTFPs like the *asaí* (*Euterpe precatoria*) and the *jatata* (*Geonoma deversa*); in the case of the former to guarantee the permanence of the species, and in the latter to reduce the growth and reproduction rates (ZUIDEMA 2002).

In summary, it is difficult to measure the level of enforcement of the public institutions pertaining to the conservation of the forests, due to the lack of information and the few legal

---

363 Personal interview with the person responsible for the SIF-Riberalta; May 13th 2002.

tools outlined by the reforms. Nevertheless, some conclusions are: 1) the laws promote the sustainability of resource use more than the conservation of the ecosystem; 2) the drawing up of the management plans does not necessarily guarantee SFM, because the main objective is the awarding of the rights over the resources and/or the lucrative exploitation of the forests; 3) the laws have not completely incorporated the conservation advantages represented by the extraction of NTFPs and 4) the commitment to the enforcement of the environmental dimension of the reforms by most of the regional actors is low, being the least popular aspect of the reforms (see figure 40).

7.2.4 Social dimension

The social dimension of the reforms includes all those legal actions directed towards improving the unequal distribution of the natural resources among local users, to integrating all the traditional users and to reducing the incidence of conflicts over forest use.

Success of and progress in the reform enforcement

The enforcement of new classes of land tenure under the Forest Law (ASL and 'authorisation of forest use in private property') and the reform of community tenures contained in the INRA Law, have contributed to diminishing the disparities in the distribution of resources. In the northern Bolivian Amazon, the enforcement of the new institutions has caused a true 'forest reform'; according to official INRA data on the *saneamiento*, the community area could increase from 60,000 hectares in 1992 to more than 3 million hectares by the end of the *saneamiento*.[364] Five years spent implementing Decree 25848 have consolidated the expectations of the rural communities, expectations left unattended during more than 40 years of the first Land Reform Law.

Since 1996, the area assigned to the rural communities has grown at the expense of the area controlled by the forest entrepreneurs. At local level to date, Bolpebra is the municipality that best illustrates the changing control over the forests. Until early 2000, 65% of the municipal area was controlled by two forest enterprises. With the Decree 25848 enforcement, 50% of the area assigned to the forest enterprises in 1997 was redistributed amongst indigenous people and peasants. With the new distribution of resources it is expected that from 2005, 52% of the area of Bolpebra will become the property of the community users belonging to nine peasant communities and one TCO (see RUIZ 2004b).

The most important social change in the study area is the loss of forest area held by the *barracas* for extractivist production. With the approval of Decree 25532 at the beginning of 2000, the *barraca* holders expected to control 3.5 million hectares. This expectation has now decreased by approximately 50% (see figure 23, chapter 6). The law also integrated the legal basis for granting TCO titles to an important group of 'legally unprotected' indigenous people, as is the case of the *Yaminagua, Machineri, Cavineño*, *Tacana* and *Ese ejja*.

364 For more information see chapter 4.

The increased control over the forests by the communal groups means an increase to the power of peasants and indigenous people in the regional political and social sphere. Several rural leaders, who promoted the reforms now occupy important positions as national parliamentarians, municipal mayors, municipal councilmen, etc. Contrary to the situation in the past, nowadays each institutional change demanded by the *barraca* holders is discussed with the representatives of the peasants and the indigenous. At local level, the rural inhabitants can demand higher prices for Brazil nuts and timber from the forest entrepreneurs with greater success.

The latest decrees approved have shown a degree of sensitivity towards the possible emergence of conflicts as a result of the redistribution of resources, institutionalising the 'Reconciliation, Arbitration and Conflict Resolution Commission' in the region. Due to the recentness of this proposal (June 2004), it is not possible to evaluate its success as yet.

Failures of and challenges facing the reform enforcement

The reforms do not undertake to provide a solution to the existing disparities within the rural communities; this issue is considered another important institutional vacuum within the laws. In all types of resource allocation at community level (collective, mixed and individual) both peasants and indigenous face great inequalities, usually favouring local elites such as the old *patrónes*, certain families and community leaders in charge of distributing and administering the resources. Cases of unequal rights in community 'collective' models include:

- Land for cultivation is free for all community members, but resources with high commercial values, such as timber and Brazil nuts, belong to the elite group;
- The members of influential families hunt and fish for commercial purposes, restricting the meat consumption of the other community members;
- The members with better market links and with influence in community decisions frequently sell the community right to Brazil nut extraction to external contractors, without obtaining the consent of the whole community, and obtain the greater part of the earnings.[365]

Examples of imbalances in the distribution of resources in community 'mixed' and 'individual' models are:

- The most extensively used plots, with the lowest resource output, are distributed to new community members or those members of the community with the least influence;
- Often one family possesses more than one plot of land, generally corresponding to the areas with the greatest abundance of natural resources and
- Each member of the influential families (father, mother, children, in laws, etc.) receives a plot of land.

365 Cf. MANZANEDA 2003.

In all cases, the two main reasons for the inequalities relate to the traditional rules and to the strong power relationships inside the communities. The internal rules do not clearly define individual rights, such as plot size, the criteria for resource allocation (surface or volume), and the exclusion of other communal members.

One of the objectives of the reforms that has not been achieved is the integration of other traditional user groups who are neither peasants nor indigenous. The most affected in this respect are the *motosierristas* and the *fregueces*. The former group suffers the consequences of the little political will on the part of the national authorities to further the establishment of ASLs, and the 'weakness' of its rights compared with the rights of the rural communities (communal ASL concession versus community property). The *freguece* group, mainly in the most peripheral areas, remains isolated and is without the legal support of public or private organisations to improve its land tenures.

In spite of the increase in the area of community property, most of the rural communities do not have the capacity to engage in commercial forest use without the support of other interest groups.

Those community members interested in timber logging must complete at least 12 steps before obtaining forest benefits (DE JONG *et al.* in prep.).[366] Most of the 300 regional rural communities have formulated their demands for land (steps 1-4). Regarding the consolidation of these demands (steps 5 and 6), in Pando all rural communities were surveyed during the land titling process. By mid 2004, however, only 10 % of all peasant communities have received land title. And in terms of forest exploitation, by the end of 2003, only three peasant communities were preparing FMPs for a total area of 80,000 ha; only 2,700 ha of which has been approved by the SIF, due to the presence of conflicts or faulty public rights. Part of the problems of the stagnation of the process also lies with the communities. Community members and leaders are poorly prepared to take over the professional planning and the technical, administrative and commercial tasks of forest management (steps 8, 9, 11 and 12).

A lack of experience of and information needed for compliance with legal requirements (resulting in high transaction costs), the absence of adequate models of 'communal forest management' for commercial purposes, diverging interests and distrust within communities in relation to the benefits from forest management, and internal social conflicts are the main obstacles (HENTSCHEL 2004; RUIZ & BECKER 2003). The contracts between communities and

366 The 12 steps towards to community forest management are: 1) the decision of neighbouring rural families to establish a settlement; 2) establishment of an internal self-administration for the settlement (regular reunions, election of leaders, formulation of a statute, registration of all members of the settlement etc.); 3) official recognition of the settlement as a legal entity (OTB) by the municipal administration; 4) formulation of a communal land claim; emergence of conflicts with third parties; 5) clarification of the land claims, settlement of the conflicts; 6) land titling by the INRA; 7) internal decision within the community concerning the use of the assigned land area; 8) preparation for community forest exploitation, especially with respect to the extraction and marketing of timber; 9) forest inventory and drafting of a FMP with professional assistance; 10) approval of the FMP by the SIF; 11) start of forest management and timber marketing; 12) households in the community receive monetary income as forest workers and from the distribution of surplus profits from timber sales (DE JONG *et al.* in prep.).

companies can potentially aggravate conflicts within the communities with regard to the appropriate forms of 'communal forest management' and the distribution of benefits derived from the timber sales. In addition, political impulses and resources for steering the development of community forest management in another direction are still lacking (DE JONG *et al.* in prep.).

Although in this study the emergence of conflicts is considered a positive aspect overall, contributing to equilibrating the power relationship, for example, when disparities in the access to resources are reduced, in this section conflict is perceived as a failure of the law enforcement given its high incidence. Six from ten interviewees declared that they are in conflict with their neighbours, a proportion that could increase if the conflicts occurring within the rural communities were also to be taken into consideration. The high incidence of conflict is not closely related to the low rural population density (0.6 inhabitants/km^2), but has rather more to do with the fact that the public institutions, particularly those of the second period, have influenced an increase in opportunistic behaviour amongst the forest users, who are seeking to embrace territories greater than their entitlement. Therefore, due the high incidence of the conflicts and the heterogeneity it is expected that the work entrusted to the new 'Arbitration and Reconciliation Commission' will have little impact. The main problem to solve will be the level of genuineness that the local population and the public organisations themselves grant to the resolutions proposed by the members of the commission. The experience of the municipality of Bolpebra indicates that even the users with title granted by the state are not willing to submit to the decisions of the public authorities, and so often the conflicts over the use of resources move to other social or administrative spheres, be it inside the rural communities, involving another type of local actor, or other legal authorities that cannot easily be controlled by the rural representative.

Summarising the social environment, since beginning in 2000 the *saneamiento* has favoured the tenure of the rural communities over that of the forest enterprises and *barraca* holders, which has contributed to reducing the existing inequalities of resource distribution. As a product of the institutional enforcement it is estimated that the individual forest users, previously 'owners' of the forests, now control the same or even a smaller forest area than the 'new' community users. Despite the advances at regional level, the reforms do not undertake to solve the disparities in relation to the access to the forest existing within the rural communities, nor to integrate informal user groups, mainly *motosierristas* and *fregueces* who remain on the margins of society.

7.2.5 Synopsis of the evaluation

Starting from the weaknesses of the previous regime, the reforms have contributed to improving the administration of the natural resources significantly (see figure 40).[367]

[367] Figure 40 helps to evaluate and to visualise the conclusions arrived at in each of the four dimensions, containing the successes or failures in the execution of the available parameters every two years, beginning in 1996. By way of evaluating the successes and failures a scale with five values is established, going from very good where the achievement of the objectives has been satisfactory, to very bad where the objective has not been met. In addition, projections (until 2010) are made, based on current tendencies and on the external and internal factors influencing the enforcement. Finally, each context receives a final grade, determining its position in the final evaluation, when compared to the others.

Figure 40 Evaluation of the enforcement of the reforms and projections

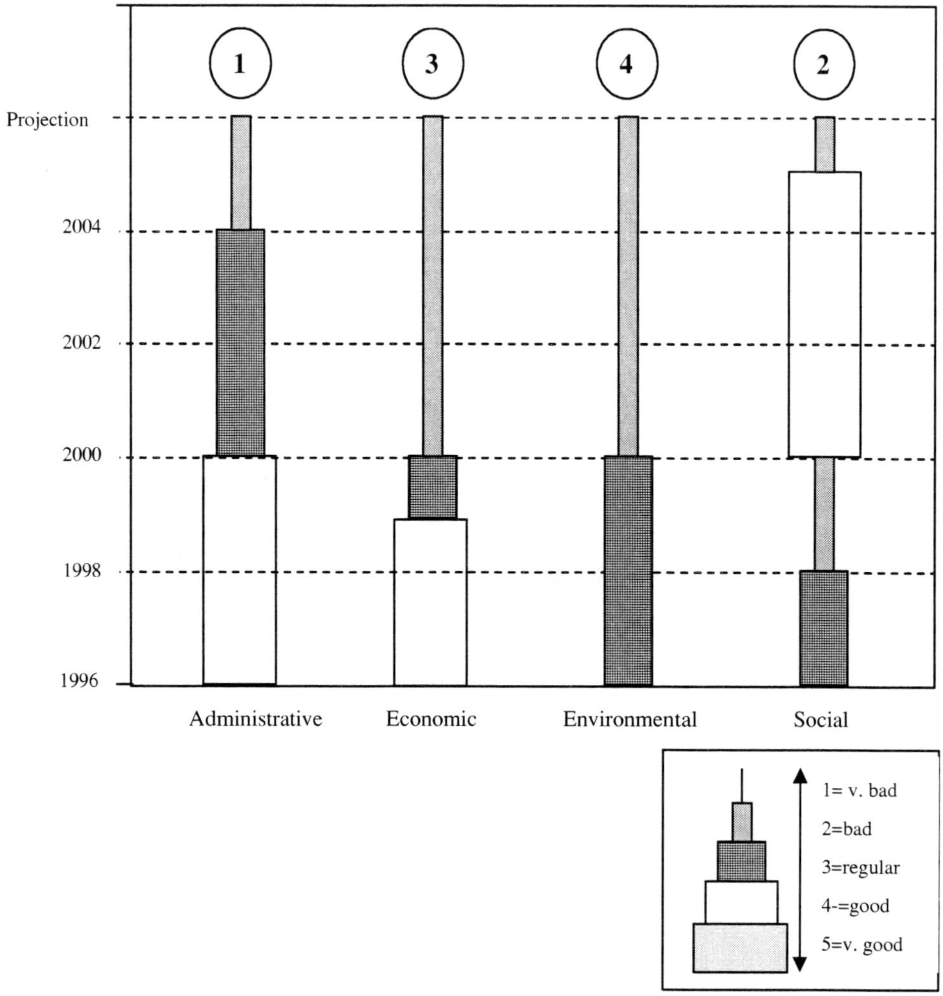

Since 1996 the situation in the four dimensions analysed has surpassed the levels established by the old public institutions. However, the legal enforcement cannot be considered successful in any of them. Even in the case of the most successfully implemented aspect of the reforms, the administrative, the achievement of its objectives has been influenced by other factors such as the Bolivian economic and political crisis. The partial success in this respect is thanks to the intentions of public agents, both in the ambitious formulation of its contents, and in their interest in its enforcement. The social dimension occupies the second place, having been helped in the case of the study area by the 500 ha Decree enforcement applied to the peasant families. Its 'success' lies in the partial incorporation of Brazil nut extraction in the national legislation. The economic dimension is in third place, where the vagueness of some tenure characteristics fails to guarantee the development of the forest sector, and where the reduction of the incomes of the public organisations compromises the control and enforcement of the institutional changes. The environmental dimension occupies the last place, as the proposed legal tools are mainly designed to regulate the form of access and the use of the resources, ahead of guaranteeing the sustainability of the system. Figure 40 also illustrates a close relationship between the outcomes of each dimension analysed.

The administrative progress in the first four years is directly related to the increased revenues obtained by the SIF and the local governments. This situation in turn means greater control over forest use, favouring the progress, however limited, of the environmental dimension. The success enforcement in the social dimension since 2000 is directly related to the execution of the land titling process, which favours the rural communities. Nevertheless, the peasants and indigenous still depend on forest companies' logging operations, which means that no increase is evident in terms of economic development. This is true mainly in the rural areas, at least for the near future. Nor is it expected that the progress in the social dimension will impact positively on the conservation of resources, because the private institutions within the communities are not sufficiently developed for this purpose.

Interpreting figure 40, the place obtained by each one of the four dimensions reflects the bargaining power between the interest groups. The administrative dimension has the backing of public agents who are motivated to achieve more control over the resources; they are also interested in improving the public revenues from the forest taxes. The 'success' of the administrative dimension reflects the strong influence of the Bolivian Government during the approval of the reforms. The advances achieved in the social dimension are due to the bargaining power of the rural communities who have been able to control greater forest areas, claiming their traditional tenures. The third place, occupied by the economic dimension, can be argued on the basis of the apathy and to a certain extent the political attenuation of the entrepreneurial sector. Lastly, the 'failure' of the environmental dimension of the reforms is attributed to its perceived irrelevance, either with the necessary lobby groups inside the political sphere for changing the laws, or with the local pressure groups fighting against the destruction of the forests. If these groups exist, they are still so weak that they have not been able to impose their interests.

This evaluation is not necessarily applicable to the rest of Bolivia, especially as refers to the advances in the social dimension, where the rural communities, mainly indigenous, still continue to claim their right to access the resources. However, many of the evaluations applied in the administrative or environmental dimension could be similar to the conditions found in the rest of the country.

Future projections

Adopting a sceptical position, a future drop in the advances of the legal enforcement in all four respects is expected, above all if the following tendencies continue:

1) In the administrative dimension:

- Increase of the administrative load of the public authorities, as a product of the social pressure exerted by the forest users;
- Lack of commitment and government will to formulate and to apply policies to support SFM and
- Competition of functions and interests between the public authorities of the agrarian and forest sectors resulting in poor administrative coordination.

2) In the economic dimension:

- Stagnation of private regional investment; a product of the lack of interest and shortcomings of the government's technical capacity to adjust the parameters of property rights as they pertain to extractivist activities and timber exploitation; true for the forest concessions, *barracas* and rural communities;
- Stagnation of government revenues; a product of the reduced collection of taxes, which results in a technical and financial drain of the regional government authorities and the neglect of their duties and
- Dependence of the forest users on other regional interest groups (sawmills, NGOs, social unions, public agents) to reduce their transaction costs in exercising their rights, particularly to access information, apply technical tools or to administer their resources.

3) In the environmental dimension:

- Increased social pressure on the forests, without institutional development or the adaptation of norms that guarantee effective social and legal control to conserve resources;
- Lack of technical, political and financial capacity of the SIF to apply legal sanctions to the offenders against the forest regime, according to the seriousness of their acts and
- Decreased control and public inspection of forest use.

4) In the social dimension:

- Stagnation of the public and private institutions intended to reduce inequalities in the distribution of resources inside the rural communities;
- Increase in the seriousness of the disputes over the use of the forests and little will of the forest users to resolve the conflicts;
- Lack of political will to integrate other still informal user groups, mainly chainsaw workers or illegal logging merchants, and eventually new migrants from outside the region.

Future research studies might deal with the following questions:

- To what extent do increases to the revenues of public organisations lead to improvements in the control of the use of the forests?
- Considering the dependence of communities on the forest companies, to what extent do the reforms improve the incomes of rural communities?
- On what factors does the unequal distribution of land within rural communities depend?

7.3 Discussion

The question that structured the discussion is whether the theoretical framework used was appropriate to understand and explain the outcomes of the reforms. To answer, two theoretical elements will be used; the functions of the institutions will be presented in section 7.3.1 and the rent-seeking behaviour in section 7.3.2.

7.3.1 The function of the institutions

At the most fundamental level, rules find their reason in the people's never ending desire to live in peace and harmony, without the continuous 'HOBBES' struggle' of one against the rest (BRENNAN & BUCHANAN 1985). Beyond supporting the ideas of the romantic jurists in their arguments that '*the institutions can do everything*', at least from the 18th century when ADAM SMITH recognised the influence of rules on social results, nobody doubts that institutions determine the interactions between individuals. However, given the influence of interest groups in both institution formulation and the enforcement process many of the institutional functions may be retained only for theoretical purposes: institutions unbalance the social relationships, once they favour a given power group more than others.

One of the main functions of the institutions is to regulate the expectations of the individuals and to reinforce the predictability of human behaviour: 'institutions should be able to put limits on our expectations, giving rise to the interests of others'. The Bolivian Agrarian and Forest Laws only fulfil this function in part, as they are not formulated precisely enough, mainly in their description of the tenure characteristics. They leave open several alternative avenues of interpretation, according to the interests of each user group. The impression left by the reforms has contributed to increasing the local actors' speculation over the access to the forests: not even amongst users belonging to the same group have the reforms been able to clarify which resources the members of this group may expect to receive. Thus, conflicts are observed in the overlap of tenures belonging to peasant communities, because their demands often exceeded the areas occupied originally. This is also a valid characterisation of the relationships between other groups, such as the indigenous inside the TCO, the *barraca* holders and the ASL. In the study region few can predict the extent of their neighbour's entitlement exactly, or how big their own forest right might be. As is to be expected, unpredictable behaviour as a source of the current land conflict is becoming increasingly common and growing more intense between heterogeneous groups, such as between the *barraca* holders and the indigenous or the concessionaires and the peasants. However, the reforms alone are not entirely responsible for encouraging conflict; there are also other historical aspects such as the traditional struggle for land between the *frequeces* and *patrones*, aimed at limiting the opponent's access to land. The fault of the reforms lies in the fact that the contents ignore this historical conflict and its heritage.

Opportunist behaviour also occurs inside community settlements, where the reforms don't establish limits regulating the internal redistribution of land. The reforms leave the responsibility for this in the hands of private rules that regulate only superficially the tenures amongst the community members. This fact leads to inequalities in the control and use of resources, whereby a few community members make use of large forest areas, affecting not only the whole community economy, but also the economy of those forest users, who waive their rights, intentionally or not. Inequalities in the use of community resources coincide with the ideas presented by HARDIN in his publication '*The tragedy of the commons*' (1968), where he confuses 'open access' with 'community property', due to the poor communal systems of law enforcement. This is valid especially for young communities or where there are strong family relationships between the community members, where all of the resources belong to all members (collective community model referred to in figure 35), but few members assume responsibility for the conservation of the forests. In this context, the reforms also fail to solve a second institutional function, as there is nothing to impede opportunistic behaviour such as 'free riding'.

Looking at another function, the reform enforcement often occurs as a result of strategies employed by forest users involving compliance with the laws instead of simply ignoring them. In this instance the public institutions are fulfilling the function proposed by KNIGHT (1992:17), namely that they influence a rational choice in given situations. This statement contradicts the expectations of other authors who claim that obeying the rules goes against the 'rational choice theory' (PRIDDAT 1996). With or without institutions, human beings are confronted by a limited rationale, i.e. that we may not be optimising our capabilities at all, and cannot even guarantee the consistency of our decisions (IBARRA 2003:14). In other words our rationale is limited by incomplete information, which consequently does not allow us to establish a valued listing of preferences. Individuals live in a system characterised by uncertainty; they are strongly influenced by their feelings, which do not allow them to calculate situations in advance (ELSTER 1989).

Under these circumstances, we have no option other than to define 'rational behaviour' as the best means of satisfying expectations selected from a group of feasible alternatives. Aware that the rules often limit the rational choice an individual can make, there are contradictions evident in many of the statements made by other authors (KNIGHT 1992; NORTH 1990; MUMMERT 1998; FISCHER 2004) who claim that the institutions are characterised by offering provisional information and incentives, contributing to reducing the cost of human interactions. It is my view that the restriction of rational choice depends on the type of institutions, the beneficiary group and the context.

To explain these ideas, two types of institutions are distinguished here: the coercive ones based on categorical commandments (either black or white) and the pro-positive institutions, involving alternative choices (if..., then....). The coercive institutions clearly differentiate the prohibited from the permitted without leaving the individual any alternative other than to accept or to reject the rule. An example of these institutions are traffic rules, such as the traffic lights, which categorically forbid the crossing of the street at a red light, only allowing us to cross when the light changes to green. The pro-positive institutions, although they have an obligatory character, offer other alternatives to the individuals, alternatives possibly representing a better option for them to maximise their benefits in many cases. An example taken from this study is the categories of community property proposed by the INRA Law (the peasant members of a community are entitled to 500 hectares per family, the individual peasants to only 50 ha, and the right of the indigenous is based on demonstrating the control over and the traditional use of the resources). In coercive institutions, when the individual submits to the rule, even when this does not satisfy his interests, his rational choice is restricted; for example, not being able to cross the street at a red light, even when there is no traffic. Pro-positive institutions do not necessarily restrict rational choice, once they offer alternatives to the recipients, for example, to *barraca* holders who before losing everything decide that it is preferable to keep 50 hectares changing their status.

Given the distribution of resources in the region, social transformations in favour of the traditionally excluded groups have been evident, a situation that contributes to the execution of another institutional function, that of "*balancing demands and preferences in the negotiations between social actors*" (HANISCH 2003:8). Although the traditional power groups still maintain their power, the reforms have facilitated the emergence of another type of actor, even allowing negotiations over the access to, use and trading of forest products. The old rules favoured the local elites, but when successfully overcoming the traditional regime the reforms force the 'losers' to look for other strategies, contrary to the law, in order to maintain their power, usually in economic or political terms. If the rules can influence the results, and some results are better than others, it means that the institutions are subject to choice. Thus, the study of the comparison of institutions becomes an appropriate object of our attention (BRENNAN & BUCHANAN 1985:2), and the formulation of institutions becomes an art, where the decision-makers are obliged to incorporate in the rules sufficient elements, facilitating the enforcement of the law. Hence, the functions of the institutions are not given *per se* at the time of approval, but rather are subject to their elaboration. Institutional change not only requires political actors interested in incorporating their interests, but also 'institutional artists' who are able to lead on the desired changes and attendant aspects such as: 1) defining all their characteristics, for example determining the property rights clearly; 2) reducing the transaction costs;[368] and 3) generating the

[368] From the point of view of the efficiency theory, the concept of transaction costs is one of the most important theoretical elements that not only explains the process of the institutional changes, but also their enforcement. That is to say, the choice to continue or to ignore the institutions is very much related to the desire to reduce these costs. For example, if the individuals have three institutional alternatives (A, B and C), all of them characterised by different transaction costs, individuals will consolidate the institution that involves the lowest transaction costs (SCHLÜTER 2000:35). Transaction costs originate from five derived market activities: the search for information, the negotiation costs, the costs of decision-making, the control costs, and the sanctioning costs. IBARRA (2003) on the other hand, following the recommendations of KERR & MARE (1996; 1998), also included the 'costs of optimisation', related with the costs of learning of norms and rules. In short, transaction costs are all types of 'effort', however quantifiable in units of time or money, or non-quantifiable, such as the availability of knowledge, the cost of learning, the access to markets or the capacity to access information and contacts.

institutional synergy derived from the combination of the comparative advantages that each rule offers separately.[369]

Without an understanding of how individuals interact within a certain social group and how the different institutional arrangements affect their interactions, it is impossible for the protagonists of the institutional changes to transform the existing rules or even to behave advisably with regard to the preservation of those rules shown to be effective in the functioning of society.[370]

7.3.2 Rent-seeking behaviour

A series of political and social phenomena, such as the distribution of resources, can be interpreted based on rent-seeking behaviour, insofar as the interest groups realise the possibility that the allocation of resources depends on political and not necessarily social criteria. The dimension of rent-seeking is in direct relationship to the size and the participation of the state in the economic activities, and to the importance of the public sector (BUCHANAN 1980:9). In Bolivia, a number of laws implemented since 1994 have reduced the state's role in the national economy.[371] However, in the case of the agrarian and forest sectors, the reforms have increased the participation of the state, at least in its function as distributor of property rights and controller of resource use.

The emergence of rent-seeking behaviour is also influenced by the political culture,[372] defined as the manifestation of bias and the typical and traditional attitudes of the members of a society (BERG-SCHOLOSSER & STAMMER 1995:181 cited in PRITZL 2000:78). MANSILLA (1990)[373] referred to a culture of authoritarianism in Latin America, which he defined as "*that political system in which the individual or group of individuals make an effort to assure their personal and political survival, seeking to obtain the support or at least the political tolerance of important social groups, and at the same time to discourage other people or groups from disputing it*". The primary goal of authoritarian regimes is to remain in power, with the political sciences distinguishing between 'excluding authoritarian systems' and 'including authoritarian systems'.[374] Under the 'excluding systems', power is preserved through the political backing of minority and elitist social groups with the help of a specific policy dedicated to privileging these interest groups, as well as developing different types of *clientelismo* or patronage. The approval of Presidential Decree 25532 in 1999 in the

---

369 For more information see section 4.5.

370 Cf. BRENNAN & BUCHANAN 1985:2.

371 For example, the Law of Capitalisation obliged the sale of 49% of the public enterprises to private industrialists, reducing the participation of the state in the national economy.

372 Political culture includes the opinions, actions and values that characterise the political and social conduct of the members of a community (PRITZL 2000:78).

373 Cited in PRITZL 2000:208.

374 The distinguishing criterion of both systems is the participation of the population in the process of social development and political decision-making (PRITZL 2000:216).

barraqueros' favour represents an example of an 'excluding system'. In the case of 'including systems', on the contrary, the rulers try to obtain the approval of the important sectors of the population, promoting a strongly populist policy with a clear paternalistic slant. In the context of the situation discussed here, the redistribution policy of the state does not necessarily benefit the population overall, being limited to those powerful sectors of society upon which the rulers depend (PRITZL 2000:216). The approval of Decree 25848 in favour of the rural communities in 2000 is an example of this type of system.

On the basis of observations made during the fieldwork phase, both 'excluding' and 'influential' authoritarian systems are not dependent upon the type of government, but rather on the pressure the public agents and politicians must endure to remain in power. In Bolivia, Banzer's government (1997-2001) came to the power thanks to the support of important regional elites, who forced politicians to grant political favours in return. At the same time, to keep power the rulers had to overcome great pressure from the public, such as the demonstrations by the rural Amazon inhabitants.

Another type of institution enacted at regional level that can be explained by rent-seeking behaviour is the adaptation of the Forest Law approved by the SIF in 1999, specifically the approval of POAFs on untitled properties and the extraction of old timber left over from the previous regime. The enforcement of the law allowed the local groups to use the forests; thereby sidestepping the agrarian legislation, and to a certain extent legitimising the illegal extraction of timber. The 'exception regime' has also led to a reduction of the social pressure on the public agents, exerted mainly by *barraca* holders and forest entrepreneurs, facilitating and ensuring the exercise of their work.

However, it was determined in the course of this study that rent-seeking behaviour is more widespread at the level of the regional actors, mainly the municipal agents, who often execute their duties with an eye to improving their own situation or the position of certain other users. Empirical findings reveal that the municipal agents: 1) facilitate the *barraca* inhabitants' receipt of 'legal personality', and seek to arrange funding for social projects (construction of a clinical post, refurbishing the school, etc.)[375] in order to win votes, rather than working to free the inhabitants from the control of the *patrón*; 2) delay the delivery of 'legal personality' to the rural communities in order to slow down the process of land distribution, in order to benefit elitist entrepreneurs; and 3) grant 'settlement certificates' in favour of private landholders (individual and collective) involved in conflicts, often ignoring old municipal political boundaries, as well as the delimitations of ARFMs.

Some municipal agents engage in rent-seeking activities because of the little knowledge and information they possess, without discarding the possibility that they receive corrupt payments to favour the position of their clients. Although the essential aspect of rent-seeking basically involves an endogenous functioning of the state (BUCHANAN 1980; PRITZL 2000;

[375] The municipality can only invest in municipal spaces recognised by the municipal government, through the granting of legal personality.

FISCHER 2004), it would not be fair to accuse solely the public agents and politicians of widespread rent-seeking practices. Rent-seekers also include those power groups who exert pressure so that the state recognises their demands, or grants them comparative advantages over other groups with respect to the distribution of public property.

One can illustrate the rent-seeking behaviour of forest users using an example similar to that referring to the car industry presented in chapter two. Quantitative or qualitative criteria, or parameters determining whether an individual or group is to be considered a rent-seeker or not, are necessary. In the case of the *barraca* holders there are two criteria: 1) the tenure of the resources in the form of ownership or as a concession (*usufruct*) and 2) the difference in the area occupied by the *barracas* in the two periods for which data is available (1984 and 2000).

In the first case, rent-seeking is considered the outcome of Decree 25532, and relates in this case to the refusal to surrender land entitlement claims made to large productive estates. In this context, the Bolivian state recognised the large estates (*latifundio*) in the northern Amazon region, distributing the land based on extractive activities, which according to domestic legislation should in fact be granted as forest concession. In other words, rent-seeking by the *barraca* holders in this case relates to the improvement of their legal entitlement to the forests.

The second case deals with a doubling of the area occupied by *barracas*, from 1.5 million hectares in 1984 to 3.5 million hectares in 2000, without there necessarily having been a great many new *barracas* established in the region. This increase is relates more to the rise of the expectations of many *barraca* holders, mainly large *barraca* holders or entrepreneurs.[376] The territorial expansion of the *barracas* was possible because Decree 25532 didn't limit the size of these areas. The difference of 2 million hectares between both periods (1984 and 2000) can be considered rent-seeking.

For the peasant communities there are three established criteria: 1) the difference in the legal limits established by the Agrarian Law of 1956 and by Decree 25548 (50 ha and 500 ha respectively); 2) the average of 20 - 80 ha for each peasant plot prior to approval of the Decree (ASSIES 2002) and 3) the peasant communities' demand for land, exceeding the average of 500 ha per each family since the execution of the land titling process (2000)

With respect to the first point, the demand for peasant plots in the region is more ten times greater than in the rest of the Bolivian Amazon region. Regional stakeholders argue in defence of this difference on the basis of the need to carry out extractive activities. Similar to the example of the *barraca* holders, the state is distributing land titles in the study area based on forest use. Legally public agents have to grant 50 ha to each peasant family plus an area dedicated to forest activities as a forest concession. The size of the community concession could also have been 500 ha per family. Rent-seeking by peasants involves obtaining property rights based on the development of extractivism.

---

[376] According to empiric data it is estimated that in the last 20 years 5% of the whole *barracas* statements are settled down in the region, i.e., around ten new *barracas*.

With respect to the second and third point, many of the peasant communities in Pando have considerably increased their original area occupied after the approval of Decree 25848. Here there is one legal and one illegal example of rent-seeking. The legal rent-seeking has allowed some communities to increase the average land entitlement per family from 80 ha to 500 ha. The illegal form of rent-seeking, which is not very widespread, concerns the desire of some community members to monopolise an average area of land greater than 500 ha per family, in some cases in excess of 2,500 ha per family.

Rent-seeking behaviour is not only characteristic of the *barraqueros* and peasants, but rather of all regional forest user groups, mainly forest concessionaires, indigenous people, private landowners and ASL members, who seek entitlement to the largest quantity of state resources when they claim to control forest areas greater than that which traditionally corresponded to them, or than is possible for them to manage. As a result of the widespread rent-seeking behaviour, approximately 75% of the study area will be occupied in the coming years. The true conflicts will begin when the region's population increases and when other Bolivian inhabitants also start to demand rights to land in the northern Bolivian Amazon.

Other rent-seeker groups are the entrepreneurs from the forest industry, when they sign timber sale and purchase contracts, in spite of the informal nature of their tenures; or when they take advantage of the forest products in an illegal or semi-legal way, paying less forest tax, exceeding the yields cited in their management plans, to be compensated by exploiting other uncontrolled areas, or when falsifying the documents required by law to access the forests.

Rent-seekers could theoretically also include influential regional NGO staff who support dubious demands made by forest users, aware of their 'illegality', manipulation and technical failures, in order to strengthen their own positions or to safeguard their work in the future. Current studies also demonstrate that due to their high dependence on external financing and the change of policy and institutions, NGO representatives are willing to change their priorities in order to guarantee their survival in the system.

Contrary to tradition, whereby only politicians and corrupt public agents are considered rent-seekers, the opportunistic entrepreneurs and *latifundistas* were also deemed as such in this study, an extension of the group of actors usually charged with seeking benefits. Certain peasants, indigenous and NGO representatives are also 'rent-seekers', since they take advantage of the political weakness of the national government to demand changes to agrarian legislation, increasing by tenfold the claims of the Amazon peasants, in comparison to other Bolivian regions.

A finding of this study is that the rent-seekers are not only interested in availing of public transfer in the process of the formulation and approval of public institutions. They are also sufficiently motivated to attempt to derive public benefits during the law enforcement, especially when the public institutions do not include rigorous sanctioning mechanisms and are broadly formulated, and when they perceive that the public organisations do not have adequate means of control at their disposal.

Although the rent-seeking activities in the region generate 'negative' impacts in the social and political dimensions, it would be incorrect to judge rent-seeking as an unproductive activity from the outset, a view shared by other authors (LEWIS, PRITZL, FISCHER, and TULLOCK). These authors highlighted, for example, that the social contract on which society is based should be open and allow the struggle for the recognition of property rights (PRITZL 2000:265). In the same context, rent-seeking has also been recognised as being "*in tension with more efficient resource allocation*", contributing both to the reduction of conflicts and to increasing stability (LEWIS 1994: 424, cited in FISCHER 2004:144).[377]

When applied to the northern Bolivian Amazon, these statements reveal that the rent-seeking behaviour revealed by the forest entrepreneurs and *barraca* holders has contributed to reigning in the expectations of the rural communities, currently strengthened by the reforms. And conversely, that the large forest areas handed over to the forest concessionaires, through non-transparent procedures, should now be redistributed to the rural communities. Rent-seeking is an effective strategy, employed by some forest users to gain access to the forests, and which contributes to creating a balance in the relationships over property rights between conflicting interest groups.

As observed in the study area, the intensity of rent-seeking also influences the degree of violence of the conflicts. In already established conflicts, moderate rent-seeking behaviour can at times act as an absorber, reducing social pressure, insofar as it represents an alternative for the improvement of the rights of the actors 'unprotected' legally.

The reforms have also served to distribute state incomes between a greater number of 'beneficiaries'.[378] In the past, rent-seeking was a privileged interaction, only for those public agents and national politicians with contacts to the powerful forest entrepreneurs; money and material resources flowed between both groups, along with political support in exchange for the allocation of resources and leniency in the extraction of the products. At present, a socialisation of rent-seeking is taking place, a process integrating the new regional and local public agents and other traditional user groups; at least the rights to receive benefits from the state have been opened up to the local population. Such interpretations may go against ethics and political morals. However, it is important to consider rent-seeking in the context of a process development and institutional change taking place in a peripheral society, where the inhabitants have not enjoyed the same political treatment as the centres of development. This process may lead to the maturing of both the civilian 'offenders' and the 'institutional experts', and the creation of effective mechanisms against rent-seeking. Even today social actors in Bolivia express their desire to put an end to the corruption of the public authorities established under the previous regime (for example in the CNRA and CDF). The remedy for these problems is not a

---

377 Nevertheless in exaggerated rent-seeking societies, this behaviour can increase both the relationship between conflicts parties and can also be a major source of political instability, as the history of many African countries demonstrates.

378 Quoting the ex-president Sanchez de Lozada (1993-1997), "the approved laws have served at least to decentralise corruption."

mechanism introduced by any international organisation, but rather one based on the experience of the Bolivians themselves ("who suffers wrong often knows what the solution is"). This concurs with the recommendations made by PRITZL (2000:341), who asserted that to avoid rent-seeking a process of social learning is needed, where each society can determine the institutional framework appropriate to meet its needs.

Some authors attribute a favourable role to rent-seeking in terms of improving access to information, which is relevant in scenarios characterised by incomplete information. This is the case in the rural areas of the northern Bolivian Amazon, where the inhabitants assume high transaction costs when acting in compliance with the laws. According to TULLOCK, rent-seeking can reveal valuable information to the holder of the rights of ownership (cited in FISCHER 2004:144). This positive factor attributed to rent-seeking seems to be important for the analysis of the property rights in the northern Bolivian Amazon. The high costs associated with formal tenures in comparison to private institutions mean that enforcement of the laws would not have been possible had the inhabitants not been able to execute traditional strategies to gain control over the resources.

Lastly, rent-seeking can be perceived as an indicator of the reform enforcement, especially in peripheral regions, long ignored by the state. The perception of rent-seeking behaviour also demonstrates the advances in the process of bringing the state nearer to the inhabitants of this region, neglected historically, as well as the interest of the local actors to adapt the new laws.

The negative outcomes of rent-seeking are better known than the positive. In authoritarian political systems, the economic policies applied by the rulers are often aimed at 'buying' the justification of their mandate, through the granting of sector privileges. Bureaucrats are primarily interested in creating social structures that stabilise their power, ahead of being rational in the economic or social sense.[379] This behaviour leads to a distortion of the social and political security within a community. Here, the villains and corrupt people surpass the talented entrepreneurs, and their objective is not to demonstrate economic efficiency in the exploitation of the resources, but rather to gain access to the same through cunning and opportunism. This environment type does not tolerate the development of ideas and policies aimed at conserving the forests, because the bad example institutionalised by the rulers does not allow them to be firm with the recipients, requiring them to enforce the rules.[380]

---

[379] Cf. PRITZL 2000:304.

[380] The freeing of individuals from the weight of the law as a form of rent-seeking on the part of government agents can be illustrated in Bolivia using the example of the payment of taxes to the state treasury: Most people argue against paying taxes, because they know that their contributions largely benefit politicians and corrupt state employees, instead of providing the social services necessary for development. At the same time, the punishments for those who violate the law are flexible and sometimes even non-existent, because the public agents have lost the legitimacy of the system. All Bolivians are faced with the problem of this 'rent-seeking symbiosis' between the tax evaders and the corrupt bureaucrats.

In the study area the reform enforcement is a result of the mixture between the enforcement of traditional rules, broadly accepted by the individuals, with those legal elements that represent lower transaction costs for the recipients. Thus, they ensure access to the resources without having to risk the seizure of the products and the incurrence of penalties or sanctions. Therefore, having a FMP or certificates of transport for products (CFOs) does not necessarily mean that the users are acting within the law, especially when both tools (FMPs and CFOs) have been obtained through rent-seeking. Here rent-seeking infringes upon the whole legal system, insofar as rent-seeking covers up illegal acts, or in forest terms, formalises illegal logging by impeding the enforcement of the control mechanisms available to the civil society or the state to combat illegal acts. In these types of 'rent-seeking societies',[381] where only income-yielding activities are developed on the political market, public statistics have a tendency to distort the reality. The example of the increased number of FMPs in Pando shows that often rent-seeking can confuse the true enforcement of the reforms. Therefore, it is recommended that institutional analysts be careful in drawing conclusions upon the laws enforcement under the interpretation of these public data. It would be instructive to learn more about the relationship between public and private agents.

Lastly, and linking up with section 7.3.1, all of the failures in the formulation of the reforms, such as the imprecise definition of the tenures, the exclusion of extractivist activities, and the discrimination against certain groups of forest users, favour the interests of rent-seekers. If it can be agreed upon that one of the main differences between developed and developing countries is the evolution of the institutions' systems, a possible cause of this lies in the presence of rent-seeking groups, and especially their influence on the approval of laws. In poor countries like Bolivia, a minority of people benefit from chaos and anarchy, including those influential politicians seeking to maintain their power, or the corrupt regional representatives seeking to increase the dependency of those they represent. This is one of the most negative aspects of rent-seeking in Bolivia, as it hinders the evolution of institutions fomenting economic development and poverty alleviation.

[381] The term 'rent-seeking society' was introduced by BUCHANAN, TOLLISON & TULLOCK (1980, cited in PRITZL 2000).

8 References

Alston, L., Libecap, G. & Mueller, B. (1997): Violence and the development of property rights to land in the Brazilian Amazon. In: Drobak, J. & Nye, J. (eds.) The frontiers of the New Institutional Economics. Academic press. 145-163.

Andaluz, A. (1997): Hacia un Marco Legal e Institucional Eficiente para Tutelar Eficazmente la Conservación y el Uso Sostenible de los Bosques y las Tierras Forestales. BOLFOR, Santa Cruz. http://bolfor.chemonics.net/Publicaciones/Simposio/andaluz.pdf. (February 2003).

Antelo, E. (2000): Políticas de estabilización y de reformas estructurales en Bolivia a partir de 1985. Serie Reformas Económicas No. 62. 5-44.

Antezana, M., Téllez, S., Mayna, J.C. & R.C., Copeticona (2001): Seguridad Alimentaria en Pando: Aprovechamiento de los recursos naturales en la alimentación de los pobladores de Pando. PIEB/Universidad Amazónica de Pando/CIPA. La Paz. 37-55.

Appendini, K., García, R. & de la Tejera, B. (1999): La transformación de las prácticas institucionales en una comunidad transnacional en torno a los recursos naturales. Paper for the Workshop: Land in Latin America. Amsterdam, 26th - 27th May 1999. CEDLA.

Aramayo, J. (2000): El Saneamiento y titulación de territorios indígenas en la Amazonía norte a 3 años de vigencia de la Ley INRA. In CIDOB: Atlas Territorios Indígenas en Bolivia. 197-199.

ASPROGOAL (18 th July 2000): Comunicado de prensa. Riberalta.

ASPROGOAL (2000): Nomina de barracas no tradicionales con trámites realizados en Riberalta. (unpublished report).

Assies, W. (1997): Going Nuts for the Rainforest: Non-timber Forest Products, Forest Conservation and Sustainability in Amazonia. Thela Latin America Series 11. Thela Publishers, Amsterdam.

Assies, W. (2002): From rubber estate to simple commodity production: Agrarian struggles in the northern Bolivian Amazon. Centro de Estudios Ruales, Colegio de Michoacán, México.

Ballivián, M. (1896): Apuntes sobre la Industria de la Goma Elástica en los Territorios Dependientes de la Delegación Nacional en el Noroeste y el Departamento del Beni. Ministerio de Instrucción Pública y Colonización. El Comercio, La Paz.

Beck, R. & Schwarz, G. (1995): Konfliktmanagement. Alling. 3-15.

Beekma, J., Zonta, A. & Keijzer, B. (1996): Base ambiental para el desarrollo del departamento de Pando y la provincia Vaca Diez. 36-54.

Bentley, A. (1908): The Process of Government. University of Chicago Press.

Birle, P. (1996): Editorial. In: Birle, P. (ed.) Bolivien – Traumland von Reformen?. Lateinamerika Analysen-Daten-Dokumentation Hamburg 13 (1996) 31. 9-14.

Bojanic, A. (2001): Balance is beautiful: Assessing sustainable development in the rain forests of the Bolivian Amazon. PROMAB scientific series 4.

BOLFOR – Proyecto de Manejo Forestal Sostenible de Bolivia (2003): Justificación técnica para la aprobación del Decreto 27024. Santa Cruz. (unpublished report).

Bonaker, T. (1996): Konflikttheorie. Eine sozialwissenschaftliche Einführung mit Quelle. Opladen. 10-25.

Bonacker, T. & Imbusch, P. (1996): Begriffe der Friedens- und Konfliktforschung: Konflikt, Gewalt, Krieg, Frieden. In: Imbusch, P. & Zoll, R. (eds.) Friedens- und Konfliktforschung. Band 1. Opladen. 63-75.

Boscolo, M. & Vargas. M (2001): Incentivos para el sector forestal de Bolivia. USAID-CIFOR.

Brennan, G. & Buchanan, J. (1985): The reason of rules. Cambridge University Press.

Bromley, D. (1991): Environment and Economy. Oxford.

Bromley, D. (2001): Property Regimes and Institutional Change. Conference of Property Rights and Institutional Change. September 2001. Fredericia, Denmark. http://www.sam.sdu.dk/fame/menu/pdf/bromley.pdf. (November 2002).

Buchanan, J. (1980): Rent Seeking and Profit Seeking. In: Buchanan, J., Tollison, R. & Tullock, G. (eds.) Toward a Theory of the Rent-Seeking Society, College Station. Texas. 3-15.

Buchanan, J. (1989): Explorations into Constitutional Economics. In: Robert Tollison & Viktor Vanberg. Economical serie No. 9. Texas A&M University 60-175.

Buchanan, J. (2002): Apatía del contribuyente, inercia constitucional y crecimiento económico. Libertas 31. Eseade.

Buckles, D. & Rusnak, G. (1999): Conflicto y colaboración en el manejo de los recursos naturales. In: Buckles, D. (ed.) Cultivar la paz: Conflicto y colaboración en el manejo de los recursos naturales. IDRC/World Bank. Capítulo introdución. http://www.idrc.ca/acb/showdetl.cfm?&DID=6&Product_ID=585&CATID=15 (January 2004).

Caballero, G. (2002): La economía política del círculo vicioso en las instituciones municipales viguesas. Claves y retos de futuro. Revista Galega de Economía, vol. 11, No 1. 1-4.

Camacho, M., Cordero, W., Martinez, I. & Rojas, D. (2001): Tasa de deforestación del departamento de Santa Cruz, Bolivia (1993-2000). BOLFOR/Superintendencia Forestal. Santa Cruz.

Cámara forestal de Bolivia (2004): Superintendente forestal destaca certificación de la empresa Inforcasa. 5 - No. 6th June 2004. Santa Cruz. www.cfb.org.bo

CEJIS - Centro de Estudios Jurídicos e Investigación Social (2000): Tercera Marcha Indígena, Campesina y de Colonizadores por la Tierra, el Territorio y los Recursos Naturales. Plataforma de demandas. Artículo Primero. 4 No. 9. http://www.angelfire.com/ok3/lfcreativa/plataformariber.html (October 2000).

CIDOB - Centro de Información y Documentación de Bolivia (1979)a: Diagnóstico Social del Norte Boliviano - Volumen I. CIDOB, La Paz.

CIDOB - Centro de Información y Documentación de Bolivia (1979)b: Diagnóstico Social del Norte Boliviano - Volumen II. CIDOB, La Paz.

CIRABO - Central indígena de la Región Amazónica de Bolivia (2000): Resultados demográficos de la TCO Multiétnico II. Riberalta, Bolivia. (unpublished report).

Cisneros, C. (2000): La Investigación Social Cualitativa en México. Forum Qualitative Sozialforschung /Forum: Qualitative Social Research [Online Journal], 1(1). http://qualitativeresearch.net/fqs (December 2000).

Coase, R. (1937): The Nature of the Firm. Economical, vol. 4. 386-405

Coase, R. (1960): The Problem of Social Costs. Journal of Law and Economics. vol.3. 1-44

Contreras, A & Vargas, M.T. (2001): Las dimensiones sociales, ambientales y económicas de las reformas en la Política Forestal de Bolivia. Forest Trends, CIFOR.

CORDEPANDO (1990-1994): Ingresos departamentales por regalías forestales. Archivos de la Corporación Regional del Departamento de Pando. (unpublished report).

Coser, L. (1956): The functions of social conflicts. New York, The Free Press.

Crespo, F. (2000): Incidencia de las reformas estructurales sobre la agricultura boliviana. CEPAL/ECLAC. Serie Desarrollo Productivo No. 98. Santiago de Chile. 5-40. http://www.eclac.cl/publicaciones/DesarrolloProductivo/5/lcl1455/LCL1455P.pdf. (September 2002).

Davalos, J. (1997): Estudio monográfico para la delimitación de la región amazónica de Bolivia. Trinidad, Bolivia. 14-33.

De Jong, W. Ruiz, S. & Becker, M. (in prep.): Conflict resolution as a pathway to sustainable forest management in northern Bolivia. In: Community-based forestry in the next decade: Towards an 'agrarian' approach?. Journal Forest Policy and Economics.

De Soto, H. (2000): El misterio del capital. El Comercio.

De Vries, A. (1998): Territorios Indígenas en las Tierras Bajas de Bolivia. Un Análisis de su estado a 1998. CPTI/CIDOB-SNV. El País. Santa Cruz.

Demsetz, H. (1967): Towards a Theory of Property Rights. The American Economic Review. Volume 57, Issue 2. May, 1967, 347-359. http://www.compilerpress.atfreeweb.com/Anno%20Demsetz%20Property%20Rights.htm (September 2001). Publication also revised in English: Hacia una teoría de los derechos de propiedad. http://www.eumed.net/cursecon/textos/DEMSETZ_teoria-derechos-propiedad.pdf (May 2001).

Denzin, N. K., & Y. S. Lincoln, (eds.) (1994): Handbook of Qualitative Research. SAGE Publications, London.

DHV (1993)a: Desarrollo de la Amazonía Boliviana - De la Actividad Extractiva hacia un Desarrollo Integral Sostenible. Estudios Agro-Ecológicos, Forestales y Socio- Económicos en la Región de la Castaña de la Amazonía Boliviana. Resumen Ejecutivo. DHV, La Paz.

DHV (1993)b: Sistemas de Recolección de Castaña en la Amazonía Boliviana. Estudios Agro-Ecológicos, Forestales y Socio-Económicos en la Región de la Castaña de la Amazonía Boliviana - Volumen C. DHV, La Paz.

DHV (1993)c: Población y Migración de la Región Castañera de la Amazonía Boliviana. Estudios Agro-Ecológicos, Forestales y Socio-Económicos en la Región de la Castaña de la Amazonía Boliviana - Volumen D. DHV, La Paz.

DHV (1993)d: Tenencia de la Tierra en la Región Castañera Amazonía Boliviana. Estudios Agro-Ecológicos, Forestales y Socio-Económicos en la Región de la Castaña de la Amazonía Boliviana - Volumen E. DHV, La Paz.

DHV (1993)e: Comunidades Indígenas en la Región Castañera de la Amazonía Boliviana. Estudios Agro-Ecológicos, Forestales y Socio-Económicos en la Región de la Castaña de la Amazonía Boliviana - Volumen G. DHV, La Paz.

DHV (1993)f: Los Sistemas Agrícolas de Pequeños Agricultores en la Amazonía Boliviana. Estudios Agro-Ecológicos, Forestales y Socio-Económicos en la Región de la Castaña de la Amazonía Boliviana - Volumen F. DHV, La Paz.

Diekmann, A. (2001): Emperische Sozialforshung: Grundlagen, Methoden, Anwendungen.

Dietl, H. (1993): Institutionen und Zeit. Tübingen. 70-101.

Elliott, C. (1997): Timber Certification: A tool for public participation and conflict management in forestry? In: Solberg, B. & Miina, S. (eds.) Conflict Management and Public Participation in Land Management. Proceedings of the International Conference Joensuu, Finland. European Forest Institute, Proceedings No. 14. 89-98

Elster, J. (1989): Social norms and economic theory. Journal of Economic Perspectives.

FAO - Organización de las Naciones Unidad para la Agricultura y la Alimentación (2001): Conflictos y manejo de recursos naturales. Roma, Italia. www.fao.org (April 2003).

Farinetti, M. (2000): Clientelismo y protesta: Cuando los clientes se revelan. Instituto de Investigaciones Gino Germani, Facultad de Ciencias Sociales de la Universidad de Buenos Aires. 1-30.

Fifer, V.J. (1970): The Empire Builders: A History of the Bolivian Rubber Boom and the Rise of the House of Suárez. Journal of Latin American Studies 2: 113-146.

Fischer, P. (2004): Rent seeking, Institutions and Reforms in Africa: Theory and Empirical Evidence for Tanzania. PhD Thesis submitted to the University of Konstanz, Germany. http://nadel.ethz.ch/forschung/rir (May 2004).

Foronda, J. (2003): Estudio integral del Sector privado en la región norte amazónica de Bolivia. SNV-Cobija. 1-33. (unpublished report).

Friedrichs, J. (1998): Methoden empirischer Sozialforschung; 9 ed. Editoral Westdeuscher. Opladen.

FSUTCP - Federación Sindical Única de Trabajadores Campesinos de Pando, et al. (2000): Propuesta del sector campesino agroextractivista del Norte Amazónico de Bolivia. Informe Técnico en el Marco de la política de "Lucha contra la pobreza". (unpublished report).

Fuentes, D., Haches, R., Maldonado, R., Albornoz, M., Cronkleton, P., de Jong, W., Becker, M. (2005): Pobreza, descentralización y bosques en el norte amazónico boliviano. Center for International Forestry Research, University of Freiburg, The Japan Center for Area Studies, National museum of Ethnology and José Manuel Pando foundation. 125 p.

Fundación José Manuel Pando (2002): Diagnóstico de la Industria Maderera en la Amazonía Sudoccidental: Acre y Rondonia (Brasil), Pando y norte del Beni (Bolivia), y Madre de Dios (Perú) - Sección Bolivia - Cobija, Pando. (unpublished report).

Furubotn, E. & Pejovich, S. (1972): Property Rights and Economic Theory: A survey of recent literature. In: Journal of Economic Literature. Vol. 10, 1972. 1137-1162.

Gamarra, P. (1992): Haciendas y Peones en el régimen hacendatario gomero boliviano. Las bases económicas de un poder regional: La Casa Suárez (1880-1940). Tesis de Licenciatura en Historia. Universidad Mayor de San Andrés. (unpublished report).

Gamarra, P. & Kent, M. L. (1992): Larecaja y la Industria de la Goma Elástica. Un mercado Regional entre 1890 y 1930. INDEAA en DATA. No. 2. La Paz - Bolivia. 197- 245.

Gamarra, P. (1993): La participación estatal en la industria de la goma elástica. Legislación fiscal y economía gomera. DATA. No. 4. 1993. Universidad Andina Simón Bolívar. 23-76.

Gamarra (2002): Norte Amazónico: 130 años de historia Transformaciones regionales y organización socioeconómica (1870-2000). SNV-Bolivia - Programa del Norte Amazónico– (unpublished report).

Garzón, A. (2002): Property Rights of the Yaminahua and Machineri Indigenous People of Bolivia. M.Sc. Thesis. University of Freiburg, Germany. Institute of Forest and Environmental policy. (unpublished thesis).

Garzón, A. (2004): El nuevo régimen legal y los derechos sobre tierra y bosque indígena. In: de Jong, W. (ed.) Retos y perspectivas del nuevo régimen forestal en el norte amazónico boliviano. CIFOR. 95-110.

Girtler, R. (1992): Methoden der qualitativen Sozialforschung: Anleitung zur Feldarbeit. 3er. Aufl. Böhlau Verlag. Viena, Colonia, Weimar.

Glasl, F. (1999): Konfliktmanagement: ein Handbuch für Führungskräfte, Beraterinnen und Berater. 6. Auflage: Verl. Freies Geistesleben. Stuttgart.

Gordillo, G. & Boening, F. (2000): El acceso a la tierra en América Latina en la década de los noventa. Grupo Chorlavi. II Conferencia electrónica "Reformas agrarias y mercados de tierras" http:www.chorlavi.cl/tierra/acceso.html. (May 2001).

Gottwald, C. (2004): Participación política de comunidades forestales en el norte amazónico boliviano. In: de Jong, W. (ed.) Retos y perspectivas del nuevo régimen forestal en el norte amazónico boliviano. CIFOR. 65-80.

Gottwald, C. (forthcoming): Institutions and organizations in forest-depended settlements: Community based approach to action and response in the northern Bolivian Amazon. PhD Thesis University of Freiburg, Germany. Institute of Forest and Environmental Policy.

Göhler, G. (1997): Wie verändern sich Institutionen? Revolutionärer und schleichender Institutionenwandel. In: Göhler, G. (ed.) Institutionenwandel. Leviathan: Zeitschrift für Sozialwissenschaft. Westdeutscher, Opladen. 21-56.

GTZ - Deutsche Gesellschaft für Technische Zusammen Arbeit (1997): Tratamiento alternativo de conflictos. LISTRA. 9-30.

Guzmán, J. (2000): De las personas, de los Bienes, de la Propiedad y de los Derechos Reales. IMPREBOL. Derecho Civil (Tomo I). Cochabamba.

Hanisch, M. (2003): Property Reform and Social Conflict - A Multi-Level Analysis of the Change of Agricultural Property Rights in Post-Socialist Bulgaria – Shaker. Band 15.

Hardin, G. (1968): The tragedy of commons. Science, v. 162. 1243-1248.

Hayek, F. A. v. (1964): Arten des Rationalismus. In: Hayek, F. A. v (1969): Gesammelte Werk von Friedrich August von Hayek. Freiburger Studien. Bd. 5. 75-89

Heidemann, C. (1995): Methodologie der Regionalplanung - Die erste und einzige kommentierte Bilderfibel der Regionalplanung. Diskussionspapiere des Instituts für Regionalwissenschaft der Universität Karlsruhe N°16. Karlsruhe.

Held, M. & Nutzinger, H. (1999): Institutionen prägen Menschen - Menschen prägen Institutionen. In: Held, M. & Nutzinger, H (eds.) Frankfurt/Main, Germany. 7-29.

Held, C. (2001): Management of woodland and tree resources in Communal Areas and Resettlement Areas in Hwedza District (Zimbabwe). Use, Institutions and conflicts. Diplomarbeit. University of Freiburg, Germany. Institute of Forest and Environmental Policy (unpublished thesis).

Held, C. (2004): Promotion of Innovations in Forest based SMEs of Developing Countries: An Actor-oriented Analysis of the Colombian Bamboo Sector. PhD Thesis University of Freiburg, Germany. Institute of Forest and Environmental Policy.

Henkemans, A. (2001): Tranquilidad and Hardship in the Forest. Livelihoods and Perceptions of Camba Forest Dwellers in the Northern Bolivian Amazon. Riberalta. PROMAB scientific series 5.

Hentschel, G. (2002) Die Veränderung institutioneller Rahmenbedingungen für die Waldnutzung durch Campesino-Siedler im bolivianischen Amazonasgebiet. Diplomarbeit. University of Freiburg, Germany. Institute of Forest and Environmental Policy (unpublished report).

Hentschel, G. (2004): El uso del bosque comunitario bajo el nuevo régimen forestal. In: de Jong, W. (ed.) Retos y perspectivas del nuevo régimen forestal en el norte amazónico boliviano. CIFOR. 81-94.

Hernáiz, I. & Pacheco, D. (2001): La Ley INRA en el espejo de la Historia. Propuestas de modificación. Fundación TIERRA. La Paz. 12-70.

Hirakuri, S. (2001): Enforcing Bolivia's forestry laws. Doctor of Juridical Science. Washington University School of Law St. Louis, Missouri, USA. ITTO Tropical Forest Update 11/1. http://www.itto.or.jp/live/Live_Server/106/tfu.2001.01(22-23).e.pdf. (March 2003).

Hocker, J. & Wilmot, W. (1995). Interpersonal conflict. Dubuque, Iowa, William C. Brown.

Honorable Senado Nacional (2003): Glosario de términos municipales. Comisión de Participación Popular, Gobiernos Locales y Descentralización. Plural, La Paz.

Ibarra, E. (2003): Private forest use decisions and state forest policy effectiveness in Costa Rica. The role of institutions, private stakeholders and the state. Institut für Forstpolitik. Freiburger Schriften zur Forst- und Umweltpolitik. Remagen, Germany. 20-150

IERAL - Instituto de Estudios de la Realidad Argentina y Latinoaméricana (1999): Las Regulaciones en la Argentina: Transformar el Estado y potenciar los mercados y la sociedad. Capítulo 1: La economía política de las regulaciones y las reformas. http://www.mercadoelectriconet.com.ar/biblioteca/regulaciones_argentinas.pdf. (May 2004).

INE - Instituto Nacional de Estadística (2002)a: Censo Nacional de Población y Vivienda 2001: Beni - Resultados Departamentales. Vol. 8. Serie II, La Paz.

INE - Instituto Nacional de Estadística (2002)b: Censo Nacional de Población y Vivienda 2001: Pando - Resultados Departamentales. Vol. 9. Serie II, La Paz.

INE - Instituto Nacional de Estadística (2002)c: Anuario Estadístico 2002. Versión disco compacto.

INRA - Instituto Nacional de Reforma Agraria (1958-2001): Registros de expedientes sobre propiedades agrícolas para el departamento de Pando, la Provincia Vaca Diez y el Municipio de Iximas. La Paz. http://www.inra.gov.bo/PortalINRA/DesktopModules/ (January 2003).

INRA - Instituto Nacional de Reforma Agraria (2002)a: Informe de Resultados Polígono 03 (Bolpebra). Unidad de Saneamiento 0142/2002. Pando, Bolivia. (17th April 2002) (unpublished report).

INRA - Instituto Nacional de Reforma Agraria (2002)b: Informe de Resultados Polígono 10 (Rapirrán). Unidad de Saneamiento 0396/2002. Pando, Bolivia. (20th September 2002). (unpublished report).

INRA - Instituto Nacional de Reforma Agraria (2004): Resultados preliminares del Saneamiento Simple de Oficio en Pando (unpublished report).

Jones, H. (in prep.): Partnerships in Problem Solving: Responses of three community forestry projects. Journal for Forest Policy and Economics.

Kapmeyer, R. (2004): Agrarian Reform and Development in El Salvador. – A Case Study from the lower Lempa River Region. PhD. Thesis. Faculty of Business Administration and Economics, Philipps University of Marburg, Germany.

Knight, J. (1992/1997): Institutions and social conflict. Cambridge University. Publication also revised in German: Institutionen und gesellschaftliche Konflikte. Tübingen.

Kundhande, G. & Luckert, M.K (2000): Towards and Analytical Framework for Assessing Property Rights to Natural Resources: A case study in the Communal Areas of Zimbabwe. CIFOR/IES/IDRC.

Kutzner, E. (2000): Fallstudien. Martens. In: Kopp, R. Langenhoff, G. & Schröder A. (eds.): Angewandte empirische Methoden: Erfahrung aus der Praxis. Methodenhandbuch. Sozialforschungsstelle Dortmund Landesinstitut. Dortmund. 53-64. www.sfs-dortmund.de (May 2001).

Lederach, J. P. (1992): Enredos, pleitos y problemas. Una guía práctica para ayudar a resolver conflictos. Clara-Semilla, Guatemala.

Leitzel, J. (1997): Rule Evasion in Transitional Russia. Section II: Institutional Change, Property Rights and Corruption. In Transforming post-Communist political economies / Task Force on Economies in Transition. Commission on Behavioural and Social Sciences and Education. National Research Council. USA. http://www.nap.edu/html/transform/contents.htm (January 2004).

Llambí, L. & Lindemann, T. (2001): Reformas del Estado y descentralización del sector público rural y agrícola. – Lecciones de la experiencia latinoamericana. FAO. Rome. http://www.fao.org/sd/2001/IN0502a_es.htm. (October 2002).

Llanque, O., Zonta A. & Milz, J. (1993): Extractivismo: Conservación y desarrollo. Encuentro Regional Bolivia Perú y Brasil. Instituto para el Hombre, Agricultura y Ecología. Instituto de Investigación Forestal de la Amazonía Boliviana; Radio San Miguel, Servicio Alemán de Cooperación social Técnica.

Llanque, O., Zonta, A., de Jong, W., Boot, R. & Bokkestijn, A. (2003): Patente forestal boliviana: crisis crónica de financiamiento. 2da. Reunión Nacional de investigación forestal. Hacia el manejo forestal sostenible: logros y estrategias para la investigación forestal en Bolivia. 11th -13th August 2003. Cochabamba.

Llanque, V. (2004): Extracción forestal, procesos migratorios y deforestación en el norte amazónico boliviano. In: de Jong, W. (ed.) Retos y Perspectivas del nuevo régimen forestal en el norte amazónico boliviano. CIFOR. 137-152.

Maldonado, R. (2002) Natural resource Management in a Tropical Protected Area – Conflicts between use and protection in the Reserva Nacional de Vida Silvestre Amazónica Manuripi - RNVSAM, Bolivia. Diplomarbeit. University of Freiburg, Germany. Institute of Forest and Environmental Policy (unpublished thesis).

Maldonado, R. (2004); Conflictos entre uso y protección de los recursos naturales, Reserva Natural de Vida Silvestre Amazónica Manuripi (RNVSAM). In: de Jong, W. (ed.) Retos y perspectivas del nuevo régimen forestal en el norte amazónico boliviano. CIFOR. 123-138.

Manzaneda, D. (2003): Un estudio sobre el uso y dependencia de los PFNM en una comunidad indígena de Pando: Implicaciones para el manejo forestal en la TCO Yaminagua-Machineri. (unpublished report).

Martínez, M. (1996): Municipios y Participación Popular: Un Modelo de Desarrollo en América Latina. CEBIAE, La Paz. 90-110.

Mayring, P. (1999): Einführung in die qualitative Sozialforschung. Beltz. Weinheim.

Mummert, U. (1995): Informelle Institutionen in ökonomischen Transformationsprozessen. Max-Planck-Institut. 1. Aufl. Contributiones Jenenses Band 2. Baden-Baden. 20-50.

Mummert, U. (1998): Wirtschaftliche Entwicklung und Institutionen. –Die Perspektive der Neuen Institutionenökonomik. E&Z. jg.39. 36-39

Mummert, U. (1999): Informal Institutions and Institutional Policy – Shedding Light on the Myth of Institutional Conflict. Diskussionsbeitrag 02-99. Max-Planck-Institut zur Erforschung von Wirtschaftssystemen. Jena.

Nittler, J. (1996): La Larga Historia del Tratamiento de la Ley Forestal. Boletín BOLFOR No. 7. June 1996. http://www.cadex.org/bolfor/BOLETIN/bolet7/2larga.htm (March 2001)

Nittler, J. (1999): Encuesta sobre la Ley Forestal y su implementación. Documento Técnico 76A/1999. BOLFOR. Santa Cruz. http://www.cadex.org/bolfor/ (March 2001)

North, D. (1981): Structure and Change in Economic History. New York: Norton

North, D. (1990/1992): Institutions Institutional change and economic performance. Cambridge University. Publication also revised in German: Institutionen, Institutioneller Wandel und Wirtschafsleitung. Tübingen

North, D. (1993). Desempeño económico en el transcurso de los años. Washington University, St Louis. Traducción del inglés de Herzonia Yáñez. Presentado en conferencia en memoria a Alfred Nobel, 9 de diciembre de 1993. Estocolmo. http://www.eumed.net/cursecon/textos/north-nobel.htm.

Olson, M. (1968): Die Logik des kollektiven Handelns: Kollektivgüter und die Theorie der Gruppen. Mohr Tübingen.

Orduna, V. (21.07.2000): Empresarios piden la mitad del departamento en concesiones forestales: Pando empieza donde termina la Ley. Tierra a Debate. www.ftierra.org. (April 2000).

Ormachea, S.E. (1987): Beni y Pando - Latifundio y Minifundio en el Norte Boliviano. Centro de Estudios para el Desarrollo Laboral y Agrario (CEDLA), La Paz.

Ormachea, S.E. & Fernández J. (1989): Amazonía Boliviana y Campesinado. Cooperativa Agrícola Integral "Campesino". La Paz.

Ortiz, P. (1996): Apuntes teórico - conceptuales para el diseño de una propuesta metodología de manejo de conflictos socioambientales a través de la forestería comunitaria. In: Ortiz, P. (ed.) Comunidades y Conflictos socioambientales: experiencias y desafíos en América Latina. FAO/FT Quito Ecuador.

Ossenbrügge, J. (1983): Politische Geographie als räumliche Konfliktforschung. Konzepte zur Analyse der politischen und sozialen Organisation des Raumes auf der Grundlage anglo-amerikanischer Forschungsansätze. - I.d.R.: Hamburger Geographische Studien. Heft 40. Hamburg.

Ostrom, E. (2000): Private and common property rights. Indiana University http://allserv.rug.ac.be/~gdegeest/2000book.pdf (September, 2004).

Ostrom, E. (2002): Governing the commons. The Evolution of Institutions for collective Action. Cambridge University. 20-98.

Otero, D.P. (1993): El Acre: Un nuevo caso de fragmentación del espacio amazónico. DATA Revista del Instituto de Estudios Andinos y Amazónicos. No. 4. 1993. Universidad Andina Simón Bolívar. 77-98.

Pacheco, P. (1992): Integración Económica y Fragmentación Social: El Itinerario de las Barracas en la Amazonía Boliviana. CEDLA, La Paz.

Pacheco, P. (1998): Pando: Barraqueros, Madereros y Conflictos por el Uso de los Recursos Forestales. In: Pacheco, P., & Kaimowitz, D. (eds.) Municipios y Gestión Forestal en el Trópico Boliviano. La Paz.

Pacheco P. (2000): Avances y desafíos en la descentralización de la gestión de los recursos forestales en Bolivia. CIFOR/BOLFOR. Santa Cruz.

Pacheco, P. & Avila, H. (2001): Amazonía boliviana. In: Urioste, M. & Pacheco, D. (eds.) Las tierras bajas de Bolivia a fines del siglo XX. PIEB. La Paz. 55-97.

Pacheco, P. (2002)a: Contribuye la descentralización a mejorar la gestión forestal? Las lecciones aprendidas del caso boliviano. CIFOR/BOLFOR/USAID. Bogor, Indonesia.

Pacheco, P. (2002)b: Avances y desafíos del régimen forestal en la Amazonía de Bolivia. CIFOR.

Paniagua, F., Aguilar, A. & Rojas A.V. (2000): Colaboración en el manejo de lo conflictos socioambientales: Manual de Capacitación y Documentación de casos. Red de Manejo de conflictos socioambientales. 1-11.

Pavez, I. & Bojanic, A. (1998): El proceso de social de formulación de la Ley Forestal de Bolivia. CIFOR/CEDLA/TIERRA/PROMAB. La Paz.

Paz, R. (1999): Dominio Amazónico. Plural/CID, La Paz.

Pejovisch, S. (1995): Economic Analysis of Institutions and Systems. Dordrecht: Kluwer Academic Publishers.

Pendzich, C. Thomas, G. & Wohlgenant, T. (1994): El papel del manejo alternativo de los conflictos en el desarrollo forestal comunitario. Organizacion de las Naciones Unidad para la Agricultura y la Alimentación.

PNUD – Programa de las Naciones Unidas para el Desarrollo (2003): Informe de Desarrollo Humano en el Norte Amazónico. Plural. La Paz.

Prefectura del Departamento de Pando (2001): Plan Departamental de Desarrollo Forestal de Pando. Cobija, Pando. 5-35.

Priddat, B. (1996): Die Zeit der Institutionen. Regelverhalten und rational choice. In: Priddat, B. & Wegner, G. (eds.) Zwischen Evolution und Institution. Metropolis. Marburg. 11-34.

PRISMA – Instituto de Políticas, Relaciones Internacionales, Sociedad, Medio Ambiente (2000): Informe sobre la situación del sector forestal.

PRISMA – Instituto de Políticas, Relaciones Internacionales, Sociedad, Medio Ambiente (2001): Informe sobre los avances y perspectivas del sector forestal

Pritzl, R. (2000): Corrupción y Rentismo en América Latina. Fundación Konrad Adenaeur. Centro Interdisciplinario de Estudios sobre el Desarrollo Latinoamericano.

PULSO (21.07.2000): Pando comienza donde termina la ley. In: Debate a Tierra. www.pulsobolivia.com. (March 2002).

Quevedo, L. (2004): Forest Certification in Bolivia. Yale School of Forestry and Environmental Studies. Connecticut, USA. 10th - 11th June 2004.

Ramirez, R. (1999): Stakeholder analysis and conflict management. International Development Research Center, Ottawa, Canada. www.arupa.or.id/papers/46.htm. (May 2001).

Real, B. (2002): Legal reforms in Bolivia in the 1990s: Challenges and opportunities for Decentralisation, Indigenous rights and forest management. Thesis presented to the graduate School of the University of Florida for the degree of Master of Arts.

Reichardt, Ch. & Cook, T (1986): Hacia una superación del enfrentamiento entre los métodos cualitativos y los cuantitativos en investigación. Madrid: Ediciones Morata.

Richards, M. (1997): Common Property Resources Institutions and Forest Management in Latin America. Development and Change Vol 28. 95-1177

Richter, R. (1994): Institutionen ökonomisch analysiert. Zur jüngeren Entwicklung auf dem Gebiet der Wirtschaftstheorie. Tübingen.

Richter, R. & Furubotn, E. (1999): Neue Institutionenökonomik. Eine Einführung und kritische Würdigung. Tübingen. 117-180.

Ruiz, S. A. (1996): Plan de Ordenamiento Territorial para la Unidad Agroforestal del PLUS (AF) al norte de los municipios de Santa Rosa y San Carlos. Prefectura del Departamento de Santa Cruz, PRODISA, Consorcio IP/CES/KMC).

Ruiz, S. A. & Becker, M. (2003): Effects of institutional change since the mid 90ies on community forestry in Bolivia's Amazon region. International Conference on Rural Livelihoods Forest and Biodiversity. May 19-23, 2003. Bonn, Germany. Poster. http://www.cifor.cgiar.org/publications/corporate/cd-roms/bonn_results/poster/T7_FINAL_MichelBecker.pdf (June 2003).

Ruiz, S. A. (2004)a. Redistribución de los recursos forestales en el norte amazónico boliviano. In De Jong, W. (ed): Retos y perspectivas del nuevo régimen forestal en el norte amazónico boliviano. CIFOR, PROMAB, COSUDE, BMZ. 25-46. Publication also available in internet http://www.cifor.cgiar.org/publications/pdf_files/Books/Retos_y_perspectivas.pdf

Ruiz, S. A. (2004)b: La nueva administración de tierras y bosques en el norte amazónico boliviano. In De Jong, W. (ed): Retos y perspectivas del nuevo régimen forestal en el norte amazónico boliviano. CIFOR, PROMAB, COSUDE, BMZ.47-64. Publication also available in internet http://www.cifor.cgiar.org/publications/pdf_files/Books/Retos_y_perspectivas.pdf

Ruttan, V. & Hayami, Y. (1984): Toward a theory of induced institutional innovation. Journal of Development Studies. Vol. 20: 203-223.

Sabatier, P., & Jenkins-Smith, H. (1999). The advocacy coalition framework: An assessment. In P. Sabatier (ed.), Theories of the policy process. 117-166

Saiegh, S. & Tommasi, M. (1998): La nueva Economía Política Racionalidad e Instituciones. Fundación Gobierno y Sociedad. Documento 10.

Salm, H. & Marconi, M. (eds.) (1992): Reserva Nacional Amazónica Manuripi-Heath. Programa de Reestructuración (Fase II). LIDEMA, CORDEPANDO PL-480. La Paz. 147-195.

Sandmo, A. (1990): Buchanan on Political Economy. A Review Article. Journal of Economic Literature. Vol. XXVIII (March 1990). 50-65.

Scharpf, F. (2000): Interaktionsformen. Akteurzentrierter Institutionalismus in der Politiforschung. Stuttgart.

Schlüter, A. (2001): Institutioneller Wandel und Transformation: Restitution, Transformation und Privatisierung in der tschechischen Landwirtschaft. Shaker. Aachen. 15-120.

Schmidt, S. (1999): Institutionenökonomische Analyse der staatlichen Forstwirtschaft in Deutschland. Institut für Forstökonomie. Universität Freiburg. Band 12.

Schneider, B. (2002): In den Tiefen des Tropenwaldes: Eine politische-ökologische Betrachtung des Gold- und Diamantenbergbaus im Südosten Venezuelas. Ididem, Stuttgart.

Schweigert, T. (1989): Land Tenure Issues in Agricultural Development Projects in Latin America. Land Tenure Center. LTC Paper 132. Madison.

Scott, J. (1985): Weapons of the weak: every form of peasant resistance. Yale University Press. New Haven. 5-50.

Seintsch, B. (2004): Regionalinitiativen der Forst- und Holzwirtschaft: Wirkungen des Regionalmarketings Forst- und holzwirtschaftlicher Akteure zur Aktivierung von regionalen Potentialen. PhD. Thesis. University of Freiburg, Germany. Institute of Forest and Environmental Policy.

SIF - Superintendencia Forestal (1997): Proceso de conversión al régimen de Concesiones: Departamento de Pando. Informe Técnico (unpublished report).

SIF - Superintendencia Forestal (1998-2001): Estadistas de Instrumentos aprobados en propiedades privadas para las gestiones 1998-2001. Cobija. (unpublished report).

SIF - Superintendencia Forestal (1999): Informe Anual de la Superintendencia Forestal Gestión 1998: Indicadores de cumplimiento. Santa Cruz.

SIF - Superintendencia Forestal (2000): Informe Anual de la Superintendencia Forestal Gestión 1999: Indicadores de cumplimiento: Santa Cruz.

SIF - Superintendencia Forestal (2001): Informe Anual de la Superintendencia Forestal Gestión 2000: Indicadores de cumplimiento: Santa Cruz.

SIF - Superintendencia Forestal (2002)a: Informe Anual de la Superintendencia Forestal Gestión 2001: Indicadores de cumplimiento: Santa Cruz, Bolivia. Capitulo 7 y 4

SIF - Superintendencia Forestal (2002)b: Deuda de patentes forestal por superficie al 31 de Diciembre del 2001. (unpublished report).

SIF - Superintendencia Forestal (2003): Informe Anual de la Superintendencia Forestal Gestión 2002: Indicadores de cumplimiento: Santa Cruz.

SIF - Superintendencia Forestal (2004): Recaudaciones efectivas de patentes forestales según el Decreto 27024. Archivos de la SIF. (unpublished report).

Silva, E., Kaimowitz, D., Bojanic, A., Ekoko, F., Manurung, T., & Pavez, I. (2002): Making the Law of the Jungle: The reform of forest legislation in Bolivia, Cameroon, Costa Rica and Indonesia. Global Environmental Politics 2(3): 63-97.

Simac, P. (1990): Lov za kometovim repom. Translated into German by Bojan Peroci. Ljubljana, Slovenija. 100-210.

Snook, L., Sabogal, C. Boscolo, M. Smith, J. Vargas, M.T., Quevedo, L. et al. (2003): Are Sustainable Practices Applied in Tropical Forests? Why or why not?. CIFOR.

Stahl, J. (2003): Rationalities in Cavineño Livelihood Strategies. A Case Study from the Bolivian Amazon. M.Sc. Thesis. University of Freiburg, Germany. Institute of Forest and Environmental Policy (unpublished thesis).

Statz, J. (2000): Nutzung von Nicht-Holz-Waldprodukten als Handlungsfeld der Entwicklungszusammenarbeit. Freiburger Forstliche Forschung. Vol. 11.

Stoian, D. 2000. Variations and Dynamics of Extractive Economies. The Rural-Urban Nexus of Non-Timber Forest Use in the Bolivian Amazon. PhD Thesis University of Freiburg, Germany. Institute of Forest and Environmental Policy.

Taylor, G., Nittler, J., & Kraljevic, I. (2003): Global Initiatives, Public Policies and Private Forestry in Bolivia: Lessons to Date and Remaining Challenges. In: Teeter, L., Cashore, B., Zhang, D. (eds.) Forest Policy for Private Forestry: Global and Regional Challenges. CABI. 67-80.

Thiel, A. (2003): Soziale Konflikte. Transcrip. Bielefeld.

Thomson, J. & Kanaan, R. (2003): Conflict Timber: Dimensions of the Problem in Asia and Africa. Volume 1: Synthesis Report. Final Report Submitted to USAID, Washington DC. 2-21.

Tollison, R. (1982): Rent Seeking: A Survey. In: Kyklos. Vol. 35. 575-602.

Torres, C. (1930): Las maravillosas tierras del Acre (en la floresta amazónica de Bolivia). Don Bosco. La Paz. 130-160.

Urapontina, J. (2002): Concesiones forestales o latifundios modernos. http://www.ftierra.org/Tierra%20a%20Debate/Pulso/02-01-11.htm. (January 2004)

Urioste, M. & Baldomar, L. (1998): Participación popular, descentralización y ley de tierras: Políticas diferenciadas para el desarrollo rural. Dataterra. Seminario Reforma Agraria e Democrazia. Rio de Janeiro. http://www.dataterra.org.br/semrario/urioste.htm (August 2002).

Urioste, M. & Pacheco, D. (1999): Bolivia: Mercado de Tierras en un Nuevo Contexto (Ley INRA). Fundación Tierra. http://www.ftierra.org/docs_trabajo.htm. (September 2001).

Walker, G. & Daniels, S. (1997): Foundations of natural resource conflict: Conflict theory and public policy. In: Solberg, B. & Miina, S. (eds.) Conflict Management and Public Participation in Land Management. Proceedings of the International Conference Joensuu, Finland. European Forest Institute, Proceedings No. 14. 13-36

Walker, Tjip. 1998. Both Pretense and Promise: The Political Economy of Privatization in Africa. Bloomington, IN, University of Indiana: Department of Political Science, unpublished Ph.D. dissertation.

Wasmuht, U. (1996): Friedensforschung als Konfliktforschung. In: Imbusch, P. & Zoll, R. (eds.) Freidens- und konfliktsforschung. Ein Einführung mit Quellen. Opladen. 175-187.

Williamson, O. (1975): Markets and Hierarchies: Analysis and Antitrust Implications. New York: Free Press.

Williamson, O. (1985): The Economic Institutions of Capitalism. New York: Free Press.

Williamson, O. (2000): The New Institutional Economic: Taking Stock, Looking Ahead. Journal of Economic Literature XXXVIII (3). 595-613.

ZONISIG - Proyecto de Zonificación Agroecológica y Establecimiento de una Base de Datos y Red de Sistema de Información Geográfica en Bolivia (1997): Zonificación Agroecológica y Socioeconómica y Perfil Ambiental del Departamento de Pando. ZONISIG, La Paz.

Zuidema, P. (2002): Demografía y Explotación de la Castaña (*Bertholletia excelsa*), Asaí (*Euterpe precatoria*) y Jatata (*Geonoma deversa*) en el Norte Amazónico de Bolivia. Primera Reunión Nacional sobre Investigación Forestal. Avances y Perspectivas para la investigación forestal en Bolivia. 25th - 27 th June 2002. Santa Cruz.

Laws and Bylaws:

Gobierno de Bolivia (24.11.1883): Ley de arrendamiento por *estradas.*

Gobierno de Bolivia (13.11.1886): Ley de Colonias y tierras del Estado.

Gobierno de Bolivia (15.05.1893): Decreto reglamentario de la Ley de concesiones de estradas gomeras.

Gobierno de Bolivia (07.12.1895): Ley de impuesto de la goma: Se eleva su cuota.

Gobierno de Bolivia (12.12.1895): Ley Explotación de la Goma adjudicación de estradas gomeras: requisitos para obtenerlas.

Gobierno de Bolivia (30. 06.1896): Decreto Estradas Gomeras Reglamento de la Ley de explotación de goma.

Gobierno de Bolivia (18.12.1896): Ley de impuesto a la explotación de la Goma.

Gobierno de Bolivia (1.09.1897): Decreto derechos de los indígenas.

Gobierno de Bolivia (25.04.1905): Decreto de declaración del Territorio de Colonias como zona reservada para la colonización.

Gobierno de Bolivia (26.10.1905): Ley de tierras baldías.

Gobierno de Bolivia (20.06.1907): Reglamento de tierras baldías.

Gobierno de Bolivia (8.11.1917): Ley de Compra de las tierras ocupadas por las *barracas.*

Gobierno de Bolivia (31.01.1919): Decreto Supremo sobre la determinación de los títulos en la proposición de 75 ha por estrada gomera.

Gobierno de Bolivia (06.09.1925): Decreto que prohibe el derribe del árbol productor en la explotación del caucho.

Gobierno de Bolivia (02.07.1939): Decreto Supremo que establece el sistema de explotación forestal.

Gobierno de Bolivia (11.11.1941): Decreto Supremo que establece que los interesados en explotar árboles y arbustos deberán presentar sus solicitudes a las prefecturas de los departamentos respectivos.

Gobierno de Bolivia (02.08.1953): Decreto Ley No. 3463 de la Reforma Agraria.

Gobierno de Bolivia (30.08.1974): Decreto Supremo No. 11686 de la Ley Forestal General de Bolivia.

Gobierno de Bolivia (4.10.1982): Decreto Supremo 19190. Gravamen de regalías madereras del 11% para los departamentos.

Gobierno de Bolivia (11.01.1990): Decreto Supremo 22407. Pausa ecológica histórica de 5 años.

Gobierno de Bolivia (27.04.1992): Ley General del Medio Ambiente. Ley No. 1333.

Gobierno de Bolivia (20.04.1994): Ley de Participación Popular. Ley No. 1551.

Gobierno de Bolivia (06.02.1995): Constitución Política del Estado. Ley No. 1615

Gobierno de Bolivia (1995): Ley de Descentralización Administrativa. Ley No. 1654

Gobierno de Bolivia (12.07.1996): Ley Forestal. Ley No. 1700.

Gobierno de Bolivia (18.10.1996): Ley del Instituto de Reforma Agraria (INRA). Ley No. 1715.

Gobierno de Bolivia (05.10.1999): Decreto Supremo 25532. Conversión de establecimientos gomero-castañeros en concesiones forestales.

Gobierno de Bolivia (22.09.2000): Decreto Supremo 25906. Reordenamiento jurídico de la "Reserva Nacional de vida silvestre Amazónica Manuripi".

Gobierno de Bolivia (10.07.2000): Decreto Supremo 25838. Abrogación del Decreto Supremo de Conversión de establecimientos gomero-castañeros en concesiones forestales.

Gobierno de Bolivia (10.07.2000): Decreto Supremo 25848. Modificación del Decreto Reglamentario de la Ley INRA.

Gobierno de Bolivia (06.05.2003): Reducción del pago de la patente forestal.

Gobierno de Bolivia (17.06.2004): Decreto Supremo 27572. Modificación al D.S. 25848.

Newspapers

La Razón, 23th February 2000: Tensión en el norte amazónico. La Paz.

La Razón, 14th July 2000: Habla el Presidente del Senado: No fue buena idea anular el Decreto. La Paz.

La Razón, 14 th July 2000: La Defensoría del pueblo argumenta que el ejecutivo violó la constitución: El Gobierno responsabiliza a un senador por tramitar tierras Fiscales. La Paz.

La Razón, 12th January 2003: El Poder dio tierras como le convenía a sus intereses: El INRA reveló cómo se manejo la tierra desde el poder político.

La Razón, 24th August 2004: La Amazonía hace un pacto para distribuir sus tierras. La Paz.

Presencia, 18th November 1993: In Pando se otorgaron nuevos permisos para aprovechamiento forestal.

Curriculum Vitae

Sergio Antonio Ruiz was born in Tarija, Bolivia on October 15, 1968. After graduating from high school in 1985, he studied agricultural engineering until 1990 at *Escuela Agricola Panamericana*, "*El Zamorano*" in Honduras, where he prepared a thesis on pig breeding.

Between 1991 and 1995, he completed two postgraduate studies, the first one in Colombia, at the Institute of Remote Sensing "*Agustín Codazzi*" and later in Germany, at the Institute of Regional Planning, University of Karlsruhe. In both studies, he achieved solid qualifications in areas such as land use planning and sustainable use of natural resources.

After returning to Bolivia in 1996, he worked as an advisor for various projects carried out by the German Agency for Technical Development Cooperation (GTZ) and for the Friedrich Ebert Foundation until 2000. One of his tasks was the preparation of the first land use plan at local level for the region of Chore in Santa Cruz (published in July 1996). In 1998 and 1999, he was co-ordinator of the GTZ 'Legal basis for land use planning' project. Other major tasks included working with national and local governments, peasant and indigenous communities as well as with national NGOs in the enforcement of Bolivian land reform, forestry and administrative decentralisation.

Between October 2000 and May 2005, he joined the CIFOR project "Developing institutions for sustainable use of non-timber forest products" as a PhD researcher with the Institute of Forest and Environmental Policy, University of Freiburg, Germany. He spent a period of one year in the northern Bolivian Amazon, working out of the PROMAB office (Programme for the Management of the Bolivian Amazon Forests) in Riberalta and out of the SNV office (Dutch Organization for Development Cooperation) in Cobija. His research topics included enforcement of reform programs in peripheral regions, multi-stakeholder analysis in conflicts situations, forest policy and rent-seeking behaviour.

He has also attended several international courses on rural development, management of protected areas and buffer zones, participative planning, illegal logging and non-timber forest products.

Sergio Antonio Ruiz has various publications in fields such as land use planning, institutional change, the impact of decentralisation on local governance, communal forestry and land conflicts.